Global Outsourcing Strategies

Global Outsourcing Strategies

An International Reference on Effective
Outsourcing Relationships

PETER BARRAR and ROXANE GERVAIS

GOWER

Published by
Gower Publishing Limited
Gower House
Croft Road
Aldershot
Hampshire
GU11 3HR
England

Gower Publishing Company
Suite 420
101 Cherry Street
Burlington
VT 05401-4405
USA

Peter Barrar and Roxane Gervais have asserted their moral right under the Copyright, Designs and Patents Act, 1988, to be identified as the authors of this work.

British Library Cataloguing in Publication Data
Global outsourcing strategies : an international reference
   on effective outsourcing relationships
   1. Contracting out
   I. Barrar, Peter, 1946– II. Gervais, Roxane
   658.4'058

   ISBN-10: 0 566 08624 7
   ISBN-13: 978-0-566-08624-3

Library of Congress Cataloging-in-Publication Data
Global outsourcing strategies : an international reference on effective outsourcing relationships / edited by Peter Barrar and Roxane Gervais.
   p. cm.
   Includes index.
   ISBN-13: 978-0-566-08624-3
   ISBN-10: 0-566-08624-7
   1. Contracting out I. Barrar, Peter, 1946– II. Gervais, Roxane, 1963–

   HD2365.G56 2006
   658.4'058--dc22

2006013673

Printed and bound in Great Britain by TJ International Ltd, Padstow, Cornwall

Contents

List of Figures

List of Tables

List of Abbreviations

AIRC	Australian Industrial Relations Commission
ASC	Australian Customs Service
ASP	application service provider
BAe	British Aerospace
BIFU	Banking, Insurance and Finance Union
BLJ	*Business Law Journal*
BPO	business process outsourcing
CAD–CAM	computer-aided design–computer-aided manufacturing
CCT	compulsory competitive tendering
CEO	chief executive officer
CFO	chief financial officier
CFROI	cash flow return on investment
CHH	Carter Holt Harvey
CIO	chief information officer
CIS	Community Innovation Survey
CNABS	Centre for North American Business Studies
CSC	Computer Science Corporation
CSR	corporate social responsibility
DEA	data envelopment analysis
DFA	deterministic frontier analysis
DR	disaster recovery
EBIT	earnings before interest and taxes
EEA	European Economic Area
EDS	Electronic Data Systems Corporation
EFTA	European Fair Trade Association
EOI	Expression of Interest
EPMU	Engineers, Printing and Manufacturing Union

ER	All England (law) Reports
ERP	enterprise resource planning
ETI	Ethical Trading Initiative
EWC	European works council
FA	factor analysis
FDI	foreign direct investment
FRS	Financial Report Standard
FTE	full-time equivalent
FSR	Fleet Street Reports
GAAP	generally accepted accounting principle
GDP	gross domestic product
GLN	Global Laboratory Network
GM	General Motors
GRE	Graduate Record Exam
HR	human resources
ICT	information and communication technology
ICU	intensive care unit
IDC	International Data Corporation
ION	inter-organizational network
IOS	inter-organizational information systems
IPC	International Paper Company
IT	information technology
IWS	Industry Wage Survey
JV	joint venture
LR	likelihood ratio
MCA	Management Consultancies Association
MNC	multinational corporation
MNE	multinational enterprise
NAFTA	North American Free Trade Agreement
NASSCOM	National Association of Software and Service Companies
NHS	National Health Service
NSI	National Savings and Investments
ODC	offshore development centre

OEM	original equipment manufacturer
OGC	Office of Government Commerce
PC	personal computer
PC	principal component
PCM	private military company
PFI	private finance initiative
PFP	partial factor productivity
PMP	prime marketing publications
PPP	public–private partnership
PSA	patient service assistant
RBV	resource-based view
R&D	research and development
RD&E	research, development and engineering
RFT	Request for Tender
RNS	Regulatory News Services
ROI	return on investment
RTS	returns to scale
SAT	Scholastic Aptitude Test
SBS	Siemens Business Services
SEM	structural equation modelling
SCGH	Sir Charles Gairdner Hospital
SFA	stochastic frontier analysis
SGM	Shanghai General Motors
SLA	service-level agreement
SLM	service-level management
SME	small and medium-sized enterprise
SOGA	Sale of Goods Act 1982
SSC	shared service centre
T&M	time and material
TC	technical change
TCE	transaction cost economics
TCO	total cost of ownership
TCT	transaction cost theory

TFP	total factor productivity
THS	temporary help supply
TUPE	Transfer of Undertakings (Protection of Employment) Regulations 1981
UCN	University College, Northampton
UCTA	Unfair Contract Terms Act 1977
VODC	virtual offshore development centre
VSP	vertical application service provider
W/S (ratio)	wages to sales (ratio)
WTO	World Trade Organization

About The Editors

Peter Barrar is Emeritus Professor at the University of Manchester. Until recently, he held the Chair in Operations Management at Manchester Business School (MBS), where he was Associate Dean of Faculty for academic affairs and, latterly, Deputy Director. He has also held appointments as Director of the full-time MBA, Director of the Postgraduate Centre and Director of the Centre for Business Research at MBS. His research interests and publications cover the use of computer-based production management and control systems, inventory management and control, performance measurement – benchmarking and outsourcing – and the strategic use of technology in manufacturing and service businesses.

Roxane Gervais obtained her PhD from the University of Hull. She has worked for many years in diverse teams, in both the public and private sectors and in international environments. Her previous roles include working for corporations such as IBM and British Airways as well as working with different consultancy firms to organize and execute research programmes. She is a highly goal-oriented professional with strong data analytic and interpretation experience. While working in the health care industry she was heavily involved in a major organizational change programme, and assisted the organization in formulating policies to move from a centralized, free system to a decentralized fee-paying one. Roxane's research interests include the effects of outsourcing on individuals, organizational change, the influence of acculturation on behaviour, job stress and strain, job satisfaction, the effects of job loss through the downsizing process on individuals, the development of the diary methodology and individual differences. She has presented her research at international conferences.

About the Contributors

Hussam Al-Shammari lectures at the Eberly College of Business and Information Technology, Indiana University of Pennsylvania. He obtained his PhD from the University of Texas at Arlington. After obtaining his MBA degree from Yarmouk University in Jordan in 1998, he taught at the Hashemite University (1998–1999) and Yarmouk University (1999–2002), both in Jordan. Hussam's research interests include executive compensation, corporate governance and outsourcing. He teaches courses in strategic management, small business and entrepreneurship, and foundations of management.

John Benson is a Professor in the School of Management, University of South Australia, Australia. From 1994 to 1997 he was Professor of Economics and Management at Hiroshima City University, Japan. He holds a PhD from the University of Melbourne and is the author/ editor of six monographs and over 70 refereed papers and book chapters. His major research interests are Japanese management and unions, the restructuring of Chinese industry, outsourcing and knowledge work. John has recently published. with Dr Chris Rowley (City University, London), an edited volume titled *Changes and Continuities in Asian Human Resource Management: Convergence Revisited* (London, Frank Cass, 2004).

Anthony Boardman is the Van Dusen Professor of Business Management in the Strategy and Business Economics Division at the Sauder School of Business, University of British Columbia (UBC). He studied for his BA at the University of Kent at Canterbury in England and obtained his PhD from Carnegie-Mellon University in Pittsburgh. Prior to joining the UBC he was on the Faculty at the Wharton School, University of Pennsylvania. Anthony's interests are in the areas of cost–benefit analysis, privatization, contracting out and public–private partnerships. His research has been published in leading academic journals and he is co-author of *Cost-Benefit Analysis: Concepts and Practice*, which is published by Prentice-Hall. He has served as a consultant to many public- and private-sector organizations and is also President of the Norfolk Consulting Group.

David H. Brown is a Senior Lecturer in Management Science, Department of Management Science, Lancaster University. He was previously Head of the Department of Systems and also past Director of the MSc in Information Management. His teaching and research is in the area of strategy and IT, including e-business. David has particular experience of exploring these areas in the context of transitional economies, especially that of China.

Rachel Burnett became an IT professional working in system development and project management after graduating from Exeter University with a degree in sociology. After qualifying as a solicitor Rachel worked in one of the first niche IT law practices and then moved on to City of London law firms. After several years as a City partner, she now runs her own legal practice, acting for IT users and suppliers. Rachel is the author of *Outsourcing*

IT: The Legal Aspects, published by Gower, and co-author of *Drafting and Negotiating Computer Contracts*, published by Tottel and now in its second edition. She is also the editor of the series of IT Law Guides published for the Institute of Chartered Accountants. Rachel is Vice President (Forums) of the British Computer Society, a Court Assistant of the City of London Worshipful Company of Information Technologists and a former Chair of the Institute for the Management of Information Systems.

Dai Davis is a Technology Lawyer. He read Physics at Keble College, Oxford and took a Masters degree in Computing Science at the University of Newcastle-upon-Tyne before qualifying as a solicitor. He is a qualified chartered engineer and a member of the Institution of Electrical Engineers (IEE). Dai is Dai is a Partner with Brooke North LLP. Dai advises clients on intellectual property and computer and technology law subjects, including such topical matters as e-commerce issues. He is primarily a non-contentious lawyer, specializing in advising on information technology agreements, outsourcing and intellectual property licences. Dai is a council member of the Licensing Executives Society and also sits on the Executive Committee of the IEE Management Professional Network.

Mike Dodsworth is a senior HR manager responsible for UK outsourcing transitions and has 15 years' experience in Capgemini's outsourcing business. He is an expert in TUPE, the legislation that protects staff who transfer with outsourcing contracts, and is a leading practitioner in the successful integration of new employees into the company. With experience of over 250 outsourcing contracts of all shapes and sizes, Mike's implementation of best-practice processes ensures that clients benefit from smooth staff transition and continuity of service, whether transfers are from in-house departments or incumbent suppliers to new contracts with Capgemini. Mike will retire from Capgemini in 2006.

K. Matthew Gilley is Associate Professor of Management at Oklahoma State University. He holds a PhD in Strategic Management from the University of Texas at Arlington. His research interests include outsourcing, CEO compensation and corporate governance. His work has been published or is forthcoming in the *Strategic Management Journal*, the *Journal of Management*, the *Journal of International Business Studies*, the *Journal of Business Research*, among others.

Steven Globerman is the Kaiser Professor of International Business and the Director of the Center for International Business at Western Washington University's College of Business and Economics. He holds a PhD in Economics from New York University. Steven has consulted extensively for private companies, as well as governments and non-governmental agencies including The World Bank and the OECD. He served on the research staffs of two Royal Commissions for the Government of Canada and is listed in *Who's Who in Economics* and *Who's Who in International Business*.

Kathleen Goolsby has researched and written extensively about outsourcing trends, issues and best practices since 1998. She conducted an analysis of a comprehensive industry research study involving three major surveys on what causes outsourcing failures and subsequently co-authored, in 2004, a series of ten research papers presenting groundbreaking findings and conclusions. Kathleen spearheaded the Outsourcing Center's annual Outsourcing Excellence Awards research programme for four years, conducting extensive interviews of hundreds of leading C-level executives worldwide in order to identify early market trend indicators, pinpoint and evaluate best practices, and analyse success factors. She is the collaborator/

ghostwriter of *Turning Lead Into Gold: The Demystification of Outsourcing* (Peter Bendor-Samuel, Executive Excellence, Provo, Utah, 2000) and has also worked as a senior writer for *Outsourcing Journal* (www.outsourcing-journal.com). More than 100 of Kathleen's feature articles, white papers and research papers on outsourcing topics are available at www.outsourcing-center.com.

Christopher C. (Kit) Green is the Executive Director of Emergent Technologies Research and a Fellow in Neuroimaging of the Departments of Radiology and Psychiatry and the Detroit Medical Centre, Wayne State School of Medicine. Kit's specialties are real-time brain imaging and Forensic Science. He returned to medical practice in 2002 after working as General Motors' Chief Technology Officer, Asia Pacific. His interests are in neurophysiological connections of behaviour and cognition. He engages in issues relating to neurological health, neurodegenerative disease, learning, memory, language and culture that underpin 'decisions made under stress'. With Kristin Zimmerman, Kit initiated numerous academic programmes in Europe, Asia and the Middle East at numerous universities that intend to acquire science and engineering from centres of excellence globally. Of special interest were key emerging technologies in materials, manufacturing and medicine. He holds the National Intelligence Medal and serves on numerous defence and Intelligence Science Boards.

Almas Heshmati is a Professor of Economics at Seoul National University and MTT Economic Research, Helsinki, is associated with the Institute for the Study of Labor (IZA) and the German Institute for Economic Research (DIW). He was Research Fellow at the United Nations University UNU/WIDER from 2001 to 2003 and Associate Professor of Economics at the Stockholm School of Economics between 1998 and 2001. He has a PhD from the University of Gothenburg (1994) where he held a Senior Researcher position until 1998. His research interests include agricultural economics, economics of public services, economics of technology and innovation, labour, income distribution, income inequality, globalization, productivity, efficiency, economic growth and dynamics of capital structure. He has published in several journals, including *Econometric Reviews*, *Economic Theory*, *European Journal of Operational Research*, *International Journal of Industrial Organization*, *Journal of Applied Econometrics*, *Journal of International Economics*, and the *Scandinavian Journal of Economics*.

Erica Hewitt is the Director and Principal Consultant for Management Projects, a business that provides consultancy services to government. She holds a DBA and a Bachelor of Economics from the University of Western Australia. Ricki started her career in the Australian Treasury and subsequently worked as an economist and industrial relations specialist in the Legislative Research Service of the Australian Commonwealth Parliamentary Library. She has also provided consultancy services in vocational education, and training and development in Canberra. Ricki is particularly interested in promoting the nexus between academic research and public-sector decision making through the development of soundly-based analytical evaluation tools that can be used by public-sector managers.

Julian Howison is the CEO/founder of Arrk Group, a UK-based management consultancy and IT services business, with a wholly owned subsidiary in India. Prior to this, Julian spent several years working as a CIO in the UK insurance and financial services sectors. He worked as a management consultant with PriceWaterhouseCoopers, helping large corporations formulate and implement their IT and telecommunications strategies. An electronics engineer by training, he started his career working in the instrumentation sector before moving on to data communications systems software development. In 1985 he led a team in the USA developing the world's first Internet mailbridge gateways. Julian speaks and lectures frequently on offshoring issues to audiences in UK, Europe and India. His special interests include offshoring and the SME and corporate social responsibility in offshoring. He has managed IT and business operations in the UK, Ireland, France, the USA and India.

Ahmad H. Juma'h holds a PhD in Finance and Accounting from Manchester Business School (1999). He is a certified public accountant (CPA), and is a member of the Certified Public Accountant Puerto Rico chapter. Since 1991 he has worked as an auditor and consultant for small companies in Puerto Rico. As a lecturer in different universities in Puerto Rico he taught courses in accounting and finance from 1987 to 1992. In 1992 he became a member of the Faculty of Economics and Business Administration, Inter-American University, and in 1996 was appointed to the position of Associate Professor of Accounting and Finance. He has published several articles related to business service outsourcing. Ahmad's research interests include global outsourcing, materiality implications in decision matters, innovations, research and development, and behavioural finance.

Andrew Kakabadse is Professor of International Management Development and Community Director of Leadership and Organisation Development at Cranfield School of Management. He has acted as Visiting Professor at a number of US, Australian and Chinese universities. His areas of research cover boards and top teams, the governance of enterprises and governments, international relations and conflict resolution. He has published 26 books, over 145 articles and 16 monographs. Andrew has consulted and lectured in the UK, Europe, the USA, South-east Asia, China, Japan, Russia, Georgia, the Gulf States and Australia. He was also Vice Chancellor of the International Academy of Management and has been Chairman of the Division of Occupational Psychology of the British Psychological Society. He is co-editor of the *Journal of Management Development* and sits on the editorial board of the *Journal of Managerial Psychology* and the *Leadership and Organization Development Journal*.

Nada K. Kakabadse is currently Professor in Management and Business Research at the Northampton Business School, co-editor (with Andrew Kakabadse) of the *Journal of Management Development* and editor of the *Corporate Governance* journal. Nada has published widely in the areas of leadership, the application of IS/IT in corporations, corporate governance, government, boardroom effectiveness, diversity management and ethics: her publications include six books, 36 chapters in international volumes, three monographs and over 80 scholarly and reviewed articles. Nada has acted as consultant to numerous public- and private-sector organizations.

Tony Kelly has held management roles in consulting, technology and outsourcing in his ten years with Capgemini, including: manufacturing consultancy – the start-up of the company's SAP business; development of ERP service offers; and management of the package-based solutions delivery team. He also designed and managed Capgemini's UK Alliance Programme and the Third Party Product Reseller business. Tony is currently Business Development Director in Capgemini's Global Business Process Outsourcing operation.

Andreas Knabe has studied economics at the University of Magdeburg, Germany, and the University of Kentucky, USA. He is currently working as a Research Associate at the University of Magdeburg. His main field of interest is labour market theory and public policy.

Bertrand Koebel is Professor of Economics at the Louis Pasteur University, Strasbourg. Previously, he was Research Fellow at the Centre for European Economic Research (ZEW, Mannheim), University College, London, and Assistant Professor at Otto-von-Guericke University, Magdeburg. He gained his PhD from Louis Pasteur University in 1997. Bertrand's research relates to the determinants of heterogeneous labour demand, production analysis and applied econometrics.

Jane C. Linder is Executive Research Fellow and Director of Research at the Accenture Institute for High Performance Business in Cambridge, Massachusetts. She is the author of many publications including *Outsourcing for Radical Change: A Bold Approach to Enterprise Transformation* (New York, Amacom, 2004).

Nigel Lockett is the Relationship Manager for InfoLab and E-Business at Lancaster University Management School. He is the Director of the MSc in E-Business and Innovation. He teaches e-business at both undergraduate and postgraduate levels and his research interests include e-business and SMEs, IS implementation and systems thinking. With 14 years' senior management experience, including eight years as Managing Director of a healthcare supplies company and two years as Managing Director of a UK plc, he has a proven track record in managing enterprises.

Chris Lonsdale is a lecturer in supply chain management at the University of Birmingham. He has written widely on the issues of outsourcing, supplier relationship management, organizational buying behaviour, venture capital and UK government contracting policy. Over recent years he has worked with the NHS, IBM and Rolls Royce in the area of purchasing and supply. He is a member of the Chartered Institute of Purchasing and Supply.

Ronan McIvor is a Reader at the University of Ulster. He has carried out extensive research in supply chain management and information systems. He is currently involved in research projects in the areas of outsourcing and the application of electronic commerce at the buyer-supplier interface with a number of manufacturing and service organizations. He has been actively involved in the development of knowledge-based and decision support systems to assist in a variety of business applications, including a tendering and estimating system for use in an aerial surveys company and an advice tool for public-sector bodies on European procurement legislation. He has published articles in a number of leading international journals including *OMEGA*, *International Journal of Operations and Production Management*, *The Journal of Supply Chain Management* and *Decision Support Systems*. He has recently authored a book, *The Outsourcing Process: Strategies for Evaluation and Management*, published by Cambridge University Press.

Amit Mehta is a holder of an Engineering degree from India and an MBA from the UK specializing in globalization strategy. During his studies and in his professional career, Amit has maintained a keen interest in IT Offshoring, which he has researched extensively, focussing on key areas such as understanding the critical success factors for IT Offshoring on the UK SME sector. As an IT professional, he has successfully fulfilled roles in business development and more recently as a delivery manager, setting up an offshore software delivery centre for a UK-based plc. Amit comes with strong program management, consulting and process capabilities and has global experience working with blue-chip companies in Southeast Asia and the UK.

Kyösti Pietola gained his PhD at Michigan State University in 1997 on the basis of his research on agricultural economics, economic theory and econometrics. He has worked first as a researcher and then as a Senior Agricultural Economist in Agrifood Research Finland (MTT). Since 2001 he has served as a Professor and Director of the Economic Research Unit of MTT. Since 1999 he has been serving as a docent at the University of Helsinki. Kyösti's research has focused on agribusiness economics and on how different policies promote firm-level decisions that either improve economic performance of individual firms or, more generally, steer structural development in agriculture. His work involves dynamic optimization routines to solve firm management problems that usually are stochastic and have a discreet nature such that underlying data are highly censored. His publications include models on discrete technology choices, irreversible investments and entry/exit decisions from the perspective of individual firms.

David Poole is vice president for Business Process Outsourcing (BPO) Operations, Capgemini. He is responsible for ensuring optimal service delivery from all of Capgemini's global BPO locations, and oversees further enhancement of Capgemini's strategy for its BPO centres, sales support, solution design, products and BPO delivery technology. David's expertise spans a wide range of industry sectors including retail, manufacturing, pharmaceuticals and oil. His specialism is in the design and implementation of complex global BPO projects and in solving the change management issues that often arise across multiple locations.

Valeria Pulignano is a professor in the Centre for Sociological Research, Katholieke Universiteit, Belgium. Her research interests include comparative European industrial relations, systems of employee representation at both national and European levels, multinational corporations, trade union organization, employment restructuring practices and unions' response. She has published widely on organizational and industrial restructuring and unions' responses at both local and comparative European levels. She is currently responsible for the coordination of a research project on 'Trade Unions Anticipating Change in Europe' (TRACE) at the European Trade Union College (ETUCO) in Brussels. The project aims to develop knowledge and skills and built capacity within the European trade unions movement to anticipate and manage change more effectively.

Abdul A. Rasheed is Professor of Strategic Management and International Business at the University of Texas at Arlington. He obtained his PhD from the University of Pittsburgh in 1988 and his MBA from the Indian Institute of Management, Calcutta, in 1981. Abdul's areas of research interest include strategic decision processes, environmental analysis, outsourcing, franchising, foreign market entry, international comparisons in strategy and governance, and corporate restructuring. His research has been published in journals such as *Academy of Management Review, Strategic Management Journal, Journal of Management, Journal of Management Studies, British Journal of Management, Journal of Business Ethics, Journal of Small Business Management, Journal of Business Research, Management International Review, Academy of Management Executive* and *International Business Review*. He has taught also in Singapore, China, Taiwan and Hong Kong. Prior to joining academicia, Abdul spent a decade in senior positions in the banking industry in India and Bahrain.

Alison Smart is a Lecturer in Operations Management at Manchester Business School, University of Manchester. Previously she has worked at the University of Edinburgh Management School. She has a BSc and DPhil in Chemistry and obtained an MBA after several years working as an industrial research and development chemist. Her research interests include business processes, social responsibility in the supply chain and operations issues facing small and medium-sized enterprises.

Robert Stehrer studied economics at the Johannes Kepler University of Linz, Austria, and sociology at the Institute for Advanced Studies (IAS) in Vienna. At present he is Research Economist at the Vienna Institute for International Economic Studies, Vienna, and Lecturer in Economics at the Johannes Kepler University, Linz. His fields of research are international economic integration, the effects of technical change and trade on employment and wages, structural change and growth, economic dynamics and applied econometrics. His special interests concern the analysis and applications of frameworks focusing on long-term economic and social dynamics. He has published a number of theoretical, as well as empirical, articles in journals and books in these fields.

Aidan R. Vining is the CNABS Professor of Business and Government Relations in the Faculty of Business Administration, Simon Fraser University, Vancouver. He joined the Faculty of Business in 1984. He obtained his PhD from the University of California, Berkeley. He holds also an LLB (King's College, London) and an MBA and MPP. He teaches and researches in the areas of business strategy and public policy analysis. Particular areas of research interest include outsourcing, internal organizational markets, public–private partnerships and privatization. Recent articles have appeared in the *Journal of Management Studies, Industrial and Corporate Change*, the *Journal of Strategic Management Education*, the *Annals of Public and Cooperative Economics* and the *European Management Journal*, among others. He is the co-author (with David Weimer) of *Policy Analysis: Concepts and Practice*, now in its fourth edition (Englewood Cliffs, Prentice Hall, 2004) and *Cost-Benefit Analysis: Concepts and Practice* (Englewood Cliffs, Prentice Hall, 1996). He recently co-edited (with John Richards) *Building the Future: Issues in Public Infrastructure in Canada* (Toronto, C.D. Institute, 2001).

Kristin B. Zimmerman is the Manager of Environment and Energy Policy at General Motors Public Policy Centre. Kristin joined General Motors (GM) Research and Development Centre in 1993 to create GM's Global Academic Partnerships Programme. The Programme's structure, process and tools for effective acquisition of technical expertise from the academic sector became the protocol for establishing GM's Global Satellite Laboratory Network. In 1994 Kristin wrote the GM Academic Partnerships Master Agreement that helped to create the GM–Shanghai joint venture. She currently heads GM's annual global corporate responsibility project that focuses on greenhouse gas reporting policy and practices and manages GM's Atlantic Rainforest Project in Brazil. She was awarded the 1999–2000 GM Fellowship to the National Academy of Engineering in Washington DC, to work on policy development of the nation's engineering, science, and technology workforce. Kristin received a PhD in Engineering Mechanics in 1993 from Michigan State University.

1 *The Nature of Outsourcing and its Present State*

As few attempts have been made to adequately define what is outsourcing and how it is changing within the dynamic state of the work economy it has become necessary to examine whether or not one of the main economic and organizational processes of the last 20 years has stayed as a static process or has evolved to assimilate more easily into the ways in which companies progress and advance their working practices. Part 1 of this volume will therefore address the current state of outsourcing in the working environment and those factors and considerations that may impact on its development in the future.

The opening chapter of Part 1 presents an overview of the benefits that could be gained from outsourcing, as well as the costs associated with the process. The authors, Steven Globerman and Aidan Vining, examine the concept of outsourcing from a firm's perspective with a focus on its specific governance costs. They also discuss four potential outsourcing situations that centre on the dynamics of product complexity and asset specificity, with suggestions for dealing with each scenario. They conclude by outlining the benefits that outsourcing can bring to organizations.

Matthew Gilley, Abdul Rasheed and Hussam Al-Shammari are responsible for outlining the nature of outsourcing. Their chapter defines outsourcing and lists those major theoretical perspectives that researchers have used in studying the process. They end the chapter with advice on areas and concepts that may prove useful in advancing future research on outsourcing.

Chapter 3 defines the drivers that have been a part of the outsourcing experience within the business environment. In this chapter Ronan McIvor examines the effect that these drivers, such as globalization and a more demanding consumer, have had on both the public and private sectors. The examination of outsourcing across both of these sectors reveals that it is a non-restrictive process. Finally, McIvor suggests what future trends may impact on the way in which outsourcing may develop and the directions that it may take.

Tony Kelly and David Poole, in Chapter 4, investigate the ways in which outsourcing has evolved, including the change in outsourcing from a traditional to a transformational process, as well as offshoring and new technologies. These factors have refined, and continue to refine, outsourcing, and the authors provide examples of these changes within companies.

Part 1 concludes with a chapter by Andrew Kakabadse and Nada Korac-Kakabadse examining the recent developments in global information technology (IT) sourcing. The authors explore the impact that offshoring has had on outsourcing and the reservation that has surfaced in recent times towards global outsourcing. Finally, they propose those best-practice factors that could lead to a better outsourcing relationship.

1 The Outsourcing Decision: A Strategic Framework

Steven Globerman and Aidan R. Vining

The growth of outsourcing

Firms as diverse as Sun Microsystems, IBM, Mattel, Boeing and Calvin Klein all engage in extensive outsourcing. Sun, for example, currently purchases around 75 per cent of its components from external suppliers (Domberger, 1999). Estimates currently put the market value of outsourcing in the United States (US) at between US$200 and US$300 billion (Dun and Bradstreet, 2000). As outsourcing continues to grow in importance, its nature and focus is evolving. Historically, most outsourcing took place in manufacturing industries, but it is now spreading rapidly within service industries. It is also becoming increasingly cross-national and global: for example, it is estimated that only approximately 40 per cent of the production value of a North American-made automobile now comes from the US, and much of this offshore supply is outsourced.

The nature of outsourcing is diverse. Some firms now outsource core production activities so extensively that they no longer engage in production, as traditionally understood. Inbound and outbound logistics are being extensively outsourced also (Knemeyer *et al.*, 2003; Zsidisin, 2003). Other firms are extensively outsourcing secondary value-chain activities such as information technology, accounting systems, distribution, aspects of human resources management and R&D (Johnson and Schneider, 1995; Lacity and Willcocks, 1998; Odagiri, 2003; Ono, 2003).

Despite its increasing importance, many firms do not have a clear understanding of the benefits and costs of outsourcing (Smith *et al.*, 1998). Yet, the outsourcing firm is inevitably placing at least part of its destiny in the hands of other firms that are seeking to maximize *their* profits. Thus, while outsourcing is often described as an 'alliance', the contracting parties inevitably have conflicting interests (Lacity and Hirschheim, 1993). The strategic objective of outsourcing decision makers should seek to maximize the net benefits of outsourcing relative to the in-house provision of value-chain activities. In practice, this can often be simplified to minimizing the total costs of any given quantity and quality of outsourced good or activity. However, costs must be viewed comprehensively. Costs consist of expenditures for the good itself *and* the costs associated with 'governing' the outsourcing transaction. This raises a number of fundamental questions relating to governance costs. How can the firm assess *ex ante* the potential governance costs that arise with outsourcing? How, and under what circumstances, can governance costs be reduced?

In this chapter first we present a framework for assessing outsourcing benefits and costs from the firm's perspective; second, we identify the specific governance costs associated with outsourcing; third, we delineate the three major determinants of outsourcing governance costs: product/activity complexity, contestability and asset specificity; fourth, we present four standard potential outsourcing situations and suggest appropriate responses for each; and, finally, we present some brief conclusions relating to the contingent nature of the potential net benefits of outsourcing.

The benefits from outsourcing

Investors expect outsourcing to create value for shareholders (Hayes *et al.*, 2000). The purpose of outsourcing is to: (1) lower the purchase price of some input by taking advantage of external suppliers' lower costs, or (2) improve the quality of some input by purchasing some superior capability from an external supplier. In either case, the supplier's advantage will be one that is not easily imitable. If the firm could easily imitate the cost or capability advantage of outside suppliers, it could produce the activity 'in-house'. The acquisition of superior capabilities can also be thought of in cost-saving terms – superior capabilities could only be produced at the same quality within the firm at higher cost. However, it is usual in the business strategy literature to analyse each activity on the value chain in terms of the firm's ability to lower cost or to improve quality (or, more broadly, to in some way differentiate their production process). We follow that distinction in the following discussion of the potential benefits of outsourcing.

COST-REDUCING RATIONALES FOR OUTSOURCING

The costs of outsourcing must be compared to the costs of internal production of the activity. Production costs are those directly generated by the opportunity costs of the resources used to produce the good. Clearly it is impossible to design firms to take advantage of economies of scale for *all* inputs – even the largest global pharmaceutical firms do not manufacture their own computers. Many inputs are inevitably outsourced. Therefore, outsourcing is really only a further step on the continuum from purchasing and procurement.

There are a number of production cost rationales for outsourcing. The most basic is that internal production of the activity entails production at levels that are too low to be efficient – that is, to achieve minimum efficient scale (Lyons, 1995). Many goods and services for which the organization has low unit demand exhibit significant cost 'lumpiness' (McFarlan and Nolan, 1995). The most significant economies of scale may relate to secondary value-chain activities such as administrative and information systems, knowledge and learning, access to capital markets and marketing (Veugelers and Cassiman, 1999). Similarly, economies of scope are becoming a rationale for outsourcing. With the advent of flexible manufacturing, the potential for economies of scope has increased dramatically (Pine, 1993). Firms that can utilize the same production equipment for a range of products have a significant cost advantage compared to smaller, specialized firms (Besanko *et al.*, 2001). Another cost advantage is the potential to change large fixed capital costs into variable costs (Quelin and Duhamel, 2003). Other cost-based rationales for outsourcing include superior external supplier economies of learning (Hayes and Wheelwright, 1984), superior ability to introduce new product generations quickly at low cost, and greater capacity utilization (Morrison, 2003).

There are also *organizational* cost factors that can motivate outsourcing. Most importantly, especially in large multi-unit organizations, internal units are often price-inefficient. Inefficient internal prices can arise for two reasons. First, the internal production unit may be an efficient low-cost producer, with price as a monopolist (Vining, 2003). Second, the production unit may not have the correct incentives to achieve the minimum feasible production costs, resulting in too high internal prices (Button and Weyman-Jones, 1994). Competition is normally the crucial driver in forcing production costs to their lowest level, but internal production units may not be subject to much competition (although firms can try to induce competition by making internal units bid against each other for production rights). This rationale for outsourcing may be more important than minimum efficient scale issues, especially for larger, bureaucratized firms.

Finally, cost savings can result from altering obligations that a firm faces under government laws and regulations or agreements with unions. For example, firms may be obliged to pay healthcare benefits to workers classified as 'full time', whereas part-time workers are not entitled to the same level of benefits (Abraham and Taylor, 1996). Outsourcing specific activities may enable firms to 're-hire' the same workers from external suppliers as temporary employees. Certainly, if labour markets are reasonably competitive and not segmented, such cost savings may prove to be only temporary.

There is some evidence that outsourcing can reduce production costs (Kakabadse and Kakabadse, 2002; Lacity and Hirschheim 1993; McFarlan and Nolan, 1995; Quelin and Duhamel, 2003) but, as noted by Leiblein *et al.* (2002), such evidence is surprisingly limited. Nevertheless, Ang (1998) found that a large sample of banks that outsource primarily considered production cost savings in their decisions, and there is some evidence to suggest that this finding is generalizable (Benson and Ieronimo, 1996; Lyons, 1995; Saunders *et al.*, 1997; Walker and Weber, 1987). Much of the best empirical evidence comes from outsourcing by government to private suppliers where production cost savings are approximately 20 per cent, especially if competitive bidding is used (Hodge, 2000; Vining and Globerman, 1999). However, almost no empirical studies have included the costs of governing the outsourcing relationship – specifically, bargaining and opportunism costs – which *a priori* might be expected to be higher with outsourcing. Indeed, some governance mechanisms for outsourcing can be expected to raise production costs above those of internal production – for example, if cost-plus contracts are used (McAfee and McMillan, 1988; Ulset, 1996).

DIFFERENTIATION (QUALITY) RATIONALES FOR OUTSOURCING

Firm-specific capabilities are increasingly recognized as the drivers of competitive success (Wernerfelt, 1984). Capabilities that are difficult to imitate are therefore the key to sustainable competitive advantage (Barney, 1991). Capabilities may be costly to imitate internally for four reasons:

1. unique historical conditions that no longer exist;
2. path dependency;
3. social complexity; and
4. 'causal ambiguity' resulting from the difficulty of knowing what is the source of the capability (Barney, 1999, pp. 140–41).

It may also be costly or infeasible for the firm to acquire another firm that has the capability (ibid., pp. 142–43).

Whatever the reasons for inimitability, a firm may be able to acquire the capability through outsourcing. Historically, for example, many firms have outsourced specialized legal services and advertising. The evidence suggests that this rationale for outsourcing is increasing (Kakabadse and Kakabadse, 2002; Quinn and Hilmer, 1994). Specifically, Quelin and Duhamel

(2003, p. 649) argue that 'cost reductions, while important, are but one objective expected from outsourcing. Other objectives include improved flexibility, quality and control.'

Again, as with cost reduction, the systematic empirical evidence of the value of outsourcing for improving quality is still quite limited. Gilley and Rasheed (2000) and Gilley et al. (2004) have recently found evidence that outsourcing various aspects of human resources management can promote innovation, although they did not find direct evidence of financial performance improvements. Leiblein et al. (2002) present evidence of benefits from outsourcing that are contingent on the specific attributes of the contractual relationship, in terms of both the nature of the activity to be outsourced and the governance response by the firm.

We turn now to a consideration of governance costs that may potentially offset the cost-lowering or differentiating-enhancing benefits of outsourcing.

THE AGGREGATE COSTS OF OUTSOURCING

Direct purchase cost savings or superior resources may be offset by increases in governance costs (Masten et al., 1991, p. 28). Governance costs are any costs in addition to production/purchase costs. Two conceptually distinct types of governance costs are relevant in the choice between internal production and outsourcing: bargaining costs and opportunism costs.

Bargaining costs

Bargaining costs arise when both parties are acting with self-interest, but in good faith (Williamson, 1985). They include:

1. contract negotiation costs;
2. post-contract negotiation costs arising from unforeseen circumstances;
3. contract monitoring costs to ensure that the other party is adhering to the contract; and
4. the costs of disputes which arise if neither party wishes to utilize pre-agreed-to resolution mechanisms, especially 'contract-breaking' mechanisms.

Whilst only the first cost is directly experienced at the time of contracting, virtually all of these bargaining costs can be anticipated and dealt with at the time of contracting.

An advantage of 'internalizing' an activity is that bargaining costs over the *distribution* of costs within the firm are normally lower. However, as the earlier discussion of monopoly intimated, bargaining within organizations over such things as internal transfer prices can be costly (Alles et al., 1998). Thus, it is the incremental bargaining costs of outsourcing that are relevant. Recent evidence does suggest that bargaining costs are higher with external suppliers (Simester and Knez, 2002) since they include costs associated with communications. However, technological change and deregulation have reduced these costs, especially for international transactions, and have thereby encouraged international outsourcing (MacPherson and Pritchard, 2002).

Opportunism costs

'Opportunism' is any behaviour by a party to a transaction designed to change the agreed terms of a transaction to be more in its favour. Opportunism costs arise when at least one party acts self-interestedly, but in bad faith. It is more likely to occur in outsourcing contexts than in transactions within organizations, since the distribution of profit is more relevant in dealings between organizations. In addition, employees within organizations have more opportunities to 'pay back' (and therefore discourage) opportunistic fellow employees. However, as opportunism can occur also within organizations (Vining, 2003), it is, again, the incremental opportunism costs that are relevant. Opportunism is usually considered to be more likely after the outsourcing contract has been implemented, but some behaviours prior to contracting have also 'opportunism-like' characteristics.

Management should seek the regime that minimizes the sum of its production, bargaining and opportunism costs. The contention, developed in the remainder of the chapter, is that bargaining and opportunism costs can be minimized. Firm executives can do so by identifying the critical attributes of the pre-contractual environment and implementing outsourcing strategies that effectively recognize those attributes. Executives should then compare the estimated costs of outsourcing with the costs of internalization – that is, the cost of the firm producing the good itself.

The determinants of outsourcing costs

Three major factors are likely to determine the sum of bargaining and opportunism costs: product/activity complexity, contestability and asset specificity.[1] These critical attributes of the outsourcing environment are summarized in Table 1.1.

Table 1.1   A summary of outsourcing states

Case	Product/ Activity Complexity	Specific Assets (Degree)	Dominant Problem(s)	Solution(s)
1	Low	Low	Few	Rely primarily on contestability via contract termination (i.e. increase potential suppliers).
2	Low	High	Hold-up	For physical assets, outsourcing firm owns and leases assets; for temporal specificity, backloaded payments, bonuses and bonding. Use of quick arbitration.
3	High	Low	Honest disagreement about quality and other performance attributes.	Where possible, mutually agreed-upon practice guidelines.
4	High	High	Opportunism by external supplier.	Harmonize outsourcing firm and external supplier incentives through 'rent-creation'.

Source: Reproduced with kind permission from *European Management Journal*.

---

1   The next two sections draw on Vining and Globerman (1999), with kind permission of the *European Management Journal*.

PRODUCT/ACTIVITY COMPLEXITY

Product (service) or activity complexity largely determines the difficulty of specifying and monitoring the terms of a transaction. Goods, services or activities can be approximately divided into search goods, experience goods and post-experience goods (Vining and Weimer, 1988). A good is a search good if its price-performance characteristics are known before the outsourcing decision. Indeed, as mentioned earlier, decisions such as the purchase of ballpoints are simply procurement. A good is an experience good if its price-performance characteristics are approximately known soon after purchase. For example, assessing the quality of food served by an external supplier can be assessed at the time of consumption. A good is a post-experience good if its price-performance characteristics cannot be assessed for a considerable time (if ever, when full revelation is dependent on contingent events) after use. Measuring the price-performance characteristics of a complex good such as research and development (R&D) is difficult (Tapon and Cadsby, 1996; Ulset, 1996). Unique and/or new (to the outsourcing firm) goods are almost always complex.

The degree of product/activity complexity largely determines the uncertainty surrounding the contract (this affects both contracting parties equally), the potential for information asymmetry (the probability that one party to the contract will have information that the other party does not have), and the probability that there will be aspects of the transaction that will affect other firm activities (externalities). Complex goods involve uncertainty about the nature and costs of the production process itself. Greater uncertainty raises bargaining costs, both during contract negotiations and post-contractually. Information asymmetry occurs when one party has relevant information that the other party does not; it usually raises costs, especially if a contract involves post-experience goods. High task complexity raises the probability that there is information asymmetry, because it implies specialized knowledge or assets whose characteristics are initially known only to external suppliers. Information asymmetry thus raises the probability that one party can behave opportunistically.

Opportunism arising from information asymmetry can occur either at the contract negotiation stage (typically when there is information asymmetry *and* low contestability) or post-contractually, but it is most likely to be significant post-contract. Either party may generate these costs. Higher task complexity increases also the potential for production externalities – the potential for serious disruption to the rest of the firm if the outsourced service is withdrawn or degraded (Globerman, 1995). From the outsourcing firm's standpoint, product/activity complexity raises costs, both because there is uncertainty surrounding the transaction, and because potential external suppliers often have more information about attributes of the relevant transactions. Thus, it may be very difficult for outsourcing firms to ensure that the quality of services provided is appropriately high.

The empirical evidence supports the idea that product complexity raises the probability of internal production. Masten (1984), for example, found that more complex components for the aerospace industry were more likely to be produced internally than to be outsourced. Mowery and Rosenberg (1989) found that R&D outsourcing is more likely for less complex functions such as material testing and process invention and less likely for product innovation. Jensen and Rothwell (1998) found that nuclear power plants were less likely to outsource complex 'production-critical' activities and where the quality is more difficult to assess before a problem occurs. Veugelers and Cassiman (1999) found that complexity led Belgian manufacturing firms to reduce the probability of them relying exclusively on external technology sourcing. Novak and Eppinger (2001) found a significant and positive relationship between product complexity and internalisation in the automobile industry.

CONTESTABILITY

The number of firms that can supply a product or service affects the likelihood that the outsourcing firm will purchase on the 'spot' market. Hubbard (2001) found that doubling the thickness of the long-haul trucking market increases the probability that spot contracts will be used by around 30 per cent. Besanko *et al.* (2001) found that firms in competitive commodity industries pass on marginal cost reductions more than firms in industries with more differentiated products. Ono (2003) found that US manufacturing firms are more likely to outsource advertising, accounting and legal services the larger the size of the supplying market. Finally, Leiblein *et al.* (2002) found that firms in the semiconductor industry produce in-house when there are few suppliers and outsource when there are many.

In many contexts, the competitive structure of the market may be less important than its contestability (Baumol *et al.*, 1982). A contestable market is one where only one or a few firms are immediately available to provide any given service, but many firms would quickly become available if the price paid by the outsourcing firm exceeded the average cost incurred by external suppliers.[2] For example, the market for basic accounting services is highly contestable as many firms have the capability to supply such services, even if they are not currently doing so.

The degree to which the activity being outsourced is contestable affects opportunism costs. If the market is contestable, opportunism is reduced at both the contract and post-contract stages. However, low contestability raises different issues at each stage. During contract negotiation, a potential external supplier in a low contestability market is tempted to offer services at a price above marginal cost (or average cost, where average cost is declining for the good). This higher price is a bargaining cost, as it is a direct result of outsourcing. At the post-contract stage, low contestability increases the risks of opportunism, both because an external supplier cannot be quickly replaced (temporal specificity) and because there is a higher risk of contract breach externalities. This risk is especially high when the external supplier provides services that are related to a network of some kind within the outsourcing firm. For example, an external firm that provides payroll operations may threaten to withdraw service, effectively shutting down the firm. Situations where firms fear breach externalities are often defined as 'strategic' systems. However, firms do not eliminate these externality problems by internalizing these activities. As the FedEx strike in the United States illustrated, employees can behave opportunistically also by withdrawing essential services (passive breach) or even by sabotage (active breach).

Some firms unintentionally contribute to their contestability problems. If potential suppliers perceive that outsourcing firms solicit 'unreasonably low' bids or demand rebids at lower prices, a competitive market may not emerge. Similarly, some outsourcing firms encourage excessive supplier specialization. This reduces other supplier firms' capacity to provide the good in the face of unsatisfactory performance. This latter point underscores the need for firms to think broadly about the cost consequences of specific outsourcing strategies. Short-run cost savings, and even improvements in quality, associated with economies of specialization, may be achieved at the expense of higher aggregate long-run costs.

In contrast, outsourcing firms can enhance competition by expanding the geographic market. This is certainly an important impetus for the growth of cross-national outsourcing (Feenstra, 1998). This strategy is less feasible if lack of contestability from location asset

---

2   In this section, we will argue that contestability is a derivative consequence of asset specificity. Hence, Table 1.1 does not contain a specific reference to contestability.

specificity (see below), rather than sunk costs *per se*. Another potential way of mitigating competition problems is for the outsourcing firm to own the (sunk cost) assets and lease them to the external supplier. The external supplier owns only relatively fungible assets. Thus, the need for potential new suppliers to make large sunk-cost investments is mitigated and contestability enhanced.

Finally, contestability is also a function of the capability of the firm to bring the service back in-house ('backsourcing'). To effectively outsource, firms must retain a 'core' employee capacity anyway. If this capacity can be readily expanded because there are trained specialists available, the outsourcing firm can credibly threaten backsourcing. There is evidence that more firms are investing in backsourcing capabilities (Hirschheim, 1998).

In sum, neither economies of scale nor the need for sunk-cost investments are necessarily barriers to contestability. In particular, if either outsourcing firms or external suppliers are mobile, small numbers of competitors need not eliminate competition. If they are not mobile, the problem is better evaluated as one of location asset specificity. Indeed, for the remainder of this chapter, we assume that contestability can be achieved in all cases.

ASSET SPECIFICITY

A specific asset is one that has much lower value in any alternative use. There are various kinds of specificity, including physical asset specificity, location specificity, human asset specificity, dedicated assets (Williamson, 1985, p. 55) and temporal specificity (Masten *et al.*, 1991, p. 9; Pirrong, 1993). Whatever its form, asset specificity obliges one or another party to employ assets (usually capital assets, but in some circumstances human capital assets) that have little or no alternative use and raise the potential for opportunism. No matter what prices are agreed to in the contracting stage, the other party can behave opportunistically by reneging and offering lower prices that only cover incremental costs (Shelanski and Klein, 1995; Ulset, 1996).

Extensive evidence suggests that asset specificity reduces the degree of outsourcing (for a review, see Vining and Globerman, 1999; for recent empirical evidence, see Ang, 1998; Azoulay, 2002; Hubbard, 2001; Leiblein *et al.*, 2002; Saussier, 2000). Intermediate levels of asset specificity, when not leading to complete internalization, often lead to long-term contracts (Joskow, 1987; Pirrong, 1993).

Outsourcing situations and some possible strategies

Although bargaining and opportunism costs can occur during contracting or post-contractually, it is feasible and desirable for the outsourcing firm to address these costs at the contracting stage. The parties are conceptually in a multi-period game (Rasmussen, 1994). The outsourcing 'player' should anticipate what the optimal strategy in each period of the game will be for the external supplier player and (by backward induction) identify its own optimal strategy. For example, suppose the outsourcing firm is playing a game where contestability is high pre-contract, but is expected to be low post-contractually. The outsourcing firm, therefore, can predict that an external supplier will behave opportunistically or generate bargaining costs post-contractually. The outsourcing firm should therefore incorporate this expectation into its strategy. The optimal result is an initial contract that anticipates and addresses all potential opportunism costs and bargaining costs.

To do so, however, outsourcing firms must distinguish between *ex ante* mechanisms and *ex post* mechanisms to minimize costs, emphasizing that, in the case of the latter, it is only the 'trigger' that is *ex post*. This advice may seem abstract, but recent evidence from an extensive survey of information technology outsourcing suggests that detailed contract specification is *the* leading predictor of outsourcing firm satisfaction (Lacity and Willcocks, 1998). Leiblein *et al.* (2002) also find that performance outcomes are crucially dependent on taking seriously the factors described above in determining whether, and how, to outsource (see also Gopal *et al.*, 2003).

This is not to say that managers should ordinarily strive for 'fully complete' contracts. There are obviously costs, as well as benefits, to establishing a complete contract. A contract can be seen as being more complete than another contract if it gives a more precise definition of the transaction and of the means to carry it out (Saussier, 2000). The costs of striving for more completeness include the bargaining costs described earlier, as well as the costs of acquiring information requisite to undertaking comprehensive contracting.

We now apply the framework to various combinations of product complexity and asset specificity (remembering that contestability problems can be treated as being ultimately co-extensive with asset specificity problems). We consider possible combinations of these two characteristics with the goal of illustrating the conceptual framework, rather than providing a definitive guide to all outsourcing issues.

LOW PRODUCT/ACTIVITY COMPLEXITY AND LOW ASSET SPECIFICITY

This combination provides the clearest case for outsourcing. It encompasses many standard products, services and activities required by the firm. Outsourcing offers the potential for lower production costs for the good or activity, as well as minimal bargaining and opportunism costs. Low product complexity implies that the outsourcing firm has, or can easily acquire, sufficient knowledge and information to specify contract terms precisely (as there is low uncertainty about price-performance characteristics and no information asymmetry). With low asset specificity (and resulting high contestability), inefficient or opportunistic external suppliers can be quickly replaced.

LOW PRODUCT/ACTIVITY COMPLEXITY AND HIGH ASSET SPECIFICITY

Given low complexity, problems associated with high asset specificity almost certainly involve high temporal or locational specificity. There are likely to be few efficiency costs arising from high physical asset specificity if the outsourcing firm makes the relevant specific investments itself as, given this ownership, it is not costly to replace the external supplier (given high contestability). There are likely to be problems, however, if the external supplier makes the investment. Once the investment is sunk, an external supplier is vulnerable to opportunistic hold-up by the outsourcing firm, which could demand that it deliver the good at marginal cost. Given that all potential external suppliers can deduce this as a possible *ex post* outcome, they will compensate *ex ante*. They can compensate in one of two possible ways: either by raising the bid price or by utilizing a higher-cost production technology that requires less physical asset specificity. Either strategy ultimately raises the outsourcing firm's costs.

One way of avoiding these problems is for the outsourcing firm to own the specific asset and to rent it or lease it to the external firm. However, leasing specific assets is not costless. The outsourcing firm is now outsourcing *two* activities – the original outsourced service and the lease contract (Hensher, 1988). Lease contracts can also generate opportunistic behaviour, including the potential for the lessee to overutilize and run down the leased assets. Including 'reasonable usage and maintenance' clauses can mitigate this problem in lease agreements.

However, this form of outsourcing requires detailed specification of both contracts, adding to costs.

Another method of dealing with the problem is for the outsourcing firm and the external supplier to explicitly share the asset-specific investments, a form of 'mutual hostage-holding'. Jap and Anderson (2003) find that such 'bilateral idiosyncratic investments' are the most powerful safeguard of high performance outcomes.

Temporal asset specificity raises several problems (Masten *et al.*, 1991). The first arises if the external supplier fails to provide contracted performance. The outsourcing firm's usual insurance against the opportunistic exercise of contract breach is an action in tort. However, this is less desirable than having a contract that mitigates breach incentives, especially in the case of transnational outsourcing where legal activity is likely to be both more costly and less predictable than in domestic outsourcing. The outsourcing firm can, for example, write a contract that contains provisions that backloads payment (contract completion bonuses) and requires performance bonding.

The second possible problem arises if the outsourcing firm wishes to terminate because of unsatisfactory performance, but needs to maintain service until a replacement external supplier is in place. The risk is that in 'endgame' situations external suppliers will act opportunistically. The most obvious way for an outsourcing firm to mitigate this risk is to demand bonding from a winning bidder *plus* a contract agreement that specifies timely arbitration of the firm's claim for the bond because of unsatisfactory contract performance (Eaton and White, 1982).

HIGH PRODUCT/ACTIVITY COMPLEXITY AND LOW ASSET SPECIFICITY

This configuration perhaps best characterizes the supply of a wide range of services or activities that are potentially outsourceable to professionals. When assessing potential outsourcing problems it should be kept in mind, however, that firms' employment contracts with professional employees are not very different from those with formally outsourced professionals. Basically, the same issues arise under either arrangement (Garen, 1998; James, 1998). The main problem is high bargaining costs owing to honest disagreements surrounding *ex ante* specifications or *ex post* performance in relationship to *ex ante* specifications. In particular, disagreements can arise because *ex ante* specifications are sometimes costly and difficult to write, and therefore the parties often have difficulty agreeing after the fact about whether the specifications were satisfied and, if not, whether the external supplier acted incompetently or negligently. This problem can be particularly relevant for multinational firms where management–employee relationships span cultural boundaries, and honest misunderstandings are more likely. However, in this situation, opportunism should not be a significant problem, since low asset specificity implies high contestability, suggesting that switching costs will be low for both parties. Opportunistic behaviour, once identified, can be easily countered by contract termination. A related inference one might draw is that short- to medium-term contracts with suppliers should be emphasized to avoid 'contractual strangleholds' (Currie, 1998).

HIGH PRODUCT/ACTIVITY COMPLEXITY AND HIGH ASSET SPECIFICITY

The important difference between this situation and the second case discussed above is that reliance on arbitration or other third-party contract enforcement procedures is more problematic, because it is more difficult for a judging third party to identify whether contract breach has occurred. This type of problem has been discussed in the industrial organization literature. The basic solution suggested is that outsourcing firms provide external suppliers with higher than normal profits that they can expect to earn indefinitely in the absence of a verified contract breach (Mathewson and Winter, 1990). The potential loss of these profits harmonizes the incentives of the firms.

Table 1.1 summarizes the relevant issues for each of the four cases described (Vining and Globerman, 1999). It focuses on two issues: the dominant problem(s) to be expected and a general strategic approach. The table identifies different combinations of problems and alternative instruments to modify each combination. However, the overall framework emphasizes the following steps:

1. Formulate consistent expectations about the uncertainties surrounding the potential transactions at all stages of contract formulation and implementation.
2. Identify the potential opportunism at different stages of contract formulation and implementation, including the underlying sources: contestability, complexity and/or asset specificity.
3. Identify contract provisions to attenuate the opportunism and assess the consequences of the preferred strategies for the overall efficiency of outsourcing versus internal production.
4. Implement the relevant strategies prior to the initiation of outsourcing.

Conclusions

There is increasing interest in outsourcing among firms in a wide range of industries. Moreover, there is evidence that outsourcing is becoming increasingly more international, so that the benefits and costs of outsourcing are becoming an increasingly important social issue, especially in the United States and Western European countries when it involves outsourcing activities to less developed countries. As a result, outsourcing governance is increasingly likely to include managing the political and stakeholder environment, an issue we do not address here. In this chapter we have suggested that contracting strategies on the part of the outsourcing firm can mitigate many of the potential costs associated with outsourcing. We have also proposed a simple framework that relates some alternative strategies for standard problem situations surrounding outsourcing, although this framework does not deal with all strategic outsourcing issues. The outsourcing firm also has to develop information strategies so that it can continue to learn – about changing costs and other relevant factors.

A strategic approach towards outsourcing must explicitly acknowledge the game-theoretic context in which the activity takes place and attempt to condition the environment in order to minimize the governance costs associated with outsourcing. It must recognize also that, in specific circumstances, the governance costs will be so high that a firm should not outsource. This approach is distinct from a strategy that emphasizes adaptation or renegotiation in response to conflict with an outsourcing partner (Melese, 2000). In this regard, management experts have argued that managers seriously underestimate the costs associated with transitioning to a new vendor (Barthelemy, 2001), and this observation strengthens the relevance of our suggested strategic approach.

The difficulties and costs associated with implementing a comprehensive strategic approach to outsourcing should not be underestimated. However, it is important to emphasize that there are likely to be economies of scale and scope in the outsourcing activity itself. Hence, substantial efficiencies may be realized by establishing a group or department specifically devoted to integrating company-wide experiences with outsourcing and using the resources in that unit to establish project teams with expertise in specific outsourcing activities (Barthelemy, 2001).

References

Abraham, K. and Taylor, S. (1996), 'Firms' use of outside contractors: theory and evidence', *Journal of Labor Economics*, vol. 14, no. 3, pp. 398–424.

Alles, M., Newman, P. and Noel, J. (1998), 'The value of information in internal management communication', *Journal of Economic Behavior and Organization*, vol. 36, no. 3, pp. 295–317.

Ang, S. (1998), 'Production and transaction economies and IS outsourcing: a study of the U.S. banking industry', *MIS Quarterly*, vol. 22, no. 4, pp. 535–52.

Azoulay, P. (2002), 'Acquiring knowledge within and across firm boundaries: evidence from clinical development', Working Paper, Graduate School of Business, University of Columbia, New York.

Barney, J. (1991), 'Firm resources and sustained competitive advantage', *Journal of Management*, vol. 17, no.1, pp. 99–120.

Barney, J. (1999), 'How a firm's capabilities affect boundary decisions', *MIT Sloan Management Review*, vol. 40, no.3, pp. 137–45.

Barthelemy, J. (2001), 'The hidden costs of IT outsourcing', *MIT Sloan Management Review*, vol. 42, no. 3, pp. 60–69.

Baumol, W., Panzar, J. and Willig, R. (1982), *Contestable Markets and the Theory of Industry Structure*, Harcourt Brace Jovanovich, New York.

Benson, J and Ieronimo, N. (1996), 'Outsourcing decisions: evidence from Australia-based enterprises', *International Labour Review*, vol. 135, no. 1, pp. 59–73.

Besanko, D., Dranove, D. and Shanley, M. (2001), 'Exploiting a cost advantage and coping with a cost disadvantage', *Management Science*, vol. 47, no. 2, pp. 221–35.

Button, K. and Weyman-Jones, T. (1994), 'X-efficiency and technical efficiency', *Public Choice*, vol. 80, nos 1–2, pp. 83–104.

Currie, W. (1998), 'Using multiple suppliers to mitigate the risk of IT outsourcing at ICI and Wessex water', *Journal of Information Technology*, vol. 13, no. 3, pp. 169–80.

Domberger, S. (1999), *The Contracting Organization: A Strategic Guide to Outsourcing*, Oxford University Press, Oxford.

Dun & Bradstreet (2000), 'Dun and Bradstreet sees 25 per cent growth for global outsourcing', 23 February, pp. 3-4, at: www.businesswire.com.

Eaton, C. and White, W. (1982), 'Agent compensation and the limits of bonding', *Economic Inquiry*, vol. 20, no. 3, pp. 330–43.

Feenstra, R. (1998), 'Integration of trade and disintegration of production in the global economy', *Journal of Economic Perspectives*, vol. 12, no. 4, pp. 31–51.

Garen, J. (1998), 'Self-employment, pay systems, and the theory of the firm: an empirical analysis', *Journal of Economic Behavior and Organization*, vol. 36, no. 2, pp. 257–74.

Gilley, K., Greer, C. and Rasheed, A. (2004), 'Human resource outsourcing and organizational performance in manufacturing firms', *Journal of Business Research*, vol. 57, no. 3, pp. 232–40.

Gilley, K. and Rasheed, A. (2000), 'Making more by doing less: an analysis of outsourcing and its effects on firm performance', *Journal of Management*, vol. 26, no. 4, pp. 763–90.

Globerman, S. (1995), 'A policy analysis of foreign ownership restrictions in telecommunications', *Telecommunications Policy*, vol. 19, no. 1, pp. 21–28.

Gopal, A., Sivaramakrishnan, K., Krishnan, M. and Mukhopadhyay, T. (2003), 'Contracts in offshore software development: an empirical analysis', *Management Science*, vol. 49, no. 12, pp. 1671–83.

Hayes, D., Hunton, J. and Reck, J. (2000), 'Information systems outsourcing announcements: investigating the impact on market value of contract-granting firms', *Journal of Information Systems*, vol. 4, no.2, pp. 109–26.

Hayes, R. and Wheelwright, S. (1984), *Restoring our Competitive Edge: Competing through Manufacturing*, John Wiley & Sons, New York.

Hensher, D. (1988), 'Some thoughts on competitive tendering in local bus operations', *Transport Reviews*, vol. 8, no. 4, pp. 363–72.

Hirschheim, R. (1998), 'Backsourcing: an emerging trend?" Outsourcing Center, Everest Partners, L.P, at: www.outsourcing-academics.com/backsourcing.html

Hodge, G. (2000), *Privatization: An International Review of the Evidence*, Westview Press, Boulder, CO.

Hubbard, T. (2001), 'Contractual form and market thickness in trucking', *RAND Journal of Economics*, vol. 32, no. 2, pp. 369–86.

James, H. Jr (1998), 'Are employment and managerial control equivalent? Evidence from an electronics producer', *Journal of Economic Behavior and Organization*, vol. 36, no. 4, pp. 447–71.

Jap, S. and Anderson, E. (2003), 'Safeguarding interorganizational performance and continuity under ex post opportunism', *Management Science*, vol. 49, no. 12, pp. 1684–701.

Jensen, J.B. and Rothwell, G.S. (1998), 'Transaction costs, regulation, and subcontracting at nuclear power plants', *Journal of Economic Behavior & Organization*, vol. 36. no. 3. 369–81.

Johnson, J. and Schneider, K. (1995), 'Outsourcing in distribution: the growing importance of transportation brokers', *Business Horizons*, vol. 38, no. 6, pp. 40–49.

Joskow, P. (1987), 'Contract duration and relationship-specific investments: empirical evidence from coal markets', *American Economic Review*, vol. 77, no. 1, pp. 168–85.

Kakabadse, A. and Kakabadse, N. (2002), 'Trends in outsourcing', *European Management Journal*, vol. 20, no. 2, pp. 189–98.

Knemeyer, A., Corsi, T. and Murphy, P. (2003), 'Logistics outsourcing relationships: customer perspectives', *Journal of Business Logistics*, vol. 24, no.1, pp. 77–109.

Lacity, M. and Hirschheim, R. (1993), 'The information systems outsourcing bandwagon', *MIT Sloan Management Review*, vol. 35, no. 1, pp. 73–86.

Lacity, M. and Willcocks, L. (1998), 'An empirical investigation of information technology sourcing practices: lessons from experience', *MIS Quarterly*, vol. 22, no. 3, pp. 363–409.

Leiblein, M., Reuer, J. and Dalsace, F. (2002), 'Do make or buy decisions matter? The influence of organizational governance on technological performance', *Strategic Management Journal*, vol. 23, no. 9, pp. 817–33.

Lyons, B. (1995), Specific investment, economies of scale, and the make-or-buy decision: a test of transaction cost theory', *Journal of Economic Behavior and Organization*, vol. 26, no. 3, pp. 431–43.

McAfee, R.P. and McMillan, J. (1988), *Incentives in Government Contracting*, University of Toronto Press, Toronto, Ontario.

McFarlan, F. and Nolan, R. (1995), 'How to manage an IS outsourcing alliance', *MIT Sloan Management Review*, vol. 36, no. 2, pp. 9–23.

MacPherson, A. and Pritchard, D. (2002), 'The international decentralization of US commercial aircraft production: implications for U.S. employment and trade', mimeo, State University of Buffalo, Buffalo.

Masten, S. (1984), 'The organization of production: evidence from the aerospace industry', *Journal of Law and Economics*, vol. 27, no. 2, pp. 402–17.

Masten, S., Meeham, J. Jr and Snyder, E. (1991), 'The costs of organization', *Journal of Law, Economics and Organization*, vol. 7, no. 1, pp. 1–25.

Mathewson, F. and Winter, R. (1990), 'The law and economics of vertical restraints', in F. Mathewson, M. Trebilcock and M. Walker (eds), *The Law and Economics of Competition Policy*, The Fraser Institute, Vancouver, BC.

Melese, F. (2000), 'Transaction cost analysis of in-sourcing and out-sourcing', mimeo, Naval Postgraduate School, Monterey, CA.

Morrison, C. (2003), 'Cost economies: a driving force for consolidation and concentration?' *Southern Economic Journal*, vol. 70, no. 1, pp. 110–27.

Mowery, D. and Rosenberg, N. (1989), *Technology and the Pursuit of Economic Growth*, Cambridge University Press, New York.

Novak, S. and Eppinger, S. (2001), 'Sourcing by design: product complexity and the supply chain', *Management Science*, vol. 47, no.1, pp. 189–204.

Odagiri, H. (2003), 'Transaction costs and capabilities as determinants of the R&D boundaries of the firm: a case study of the ten largest pharmaceutical firms in Japan', *Managerial and Decision Economics*, vol. 24, nos 2–3, pp. 187–211.

Ono, Y. (2003), 'Outsourcing business services and the role of central administrative offices', *Journal of Urban Economics*, vol. 53, no. 3, pp. 377-95.

Pine, B. (1993), *Mass Customization*, Harvard Business School Press, Boston, MA.

Pirrong, S. (1993), 'Contracting practices in bulk shipping markets: a transactions cost explanation', *Journal of Law and Economics*, vol. 36, no. 1, pp. 913–37.

Quelin, B. and Duhamel, F. (2003), 'Bringing together strategic outsourcing and corporate strategy: outsourcing motives and risks', *European Management Journal*, vol. 21, no. 5, pp. 647–61.

Quinn, J. and Hilmer, F. (1994), 'Strategic outsourcing', *MIT Sloan Management Review*, vol. 35, no. 4, pp. 43–55.

Rasmussen, E. (1994), *Games and Information*, 2nd edn, Blackwell, Cambridge, MA.

Saunders, C., Gebelt, M. and Hu, Q. (1997), 'Achieving success in information systems outsourcing', *California Management Review*, vol. 39, no. 2, pp. 63–79.

Saussier, S. (2000), 'Transaction costs and contractual incompleteness: the case of Electricité de France', *Journal of Economic Behavior and Organization*, vol. 42, no. 2, pp. 189–206.

Shelanski, H. and Klein, P. (1995), 'Empirical research in transaction cost economics: a review and assessment', *The Journal of Law, Economics and Organization*, vol. 11, no. 2, pp. 335–61.

Simester, D. and Knez, M. (2002), 'Direct and indirect bargaining costs and the scope of the firm', *The Journal of Business*, vol. 75, no. 2, pp. 283–304.

Smith, M., Mitra, S. and Narasimhan, S. (1998), 'Information system outsourcing: a study of pre-event firm characteristics', *Journal of Management Information Systems*, vol. 15, no. 2, pp. 60–92.

Tapon, F. and Cadsby, C. (1996), 'The optimal organization of research: evidence from eight case studies of pharmaceutical firms', *Journal of Economic Behavior and Organization*, vol. 31, no. 1, pp. 381–99.

Ulset, S. (1996), 'R&D outsourcing and contractual governance: an empirical study of commercial R&D projects', *Journal of Economic Behavior and Organization*, vol. 30, no. 1, pp. 63–82.

Veugelers, R. and Cassiman, B. (1999), 'Make and buy in innovation strategies: evidence from Belgian manufacturing firms', *Research Policy*, vol. 28, no. 1, pp. 63–80.

Vining, A. (2003), 'Internal market failure: a framework for diagnosing firm inefficiency', *Journal of Management Studies*, vol. 40, no. 2, pp. 431–57.

Vining, A. and Globerman, S. (1999), 'A conceptual framework for understanding the outsourcing decision', *European Management Journal*, vol. 17, no. 6, pp. 645–54.

Vining, A. and Weimer, D. (1988), 'Information asymmetry favoring sellers: a policy framework', *Policy Sciences*, vol. 21, no. 4, pp. 281–303.

Walker, G. and Weber, D. (1987), 'Supplier competition, uncertainty, and make-or-buy decisions', *Academy of Management Journal*, vol. 30, no. 3, pp. 589–96.

Wernerfelt, B. (1984), 'A resource-based view of the firm', *Strategic Management Journal*, vol. 5, no. 2, pp. 171–80.

Williamson, O. (1985), *The Economic Institution of Capitalism*, The Free Press, New York.

Zsidisin, G. (2003), 'Managing perceptions of supply risk', *Journal of Supply Chain Management*, vol. 39, no. 1, pp. 14–25.

2 Research on Outsourcing: Theoretical Perspectives and Empirical Evidence

K. Matthew Gilley, Abdul A. Rasheed and Hussam Al-Shammari

The last two decades have witnessed a significant trend towards ever-increasing outsourcing by firms in most developed economies. This trend reverses an earlier pattern in the evolution and growth of large industrial firms towards greater levels of vertical integration that prevailed during most of the previous 100 years. This change in the evolutionary trajectory of firms has attracted significant research attention in recent years. Most academic research has focused on identifying the environmental and organizational antecedents of outsourcing as well as its performance consequences. Meanwhile, a vigorous public policy debate has swirled around the social costs and benefits of the practice of outsourcing (Cooper, 2004). Both in the academic and practitioner literatures, there is considerable controversy and very little consensus. The accumulation of empirical studies of outsourcing over the last 15 years provides us with an opportunity to take stock of the research evidence available, evaluate the often confusing and conflicting findings, and explore possible avenues for future research on this controversial subject.

The primary objective of this chapter is to review extant research on outsourcing. Since past theoretical and empirical work has addressed a multitude of research questions and has employed widely divergent theoretical perspectives, our effort is to provide an overview rather than to be exhaustive. Towards this, we have organized the chapter as follows. First, we address issues concerning the definition of outsourcing. Next, we provide an overview of the major theoretical approaches that have been used to study outsourcing and suggest additional theoretical perspectives that may be useful in further studies across countries. Third, we review past research on the antecedents and consequences of outsourcing, including various moderator variables that have been considered. Finally, we present several suggestions that may help in advancing future research on outsourcing.

Outsourcing: definition and types

DEFINITION OF OUTSOURCING

There is considerable diversity in both the terminology used and the definition of terms in outsourcing research. Terms such as 'outsourcing', 'de-verticalization', 'dis-integration', 'farming-out', 'subcontracting' and so on have been used, often interchangeably. Lei and Hitt (1995, p. 836) have defined outsourcing as 'the reliance on external sources for manufacturing components and other value-adding activities'. Similarly, Kotabe (1992, p. 103) has defined outsourcing as 'the extent of components and finished products supplied to the firm by independent suppliers'. The problem with most of these definitions is threefold. First, a good definition must provide some rules of inclusion and exclusion, whereas the above definitions are too broad and encompass all purchasing activities. Second, they do not capture the true complexity and richness of the phenomenon. Third, they fail to provide us with sufficient clarity to develop a measurement method that can guide further empirical research.

Gilley and Rasheed (2000) argue that outsourcing is more than a simple purchasing decision: no firm is completely self-sufficient, and all firms purchase some inputs from outside. Instead, they view outsourcing as a fundamental strategic decision to reject the internalization of an activity. This means that outsourcing can arise in two ways. First, it may involve the *substitution* of market transactions for internal activities. This occurs when an organization ceases performing an activity in-house and shifts it to an outside supplier. Second, outsourcing may arise through *abstention*. That is, a firm may decide never to engage in a given activity and thus abstain from it altogether, even though it is well within the firm's managerial, technical, and financial capacity to do so. For example, it is probably within Nike's ability to produce the shoes it designs, but, the company has made a conscious decision not to internalize its production activity. The advantage of this approach to defining outsourcing is that it clearly distinguishes outsourcing from procurement. When an organization has no choice but to acquire a particular good or service from an external source due to lack of capabilities and resources within the firm, it is not engaging in outsourcing.

Types of outsourcing

As we have described above, outsourcing involves the procurement of physical and/or service inputs from outside organizations either through cessation of an activity that was previously performed internally or abstention from an activity that is well within the capability of the firm. Given the broad range of activities that can be included within this definition, most prior studies have attempted to achieve greater focus in two ways. A large number of studies have focused on the outsourcing of a specific functional activity. For example, Loh and Venkatraman (1992) focus on information technology outsourcing. Gilley, Greer and Rasheed (2004), on the other hand, focus exclusively on the performance implications of the outsourcing of human resource functions. Gilley and Rasheed (2000, 2004) have suggested an alternative approach that distinguishes between *core* outsourcing – the outsourcing of strategically relevant, core activities – and *peripheral* outsourcing – the outsourcing of non-core activities having little potential to convey a long-run competitive advantage. For an automobile company, for example, engine technology represents a core competence, and therefore if it decides to procure engines from outside, that would be a case of core outsourcing. On the other hand, if the firm purchases tyres or fabric for seat covers from an outside supplier, this would be a case of peripheral outsourcing. In the final analysis, what constitutes a core or peripheral activity is a matter of judgment on the part of each individual firm, based on what it considers to be its core competency. Thus, even within the same industry, what one firm may consider as a core activity may be viewed as peripheral by another firm.

Theoretical perspectives

Although we are far from developing a general theory of outsourcing, a review of recent research provides evidence of increasing theoretical sophistication. Some of the more commonly used theoretical perspectives include the resource-based view, transaction cost theory, agency theory, institutional theory and contingency theory. In this section, we attempt a brief review of these theoretical approaches. In addition, we suggest additional theoretical perspectives that may prove helpful in studying outsourcing.

THE RESOURCE-BASED VIEW

The resource-based view (RBV) focuses on resource heterogeneity among firms and seeks to explain competitive success on the basis of resource characteristics possessed by firms (Barney, 1991). The two basic assumptions underlying the RBV are that resources and capabilities vary significantly across firms within an industry and that these differences tend to be stable across relatively long periods of time. Thus, within the same industry, firms tend to have very dissimilar value chains built on resources and capabilities that are highly firm-specific.

Every firm faces the challenge of deciding which activities to internalize and which to outsource. Given that resources are scarce and that reducing the cycle time to get a product from the drawing board to the consumer is critical in an era of fierce global competition, most firms do not have the luxury of internalizing more than a very limited set of activities. Essentially, a firm's decision to engage in outsourcing hinges on which resources and capabilities to build internally and which to access through outsourcing arrangements. Thus, the RBV provides managers with a tool that is far more valuable than the simple arithmetic of a 'make or buy' decision.

An examination of several organizations, both large and small, that have pursued successful outsourcing strategies suggests the applicability of the RBV. For instance, much of Nike's initial success was due to a clear decision to outsource the manufacturing function and to combine the venture's limited resources in a unique and inimitable fashion. The Topsy Tail Company, a Dallas-based firm focusing on haircare items and fashion accessories, generated approximately US$80 million in annual revenues with just three employees. Topsy Tail's management did this through abstention-based outsourcing; from the outset, the company focused on a very narrow set of tasks and outsourced manufacturing and order fulfilment to outside specialists. Both Nike and Topsy Tail determined that resources and activities yielding the greatest potential for competitive advantage were to be internalized, while lower value-adding activities were to be outsourced.

Despite its considerable theoretical appeal and obvious applicability, empirical research on outsourcing using the RBV has been very limited so far. This may be due to the inherent difficulties in making operational many of the basic ideas of the RBV, especially in an outsourcing context (Priem and Butler, 2001). As Brush, Greene and Hart (2001) suggested in their study of new ventures, to be successful, a firm should be able to attract a set of human, social, financial, physical, technological and organizational resources and combine them in ways that are valuable, unique and difficult to imitate. Given that most firms tend to operate with limited resources, the key is to accurately specify which resources and activities are critical to the firm's success and to internalize them. The challenge, then, is to identify the resource and competence bundles that are most likely to yield a sustainable competitive advantage and focus on developing those in-house, while outsourcing the rest. It is imperative, however, to conduct periodic evaluations of the activities that were internalized earlier. Such evaluations may lead to further outsourcing by substitution so that the firm can continue to focus on its core competencies.

TRANSACTION COST THEORY

The origins of transaction cost theory (TCT) lie in the effort to answer the question 'Why do firms exist?'. Originally introduced by Coase (1937) and subsequently developed by Williamson (1975), TCT views markets and hierarchies as alternative ways of completing a set of transactions. According to TCT, economic actors will make a choice between these two governance mechanisms based on which will yield minimum costs (Barney and Hesterly, 1996). One of the major strengths of TCT in the study of outsourcing is that it takes into consideration both the production costs and the transaction costs. As Cheon, Grover and Teng (1995) point out, outsourcing leads to lower production costs (mainly due to the economies of scale enjoyed by an outside provider) but, in many cases, higher transaction costs related to negotiating, monitoring and enforcing contracts. The move towards higher levels of outsourcing in many industries today can be seen as a result of the continuing decline in transaction costs, both domestically and internationally. Furthermore, developments in supply chain management technology and electronic inter-firm integration have enabled many large firms to realize the benefits of vertical control without vertical ownership.

In addition to focusing attention on transaction costs in the outsourcing decision, TCT also helps with identifying the sources of transaction costs. Three specific factors have been identified as most salient (Williamson, 1985). These are asset specificity, uncertainty and frequency. If an activity requires highly specific assets without any alternative use, it is unlikely that an outside provider will be willing to make those transaction-specific investments for fear of hold-up problems in the absence of contractual safeguards. Highly uncertain environments may drive up transaction costs due to the complexity of contracts. Finally, the costs of relationship building cannot be amortized if the transactions are infrequent. Alpar and Saharia (1995) provide a transaction cost theory-based conceptual framework for analysing the outsourcing of information system functions. Generally speaking, more 'commoditized' activities lend themselves to outsourcing. However, from a research perspective, it is more interesting to study the outsourcing of more idiosyncratic, firm-specific activities and identify the characteristics (both contractual and non-contractual) of the relationship that leads to the successful outsourcing of such activities. One example of a TCT-based approach to studying outsourcing is the Ang and Straub (1998) study on IT outsourcing by banks. This approach may be restricted to certain situations as Wang, Barron and Seidmann (1997) have argued that TCT does not always provide a suitable framework for studying outsourcing of custom software development.

AGENCY THEORY

Eisenhardt (1988), as well as Cheon, Grover and Teng (1995), have suggested the potential applicability of agency theory to the study of outsourcing. An agency relationship is one in which one or more persons (principals) engage another person (agent) to perform certain activities (Jensen and Meckling, 1976). Such relationships are governed by an agency contract. An agency relationship is characterized by divergence in the interests of the principals and the agents, and such divergence is reduced through monitoring or through incentive systems. Cheon, Grover and Teng (1995) point out that agency costs are determined by five factors:

namely, outcome uncertainty, risk aversion, programmability of the task delegated, outcome measurability, and the length of the agency relationship. Agency theory can be applied to the study of outsourcing in two very fundamentally different ways. First, the relationship between the firm and its outsourcer can be viewed as a principal–agent relationship, and the nature of the outsourcing agreement and its performance implications can be studied in terms of the above five characteristics. Although they did not explicitly acknowledge the agency perspective, Gilley and Rasheed (2000) and Gilley, McGee and Rasheed (2004) have investigated the role of environmental uncertainty and managerial risk aversion, respectively. Yet another level at which outsourcing decisions can be investigated is in terms of managerial incentive structures. It would be interesting to examine whether a firm's decision to outsource an activity or to perform it in-house is influenced by the incentive systems in place for top management team members.

INSTITUTIONAL THEORY

Unlike transaction cost theory or agency theory, institutional theory is based on non-economic logics that drive human action. Drawing from sociological reasoning, DiMaggio and Powell (1983) argued that organizations exist in 'fields' of other similar organizations. Within a specific field, over time, organizations become increasingly homogenous in terms of their structures, practices and even strategies. Institutional theory suggests that this homogeneity or organizational isomorphism is a result of a combination of mimetic, coercive and normative processes. As more and more firms within an industry outsource a specific activity, such as training or logistics or information systems, mimetic pressures can lead other firms within the industry to outsource. In public-sector institutions, from the universities to the military, normative and coercive pressures have, in recent times, led to unprecedented levels of outsourcing. Ang's and Cummings' (1997) research is an example of the application of institutional theory to the study of outsourcing. They examined information system (IS) outsourcing in banking and found that federal regulator influence (coercive and normative) and peer influence (mimetic) affected IS outsourcing. They found that smaller firms (banks in this case) engage in more IS outsourcing. This may be because institutional pressures are stronger for smaller firms. It seems reasonable to suggest that the more institutionalized an organizational field, the faster outsourcing is likely to spread within that field.

CONTINGENCY THEORY

Contingency theories have played an important role in the development of management literature in the last four decades. As Tosi and Slocum (1984) point out, contingency approaches are based on the assumption that performance is a consequence of the fit between several organizational attributes such as strategy, structure, systems, culture and environmental characteristics such as dynamism, complexity and munificence. The most developed stream among contingency theory-based research is the structural contingency theory (Pennings, 1992). The pervasive influence of environment on organizational strategies, structures and processes has been the subject of considerable research (Keats and Hitt,1988). Interestingly, much of the research on outsourcing has followed implicitly contingency approaches even when contingency labels have not been formally used. Gilley and Rasheed (2000), for example, examined the fit between business-level strategy, environmental dynamism and outsourcing strategy to assess its performance outcomes. Similarly, Kotabe (1990) included several industry-level variables in his study of the relationship between outsourcing intensity and the innovation intensity of the firm. A contingency approach can help in identifying the specific environmental and organizational attributes that can lead to successful outsourcing and thus holds considerable potential for arriving at prescriptive findings.

INTERNATIONAL OUTSOURCING: USEFUL THEORETICAL PERSPECTIVES

Two related developments in recent years require us to take a global perspective in the study of outsourcing. First, many of the outsourcing relationships in today's economy span two or more countries. For example, China has emerged as the country of choice for manufacturing outsourcing, while India is increasingly becoming a leader in the outsourcing of service activities. Second, outsourcing, as an organizational practice, is spreading across the world. This has resulted in the gradual emergence of a body of research examining the competitiveness implications of global outsourcing decisions (Kotabe 1989, 1990; Levy, 1995; Murray, Kotabe and Wildt, 1995). Comparative studies of outsourcing practices are also attracting growing interest (Apte et al., 1997; Kakabadse and Kakabadse 2002). The theoretical perspectives presented above, although powerful in the examination of outsourcing practices within a country, fail to provide adequate explanations for inter-country differences in outsourcing. The current state of international comparative studies is indicative of this problem. Both the Apte et al. (1997) and the Kakabadse and Kakabadse (2002) studies, while pioneering in their effort to attempt international comparisons, are descriptive in nature and are not based on any theoretical explanatory framework. In other words, these studies provide evidence of differences in outsourcing practices across countries but do not provide an explanation for why these differences exist. We suggest two theoretical approaches that may prove useful in international comparative studies of outsourcing. First, cultural differences across countries may provide some insight into the differences among countries. Second, the state of institutional development in a country may determine the feasibility of outsourcing as well as its performance outcomes. We provide an introduction to both of these approaches below.

The culturalist perspective

Research in comparative management is characterized by two competing perspectives – namely, the 'culture-free' and the 'culturalist' approaches (Lachman et al., 1994). In recent years the culturalist perspective has made significant advances through the identification of the underlying dimensions of culture and their careful measurement. The most commonly used set of cultural dimensions were proposed by Hofstede (1980). Trompenaars and Hampden-Turner (1998) and Schwartz (1992) have proposed alternative models.

Adler (1983) argued that there could be both culture-specific and culture-free aspects to a given phenomenon. Since then, a considerable body of research has accumulated, suggesting that a number of organizational choices that are commonly perceived as purely economic phenomena can indeed be better explained using a combination of culture-bound and culture-free perspectives (Delios and Henisz, 2003; Kogut and Singh, 1988; Pothukuchi et al., 2002). In the absence of any prior empirical studies that examine the role of culture in outsourcing, the important questions are whether culture plays a role in an organization's choice of outsourcing strategies and, if so, what are the relevant cultural dimensions. Al Shammari (2004) has argued that the cultural dimensions of uncertainty avoidance and power-distance may be relevant to the study of outsourcing. Firms in high uncertainty avoidance countries may engage in lower levels of outsourcing compared to firms in low uncertainty avoidance countries. This is because in high uncertainty avoidance culture, firms may choose to internalize activities in order to reduce the uncertainties associated with market transactions. Similarly, firms in high power-distance countries may prefer hierarchies to markets. These conjectures require empirical verification, however.

The institutional context

Divesting unrelated operations, focusing on core competencies and outsourcing entire segments of the value chain have become increasingly popular choices in North America and Western Europe in recent years. Quinn (1992), for example, argues that a firm must focus narrowly on what it does best and outsource everything else. In a similar vein, Prahalad and Hamel (1990) have suggested that a firm should build its businesses on its core competencies. Despite the apparent normative appeal of these exhortations, doubts have been raised about the universal applicability of such advice. Khanna and Palepu (1997, 1999) have argued compellingly that while focus and outsourcing may be great ideas in New York or London, the differences in institutional context may make them counterproductive ideas in emerging markets. According to them, emerging markets are characterized by institutional voids – that is, institutions that Western companies take for granted are yet to be fully developed in many countries. They identified five elements of the institutional context that must be taken into consideration before a firm decides to pursue a focused strategy of outsourcing. These are the state of development of the capital market, product markets, labour markets, government regulations and contract enforcement. The lack of development of institutions makes it difficult for a firm to outsource activities. For example, if a country lacks developed product markets and if the legal institutions for enforcing contracts are not fully developed, outsourcing may not be a desirable strategy. The beginnings of an institutional context-based explanation for inter-country differences in outsourcing practices can be found in Apte *et al.* (1997).

Many of the most successful business groups in emerging markets have internalized virtually every stage of the value chain within their firms and are reluctant to engage in outsourcing. The Charoen Pokphand group, Thailand's biggest conglomerate, exemplifies such internalization strategy. The group produces chicken feed, owns poultry farms and distributes its output through company-owned grocery stores as well as a nationwide chain of restaurants. This extreme level of activity internalization was imperative for the group because it had to create the entire production chain in the absence of both feed suppliers and retail stores with freezers in the Thai marketplace. Similarly, the Indian Tata group owns India's oldest steel mill as well as its biggest automotive production facility.

Antecedents and outcomes of outsourcing

There has been a steady accumulation of empirical studies of the antecedents and outcomes of outsourcing since the late 1980s. We provide a summary of these studies in Table 2.1, which is organized in terms of the theoretical approach followed by the study; the measures of antecedents; outsourcing, and outcomes used; sample and method; and findings. The table does not claim to cover all studies of outsourcing; instead, it focuses on those studies that have followed the antecedents–outsourcing–outcomes design in their research.

Table 2.1 Studies of outsourcing

Authors and Theoretical Perspective	Measures	Sample and Method	Results
Ang and Cummings (1997): institutional theory	• Antecedents Federal regulator influence Peer influence • Outsourcing: IS outsourcing (internal v. external) • Moderators Asset specificity, functional complexity, technological uncertainty, supplier presence, financial slack, production cost advantage, bank size	Questionnaire survey – 226 US banks	• Peer and federal regulator influences are significant predictors of decision to outsource. • Peer influence is strengthened by external cost advantage, functional complexity and supplier presence and is weakened by slack resources and asset specificity. • Federal regulator influence is strengthened by only technological uncertainty. • Generally speaking, small banks tend to acquiesce more to mimetic pressures than large banks.
Ang and Straub (1998): TCE	• Antecedents Production cost, transaction cost, and financial slack • Outsourcing IS outsourcing (extent of outsourcing across eight different functions such as planning, security, etc.) • Controls Firm size	Questionnaire survey and archival data – 243 US banks	• The production cost advantage offered by vendors has a strong effect on IS outsourcing. • Transaction costs have an impact, but much smaller than that of productions costs. • Financial slack has no significant effect.
Gilley and Rasheed (2000): contingency theory	• Outsourcing (peripheral outsourcing intensity/core outsourcing intensity) • Outcome Firm performance • Moderators Firm strategy (cost leadership and differentiation) Environment (dynamism) • Controls Past performance	Questionnaire survey – 94 manufacturing firms from 16 industries	• Outsourcing has no direct effect on firm performance. • Firm strategy and environmental dynamism moderate the relationship between outsourcing and performance.

Table 2.1 *Continued*

Gilley, Greer and Rasheed (2004)	• HR outsourcing (the extent to which training and payroll activities are performed by an outsider) • Outcome • Firm performance • Moderators • Firm size • Controls • Past performance, firm age and industry	Questionnaire survey – 94 manufacturing firms from 16 industries	• Outsourcing training is a significant predictor of a firm's stakeholder and innovation performance. • Payroll outsourcing is a significant predictor of innovation performance. • There is no moderating effect for size.
Gilley, McGee and Rasheed (2004): contingency perspective	• Antecedents • Environmental dynamism • Managerial risk aversion • Outsourcing; the extent to which firm's machining and assembly operations are being undertaken by outside suppliers • Moderators • Firm maturity	Questionnaire survey – 86 small manufacturing firms	• Perceived environmental dynamism and managerial risk aversion are positively related to manufacturing outsourcing. • Firm maturity moderates this relationship. Whereas newer firms engage in more outsourcing when environmental dynamism is high, mature firms engage in more outsourcing when top management teams are more risk-averse.
Grover, Cheon, and Teng (1996): transaction cost theory	• IS outsourcing (difference between a firm's current outsourcing budget and that of three years ago) • Outcome • IS outsourcing success (satisfaction with benefits from outsourcing) • Moderators • Service quality • Trust (mediator)	Questionnaire survey – senior executives in 188 firms	• Outsourcing system operations and telecommunications is positively related to outsourcing success. • Outsourcing asset-specific functions does not lead to increased success. • Service quality, vendor trust, cooperation and communication are important for outsourcing success.
Kotabe (1989)	• Outsourcing: hollowing out (ratio of US-manufactured imports from foreign affiliates of US multinational firms to their total US sale as a system for each industry) • Outcome • Global competitiveness (relative global market share) • Controls • R&D intensity, equipment and component exports	Benchmarking survey data from US direct investment abroad – 2000 US parent firms, 18 500 affiliates, 29 manufacturing industries	• The extent of 'hollowness' is positively related to global competitiveness.

Table 2.1   *Continued*

Study	Variables	Method	Findings
Kotabe (1990)	• Offshore outsourcing (806/807 import propensity) • Outcome • Innovation propensity (number of product innovations) • Controls • R&D intensity, skill intensity, concentration ratio, unionization ratio, advertising intensity, capital intensity	Archival data from various US government sources for four manufacturing industries	• There is a positive relationship between offshore sourcing and innovativeness.
Levy (1995): supply chain perspective	• Antecedents • Relational factors (the distance between one activity and the rest of the chain and the stability of the linkages that bind them) • Outcomes • Sourcing cost, demand fulfilment, inventory levels	Case study and simulation – single company in the personal computer industry	• Disruptions to an international supply chain can generate substantial and unexpected costs when shipping and lead times are long. These costs take the form of expedited shipping, high inventory levels and lower demand fulfilment.
Loh and Venkatraman (1992)	• Antecedents • Business cost structure, business performance, financial leverage, IT cost structure, IT performance • Outsourcing • IT outsourcing (ratio of IT outsourcing expenditure to total assets for each firm) • Controls • Size and industry	Archival data – 57 US manufacturing and service firms	• Business and IT cost structures are positively related to the level of IT outsourcing. • Outsourcing is negatively related to IT performance. • Business performance and financial leverage have no significant effect on IT outsourcing.
Murray, Kotabe and Wildt (1995): contingency theory	• Internal v. external sourcing (the percentage of the total value of all non-standardized components in the product sourced internally) • Outcomes • Firm performance (financial and strategic) • Moderators • Supplier bargaining power, proprietary technology, asset specificity, transaction frequency	Questionnaire survey – 104 US subsidiaries of Fortune Global 500 manufacturing firms	• Proprietary technology (product and process innovation) and asset specificity moderate the relationship between outsourcing and financial performance. • Suppliers' bargaining power and transaction frequency have no moderating effect.
Wang, Barron and Seidmann (1997): transaction cost theory	• Antecedents • Cost uncertainty • System value uncertainty • Outsourcing: internal v. external source for custom software development projects	Mathematical modelling and simulation	• Uncertainty about system value is not a significant predictor of software development outsourcing. • Uncertainty about development cost is highly significant, with greater uncertainty making outsourcing less attractive.

An examination of Table 2.1 suggests several interesting emerging patterns in the research on outsourcing:

1. The increasing adoption of outsourcing, both domestic and offshore, by business organizations is reflected in the increasing research attention to the topic.
2. Information systems researchers seem to be paying more attention to the issue of outsourcing than any other functional area. Considering that outsourcing is even more prevalent in the case of manufacturing, this is rather surprising.
3. Empirical studies are increasingly grounded in established theoretical paradigms such as institutional theory and transaction cost theory. At first sight, this might suggest that outsourcing is a phenomenon in search of a theory. However, we believe that the use of different theories suggests that the study of outsourcing warrants a multi-theoretic approach.
4. The principal source of data collection seems to be questionnaire surveys, although both case studies (Levy, 1995) and archival data (Kotabe, 1990) have occasionally been employed.
5. Recent empirical models demonstrate greater sophistication in terms of model specification through the use of a number of control variables.
6. Researchers are paying greater attention to contextual variables that may moderate or mediate the relationship between outsourcing and its performance outcomes.
7. There is considerable variation in the measurement of outsourcing across studies.

The research questions addressed by the various studies in our review can be summarized as follows:

- What set of internal and external factors motivate an organization to outsource?
- What are the organizational consequences of outsourcing?
- What factors moderate the relationship between outsourcing and performance?

In the next few paragraphs we provide a brief review of the antecedent, moderator and outcome variables considered in past research.

ANTECEDENTS

The choice of antecedent variables in most studies is driven by the theoretical perspective adopted by the study. For example, Ang and Cummings (1997) considered federal regulator influence and peer influence as antecedent factors, a direct result of the institutional theory perspective that they adopted. Ang and Straub (1998), following a transaction cost perspective, examined the role of production costs and transaction costs in the decision to outsource. Business performance, interestingly, has been used both as an antecedent variable (Loh and Venkatraman, 1992) and as an outcome variable.

MODERATORS

The moderators examined in outsourcing research can be broadly classified as either environmental or organizational. Generally speaking, the tendency has been to use external variables, especially industry variables, as control variables rather than as moderators. Environmental dynamism (Gilley and Rasheed, 2000) and technological uncertainty (Ang and Cummings, 1997) are examples of external variables that have been used as moderators.

A much larger number of organizational variables have attracted the attention of researchers. These include firm strategy (Gilley and Rasheed, 2000), asset specificity (Ang and Cummings, 1997), firm size (Gilley, Greer and Rasheed, 2004), trust (Grover *et al.*, 1996) and firm age (Gilley, McGee and Rasheed, 2004).

OUTCOMES

Although the outcome variable of interest is organizational performance, there is considerable variation in the specific aspect of performance that was used in the studies that we reviewed. Kotabe (1989, 1990) used a firm's relative global market share and its innovation propensity as performance variables. Other studies have used a firm's financial performance as the outcome of interest. Intermediate outcomes such as satisfaction with outsourcing (Grover *et al.*, 1996) and sourcing cost and demand fulfilment (Levy, 1995) have been used in some studies. Recognition of performance as a multidimensional construct can be seen in Gilley, Greer and Rasheed (2004), who make a distinction between stakeholder performance and innovation performance, and Murray *et al.* (1995) who consider both financial and strategic performance.

Conclusions and directions for future research

Our review of past research on the antecedents and outcomes of outsourcing suggests that research on outsourcing is still in its early stages. Although many antecedents of outsourcing have been identified, there is very little consensus on the performance implications of outsourcing practices. This lack of consensus has led to a move away from the examination of simple bivariate relationships between outsourcing and performance and towards a more sophisticated examination of the moderating role played by a number of contextual factors, both organizational and environmental. The preceding review has enabled us to develop a set of suggestions. These suggestions build on past research and can potentially prove useful in introducing a greater level of sophistication to future studies of outsourcing.

GREATER THEORETICAL PLURALISM

A majority of the studies that we reviewed did not specify a clear theoretical perspective. This is not unusual in the early stages of examination of any phenomenon in the strategic management area. In the more recent past, we have seen a greater propensity to build empirical research based on transaction cost theory and, to some extent, institutional theory. It may be premature at this point to restrict research to one theoretical paradigm, however appropriate that perspective may seem. Examination of outsourcing from multiple theoretical perspectives is likely to yield more insights than premature consensus on a single perspective. Furthermore, the more important issue is deciding what theoretical perspective is most appropriate to answer a specific research question. The research question must drive the choice of theory rather than a theoretical perspective drive the choice of research questions.

COMBINATION OF MULTIPLE THEORETICAL PERSPECTIVES

A comprehensive theory of outsourcing may require researchers to draw from multiple theoretical bases in a single study. This suggests the need to combine and integrate multiple theories into a comprehensive framework. Cheon, Grover and Teng (1995) have made a promising step in this direction by proposing a model that integrates RBV, resource dependence theory, agency theory and transaction cost theory.

CONSIDERATION OF INTERMEDIATE OUTCOME VARIABLES

Our review suggests that the majority of the empirical studies have focused on organizational performance as the outcome variable. Although organizational performance is the dependent variable of prime interest in much strategy research, it is important to rethink whether performance, operating as financial performance in a given year, is the most appropriate variable for a multiplicity of reasons. First, given the variety of organizational and environmental influences on financial performance, any inference of cause–effect relationships is highly problematic. Second, long-term performance implications in terms of deskilling and hollowing are unlikely to be captured in contemporaneous correlations of outsourcing and financial performance. It is unclear also whether economic motivations are the only factors that managers consider when making outsourcing decisions. It may be more appropriate to compare the results of outsourcing against the considerations that motivated outsourcing, such as greater managerial focus on core areas or improved quality of a specific input. Such intermediate outcomes are the direct consequence of outsourcing and therefore may allow more valid cause–effect inferences.

PRECISION IN DEFINITION AND OPERATIONALISM OF RESEARCH CONSTRUCTS

Systematic comparison across studies is a prerequisite for the cumulative building of knowledge about any organizational phenomenon. However, as the preceding review suggests, our ability to make inter-study comparisons is severely limited by inconsistent operationalism of the core construct of outsourcing from one study to another. The development of consensus about valid and reliable measures of outsourcing and their consistent application across studies can provide us with more meaningful insights about both the antecedents and outcomes of outsourcing over a period of time.

EXPLORATION OF NON-LINEAR RELATIONSHIPS

Our review of prior empirical work shows that most studies have implicitly assumed a linear relationship between outsourcing and performance and have therefore relied on linear estimation techniques. However, there is reason to believe that the assumption of linearity may hold good only within relatively narrow ranges. It is entirely possible that the actual relationship follows an inverted U-curve pattern when considered over the entire range. That is, some degree of outsourcing may have positive performance outcomes whereas excessive outsourcing may result in competitive decline. The examination of possible curvilinear relationships using appropriate estimation techniques can yield valuable insights about the optimal level of outsourcing for a firm.

CONSIDERATION OF ADDITIONAL MODERATOR VARIABLES

Whenever one encounters inconsistent findings in bivariate relationships, the relationship can be elaborated by introducing additional variables. Our review shows that researchers have recently begun to examine a number of external and internal variables. However, a critical variable that has not been examined thus far is the management of the outsourcing process itself. For example, two firms that follow identical outsourcing strategies may end up with very dissimilar performance outcomes because of the variance in their management processes. Outsourcing can succeed only if the firm has appropriate structural attributes and management systems. More detailed examination of suitable organizational architectures (Dess *et al.*,1995), as well as systems that encourage inter-firm coordination and relational governance, are required.

OUTSOURCING AND THE LIFE-CYCLE STAGE OF THE FIRM

A relatively unexplored area of investigation is the relationship between the firm's life-cycle stage and appropriateness of its outsourcing strategies. Most studies of outsourcing have primarily focused on large, established organizations. It is important to study firms in different stages of their life cycle before we can develop useful prescriptive conclusions. A beginning in this direction is the study by Gilley, McGee and Rasheed (2004) which examines the antecedents of outsourcing in small and medium-sized organizations.

Generally speaking, it is intuitively appealing that organizations at different stages of development will rely relatively more or less on a strategy of outsourcing because of their varying resource levels. A particularly useful theoretical foundation, then, for the study of outsourcing's relation to organization life cycle would be the resource-based view of the firm. Research on outsourcing across life-cycle stages may be also informed by transaction cost economics. Whether internalization or outsourcing represents the optimal means of structuring production probably depends on the organization's level of development. It may be that younger, smaller firms benefit more from outsourcing because they have not yet developed the managerial, technical or financial capacity to internalize.

Finally, institutional theory may also be of use in the study of outsourcing across organizational life-cycle stages. In particular, institutional pressures may result in a growing similarity of outsourcing strategies for firms in the same stage of development.

CONCLUSION

Given the relative infancy of outsourcing research, it appears premature to propose a normative theory of outsourcing. However, considerable advances have been made recently in classifying the types of outsourcing (core versus peripheral), identifying organizational and environmental antecedents of outsourcing and exploring potential moderators of the outsourcing-performance relationship. We hope our review of prior research, identification of theoretical approaches appropriate for the study of outsourcing, and the suggested directions, will help to guide and motivate future research, contributing to an improved understanding of the theory and practice of outsourcing.

References

Adler, N.J. (1983), 'A typology of management studies involving culture', *Journal of International Business Studies*, vol. 14, no. 2, pp. 29–47.

Alpar, P. and Saharia, A.N. (1995), 'Outsourcing information system functions: an organization economics perspective', *Journal of Organizational Computing*, vol. 5, no. 3, pp. 197–217.

Al-Shammari, H. (2004), 'Antecedents of inter-country variance of outsourcing practices: culture and institutional context', Working Paper, University of Texas at Arlington.

Ang, S. and Cummings, L.L. (1997), 'Strategic response to institutional influences on information systems outsourcing', *Organization Science*, vol. 8, no. 3, pp. 235–56.

Ang, S. and Straub, D.W. (1998), 'Production and transaction economies and IS outsourcing: a study of the U.S. banking industry', *MIS Quarterly*, vol. 22, no. 4, pp. 535–52.

Apte, U.M., Sobol, M.G., Hanaoka, S,, Shimada, T., Saarinen, T., Salmela, T. and Vepsalainen, A. (1997), 'IS outsourcing practices in the USA, Japan and Finland: a comparative study', Journal of Information Technology, vol.12, no. 4, pp. 289–304.

Barney, J. (1991), 'Firm resources and sustainable competitive advantage', *Journal of Management*, vol. 17, no. 1, pp. 99–120.

Barney, J. and Hesterly, W. (1996), 'Organizational economics: understanding the relationship between organizations and economic analysis', in S.R. Clegg, C. Hardy and W.R. Nord (eds), *Handbook of Organization Studies*, Sage Publications, London.

Brush, C.G., Greene, P.G. and Hart, M.M. (2001), 'From initial idea to unique advantage: the entrepreneurial challenge of constructing a resource base', *Academy of Management Executive*, vol. 15, no. 1, pp. 64–78.

Cheon, M.J., Grover, V. and Teng, T.C, (1995), 'Theoretical perspectives on the outsourcing of information systems', *Journal of Information Technology*, vol. 10, no. 4, pp. 209–19.

Coase, R.H. 1937), 'The nature of the firm', *Economica*, vol. 4, pp. 386–405.

Cooper, J.C. (2004), 'The price of efficiency: stop blaming outsourcing', *Business Week*, March, pp. 38–42.

Delios, A. and Henisz, W.J. (2003), 'Policy uncertainty and the sequence of entry by Japanese firms, 1980–1998', *Journal of International Business Studies*, vol. 34, pp. 227–41.

Dess, G.G., Rasheed, A., McLaughlin, K. and Priem, R. (1995), 'The new corporate architecture', *Academy of Management Executive*, vol. 9, no. 3, pp. 7–20.

DiMaggio, P.J. and Powell, W.W. (1983), 'The iron cage revisited: institutional isomorphism and collective rationality in organizational fields', *American Sociological Review*, vol. 48, pp. 147–60.

Eisenhardt, K.M. (1988), 'Agency and institutional theory explanations: the case of retail sales compensation', *Academy of Management Journal*, vol. 31, no. 3, pp. 488–511.

Gilley, K.M., Greer, C.R. and Rasheed, A.A. (2004), 'Human resource outsourcing and organizational performance in manufacturing firms', *Journal of Business Research*, vol. 57, no. 3, pp. 232–40.

Gilley, K.M., McGee, J.E. and Rasheed, A. (2004), 'Perceived environmental dynamism and managerial risk aversion as antecedents of manufacturing outsourcing: the moderating effects of firm maturity', *Journal of Small Business Management*, vol. 42, no. 2, pp. 117–33.

Gilley, K.M. and Rasheed, A. (2000), 'Making more by doing less: an analysis of outsourcing and its effects on firm performance', *Journal of Management*, vol. 26, no. 4, pp. 763–90.

Grover, V., Cheon, M.J. and Teng, T.C. (1996), 'The effect of service quality and partnership on the outsourcing of information systems functions', *Journal of Management Information Systems*, vol. 12, no. 4, pp. 89–116.

Hofstede, G. (1980), *Culture's consequences: International Differences in Work-related Values*, Sage, London.

Jensen, M.C. and Meckling, W.H. (1976), 'Theory of the firm: managerial behavior, agency costs and ownership structure', *Journal of Financial Economics*, vol. 3, pp. 305–60.

Kakabadse, A. and Kakabadse, N. (2002), 'Trends in outsourcing: contrasting USA and Europe', *European Management Journal*, vol. 20, no. 2, pp. 189–98.

Keats, B.W. and Hitt, M.A. (1988), 'A causal model of linkages among environmental dimensions, macro organizational characteristics, and performance', *Academy of Management Journal*, vol. 31, no. 3, pp. 570–98.

Khanna, T. and Palepu, K. (1997), 'Why focused strategies may be wrong for emerging markets', *Harvard Business Review*, vol. 75, no. 4, pp. 41–51.

Khanna, T. and Palepu, K. (1999), 'The right way to restructure conglomerates in emerging markets', *Harvard Business Review*, vol. 77, no. 4, pp. 125–34.

Kogut, B. and Singh, H. (1988), 'The effect of national culture on the choice of entry mode', *Journal of International Business Studies*, vol. 19, no. 3, pp. 411–33.

Kotabe, M. (1989), 'Hollowing-out of U.S. multinationals and their global competitiveness: an intra-firm perspective', *Journal of Business Research*, vol. 19, no. 1, pp. 1–15.

Kotabe, M. (1990), 'The relationship between offshore sourcing and innovativeness of U.S. multinational firms: an empirical investigation', *Journal of International Business Studies*, vol. 3, no. 4, pp. 623–38.

Kotabe, M. (1992), *Global Sourcing Strategy: R&D, Manufacturing, and Marketing Interfaces*, Quorum, New York.

Lachman, R., Nedd, A. and Hinings, B. (1994), 'Analyzing cross-national management and organizations: a theoretical framework', *Management Science*, vol. 40, no. 1, pp. 40–55.

Lei, D. and Hitt, M. (1995), 'Strategic restructuring and outsourcing: the effect of mergers and acquisitions and LBOs on building firm skills and capabilities', *Journal of Management*, vol. 21, no. 5, pp. 835–59.

Levy, D.L. (1995), 'International sourcing and supply chain stability', *Journal of International Business Studies*, vol. 26, no. 2, pp. 343–60.

Loh, L. and Venkatraman, N. (1992), 'Determinants of information technology outsourcing: a cross-sectional analysis', *Journal of Management Information Systems*, vol. 9, no. 1, pp. 7–24.

Murray, J.Y., Kotabe, M. and Wildt, A.R. (1995), 'Strategic and financial performance implications of global sourcing strategy: a contingency analysis', Journal of International Business Studies, vol. 26, no. 1, pp. 181–202.

Pennings, J.M. (1992), 'Structural contingency theory: a reappraisal', in B.M. Staw and L.L. Cummings (eds), *Research in Organizational Behavior*, vol. 14, JAI Press, Greenwich, CT, pp. 267-309.

Pothukuchi, V., Damanpour, F., Choi, J., Chen, C.C. and Park, S.H. (2002), 'National and organizational culture differences and international joint venture performance', Journal of International Business Studies, vol. 33, no. 2, pp. 243–65.

Prahalad, C.K. and Hamel, G. (1990), 'The core competence of the corporation', *Harvard Business Review*, vol. 68, no. 3, pp. 79–93.

Priem, R.L. and Butler, J.E. (2001), 'Is the resource-based "view" a useful perspective for strategic management research?', *Academy of Management Review*, vol. 26, no. 1, pp. 22–40.

Quinn, J.B. (1992), *Intelligent Enterprise*, Free Press, New York.

Rasheed, A. and Gilley, K.M. (2004), 'Outsourcing in entrepreneurial ventures, in M. Hitt and D. Ireland (eds), *The Blackwell Encyclopaedic Dictionary of Entrepreneurship*, Blackwell Publishers, Oxford.

Schwartz, S.H. (1992), 'Universals in the content and structure of values: theoretical advances and empirical tests in 20 countries', in M.P. Zann (ed.), *Advances in Experimental Social Psychology*, Academic Press, San Diego.

Tosi, H.L. and Slocum, J.W. (1984), 'Contingency theory: some suggested directions', *Journal of Management*, vol. 10, no. 1, pp. 9–26.

Trompenaars, F. and Hampden-Turner, C. (1998), *Riding the Waves of Culture: Understanding Cultural Diversity in Global Business*, McGraw-Hill, New York.

Wang, T.G., Barron, T. and Seidmann, A. (1997), 'Contracting structures for custom software development: the impact of informational rents and uncertainty on internal development and outsourcing', *Management Science*, vol. 43, no. 12, pp. 1726–44.

Williamson, O.E. (1975), *Markets and Hierarchies: Analysis and Antitrust Implications*, Free Press, New York.

Williamson, O.E. (1985), *Economic Institutions of Capitalism*, Free Press, New York.

3 Outsourcing: Drivers and Future Developments

Ronan McIvor

The increasing prominence of outsourcing across both the private and public sectors of many countries has led to the concept receiving a significant amount of attention from both academia and practitioners. Outsourcing has progressed from focusing initially on areas such as information technology services and facilities management to encompassing almost every organizational function (Barthelemy, 2003). Its growth has further been accelerated by rapidly developing product and service markets, both locally and offshore (McIvor, 2005). It has also become an extremely political issue in the developed economies of the world as organizations increasingly outsource many production- and service-related activities to developing economies in order to take advantage of lower labour rates and more favourable employment legislation. In addition, many governments in developed economies have been employing outsourcing as a means of reducing the scale of large public-sector organizations and accessing the capabilities of product and service providers in the private sector.

This chapter outlines a number of developments in the business environment that have been driving the outsourcing phenomenon. These drivers include advances in information technology, globalization, more demanding consumers and reforms in the public sector – changes that have forced organizations to become more flexible and responsive to customer needs. As a result, many hierarchically-controlled organizations that previously performed the majority of their business activities internally have been forced to create more network-oriented organizational structures, which involve outsourcing activities to specialist suppliers. The chapter then goes on to identify a number of potential future developments in the area of outsourcing.

Drivers of outsourcing

The trend towards outsourcing has been driven by a number of factors in the business environment, as discussed below.

DEVELOPMENTS IN INFORMATION AND COMMUNICATION TECHNOLOGIES (ICTs)

Advances in telecommunications and information technology have been a major facilitator of the trend towards outsourcing. Innovative information and communication technologies (ICTs) have been increasing in importance for economies and societies and, over the last few decades, have had a radical impact on the way in which business is performed as well as on the way in which organizations compete in many industries (Porter, 2001). Most organizations cannot compete effectively without employing information technology, which can create efficiencies in a number of business areas ranging from design to marketing to finance. In addition, ICTs have enabled organizations to globalize production and access new product markets. In particular, the advance of the Internet, with its vast range of potential services and applications, has led to a transformation of corporate strategy since the mid-1990s (Picot *et al.*, 1997). Traditional industry boundaries are blurring as, increasingly, many industries – information technology industries, in particular – converge or overlap (Bettis and Hitt, 1995). Companies such as Amazon compete across a number of traditional industries by offering a range of products that includes CDs, DVDs and books. The benefits of the Internet – making information available; reducing procurement, marketing, and distribution costs; allowing buyers and suppliers to transact business more easily – also make it more difficult for organizations to profit from these benefits. For example, the Internet allows consumers to search more comprehensively at negligible costs for the most competitive price for a range of products or services. A major challenge for management in exploiting the Internet is to realize that these fundamental changes are creating a situation where organizations are operating in an increasingly global, technologically interconnected and information-driven world (Sampler, 1998).

Advances in ICTs have also acted as a key enabler in allowing organizations to adopt radically altered structures, which in itself has been a major driver behind the trend towards increased outsourcing. This is because developments in ICTs have significantly increased both the complexity and amount of information that can be transmitted while at the same time reducing both the cost and the time it takes as well as effectively eliminating the geographical constraints associated with physical information transmission mechanisms. All of these developments have led to a reduction in the costs of internal and external information dissemination for organizations. Consequently, many organizations have redesigned their organization structures and have used ICTs to coordinate and integrate the various elements of the business.

New Internet technologies, such as intranets and extranets, have also facilitated information exchange both vertically and horizontally in the organization hierarchy as well as externally in the business network. For example, within large organizations, the emergence of open standards for exchanging information over intranets fosters cross-functional teams and has the potential to accelerate the demise of hierarchical structures and their proprietary information systems (Evans and Wurster, 2000).

Developments in ICTs have also led to the creation of virtual corporations – that is, organizations comprising a number of business partners (ideally the most competent available in the chosen specialist area) who share costs and resources in the development, production and delivery of a product or service. The virtual corporation aims to create a high level of trust and eliminate the potential for opportunism through making the organizations involved more dependent on one another, and its creation and operation depend heavily on using information technologies to enable rapid communication and collaboration between each business partner in the value chain. Developments in Internet technologies such as extranets – networks that link one organization with another over the Internet – facilitate the operation of the virtual corporation. Extranets can provide a secure connection between an organization's own intranets and those of its business partners, materials suppliers, financial services, government and customers. The protected environment of the extranet allows groups to collaborate, share information exclusively and exchange it securely.

GLOBALIZATION

The outsourcing phenomenon has become increasingly associated with globalization. In recent years the business environment has become increasingly global for many industries. Regional agreements such as the North American Free Trade Agreement (NAFTA) between the United States (US), Canada and Mexico and the development of the European market with a single currency facilitated the development of trade on a global basis. This trend has led organizations to expand the geographical scope of their business operations in terms of the markets they serve and the production sources for product manufacture and service delivery. These changes have presented organizations with a number of opportunities in terms of achieving greater economies of scale, sharing investments in research and development (R&D), selling in a wider range of markets, and accessing lower-cost labour sources for both the manufacture of their products and delivery of their services. In addition, many organizations have been able to build internationally recognized brands for their products and services. Throughout the developed economies of the world, including the US, Europe and Japan, standardized consumer products in areas such as electronics, computers and cars have become increasingly prominent. Nevertheless, globalization has also presented many challenges. Establishing a global presence can involve managing a complex network of manufacturing, distribution and retail sources. Differences in language, culture, legal requirements and currency movements can further increase the complexity of this process.

Increasing deregulation across a range of industries, including telecommunications, air travel and utilities, has led to the globalization of the external environments in which many organizations compete. For example, increasing competition from low-cost carriers such as Ryanair and easyJet in the European airline industry has been very much driven by deregulation. Globalization has also been increasing the intensity of competition in many industries. In the past, organizations operated in a national market with three or four established companies and a low level of competition. Nowadays, as they extend their boundaries globally they face competitors in both home and international markets. This increased intensity of competition has forced many companies to reduce costs, and improve customer responsiveness and product quality. Many organizations have also been forced to accelerate the development of new products and services and restructure business processes in order to reduce costs and eliminate inefficiencies.

Globalization has had also significant economic effects. The liberalizing of global trade has facilitated many countries' economic development. For example, export-led growth has been central to the industrial policy of many Asian countries; this, in turn, has raised the living standards of their populations. The arguments for free trade are based on the law of comparative advantage proposed by the English economist David Ricardo (1772–1823). This law states that countries should specialize in producing and exporting the products or services that they produce at a lower relative cost to competing countries. However, the liberalization of trade has led to the loss of many jobs in developed economies as companies increasingly outsource manufacturing- and service-related activities to developing economies with lower labour costs – a trend which is sometimes referred to as offshoring. Offshoring involves transferring organizational activities carried out locally to service providers in other countries. The trend towards offshoring has been particularly pronounced in the areas of telemarketing services and software development. For example, many UK, US and Australian organizations have now outsourced much of their call-handling activities, ranging from after-sales support to direct marketing. Much of this outsourcing has involved the use of both local call centres and offshore call centres in a range of locations including India, Malaysia and Jamaica. The motivation behind the outsourcing of these telemarketing-related services to offshore locations has often been a desire to access service providers with considerably lower labour costs.

MORE DEMANDING CONSUMERS

Consumers in many business sectors have become more sophisticated and demanding as they have become more knowledgeable on issues such as price, reliability and availability. Not only are they demanding a more customized product and service at a lower price, but they are also much more mobile in terms of ease of access to alternative sources of supply as a result of increased competition in many markets and the advent of the Internet. With global access through the Internet to more products and services than ever before and with instant communications, typical constraints, such as time and distance, are rapidly disappearing. As a result, consumers' loyalty to product and service providers is diminishing. This has forced organizations to become more responsive to customer needs in a range of areas. In some consumer markets, it is now possible for the consumer to describe exactly what they want by actively modifying and adding features to the product virtually. For example, on Nike's website – nike.com – the customer can design and choose features to create their 'favourite' running shoe. Car manufacturers, too, allow potential customers to create their preferred car on-screen and access immediate prices for any extra features required.

Such changes are not only affecting commercial organizations but are also having major implications for public-sector organizations. Consumers are increasingly demanding higher levels of service and responsiveness from public-sector organizations as a consequence of their more information-enriched and interactive relationship with commercial organizations. This means that public-sector organizations have now to respond innovatively in terms of the way in which they interface with citizens in order to achieve greater accessibility and efficiency. Academic institutions are already using the Internet to interact virtually with students, and, many of them allow students to carry out activities such as submitting applications for courses, enrolment and accessing teaching materials and results over the Internet. In the past, many public-sector organizations have been 'protected' from the harsh commercial reality of competition and an ever increasingly demanding customer. However, consumers' expectations will continue to rise with the increasing use of online trading which allows business to be conducted at any time of the day.

PUBLIC-SECTOR REFORMS

Wide-ranging reforms occurring in public-sector organizations in many countries have also influenced the trend towards outsourcing. Governments in the US and UK have pursued radical public-sector reforms which have placed the use of competitive market mechanisms at their heart. Proponents of competitive market mechanisms argue that assets and activities should be transferred from the public sector to the private sector in order to improve performance. Moreover, they argue that the public sector should aspire to the levels of performance attained in the private sector. Much of the force behind this trend has been the prevailing belief that best value is achieved through the use of competitive market solutions for service provision. For example, the impetus for greater application of market forces to the public sector in the US came from the publication of *Reinventing Government* (Osborne and Gaebler, 1992), which emphasized the benefits of competition and customer choice as a means of delivering better and more cost-effective services to citizens. In the UK, during the 1980s and 1990s, successive governments pursued policies which encouraged free market mechanisms in the public sector and discouraged state intervention where possible. The most prominent concept associated with using the market in the public sector has been the privatization of publicly owned organizations, although, the introduction of internal markets and the outsourcing of public-service services such as refuse collection, building, catering and cleaning have become very prominent too. In the UK, outsourcing began in local government in the 1980s and subsequently spread to central government in the 1990s, following the publication of the White Paper, *Competing for Quality*. A key initiative was compulsory competitive tendering (CCT) which required regular re-tendering and the achievement of a stated minimum rate of return on the value of the contract that involved agreeing a formal contractor–client split. A further development has been the public–private partnership (PPP) philosophy, which has attempted to create a climate of cooperation between the public and private sectors in the form of an inter-organizational partnership. PPPs involve not only the introduction of market mechanisms to public-sector management, but also the use of partnerships to integrate the strengths of both the public and private sectors in order to achieve a common set of objectives.

A major element of PPPs in the UK has been the private finance initiative (PFI) which involves replacing the purchase of an asset by the public sector by the purchase of a service for an annual fee paid to a contractor (Akintoye *et al.*, 1998). The structure of a PFI project involves a number of elements including a concession agreement, a contract between a public-sector organization that grants a promoter a right or privilege to undertake construction works, along with an obligation to undertake those works for a specified time period.

The constant drive for cost reduction and the efficient use of resources has also forced many public-sector organizations to consider reducing the scale of government departments and public services. This trend towards radically changing the large hierarchical nature of public-sector organisations to more responsive customer-oriented network structures reflects the changes occurring in many commercial organizations. However, these developments in the public sector have been very controversial, and, the high level of unionization in the public sector has hindered the freedom with which governments can pursue such reforms.

Future trends

Although the practice of outsourcing is already well developed in the private sectors of many countries and gaining prominence in the public sectors, it still has some way to go before it reaches the level of development as that of the private sector. The increasing use of outsourcing in the public sector has been directly attributable to the introduction of the free market mechanisms by governments in the UK and the US during the 1980s. Many governments have continued to view outsourcing as an appropriate way of achieving performance improvements in services and greater choice for their citizens. However, the extent to which public-sector organizations can pursue outsourcing relative to the private sector is, and will continue to be, constrained by the presence of political influences. In the previous section, a number of outsourcing drivers were identified, including developments in ICTs, globalization, more demanding consumers and public-sector reforms. Although the pace of outsourcing is difficult to predict, these drivers will continue to influence the trend towards outsourcing by both public- and private-sector organizations. In many cases, these trends are interrelated. Also, the development of outsourcing will be influenced by the success of current outsourcing efforts. This section outlines some of the potential future developments in the area of outsourcing.

MORE DEMANDING SOURCING ORGANIZATIONS

As has been stressed, organizations are already dealing with extremely sophisticated and demanding consumers, who will continue to be further empowered by the increasing level of competition and the further development of the Internet as a channel for communication and trading in many industries. Consumer demand for growing product and service complexity is likely to further accelerate the trend towards outsourcing. The increasing demands placed by consumers on organizations are also impacting upon the suppliers of these organizations. Although many organizations are increasingly outsourcing more critical business activities, most currently outsource only peripheral business activities. As they outsource a greater range of activities and a higher level of value associated with each activity, suppliers will have to deliver a broader range of services. Rather than employing outsourcing to deliver solely cost reductions, more organizations will outsource activities in order to obtain a higher level of value from suppliers in areas such as greater responsiveness and flexibility. Of course, a potential risk associated with outsourcing a broader range of activities is that suppliers will be unable to keep pace with the demands of customers. For example, in many supply markets the complexity of the demands by organizations has posed challenges and, in some cases, outpaced the capabilities of suppliers. In future, organizations will be forced to place more emphasis on evaluating supplier performance and supply market developments. The ability of organizations to manage suppliers is a key element of any outsourcing strategy. As organizations outsource more critical business activities, the approach to supplier management will become even more critical. The organizations that will gain most from outsourcing will be the ones that can unlock the potential opportunities that exist in supply markets.

GREATER OUTSOURCING COMPLEXITY

With the outsourcing of more critical business activities, the processes of selecting suppliers, negotiating contracts and managing the transfer of assets and operations to the supplier are likely to become more complex and costly to implement. Contracts will become more sophisticated in terms of performance measurement mechanisms, asset transfer management and the development of clauses to allow for outsourcing failure. Also, the tendency to use more external suppliers will become more prevalent as many supply markets develop to offer a wider range of business services – both locally and offshore. Indeed, many organizations will reach the point at which almost all the activities required to produce and deliver their product and service portfolio can be performed entirely by external product and service providers. A key element of business strategy, therefore, is determining the scope of organizational activity that can create competitive advantage both currently and in the future. Indeed, the process of outsourcing evaluation and management has become a critical activity for organizations. Developments in ICTs are further fuelling the move towards the adoption of alternative relationship configurations such as network organizations and virtual corporations. As well as accessing the capabilities of suppliers, organizations will continue to employ outsourcing as a means of reducing financial risk in areas such as new product development. For example, in the past, many original equipment manufacturers (OEMs) shouldered most of the burden of R&D expenditure for new products. However, OEMs are now encouraging suppliers to invest resources in research and design in return for longer-term contracts.

OFFSHORING

Many organizations have decided against offshoring because they believe that foreign service providers cannot provide comparable levels of service to that of local service providers. Indeed, Dell decided to bring back in-house some customer service activities outsourced to India as it had received complaints from its business customers about poor service from operators. However, despite the difficulties experienced by some organizations with offshoring certain activities in terms of service and quality levels, this trend is set to continue. This trend is, however, likely to be more prevalent amongst private-sector organizations than public-sector organizations. Indeed, in some countries, such as the US, legislation has been enacted to prevent the outsourcing of public-sector activities offshore. Nevertheless, many private-sector organizations will continue to engage in offshoring in order to obtain the potential cost savings and productivity gains. Many offshore locations for product- and service-related activities are aggressively marketing their regions to both private- and public-sector organizations in the developed economies. India is no longer the main source for outsourcing services; other countries are now competing for this business, and China, Malaysia and some parts of Eastern Europe, for example, are increasingly becoming suitable locations for such services. Indeed, a major concern for developed economies is that high value-added jobs are coming under potential threat from offshore locations. This is a legitimate concern as many developing economies continue to develop their skills base through investment in training and higher education. For example, some of these countries, such as India, are now offering design as well as product manufacturing and service delivery capabilities. Therefore, a major challenge for developed economies is to increase the level of added value and innovation capacity in order to compensate for the decline in jobs as a result of offshoring in manufacturing and service areas.

THE CHANGING ORGANIZATION–EMPLOYEE RELATIONSHIP

Organizations are increasingly adopting a range of different working arrangements, including the employment of external consultants and temporary workers. As a result of these more flexible working arrangements, the relationship between many organizations and their employees has radically changed. In particular, many individuals have begun to specialize in one area of expertise and are no longer loyal to a single organization. In turn, the paternal role of the organization in its relationships with its employees has been gradually disappearing. The development of specialist organizations in outsourcing supply markets has presented opportunities for individuals to develop specialist expertise. Research on information technology professionals in the US has found that contract arrangements in some cases increased skill levels through experience of different workplaces, friendships and collaborations (Grugulis et al., 2003). As a result of these developments, the responsibility for career development has shifted from the organization to the individual. Due to the lack of job security and the increasing prevalence of flexible working arrangements, individuals will have to develop knowledge and skills that allow them to contract with successive employers. Clearly, a major concern with this trend is that these conditions are not conducive to allowing individuals to develop their knowledge and skills base. Indeed, Mallon and Duberley (2000) found in a study of career professionals employed on a consultancy basis that these individuals were still relying on knowledge gained at the start of their careers. In the paternal organizational model skills development was supported through a range of mechanisms such as training, promotion, mentoring and development. Although, organizations are seeking greater flexibility and lower costs through outsourcing, a concern is that they are reducing the skills base available in their respective labour markets.

Conclusions

The trend towards outsourcing is set to continue as organizations are expected to do more with fewer resources. Outsourcing is not limited to the peripheral areas of the business but is increasingly impacting on business areas that can contribute significantly to competitive advantage. Studies have shown that organizations are becoming more ambitious and sophisticated in both their objectives and approach to the outsourcing process. For example, Saunders *et al.* (1997) found that, in many cases, the principal motives for outsourcing were technological and strategic and not cost reduction. They also found that outsourcing allowed organizations to achieve a number of strategic benefits ranging from the more rapid adoption of new technologies to becoming more responsive to customer needs by better coping with variations in product demand. PricewaterhouseCoopers found that the motivation for outsourcing has moved from searching for efficiencies and improvements in a single process or activity to reconfiguring entire processes in order to obtain greater value across the organization (Yankelovich Partners, 1999). In addition, further developments in ICTs will accelerate the trend towards the adoption of virtually integrated relationship configurations. In effect, organizations are responding to changes occurring in the business environment. Increasingly, the ability of organizations to reduce costs is regarded as a prerequisite for participation in many industries, whilst innovation and responsiveness to customer needs are regarded as potential sources of competitive advantage. Outsourcing strategies are becoming more ambitious in order to meet these challenges.

References

Akintoye, A., Taylor, C. and Fitzgerald, E. (1998), 'Risk analysis and management of private initiative projects', *Engineering Construction and Architectural Management*, vol. 5, no. 1, pp. 9–21.

Barthelemy, J. (2003), 'The seven deadly sins of outsourcing', *The Academy of Management Executive*, vol. 17, no. 2, pp. 87–98.

Bettis, R.A. and Hitt, M.A. (1995), 'The new competitive landscape', *Strategic Management Journal*, vol. 16, pp. 7–19.

Evans, P.B. and Wurster, T.S. (2000), *Blown to Bits: How the New Economics of Information Transforms Strategy*, Harvard Business School Press, Boston, MA.

Grugulis, I., Vincent, S. and Hebson, G. (2003), 'The rise of the "network organisation" and the decline of discretion', *Human Resource Management Journal*, vol. 13, no. 2, pp. 45–59.

McIvor, R. (2005), *The Outsourcing Process: Strategies for Evaluation and Management*, Cambridge University Press, Cambridge.

Mallon, M. and Duberley, J. (2000), 'Managers and professionals in the contingent workforce', *Human Resource Management Journal*, vol. 10, no. 1, pp. 33–47.

Osborne, D. and Gaebler, T. (1992), *Reinventing Government: How the Entrepreneurial Spirit is Transforming the Public Sector*, Addison-Wesley, Reading, MA.

Picot, A., Reichwald, R. and Wigand, R. (1997), *Information Organisation and Management: Expanding Markets and Boundaries*, Wiley, New York.

Porter, M.E. (2001), 'Strategy and the Internet', *Harvard Business Review*, vol. 79, no. 2, pp. 63–78.

Sampler, J.L. (1998), 'Redefining industry structure in the information age', *Strategic Management Journal*, vol. 19, pp. 345–55.

Saunders, C., Gebelt, M. and Hu, Q. (1997), 'Achieving success in information systems outsourcing', *California Management Review*, vol. 39, pp. 63–79.

Yankelovich Partners (1999), 'Global top decision-makers study on business process outsourcing', PricewaterhouseCoopers LLP, New York.

4 *The Evolution of Outsourcing*
Tony Kelly and David Poole

The evolution of outsourcing is helping to define the shape of the corporate economic model in the early twenty-first century. Changes in the last 20 years show a dramatic shift in the global economy. In the UK in the early 1980s, the mix of businesses included heavy industry and manufacturing, but today the services sector dominates the economy, with raw materials and products largely imported from lower-cost countries.

In addition, the services sector has changed. The transfer of non-core operations to third-party specialists who then supply services more effectively at lower cost has created new business models. Catering, cleaning and switchboards are among the aspects of running a business which are now rarely managed in-house. The outsourcing of services is a well-established business strategy, and, if taken to its limit, outsourcing has the potential to leave a business with only its board of directors and a unique business plan. Experts brought in from external companies would do everything else, from legal services to product development and sales.

The Connaught Motor Company is an example of the first virtual car company. This British company, founded by two former Jaguar engineers, had relatively low start-up investment costs, because it outsourced the manufacturing components and retained the design and project management in-house. The company's first project – the hybrid Type-D sports coupé – was launched in July 2004, having received almost half a million pounds worth of funding from the Energy Saving Trust. It has no less than 17 patents pending on its groundbreaking technology. However, most corporations will always retain more than just the board, although areas that impact upon competitive advantage, such as the successful and innovative application of technology, are outsourced to specialists.

The difficulty of recruiting, retaining and training information technology (IT) staff, whose skills help drive efficiency improvements, is one of the reasons for the growth of the IT services sector. In this sector, the management of the IT infrastructure and business process outsourcing (BPO) are now growing faster than other areas such as the implementation and integration of new systems. Globalization, the driving force behind the shift in manufacturing from Europe and America to the East, is also key to understanding the evolution of IT services. Outsourcing in the IT sector started with the servicing of hardware. Then, as software became standardized and developed into a commodity it became possible to manage and support applications offshore. The ability to produce personal computers (PCs), mainframes and related components at ever lower prices because they were being manufactured in low-cost locations, fuelled the explosion of corporate networks and economies of scale achieved by using third parties for service provision.

The next phase in this evolution was the move by Western companies to use offshore providers. Initially, small teams of skilled IT developers in countries like India were used to build and test new applications. Then, largely because of the development of remote support applications technology and improvements in communications infrastructures and large-capacity networks left after the dot.com boom, IT service management outsourcing became possible from different parts of the world, unconstrained by geography. In parallel to this trend towards offshore services, IT outsourcing is spreading into the outsourcing of business processes, together with the IT that supports them. Business functions such as payroll, call centres and accounting can now be provided as remote services. Companies seeking to make a significant impact on their cost base but, increasingly and perhaps more importantly, to re-engineer and transform the flexibility, agility and responsiveness of their corporate processes, can have the management of these business processes delivered offshore. Just as with IT outsourcing, companies have access to well-educated multilingual staff and excellent IT infrastructure, combined with deep process and industry expertise from around the world.

There are two distinct themes that aid in understanding this shift and its implications: first, the change in IT and business process outsourcing from a being a cost reduction tool to being an enabler of business change and, second, the globalization of service management provision.

From conventional cost reduction to fundamental change

Traditionally, outsourcing has tended to be seen as a relatively straightforward cost reduction tool with a clearly defined and limited scope – something to be used to reduce the cost of non-core activities. Increasingly, however, outsourcing is regarded as a means of achieving a step change in performance, agility and customer service. Transformational outsourcing – bundling technology, transformation skills and outsourcing into an affordable commercial package – is emerging as a way of achieving substantial technological and organizational change. Increasingly, cost-saving objectives are being superseded by other factors. Two 2004 surveys highlight this change: a Capgemini Pulse Survey of chief financial officers rated improvements in operational efficiency as the top advantage of outsourcing (Capgemini, 2004a) and the Management Consultancies Association (MCA) ranked access to specialist skills above cost saving (MCA, 2004).

Conventional outsourcing adds value by accessing best practice and economies of scale in non-complex and non-core areas. Under conventional outsourcing, performance improvement is operational in nature rather than strategic: doing the same things a bit better, a bit faster or a bit cheaper. To some extent, a shift from fixed to variable costs is both practical and achievable, and more tightly defined service level agreements are typically achieved. But often there is little or no scope for significant and fundamental business change – for which conventional outsourcing does not aim. It is tactical rather than strategic.

Transformational outsourcing, on the other hand, is evolving because companies need responsive systems architectures and business processes that are not hardwired to the past. For them, it is becoming less practical to outsource the as-is for efficiency-driven cost reduction alone. Outsourcing providers are responding with skills in technology, operations and business transformation to offer innovative financing models that can reduce the need for significant upfront investment and move fixed costs towards variable costs. Moreover, dramatically enhancing the business's ability to provide services to its customers and supporting greater visibility and accountability in the back office is consistent with the new wave of compliance requirements (for example, the Sarbanes-Oxley Act 2002 in the US, which addresses compliance and aims to make corporate governance more transparent).

Whereas conventional outsourcing was about doing the same things but doing them better, faster and cheaper, transformational outsourcing is about helping to create a new business model and a new management approach. Whereas conventional outsourcing was contracted on the basis of long-term stability, transformational outsourcing is predicated on change, shared risk and reward, and increased shareholder value. Successful transformational outsourcing depends on forging strong links between the 'strategic' boardroom and the 'operational' systems and process functions that make the organization tick. The collaborative relationship is closer, with more joint teams working together more deeply and broadly across a wider range of issues and functions – and because of the nature of the commercial model, the contract is typically longer

Dairy Farm International Holdings is a retailer in Asia Pacific, which operates brands including 7-11, Ikea and Starbucks in ten territories. In the late 1990s, in the face of fierce competition, Dairy Farm restructured to strengthen core competences and reduce operating costs while growing revenue. It was important to avoid capital outlays in non-core areas, so Dairy Farm outsourced its accounting, finance and procurement services as a joint venture. Their solution transferred finance, payroll and procurement activities to their outsourcing partners' delivery centres. In doing so, they achieved 70 per cent cost savings during a period of rapid growth (30 new stores in key markets); achieved nearly 50 per cent overall reduction in finance and accounting staff, and 40 per cent reduction in associated costs; and negotiated more than $5 million savings in the procurement of operating supplies. In other words, the outsourcing project was the engine for supporting and enabling Dairy Farm's growth and expansion objectives.

Transformational outsourcing needs the client and supplier to have a shared vision. In the case of Virgin Trains (thetrainline.com – rail retailing) this was cemented through shared-risk, shared-reward contracts. Because thetrainline.com needed to improve sales, its transformational outsource applied leading-edge techniques of advanced speech recognition and voice-data integration into sales centres. This automated and speeded up a large proportion of the sales process, resulting in a three-fold increase in revenue and a reduction of over 70 per cent in missed customer calls.

Both these case studies focus on transformational business process outsourcing and reinforce the fact that this rapidly maturing market is making its mark as a prime mover in cutting costs and generating efficiency, already well proven in IT outsourcing. A recent survey carried out by Capgemini (2004b) estimates a 7–10 per cent BPO market penetration amongst large European organizations. There is a long-standing track record of success: 61 per cent of companies with BPO experience have been outsourcing for over four years. What is more, these companies are extending the scope of their contracts. A quarter of extensions are to a new process area – for example, from finance and administration to procurement.

Many of the companies that are now outsourcing their business processes started with a shared service centre (SSC) for internal process improvement and are now completing the evolution by outsourcing their SSC. Their successes, and the continued market pressure to reduce cost and increase shareholder value, is creating the confidence for organizations to move directly to outsourcing back- and front-office processes, without the need to go via an internal SSC.

The globalization of service management provision

Outsourcing to offshore locations is one of the fastest-growing and most controversial sectors of the global economy. As organizations seek relentlessly to reduce costs and become more efficient, the labour-cost advantage from offshore outsourcing is compelling.

The decision to move activities offshore involves far more than simply searching out the lowest-cost location. Activities are located where they function most efficiently and effectively with the right balance of cost, flexibility and risk. This might mean locating some activities in a farshore environment, but more typically it will mean siting a blend of capabilities in various locations, be they on-site, onshore delivery within the same country, nearshore delivery from nearby countries, or in farshore delivery from different continents. The mix must be tailored and coordinated to meet specific business goals (see Figure 4.1).

The right decision about where to locate delivery takes into account the best configuration for a particular company's processes, services and functions, making the most of labour arbitrage opportunities while ensuring that the appropriate skills and services are provided from the most efficient locations. If a support process demands unique skills and close or frequent customer contact, the best decision might be to keep that process, or a portion of it, onshore or even on-site. Other activities, such as applications or network management, might be more efficient if performed in countries close by or on nearshore sites. Similarly, to take full advantage of the available labour and site cost differentials, routine, standard processes are often prime candidates for farshore outsourcing. The key to success lies in making the right decision in each case.

India is the best-known offshore outsourcing location, but many other countries have a significant role to play. In August 2003, *Business Week* reported that, while China supplies back-office support primarily to neighbouring Asian countries, its global reach is extending. According to *Business Week*, '[i]t is making inroads as an outsourcing base principally for

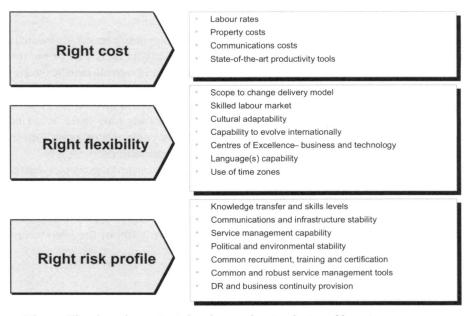

Figure 4.1   The three key principles that underpin choice of location

English-speaking nations, a business dominated by India, because of the influx of western multinationals that are now bringing back-office work to China (Einhom and Kripalani, 2003). Some believe that China will eventually reach parity with India in terms of the provision of call centre and back-office activities. Equally, Poland's services market is also on the increase and becoming well positioned to become the BPO centre for Europe.

The labour-cost advantages of farshore locations are well known, but this is only part of the story. The problem with arbitrage is that it is temporary in nature. Arbitrage is defined as the sale of essentially identical goods, services or assets in one market at a significant price advantage in another market. But basic economics tells us that arbitrage is ultimately temporary, if not transient, and it is corrected through supply and demand forces in the market. Clearly, the economies from which this differential exists tend to be large and the closing trend will be far from immediate, but nonetheless the gap will close with a tidal inevitability. So, although labour arbitrage does have a role in the near term, few organizations have the will, scale or resources to operate networks with multiple connected centres in order to spread the risks of any one location and leverage the future economic shifts that inevitably will take place.

It is questionable whether any organization should be making offshore decisions based on any model that focuses on a particular single location. Indeed, it will be difficult to imagine why anyone other than an outsourcer would make the investments required in technology and telecommunications to enable the shifting of workload and capacity between centres based on the specific requirements of the clients at any point in time. Labour arbitrage will be around for many more years before service costs and risk premiums equalize the market. Outsourcing providers and their clients that leverage multiple offshore locations and seamlessly transfer workload and capacity from one location to another will have the long-term advantage.

Future projections

Technology leverage is the next big wave in the evolution of outsourcing, with standardization driving utility process provision. Technologies like adaptive and open architecture, on-demand business services, agent technology, automated server management, server virtualization and a whole host of others are rapidly emerging.

These technologies are targeted at reducing total cost of ownership either through the creation of more open communications between systems or by reducing the effort of managing applications and hardware. By reducing complexity and cycle times of business processes with technologies which connect disparate data sources from trading partners, web e-commerce applications and legacy systems, easier access to real-time management data is possible.

The standardization of processes and the underpinning technology will make it possible for companies to buy on-demand services. Ultimately, utility computing and utility services will be comparable to other utilities such as electricity, where businesses do not own the power generators and just buy electricity on demand. The end-game is for clients to vary capacity because outsourcers take on business processes, the enterprise applications and the infrastructure and offer the services amortizing the investment across a wide cross-section of clients on an industrial scale. The melding of process and IT outsourcing services to deliver end-to-end business processes, such as purchase-to-pay, from integrated IT and business process management infrastructures will give greater control over activities that were previously loosely linked. Outsourcers' investment in multiple processes across common IT architectures from low-cost, highly automated SSCs will provide process and data management efficiencies that cannot be achieved through disparate data flows.

There are many companies counting the cost of the last wave of IT investments they made. Huge depreciating assets, combined with the trend towards mass standardization, make it more difficult for companies to justify keeping back-office processes in-house. The challenge for European businesses and workers is how to maximize gain and minimize pain through this evolutionary period. Fighting the economic trend will leave companies uncompetitive. In the longer term, understanding the evolution of outsourcing and embracing the growth-enhancing benefits it can bring can only contribute to building healthier businesses which must be the best way of securing long-term economic growth and more, if different, employment prospects.

References

Capgemini (2004a), 'Survey of CFOs finds value of information technology goes well beyond regulatory compliance', press release, 29 September at: www.us.capgemini.com/news/current_news. asp?ID=413&PRyear=2004 (accessed August 2006).

Capgemini (2004b), *Business Process Outsourcing Adoption and Perspectives in Western Europe*, Survey, June.

Einhom, B. and Kripalani, M. (2003), 'Outsourcing: make way for China', *BusinessWeek Online*, 4 August, at: www.businessweek.com/magazine/content/03_31/b3844132_mz033.htm?chan=search (accessed August 2006).

MCA (2004) *National Management Survey on Transformational Outsourcing*, Management Consultancies Association and PMP, at: www.mca.org.uk/mca/pdf/Transformational%20Outsourcing%20Summary. pdf (accessed August 2006).

5 Global IT Sourcing: Analysis, Developments and Best-Practice Considerations[1]

Nada Kakabadse and Andrew Kakabadse

Despite the fact that outsourcing is a relatively new term in management, the phenomenon of outsourcing has existed in various forms since Roman times, notably for tax collection and highway maintenance (Kakabadse and Kakabadse, 2000, 2001). Since its resurgence in the 1980s, outsourcing has become a popular managerial tool (Kakabadse and Kakabadse, 2000, 2001) to the point where global sourcing, commonly referred to as offshore outsourcing, has become an emerging phenomenon.

One critical reason for this is the proliferation of information and communication technologies (ICT) in the workplace. Seventy-five per cent of UK employees now use a PC or other forms of information communication technologies (ICT) in their work. Nine out of ten new jobs demand IT skills, whilst in most firms a range of standard processes are now computerized, confirming the high-tech trajectory move. However, research suggests that investment in ICT no longer merely provides a competitive edge but has now become a necessity for maintaining operational functionality. Therefore, in order to achieve differentiation and competitive advantage, organizations are increasingly searching to reduce the operating costs of ICT through a variety of strategic options.

With the cost competitiveness imperative in mind, this chapter presents findings from a number of studies into outsourcing in general and IT sourcing in particular, both pursued at Cranfield University, School of Management, as well as from an ongoing study into the governance of offshore sourcing arrangements conducted at Northampton Business School, University College Northampton (UCN). In particular, the chapter examines recent global sourcing trends, paying special attention to global IT outsourcing and the nature of IT offshoring. It then goes on to discuss the resistance to offshoring as well as the gains and challenges to both outsourcing and offshoring. The chapter concludes with a discussion of the crucial skills involved in best-practice outsourcing.

Global sourcing trends

There are no more sacred cows. R&D used to be one but that has changed, even in the pharmaceutical industry. What is a sacred or core activity, needs to be debated and agreed by the top team and even then we have to consider various political influences such as our

---

1   We wish to thank Sergiy Zatolyuk, Northampton Business School, for his involvement and comments in the writing of this chapter.

government polices in relation to our host suppliers. We operate now in a much more complex way, where external as well as internal influences can alter corporate course of action. (Vice President, pharmaceutical corporation)

Although previous studies (Kakabadse and Kakabadse, 2000, 2002a, 2002b, 2002c, 2002d, 2002e) show that the cost-savings argument for outsourcing is not nearly as compelling as the potential improvements to be gained from quality of service or resource utilization flexibility, emerging results suggest that offshore outsourcing is in fact primarily driven by cost considerations (Hutchins, 2004). However, one area not so determined by the cost argument is the accelerating sophistication of military grade software, hardware and ICT adapted for civilian usage. For example, the high-tech weapon systems used to such devastating effect in Afghanistan, former Yugoslavia and Iraq are so complex that combat units in the field have no choice but to depend on expert civilians to maintain and, in many cases, operate them during periods of combat. The F-117 stealth fighter, the M1A1 tank, the Patriot missile and the Global Hawk unmanned drone are all heavily dependent on civilian contractors (Bianco and Forest, 2003). Further, during the Balkan war, civilian service providers supplied most of the military communications for UK and allied forces. Similarly, in the USA, the Defense Department is the military industry's biggest customer, but it is not the only buyer in what is a truly global market. Advanced technology, alternatively sourced, provides US armed forces with an astounding array of new high-tech weaponry that replaces tens of thousands of soldiers with highly specialized, local or remote civilian workers. In fact, on the military side, there are currently some 90 private military companies (PMCs), predominately USA-based, followed by British, South African, Israeli and Russian companies providing services to 110 countries (Bianco and Forest, 2003). Many of these weapons technologies are now finding industrial usage, thus accelerating the outsourcing/offshoring trend.

Nevertheless, for most activities, the spectrum of outsourcing covers basic services such as building maintenance, information technology (IT), business process outsourcing (BPO), drug trials management, and so on. On the IT side, the shift from purchasing or leasing software as a product to purchasing application service on demand is growing in momentum through the use of such intermediaries as application service providers (ASPs). ASPs lease and manage technology – namely, commercially available proprietary applications and other computer services – from remotely located (that is, local and/or offshore) data centres and deliver services to multiple users via the Internet, wireless, or other private or dedicated networks (Kakabadse and Kakabadse, 2002c; Kakabadse *et al.*, 2004). For example, the Synxis Corporation, an ASP in Denver, provides services for the hospitality industry using Bulgarian software programs to develop and maintain vital online hotel reservation systems for its clients. Similarly, the Pizza Hut fast food chain in the UK uses FutureLink for its business management applications. In fact a range of ASPs exist, varying by business specialization and functional focus; these include enterprise ASPs, generic business ASPs, vertical market ASPs, aggregator ASPs among others. Many ASPs are supported by large IT companies such as Microsoft, Cisco and Oracle (Kakabadse and Kakabadse, 2002c).

The main difference between IT outsourcing and sourcing via ASP software delivery is determined according to applications and basis of charging which may be either per-use or by subscription (see Table 5.1).

Table 5.1   Outsourcing trend

IT outsourcing	Sourcing via ASP
• Replaces people	• Does not replace people
• Customization as necessary	• Minimal customization
• Software belongs to host organization	• Application is rented
• No change in service delivery	• Internet, leased/dedicate lines or wireless service delivery
• Investment in hardware/software infrastructure	• Rental service, includes upgrade
• Product orientation	• Service orientation
• High upfront costs/gains	• Predictable costs

Source: Compiled from Kakabadse et al. (2001).

Global IT outsourcing

Companies are increasingly under pressure to cut costs and create value and offshore outsourcing offers compelling savings. So we are increasingly willing to take a risk regarding copyright and data protection. The question for us now is not whether to send more work offshore, but under what circumstance and how to minimize potential exposure to risk.

(IT Director, software engineering)

Globalization, otherwise termed 'market and capital liberalization', and advances in information technology have all facilitated global sourcing as a distinct corporate strategy. Many American, UK, Australian and certain European enterprises have outsourced a variety of IT activities from maintenance of mainframe computers and desktops to the designing and development of new worldwide information systems (Table 5.2).

In the past, IT products and/or services were outsourced on a cost/commodity basis. A firm attained differentiated advantage by placing reliance on external suppliers to provide an IT service more cheaply and of greater quality so that the host organization could redirect its own capabilities to other high value-adding areas. Now, even the most innovative IT services, such as design, are being outsourced globally. In effect, once a job is defined and its requirements codified, an external supplier can provide the product or service according to best-value criteria. Even delivery now holds commodity characteristics, particularly in the case of software coding and programming, much of which has been shifted to India (Engardio, 2003).

Moreover, the IT sourcing market has moved from a 'one-size-fits-all' model, in which the entire IT operation is handed over to what is termed a 'best of breed' supplier, to specialist suppliers in areas such as networks, desktops, call–centres and data centres, taking on one aspect of the IT operation on behalf of the host organization (see Table 5.3). In the USA and UK the question is no longer whether to utilize global sourcing facilities but rather which one for which task?

Table 5.2   Activities most commonly outsourced offshore

Functions	Activities
IT products and services	• Software/product development – design, development, testing, packaging • IT architecture • Product implementation • Application maintenance • Application enhancement and upgrades • Software conversions
IT-supported sales and marketing	• Telesales and marketing • Telesales support • Data mining and market research • Customer service – call centres, electronic messaging (e.g. e-mails)
IT-supported finance and accounting	• Accounting transaction management • General accounting • Billing • Financial analysis • Credit card processing • Claims processing • Transaction processing

Source: Compiled from Kakabadse and Kakabadse (2002c).

Table 5.3   Global IT sourcing

Drivers	Strategy	Benefits	Risks
Efficiency	Operational effectiveness	• Global economy of scale and comparative advantage of location improve technical and allocative efficiency (e.g. low cost of input factors – labour, capital)	• Unable to sustain internalization at firm, industry and political level • Untested management capabilities • Cultural differences (e.g. language, standards – ISO 9000:2000)
Knowledge leverage	Innovation	• Global use of skills, competencies and ideas	• Incompatibility of legal system (e.g. contract law and copyright protection – data protection, privacy) • Incapacity for knowledge dynamism
Responsiveness	Customer targeting	• Good adaptation to local customer demands	• Unable to integrate global/local activities and/or processes (e.g. availability of infrastructure)

Source: Compiled from Kakabadse and Kakabadse (2001).

OFFSHORING IT SERVICES

As outsourcing has now reached such momentous proportions, it is important to understand the difference between 'offshore outsourcing' and 'global sourcing'.

> *The reality is cost reduction. We are outsourcing to low cost suppliers who employ only non-union labour, or to offshore suppliers in Bangalore that are thousands of miles away with a different culture, legal system, value and high level of piracy rate and experts who work for a fraction of the average salary in UK. Whatever others tell you the reality is that cost is the first and foremost driver in global sourcing. It feeds our zeal for cost cutting as the company can make huge savings by outsourcing work offshore and making use of modern telecom links.*

> (CIO, telecommunications)

As can be seen from the comments above, offshore outsourcing is closely associated with reducing operations costs through labour arbitrage (Lane, 2003). In order to make resource savings, enterprises contract out labour-intensive but well-defined IT processes to companies located in low-cost countries (see Table 5.4). Often, members of the suppliers' staff are temporarily assigned to the client's site in order to facilitate a faster transfer of activities to be outsourced. In contrast, global sourcing is more about flexibility and efficiency. The selective application of resources to specific projects offshore is inherent in this type of outsourcing whereby specific skills and expertise are relocated taking into account labour costs, degrees of risk which certain global locations create, flexibility and the utilization of best-in-class capability. Thus, companies can undertake complex IT initiatives involving package configuration and/or integration of large-scale systems projects while maintaining reasonable operations costs through the adoption of an offshore workforce.

However, the decision to adopt an offshoring sourcing strategy has an impact on local employment. Offshoring often leads to job cuts and lay-offs as evidenced by BT's decision to outsource many of its services to India, followed by Barclays Bank's announcement in 2003 that it was signing a £450 million outsourcing deal with Accenture that could involve over 1000 software development jobs moving to India (Morgan Cole E-Business Team, 2004). Barclays is also planning to move part of its call centre operation to India, which involves some 5000 jobs, as are National Rail Enquiries, which will affect 600 jobs (Warren, 2006). Financial institutions such as HSBC and American Express, as well as other large-scale enterprises such as Microsoft, Intel and GE, have already transferred many of their activities to India (*The Economist*, 2004). Approximately 50 000 British call centre jobs were relocated to India between 2001 and 2003 (*Gulf News*, 2003; *The Economist*, 2004). Although the call centre industry still employs some

Table 5.4   The low-cost advantage of IT labour

Country	Per capita income (US$)	Salary of university-educated IT professional as multiple of per capita income	Salary of university-educated IT professional (US$)	Salary of university-educated IT professional, purchasing power parity (US$)
US	34 280	2.2	75 000	75 000
UK	25 120	3.8	96 000	93 120
India	460	55.4	26 000	159 380

Source: Compiled from NASSC (2003).

600 000 personnel, it is expected that around 100 000 jobs will be transferred in the next five years to India, South Africa, Eastern Europe and the Philippines. About 15 per cent of FTSE 100 companies and 35 of Fortune 500 companies have taken advantage of low-cost call centres in developing countries (*Gulf News*, 2003). In India, for example, the average salary for a call centre worker is £1200 per year whereas the UK average is £12 000 per year (NASSC, 2003; *Gulf News*, 2003). In 2002 Gartner, a market research and consultancy firm, estimated that more than 300 of the Fortune 500 firms had business relationships with Indian IT service companies and that, by the end of 2004, more than 80 per cent of US companies would be considering using such offshore IT services (Frauenheim, 2002). In the same year, Forrester Research estimated that the number of computer-related jobs in the USA being outsourced globally would grow from 27 171 in 2000 to a cumulative total of 472 632 by 2015 (Frauenheim, 2002). Continental European firms are also similarly inclined but tend to outsource IT-related work to Eastern Europe, including the Czech Republic, Hungary, Poland, Romania, Russia and the Ukraine (McCue, 2003).

In addition to service provision activities, such as call centres, other activities are also being globally outsourced, including: IT-supported services such as financial analysis, which are increasingly being transferred to India; bookkeeping to Ireland, India and the Philippines; computer chip design to China and India; computer-generated sketches for drafting to the Philippines, Hungary and Chile; and customer service centres currently to India and the Philippines. Other white-collar professional activities are forecasted to follow this trend, including legal services and jobs in the life sciences. Overall, it is estimated that, by 2015, a total of 3.3 million jobs and $136 billion in wages will be transferred from US service providers to China, India, Russia and the Philippines (Frauenheim, 2002). Such predictions seem accurate as one report indicates that 43 out of 50 US states have one or more offshoring programmes (Ganjoo, 2006). The offshoring of service jobs follows the pattern of outsourcing in traditional industries, such as manufacturing and agriculture.

THE NATURE OF THE GLOBAL IT OUTSOURCING MARKET

Currently, global IT outsourcing is championed by Indian software companies which, by 2002, had attracted approximately 80–95 per cent of the total software export value (NASSCOM, 2002). India dominates, and is expected to continue dominating, the offshore market (NASSCOM, 2002; Terdiman and Berg, 2001). Between 1997 and 2002 its IT exports grew more than 55 per cent per year (NASSCOM, 2002). Such success was critically dependent on the Indian national and state governments who liberalized business policies, introduced tax exemptions, funded world-class satellite telecommunications projects and provided incentives for ISO and SEI certification. Despite the fact that India has masterfully evolved a powerful reputation for product and service quality, specialists have noted the growing challenge of being able to sustain such a level of high quality with an industry that, by the end of the 1990s was growing at 50 per cent per year (McCaffrey, 1999). A substantial growth rate is still being realized: NASSCOM, the champion of the IT software and services industry in India, recorded a US$23.6 billion result for 2005–06 – an increase of 33 per cent on the previous year (NASSCOM, 2006).

Ireland is the second largest software exporter in the world (Terdiman and Berg, 2001). Although Ireland does not compete with other countries on price, it has an excellent reputation for product quality and political and economic stability. Ireland's success is attributable to its well-educated workforce, active government support, an innovative and flexible private enterprise sector and its geographic location. The Irish government's multibillion-dollar investment in a modern telecom and industry infrastructure was also a critical factor in the 'Celtic tiger' success story.

Major contenders for offshore IT services provision include China, Russia, Pakistan, Ukraine and a number of Eastern European countries. Although this group of countries is in the early stage of developing a competitive outsourcing industry, it has substantial potential to compete. These countries 'have talented, innovative programmers, but the poor infrastructure discourages many prospective customers' (Terdiman and Berg, 2001, p. 15). However, although they have the skills and knowledge, they face a challenge in effectively promoting themselves because of their lack of marketing experience, poor onshore assistance expertise and lack of exposure to Western business practice (Gupta, 2002). An additional weak point is lack of English-language skills.

Resistance to offshoring

Many state governments in the USA have been pressured by lobby groups to legislatively restrict private contractors from globally outsourcing employment under state contracts, a practice that has already sent thousands of publicly paid jobs overseas (Gruenberg, 2003b). For example, intense lobbying and public pressure in New Jersey forced the state government to return nine white-collar jobs (a 'help-line' for welfare recipients) that a private contractor had outsourced to India back to Camden, an area of high unemployment (Gruenberg, 2003a). Moreover, the state of Maryland, like other states across America, has introduced legislation banning state agencies and contractors from exporting IT jobs to other countries (Gruenberg, 2003a).

At the national level, by 2003 the US House of Representatives' Small Business Committee had already held two hearings on the issue of global outsourcing and its impact on American job losses in the IT industry (Gruenberg, 2003b). In addition, the US Congress has initiated a legislative response to global outsourcing. On 30 September 2003 it allowed the upper limit on H-1B visas issued to foreign high-technology workers to revert from 195 000 annually to its previous level of 65 000, largely to ensure that more of these professional positions are filled by US citizens (Reich, 2003). Furthermore, the president signed the Omnibus Appropriations Bill into law on 24 January 2004, forbidding the outsourcing of federal contracts overseas. In effect, the USA, with its flexible labour markets, is increasingly refusing to play the global multilateral trade agreement game, but simultaneously pursues a desire to identify foreign scapegoats for its domestic economic difficulties, resulting in disruptive protectionist trade wars (Pfanner, 2004).

Although many UK companies have relocated their operations, including application development and call centres offshore as a distinct element of their cost-discipline strategy, local and central government are not likely to follow this trend according to the Office of Government Commerce (OGC). The head of the OGC has assured unions that jobs would not go overseas due to data security concerns as the public sector has to be 'very careful about the extent to which customer data actually moves offshore' (Morgan Cole, E-Business Team, 2004, p. 1).

Countries that are recipients of global outsourcing are increasingly aware of the potential political backlash growing in the USA and Western Europe. The National Association of Software and Service Companies (NASSCOM), one of India's largest business associations, recently released a report that it had commissioned with Evalueserve, a USA business research and intellectual property service firm, evaluating the impact of IT offshoring and increased globalization on the USA economy and warning of the political dangers that are likely to occur (NASSC and Evalueserve, 2003).

Balancing the gains

As highlighted above, outsourcing involves contracting to a third party the responsibility for providing goods and services that would otherwise have been available in-house on the basis that greater value can be realized from having so repositioned such resources.

Two schools of thought surround the value to be gained from it:

- Economies of scale. As repeatedly highlighted in this chapter, one of the key benefits an organization can gain from outsourcing is cost reduction and the attainment of greater internal efficiencies.
- Competitive advantage. The outsourcing of peripheral activities allows management to focus on the core competencies of their organization and on establishing clear differentiation from its competitors.

Thus, outsourcing can exercise additional leverage and/or new value for the host organization in terms of differentiation by:

- reducing transaction costs and the level of financial and practical risk associated with the purchase of capital equipment or particular services;
- improving process expertise;
- better access to capital, expensive technology and cheaper labour.

Moreover, the strategic cooperation between host and suppliers allows them to gain critical information about each other, and this positive relationship fosters innovative approaches to solutions combining economy of scale and competitive advantage gains, particularly in the case of multiple supply chain relationships.

However, in order to realistically benefit from outsourcing, a reality check needs to be introduced. The stated advantages of cost reduction and quality improvement of service need to be considered against the disruptive effect of outsourcing:

> ... at the end of the day, every organization that goes into any form of outsourcing option has to ask themselves what they are hoping to get out of it; what is going to be the effect; and what are the cost-benefits and risk associated with it? And basically, are these risks worth taking? (IT Infrastructure Manager, retail services)

The biggest disadvantage of outsourcing is loss of skills and expertise. For example, outsourcing the IT department to suppliers may leave the host organization locked into difficult long-term agreements as happened to the Australian Customs Service (ACS). The ACS outsourced its whole IT department to the Electronic Data Systems Corporation (EDS) thereby removing an IT expertise that had been established over 30 years. When EDS, together with its supplier, installed two servers that were deemed to perform unsatisfactorily, the ACS was unable to terminate the contract because it would have had to negotiate the return of all of its former assets that were transferred to EDS's control, and even if it achieved that, it could not rapidly reacquire those lost skills (Hutchins, 2004).

With the potential loss of skills come questions about the level and quality of physical and data security, particularly issues of privacy and copyright (see Table 5.5). Consequently, maintaining a positive and workable relationship with suppliers is emerging as a competence in its own right. Yet even when relationships are positively established and maintained, focusing on economies of scale has its drawbacks as the delivery of low-cost solutions, particularly in computing, may lack the agility desired. Leasing models lack the flexibility for innovation. This means that, in order to address the situation and increase service flexibility, contract service level agreements have to be renegotiated, thus increasing costs. Organizations may outsource infrastructure and services but should not allow themselves to outsource responsibility and accountability. If vigilance is not maintained, a strategy of driving costs down for an increased level of service may backfire as the supplier may not be able, or may not wish, to give the required level of attention to the host.

Table 5.5   Case-study examples of challenges associated with outsourcing

Client	Service provider	Year	Problems
USA: Internal Revenue Services (IRS)	Computer Science Corporation	2003	The late delivery of elements of the overhaul of the IRS record-keeping system. This project, costing US$8 billion, is more than two years behind schedule.
USA: US Navy	EDS	2003	Missed milestones on a project to install a new communication network resulted in a delayed payment of US$1.6 billion to the supplier.
USA: State of Georgia	Affiliated Computer Services (ACS)	2003	The state government terminated part of a US$300 million medical claims processing project after ACS missed a key deadline.
Australia: Australian Customs Service (ACS)	EDS	2003	Two ACS server computers were 'stolen' by an EDS employee and an accomplice after ACS outsourced its whole IT department for AUS$250 million.
South Korea: South Korean Authority	IBM	2003	This project resulted in corruption charges – bribing government officials in order to win US$55 million worth of procurement contracts from agencies such as the South Korean Information Ministry and National Taxation Office.
USA: The Pentagon	Halliburton	2003	Accusations of fraud and/or incompetence over a dining-hall-service bid in which Halliburton estimated its payments to a subcontractor as over US$200 million, whilst it had already reached a deal with a subcontractor for nearly US$70 million less – an overestimate of almost 50 per cent.

Source: Park *et al.* (2003); Hutchins (2004); Jung-a (2004); *Business Week* (2004).

Although the examples listed in Table 5.5 are from the public sector, private-sector organizations experience similar challenges. However, it is difficult to identify specific case examples because firms have displayed more reluctance to disclose their misfortunes than government organizations, which are accountable to the public and thus more transparent.

Globally outsourced projects also present exposure to risks of cultural differences between customer and supplier (Rae, 2002). Almost all projects are subject to unforeseen problems, misunderstandings and incorrect assumptions. An awareness of cultural inclinations helps shed light on some critical areas of confusion that may occur between customer and offshore vendor. In fact, the Gartner Group warns against underestimating the impact of cultural differences (Terdiman and Berg, 2001). Their survey report clearly emphasizes the need to understand cultural differences and to invest in learning how to address such concerns project-by-project. As can be seen, communication has been a difficult aspect of outsourcing relationships: 'Small communication failures can add up to big disaster' (Gupta and Raval, 1999, p. 22). Experience of well-established offshore relationships shows that early and frequent communication can benefit both sides of the partnership (Mayor, 2000).

Best-practice outsourcing

Many organizations generally underestimate the amount of work before and after the deal is signed and the level of skills that are required. You need to have shared agreement at the top; a good strategic oversight and continuous focus on relationships. You need a clear idea of the objectives of your organisation and how an outsourcing deal can support these objectives. (CIO, communications)

In order to achieve the desired benefits from any sourcing-driven interaction, attention needs to be given to a number of critical success factors; shared vision, clear strategy, choice of supplier/partner, the nature of outsourcing arrangements, the clarity of service-level agreements (SLAs) and their governance, and ongoing relationship management. Of these, shared vision, developing a clear strategy and ongoing relationship management are considered as critical (see Table 5.6).

SHARED VISION

The very essence of success in outsourcing, or any other strategic activity, lies in the top management agreement regarding the company's vision and corresponding strategies for its achievement.

(CEO, financial services)

Shared vision in respect of what are the core activities that create value and, in turn, competitive advantage prevents the emergence of organizational malaise, such as lack of clear goals and objectives, poor levels of trust and opportunistic behaviour. Top team failure in building a shared vision and commitment to corporate purpose often leads to the maladaptive behaviours that are evident in low-performance organizations. Such a range of positive and negative characteristics are an equally potent influence on sourcing contracts, particularly those that have a distinct strategic impact on the host organization.

Table 5.6   Three steps to successful outsourcing

Steps	Activities	Operationalization
Shared vision	• Building a vision shared by the top team regarding the organization's core capabilities	• Hold regular meetings and an ongoing discussion at the top-team level regarding what is core capability
Clear strategy	• Choosing a business model (e.g. ownership arrangements, type of outsourcing arrangements) • Forecasting contractual costs and service-level agreements (SLAs), monitoring and residual costs • Choosing supplier(s)/ partner(s) and location – outsourcing arrangements • Integrating outsourced activity within the host organization • Implementing performance measures: compensation: composition, level and functional form (rewards, penalties) • Establishing evaluation systems • Establishing a conflict resolution system	• Ensure cultural fit: corporate governance, management style, skills, language • Establish a market position: CSR, ethics • Set a price • Offer performance incentives • Set up inclusive performance to promote accountability
Ongoing relationship management	• Coordination • Multilevel relationships management • Managing risks • Mentoring/feedback • Benchmarking performance (i.e. transparency)	• Adequately resource relationship(s) with the service provider/partner at all levels • Build relationships with the supplier across management levels • Exercise contingent intervention • Actively monitor and review benefits and the viability of the relationship

Source: Compiled from Kakabadse and Kakabadse (2002c).

CLEAR STRATEGY

Not all corporations are good at figuring out which jobs really should stay close to home and which are dispensable. If you are exporting good jobs simply to save money then it is most likely your strategy will not get support in your organization. (HR Director, consultancy)

The decision to outsource often requires a re-evaluation of the organization's business model. The following all require careful management:

1. Strategic planning.

---

2   TCO calculates the total costs for purchases from different suppliers.

2. Examining alternative outsourcing arrangements.
3. Using structured tools as SEM (structural equation modelling) and TCO (total cost of ownership),[2]
4. integrating the outsourced service with the activities that remain in-house,
5. and minimizing any negative impact on employees, on the internal and external work groups who will interface with the supplier after the transition,

the complexity of the outsourcing process and the legal, economic and social impact on the contracting/partnering parties involved in the outsourcing all require careful management. Benchmarking is useful in evaluating both the production costs of the activity prior to outsourcing as well as establishing comparative production and transaction (bargaining, monitoring, contractual opportunism, management, specificity/complexity of relationships and outsourcing process) costs of each outsourced process/activity. For example, outsourcing activities that require specific assets such as technical competencies often harbour hidden costs in monitoring and defining contract terms and conditions.

Choice of supplier/partner

> *The most important factor in deciding whether to use a local or offshore supplier is whether that strategy adds significant value to the company in the long run as well as whether there is a cultural fit between the parties.*

> (CEO, manufacturing)

Cultural fit with the service provider, as much to enhance the relationship as well as to avoid damaging tensions, is an equally important consideration. It is particularly important if the service is sourced globally simply because different cultures operate in different ways. For example, US enterprises tend to evaluate performance on the basis of profit, market share and specific financial benefit. In contrast, Japanese, Swedish and most continental European organizations tend to view performance primarily on how the sourced relationship helps build the host company's strategic position, particularly in terms of skill improvement (Daniels and Radebaugh, 2001). Further, certain studies reveal that US companies operating in Europe and Japan aim for a 51 per cent shareholding in any partnering venture, thereby ensuring a majority position and control over personnel, brand decisions and investment choices (Ohmae, 1992). However, such a level of control does not guarantee an effective partnership as no sound relationship works on the basis of control but, rather, on commitment, trust and a continuous effort to achieve agreed benefit. Establishing an effective working relationship with a new supplier, whether local or offshore, requires time and effort. Analysis of the supplier's market position, industry expertise, prices, technical quality, ability to manage client relationships, management style, track record of effective client relationship management and quality of previous service provision is necessary. Research findings indicate that local and offshore suppliers require equal attention (Kakabadse et al., 2004).

> *Many of our clients that are users of ASP services were quite alarmed when some 30 ASP vendors were investigated for alleged selling of their customer data. However, none of them carried out the due diligence on the selected vendors and only came for advice after the alarms went off.*

> (Legal Professional, legal services)

Outsourcing arrangements

Anything that leverages outside resources, whether by minimizing overheads, increasing efficiency, speed, flexibility, quality or value adding, that does good to your organization and enables it to achieve market share by adopting price and/or product/service leadership, is a form of outsourcing. Do it – it helps your company.

(CEO, finance sector)

Despite the growing popularity of 'offshore outsourcing', described by Lacity and Willcocks (2001) as sourcing information technology into foreign countries in order to take advantage of favourable prices and competent skills/performance, numerous models of sourcing arrangements have arisen (Lane, 2002).

Some of the more popular are:

- *Single provider:*
  - Strength: vendor understands client needs and offers better service.
  - Challenge: the 'loss' of a 'best-of-breed' performance.
- *Multiple vendors* (more than one supplier managed by the client):
  - Strength: allows for improved service and lower cost
  - Challenge: requires a significant effort to monitor and coordinate vendors.
- *Integrated suppliers* (number of suppliers managed by a single or main service provider):
  - Strength: reduces outsourced client coordination challenges, as interaction with the main service provider who is responsible for the performance of all suppliers, is required.
  - Challenge: attaining appropriate mix of suppliers.
- *Spot contracting* (temporary relationship): usually involves a short-term contract for one activity.
- *Strategic partnering*: a long-term relationship driven by brand enhancement, competitive advantage and differentiation requirements.
- *Private finance initiative* (PFI): whereby a private-sector operator undertakes designing, building, financing and operating one or more required services on behalf of a public-sector body in order to achieve value for money. Although many billions of pounds worth of contracts have been signed in the UK, politicians often perceive PFIs as a vehicle for building public projects that disguise the effect of government borrowing and the real public debt (*Financial Times*, 1998).

Table 5.7 provides a more in-depth analysis of the range of current sourcing contracts and their level of usage, now and into the future.

Table 5.7   Current and future outsourcing arrangements

Nature of sourcing arrangements	Current (%)	Future (%)	
Preferred/trusted supplier(s)	55.0	50.0	Down
Performance-based contract(s)	32.2	40.4	Up
Partnerships (joint risks/liabilities and rewards)	17.0	40.2	Up
Strategic alliances	20.1	34.2	Up
Single contracts	54.9	33.5	Down
Multiple suppliers providing seamless service	19.4	24.6	Up

Flexible pricing contracts	17.4	21.4	Up
Rolling contracts	28.1	21.2	Down
Partnerships with cross equity/JVs	12.8	20.9	Up
Shared sourcing consortia	5.6	11.3	Up
Public–private partnership (PPP/PFI)	7.8	11.2	Up

Source: Compiled from Kakabadse and Kakabadse (2001).

Service-level agreement (SLA), governance and efficiency curves

The most important issues facing outsourcing are related to governance of outsourced activities. Good governance cannot be imposed externally through legislation, contract or measures, but good governance comes from within the contracting parties. Both parties have to believe in it and have a will to pursue it.

(Senior Partner, legal services)

Critically important to an SLA, namely a commitment between the host enterprise and the respective supplier of goods/services relating to quality standards, is the ability to meet date of delivery, logistics and data security. SLAs must clearly define the agreed service levels of the outsourced activity and the nature of the commitments between the contracting parties. SLAs need to specify minimal acceptable standards as well as expected technical qualities, total service availability (for example, service availability for the product, network, centre availability, application availability). They must also define the governance style, for example, ownership arrangements, governance processes, monitoring and reporting procedures, financial stability, emergency procedures, organizational arrangements or model of service provision and contractual specifications. Such arrangements will involve monitoring the suppliers' performance according to appropriate indices or efficiency curves inclusive of targets to be achieved and quality of performance during the implementation phase.

ONGOING RELATIONSHIP MANAGEMENT

The problem is that only a few firms are very good at managing networks of relationships at all levels, from the support staff, R&D specialists, to executives that are dispersed around the globe. Those that now have these capabilities will gain competitive advantage in terms of global sourcing over others. (Director, global contracting)

Ongoing relationship management or service-level management (SLM), requires a constant effort from both parties across multiple levels. Both host and supplier(s) will require expertise in monitoring, controlling and evaluating, service levels while at the same time cooperatively managing contractual relationship(s). Particular attention needs to be given to:

- the management of performance risks (external factors, market factors and internal factors) through the establishment of measurable and achievable goals and objectives;
- coordination – namely controlling coordination costs and managing differences in operating procedures and differences in standards with regard to corporate social responsibility and ethics;

- levels of openness between parties, involving the sharing of information/activities with others, data protection and integrity, providing feedback and generating a willingness to learn from each other;
- relationship skills – investing the time to generate positive relationships with new suppliers/partners, being flexible and responsive and developing the capacity for conflict resolution.

Conclusion

Although whatever is necessary for a firm to survive and prosper is context dependent, the firm's strategy needs to consider and balance the needs of its stakeholders. I think the firm should not do what is necessary to increase its profit or even its survival if that is harmful to the majority of its stakeholders.

(HR Director, health services)

Successful outsourcing, including that of global sourcing and offshoring, is dependent on the maintenance of effective relationships between the parties involved. Generating such relationships is essential if benefits from outsourcing are to be realized in an increasingly complex and turbulent environment. Unfortunately, although governance disciplines may add extra levels of structure and thereby create a stronger base for effective interaction, they tend to focus on performance-based results and benchmarking. Irrespective of the reasons for outsourcing, the skills required to manage such arrangements are becoming an ever more prominent concern.

References

Bianco, A. and Forest, A.S. (2003), 'Outsourcing war', *Business Week*, 6 September, pp. 27–28.
Business Week, (2004), 'Contracting Trouble', Special Report, 12 January, p. 53.
Daniels, D.J. and Radebaugh, L.H. (2001), *International Business* (9th edn), Prentice-Hall, Englewood Cliffs, NJ.
Engardio, P. (2003), 'Online extra: perilous currents in the offshore shift', *Business Week Online*, 3 February at: www.businessweek.com:/print/magazine/ content/ 03_05/b3818051.htm?mz (accessed October 2004).
Financial Times (1998), 'Call to Account', 10 September, p. 3.
Frauenheim, E. (2002), 'U.S. firms move IT overseas', *CNET News.com*, 11 December at: http://news. com/2102-1001-982839.html (accessed October 2004).
Ganjoo, M. (2006), 'Most US states offshore govt's IT work', Rediff.com Business, Silicon Valley, 17 April at: www.rediff.com/money/2006/apr/17bpo.htm (accessed August 2006).
Gruenberg, M., (2003a), 'MD state lawmakers to fight export of jobs', *Press Associates Union News Service*, 20 October at: www.washtech.org/wt/printer.php?ID-Content=4623 (accessed October 2004).
Gruenberg, M. (2003b), 'White-collar job flight concerns lawmakers', *Press Associates Union News Service*, 24 October at: www.washtech.org/wt/printer.php?ID-Content=4624, (accessed October 2004).
Gulf News (2003), 'Barclays may shift 5,000 call-centre jobs to India', 30 December, p. 35.
Gupta, S. (2002), 'Riding the offshore wave', *White Paper*, PriceWaterhouseCoopers, www.pwcglobal.com/ (accessed April 2004).
Gupta, U.G. and Raval, V. (1999), 'Critical success factors for anchoring offshore projects', *Information Strategy: The Executive's Journal*, vol. 15, Part 2, pp. 21–27.
Hutchins, D. (2004), 'Outsourcing the Commonwealth', *Information Week*, December–January, pp. 26–31.
Jung-a, S. (2004), 'Soul threat to impose ban on IBM contracts', *Financial Times*, 6 January, p. 30.
Kakabadse, A. and Kakabadse, N. (2001), 'Outsourcing in the public services: a comparative analysis of practice, capability and impact', *Public Administration and Development*, vol. 21, no. 4, pp. 401–13.

Kakabadse, A. and Kakabadse, N. (2002a), 'Outsourcing: current and future practice', MORI-Xerox Survey Report, Xerox Europe, Uxbridge.

Kakabadse, A. and Kakabadse, N. (2002b), 'Trends in outsourcing: contrasting USA and Europe', *European Management Journal*, vol. 20, no. 2, pp. 189–98.

Kakabadse, A. and Kakabadse, N. (2002c), *Smart Sourcing: International Best Practice*, Palgrave, Basingstoke.

Kakabadse, N. and Kakabadse, A. (2002d), 'Application service providers (ASPs): new impetus for transformational change', *Knowledge and Process Management*, vol. 9, no. 4, pp. 205–18.

Kakabadse, N. and Kakabadse, A. (2002e), 'Software as a service via application service providers (ASPs) model of sourcing: an exploratory study', *Journal of Information Technology Cases and Applications* (JITCA), vol. 4, no. 2, pp. 26–44.

Kakabadse, A. and Kakabadse, N. (2003), 'Outsourcing best practice: transformational and transactional considerations', *Knowledge and Process Management*, vol. 10, no. 1, pp. 60–71.

Kakabadse, A., Kakabadse, N. and Macaulay, S. (2001), *Outsourcing Current and Future Practice*, Report, Cranfield School of Management, Cranfield.

Kakabadse, N. and Kakabadse, A. (2000), 'Outsourcing: a Paradigm shift', *Journal of Management Development*, vol. 19. no. 8, pp. 670–728.

Kakabadse, N. and Kakabadse, A. (2002a), 'Application service providers (ASPs): new impetus for transformational change', *Knowledge and Process Management*, vol. 9, no. 4, pp. 205–18.

Kakabadse, N. and Kakabadse, A. (2002b), 'Software as a service via application service providers (ASPs) model of sourcing: an exploratory study', *Journal of Information Technology Cases and Applications* (JITCA), vol. 4, no. 2, pp. 26–44.

Kakabadse, N., Kakabadse, A., Ahmed, P. and Kouzmin, A. (2004), 'The ASP phenomenon: an example of solution innovation that liberates organisation from technology or captures it?' *European Journal of Innovation Management*, vol. 7, no.2, pp. 113–27.

Lacity, M.C. and Willcocks, L.P. (2001), *Global Information Technology Outsourcing*, John Wiley and Sons Ltd, Chichester.

Lane, S. (2002), 'Analyst presentation: Steve Lane on IT services and the growth of offshore suppliers', Report, Aberdeen Group, Inc., available at: www.aberdeen.com/ab_company/hottopics/insider/analyst071202.htm (accessed June 2002).

Lane, S., (2003), *Focusing of the 'Global' in IBM Global Services*, Report, 27 August, Aberdeen Group, Inc., Aberdeen.

McCaffrey, M. (1999), 'Offshore outsourcing: the alternatives, key countries, and major challenges', *Cutter IT Journal*, vol. 12, no. 10, pp. 29–34.

McCue, A., (2003), 'India's new outsourcing rival – Romania?', *CNET News.com*, September 11, http://news.com/2102-1001-5074725.html, (accessed October 2003).

Mayor, T. (2000), 'Hands across the waters', *CIO, Framingam, MA*, vol. 13, Part 23, pp. 94–107.

Morgan Cole E-Business Team (2004), 'Legal column: December 2003 – public sector not following the offshoring trend', *Morgan Cole E-Business Bulletin*, 14 January at: www.itsecurity.com/archive/papers/eb21.htm.

NASSC (National Association of Software and Services Companies) (2003), *The Impact of Global Sourcing on the U.S. Economy*, October, Delhi, India.

NASSC (National Association of Software and Service Companies) and Evalueserve (EVS) (2003), 'Impact of global sourcing on the US economy, 2003–2010', NASSC–Evalueserve report at: www.evalueserve.com (accessed May 2004).

NASSCOM (2002), *McKinsey Report 2002*, National Association of Software and Service Companies, Delhi, India.

NASSCOM (2006), 'IT software and service exports grow by 33% in FY 2005–06', Embassy of India, Athens, at: www.indembassyathens.gr/Business/Indian%20IT%20exports%20grow%20by%2033%20%25%20in%202005-06.htm (accessed August 2006).

Ohmae, K. (1992), *Transnational Management*, Irwin, Chicago, IL.

Park, A., Foust, D. and Magnuson, P. (2003), 'Looking who's souring on outsourcing', *Business Week*, 29 December, p. 37.

Pfanner, E. (2004), 'Global economic outlook: the worrying unknowns cloud an otherwise brighter future', *International Herald Tribune*, 21 January at: www.iht.com/articles/2004/01/21/rover_ed3_.php (accessed July 2006).

Rae, S. (2002), 'Offshore resourcing: once adventurous, now essential for financial services firms', PWC Consulting, available at: www.pwcglobal.com (accessed May 2004).

Reich, R.B. (2003), 'High-tech jobs are going abroad! But that's okay', *The Washington Post*, 3 November, p. B3.

Tenon techlocate (2006), 'Outsourcing and offshoring – East Midlands shows the way', Special Report at:

2 *The Impact of Outsourcing on Organizational Structures*

Part 2 addresses the ways in which outsourcing directly and indirectly influences how organizations alter as a result of contracting out services. Although organizations utilize the outsourcing process in order to make themselves leaner and more competitive, any such change has consequences. This makes it necessary to examine how organizations cope (or attempt to cope) with internal changes, which may include assessing how individuals within organizations deal with outsourcing or what an organization needs to do to maintain a competitive advantage.

Part 2 starts with a chapter by Kristin Zimmerman and Christopher Green, who provide an overview of the ways in which a company can benefit from insourcing needed skills rather than outsourcing services. They illustrate the usefulness of a Global Laboratory Network (GLN) through which intellectual equity (person knowledge) is sourced for an organization. The GLN, as it can be applied across countries, is able to capture the resources that are needed while maintaining 'control' over its assets.

Next, Almas Heshmati and Kyösti Pietola provide a comprehensive assessment of how outsourcing is affected by corporate competitiveness strategy, innovation, increased efficiency and productivity growth. They give a comprehensive review of the literature, and present an analysis of Swedish firm-level innovation survey data. They find that the size of a firm was a determining factor in their analysis, while outsourcing was positively related to growth in value added indices. The chapter highlights the differing components, in addition to outsourcing, which are able to influence a firm's performance level.

It is important to acknowledge the changes that workers undergo during an outsourcing project. Such changes are rarely assessed as part of the outsourcing process. The chapter by Mike Dodsworth and Mike Constable addresses those concerns that workers may find difficult to voice when a company decides to outsource any aspect of its business. In addition, they highlight the limited knowledge that workers have about their employment rights during the outsourcing process. Their chapter tackles an aspect of outsourcing that is infrequently addressed in the literature – that of employee concerns.

Part 2 ends with a chapter by John Benson who examines the impact of outsourcing on employees and looks at their organizational commitment levels, among other factors. He notes that workers' commitment levels tend to decrease the longer an employer outsources services and that outsourcing was less likely to lead to an improvement in conditions or services within those organizations surveyed. He states that management needs to take a more strategic approach to the outsourcing process in order to gain the maximum benefits.

6 Global Technology Transfer: Personal Experience from GM and the Private Sector

Kristin B. Zimmerman and Christopher C. Green

The development of the ideas for this discussion is rooted in experiences gained from the authors who have spent many years in technology acquisition and deployment in the academic, governmental, industrial and private sectors. The specific examples used are from direct and personal experiences in industrial manufacturing and academic research from the mid- to late 1980s through to the present day. The experiences began, however, in the early 1970s with exposure to foreign scientific intelligence by one of the authors while in the US government.

However, as the title of this chapter suggests, there are many other attributes to the subject that are now coming into global societal awareness and are provoking renewed discussion and controversy centred on an 'us versus them' nationalistic debate. Consequently, we will use as its starting point lessons actually learned from industry. Then, we move towards science and technology policy and philosophy that are now becoming practice and affecting social balance through labour force shifts and the inability to manage intellectual property in the same way as was done in the past.

The discussion of an approach to managing global intellectual equity and the role of the 'person' in the global technology equation is an experiential one. We do not intend that the opinions incorporate (necessarily) those of our current or past employers. Indeed, in many cases, they do not.

The beginning of change: the Asian Model

The 'insourcing / outsourcing dimension' in fact comprises three separate substantive tracks of change. They have merged only in the past five or so years as a result of dramatic public policy debate. The two core opposing tracks that relate to the topic of this chapter include, first, the USA's diminishing capability in progressing its science and technology education into the US manufacturing technology base and, second, the contemporaneous increase in (primarily) Asian–Pacific Rim outsourcing.

But these two elements mutually influence the third track, the rapid change in industrial applications and engineering education in the USA itself. This 30-year process began in the East, which invested in science-focused education, in contrast to the USA, which invested in programmes focused more heavily on social needs and demographic equilibrium. In addition, the value of the teaching professions in terms of both generous governmental subsidy and popular public reverence has similarly reversed.[1]

Significantly, in the USA in the early 1980s, a dramatic shift in the relative numbers of job applicants began. No mystery here, because, at the same time, the numbers of foreign graduates seeking employment mirrored the foreign student numbers matriculating in US graduate programmes in science and engineering (Rai, 2004).

US industrial employers found receptive audiences in Asian universities for investment and training, initially in engineering support programmes and maths-intensive development programmes for which there was a decreasing demand in the USA. The pressure to perform in new growth markets stimulated the programmes discussed below (for example, in both the automotive and medical sectors).

In both educational 'markets', however, companies dependent on science and mathematics have the same experience whether they operate in the USA or in Asia. Even though US citizens owned 94 per cent of the shares in Compaq, Microsoft, Carrier and Lucent (Coca Cola and General Motors), the exports of those companies in the aggregate increased from US$2.5 billion in 1990 to US$4.0 billion in 2002, suggesting that the technology no longer resides only 'at home' (Friedman, 2004). In a recent analysis of global educational trends in manufacturing, eighth-graders (average age 13) in Singapore, South Korea, Thailand, Hong Kong, and Japan (China and India were not surveyed) scored first through fifth in standardized maths scores. The USA came seventeenth, behind Latvia in sixteenth place (Kristoff, 2004).

A strategy for change

In the real world of engineering, it is often taught that new programmes can be planned to 'have low cost, high quality and on-time delivery...pick any two'. The suspicion began to grow in the early 1990s that it may be possible, just possible, to have all three by using Asian capabilities. While we now realize that issues of 'quality' are responsible for the indirect costs of warranty and repair when they are less than the standards set, it is much easier to improve quality with on-site inspection and rigorous attention to in-plant training than it is to drive down infrastructure costs that flow directly to the bottom lines of new programmes. In other words, high-quality manufacturing issues can be improved on-site whereas infrastructure costs derived from a decreasing talent pool of design engineers in the USA, demand for high starting salaries and retraining in science and mathematics cannot. At least when operating in the host country, abiding by foreign rules and standards, it is possible to have 'all three'. Manufacturers, deploying what may be considered disruptive technologies, are willing to wait for quality to improve, and influence that growth in quality by resourcing low-cost, high value-added training programmes in foreign operations. Evidence of success in this strategy, in terms of improvements in profitability, has been seen in virtually every high-technology business over the past few years (Christensen, 1997).

The experience has been dramatically different with low-tech and service-oriented industries that attempt to 'outsource' when the focus is primarily on short-term programmes and profits (Stone, 2004). Companies' failure to understand the very concept of 'insourcing intellectual equity' (described in detail below) with their attendant focus on capitalizing on

---

1   Although this analysis and personal view does not encompass Western European educational and manufacturing experience, it is interesting in passing that similar outsourcing issues are less controversial in Western Europe, where outsourcing options to insourcing pressures do not assume the same gravity of public policy debate).

new technology talent with young students and entry-level engineers is leading to many cases of what is being called 'onshoring' since the jobs (as opposed to the innovations) are being returned to parent companies in the USA. As US companies learn to balance expectations with growth markets, and continue to invest in technology programmes in overseas markets where willing students are anxious to learn and be taught continuously, 'right-shoring' will result. One example of a company that got it right follows.

GENERAL MOTORS (GM): A CASE STUDY

Beginning in 1993, General Motors (GM) created a novel operating concept called the Global Laboratory Network (GLN) within their traditional automotive science and technology laboratories. Traditional GM researchers initially thought that the notion was all about *outsourcing*. Instead, what GM had really designed was a model for *insourcing* intellectual equity (person-knowledge) to enhance their research, development and engineering (RD&E) portfolios of projects and programmes, specifically aiming for the greatest level of productivity and return on investment around the globe.

The GM Global Science and Technology Policy Vision was truly a global vision. Within two years, the GLN was implemented throughout North America, Europe and across Asia, and became a cornerstone of the negotiations for GM's joint venture in Shanghai China called Shanghai General Motors (SGM). Over time, the GLN set up local/regional nodes to acquire science and technology to insource local talent to support its burgeoning new business ventures, rather than shipping talent and knowledge from the USA overseas in either its physical or electronic state.

The GLN started out as a very 'top-down' vision but soon was defined and made real by GM scientists and engineers, not by management. The GLN system of knowledge management put GM personnel in cultural and 'learning' satellites – or virtual communities – in order to join creative minds with strong-pulling local business needs. 'Insourcing of Intellectual Equity' was the theme of the GM programme.

The concept of the GLN fits the defining characteristic of Asian science, engineering, and technology – the passion to operate as fast as possible, but not faster, with just the right amount to move an invention into practice.

The GM experience

In 1993 GM created the Directorate for Partnerships and Leveraging which encompassed three sectors: industry, government, and academia. Its structure was quite different from the traditional process for pursuing areas of needed research by contract. The new programme understood how the rate of discovery in science and engineering was accelerating; how no one lab, even the 'best-of-the-best', could keep up with the asymptote of incremental discoveries by patenting everything; and how even GM could not afford the costs in time – typically several years from a concept in a lab notebook to filing a patent – and the legal fees to maintain the patents.

Technical education and electronic communication between scientists globally were supplanting many conferences and traditional face-to-face communications. Global marketing was making obsolete the old and failing approach to innovation of 'invent something good and throw it over the wall'. Understanding that the engineers on the other side of the walls had their own busy agendas – like applying maths-based tools to design cars and trucks – was a tough lesson to learn.

'Good,' and even 'better' innovation isn't competitive unless it is put into practice. 'Innovation' was recognized as patent put into practice. Therefore, discovery not only had to be applied to a business need, but also had to increase value by increasing quality or throughput in the company; otherwise there was little value in, or return on, the research dollars being spent.

The virtual global laboratory network (GLN): what is it?

As stated earlier, many of GM's scientists and engineers thought that the creation of a GLN was all about *outsourcing* – they could not have been more wrong! What it was really about was *insourcing* intellectual equity (the experiential base of the persons involved) to enhance the RD&E portfolios of projects and programmes, specifically aiming for the greatest return on investment. The scientists and engineers thought that those people who were beginning to talk about spending ever-diminishing material, or project dollars, outside GM's Warren Michigan Lab – in laboratories in China, India, Korea, Israel and even Ann Arbor, for heaven's sake – were crazy. The hostility was often palpable. Some friends were lost.

The new GLN notion created diverse, cultural, learning satellites, or virtual communities, which joined creative minds with strong-pulling business needs. This is real technology acquisition and deployment, not outsourcing of research, but rather what we refer to as the 'insourcing of intellectual equity. Previous notions of the words 'global lab' missed the whole point of diversity as the strength to unite partners, and typically only worked within the traditional outsourcing model.

GM's Global Science and Technology Vision was truly a global vision – and what was learned was that it worked best in Asia. It started as a very 'top-down' vision, but became defined and made real by the partnering scientists and engineers, not by GM management.

A GLN is created using a four-step process:

1. Find a university, national lab or person with technology competencies in a country in which you do business. Use templates, metrics and 'scorecards' that are flexible, and include not only patents but also, and more importantly, faculty expertise, graduate study areas, fellowship profiles and publications, including electronic publishing on the Internet by faculties at the institutions. Identify which GM scientists and engineers are familiar with, or are graduates from, these programmes. Send them on detailed site visits to meet face-to-face with the identified expertise – fast.
2. Matrix the findings against GM's business, technology, public policy, and emerging and emergent needs; debate the findings across internal technology intelligence and science advisory personnel; and determine the 'missing capability' cells, or voids, of a second matrix by utilizing RD&E and design centre expertise.
3. Negotiate the GM Master-Academic Partnership Agreement[2] with the institutions, or people who provide capabilities that fit specific needs. Be sure to negotiate intellectual property rights upfront, and design in 'off-ramps' that allow, at any time, the movement of maturing projects into totally proprietary cells of work.

---

2   The GM Master Agreement was written by Zimmerman and her team in 1994. The agreement is a legal instrument used to protect the publishing rights of the persons participating in the research and technology exchange, as well as protect intellectual property rights, and it is used as an addendum to a GM purchased services agreement.

4. Assign members to the labs, and appoint researchers or engineers from GM business/ operating units to be project monitors. Audit the work every six months face-to-face. Build in exchanges, fellowships, awards, recognition, recruiting schemes for eventual employment, and more.

The important overarching principle is twofold: couple the business, technology and public policies of the corporation to the products and services that are being jointly developed; and 'send projects chasing dollars, not dollars chasing projects'. These principles are at the core of the GLN model.

Asia – GM's learning example

In March 1994, Mr Jack Smith, chairman of GM, Mr Harry Pearce, vice chairman of GM, and Madame Shirley Young, vice president of GM Marketing for China, made numerous statements at shareholder meetings and at trade missions in Asia. For example, in July 1994, Mr Rudy Schlais, GM vice president for GM China, in Beijing, articulated five principles for GM operating in China during initial negotiations at Shanghai Automotive Industries Corporation. He later made the principles public in the form of his vision statement for Asia in various trade and public conferences. They remain some of the most powerful words in the automotive world because they are action words, not platitudes. They are controversial. They have been called anti-Western and worse. The five principles encompass these ideas:

*   GM will take its best technology to Asia and keep it current.
*   The technology will not, however, be one-way. A 'win–win' strategy will include technology acquisition as well as deployment, quality that is exportable in GM products from the region, and which will serve other regions' manufacturing and product needs.
*   The practice of automotive engineering will be, for GM, regionally based, with local nationals as full partners.
*   These partnerships will include every single aspect of GM's business. Every single one. That includes, especially, research and engineering.
*   The partnerships are based on core human values – including above all, respect for the differences in approach, education, business needs and the differences in people. Therefore, diversity is its core strength.

There are a few Asian GLN examples worth noting. GM now builds several of its highest-quality vehicles in Asia, and will design and build more vehicles for export in the future. The company saves millions of dollars by using a manufacturing system in Michigan that was invented in a Chinese lab. A set of software solutions from India aid the design of a North American platform and serve to reverse engineer the changes needed to adapt a European platform to Indian standards and needs.

Operating in Asia: the downsides

What are the 'going-in' risks or downsides of an Asian technology example, other than, of course, incurring the wrath of current cable news programmes? For example, we know that Asian business practices are often perceived as generating a reputation for seeking economic advantage in the face of Western perceptions of contractual obligations.

The Eastern concept that 'to copy is to honour' is not viewed in Western culture as honourable. This is especially true for labour-rich automotive suppliers who see their loss of jobs not so much as a result of increased productivity, as they do the 'stealing' of intellectual property – usually designs of products and/or manufacturing performance specifications. Curiously, however, the number of actual patent priority infringement cases in Asia and (even high-profile) lawsuits remains small in comparison with US company tort battles.

Part of the reason for this may be the immaturity of the relationships to date, as well as an intense desire on the part of both sides not to rock the otherwise proverbial stable boat and sink it as it displaces more and more profit loss. Another just as likely reason is due to cultural factors, as described elsewhere in this analysis: in Asia (especially China) a contract signed after negotiation is seen by the Western partner as setting parameters for production. For the Asian partner it defines the subjects for continuing intellectual 'equity' negotiation that bounds the relationship in time.

What this means for both partners is simple: recognize these distinct cultural traits as values and strengths, not as infringements. For the Western company, however, it also means something else that, indeed, can be a downside in outsourcing to Asia: the property of greatest value may be appropriated not by *your* Asian partner but by your Asian *partner's* in-country competitor or supply chain!

With the newly emerging legal protections (compared to in the West) this means that companies need to be willing to risk copy infringements by continuous product, design and manufacturing improvements – to make themselves obsolete. The alternative, of course, is to have a deep pocket and attempt to sue in foreign courts, control all the software with embedded business practices and design specifications, double the information technology (IT) firewalls, or choose not to partner in the first place.

For a company manufacturing a small number of designs that are information-rich and somewhat static, the risks may simply be too high. Partnering in Asia is neither for the culturally faint-hearted nor for the company that does not have a rich and dynamic technology portfolio.

The defining characteristic of Asian science, engineering, and technology is its passion to operate as fast as possible – but not faster – just the right amount to move an invention into practice. It is more appropriately called *technology elegance*. More than excellence, it recognizes something more profound. The Asian labs, like no others, seem to capture the notion that a learning organization is distinguished from a knowing organization because it is dynamic (ever-changing and growing) and not measured in a patent priority or a single licence or sale. The improvements to any scientific discovery are most efficiently achieved from practice. It may not make perfect, but it stands a better chance of getting on to the next task that stretches towards perfect science and technology policy and practice.

No structure of research on the globe seems to understand that as well as do the distributed centres of excellence and labs, the GLNs, in Asia. The absolute insistence on relevance and speed, and not on perfection and obsolescence, is what organizations like GM need, and is what Asia has to offer.

We can summarize with a prediction: if you are wearing an industry hat then you must avoid the strong temptation to bring all the projects back inside your own 'patent protected' organization, or into a small 'NEWCO' (a planned new start-up technology company) where you will lose the economies of scale, low overheads and a 24-hour mentality. It is likely that an Asian GLN will surpass others in size and scope, though not necessarily in importance, in a very short time. All the elements are present: a passion to do the right thing, not just feed contracts; to be relevant, not spin research webs that are not attached to the business; and, most important, to be elegant, not just fast.

The implementation process: lessons learned

There are three very important lessons generated from the GLN model with its overarching 'projects chasing dollars' principle. The first is that virtual satellite centres of excellence are created in order to leverage knowledge and expertise across several people, universities and national labs. Therefore, the investment, public relations effects and access to learning instead of single-lab knowledge grow exponentially.

Second, decentralized research in highly diverse global locations, but with retention of central management by researchers and engineers working on the product and manufacturing programmes, means very low overhead costs. And, the people doing the management have a personal stake in seeing that the work gets done on time.

Third, the success of any laboratory, programme, project or, for that matter, one's own individual career path depends on having a sponsor (sometimes called their champion or angel) to guide and support the vision. The sponsor must have fiduciary responsibility as well as access to, or membership of, the top ranks of the organization. A mentor, on the other hand, is very helpful also, but not necessary. Note that under the GM model the scientists and engineers directly involved in an insourced project are essentially mentors for the people involved.

As a case in point, in the 27 GLN partnership programmes audited, 25 came in under budget and 15 ahead of schedule. These included a project in an Asian consortium to work on fuel cell hydrogen storage and catalyst materials – maybe the most 'basic' research in physics and materials that GM had ever undertaken. There are many projects that, ten years ago, would have been called 'basic' research and which today are thought of as targeted.

Just as 'form follows function' in biology, in leveraging, 'projects should chase dollars' and, in science and technology policy management, 'the business should define the process'. The secret is to align your targeted RD&E portfolios with your organization's business needs. From an academic perspective: be sure to observe the global economic and RD&E trends, and be ready when industry comes knocking on your door with dollars and a specific one-to-three-year RD&E need.

CONTROLLING THE TRANSFER: WHAT SHOULD BE DONE – AND NOT DONE?

There is no doubt that the quality and the cost metrics of doing science and engineering in Asia are very favourable. Other companies, although not as many as reported in the press, are putting fairly large resources in single places. This includes companies that have persuaded their own research communities that it makes sense to centralize functionalities, invest a significant sum – say, 1 to 50 million – and then send 'job-shop' activities over on a 24-hour basis. A worse option is to co-locate the projects to your existing RD&E facilities and pay US overhead rates. This should be done only when and if there is a central engineering or software need or where there are unique capabilities in software, computer-aided design–computer-aided manufacturing (CAD-CAM) or other graphics – for instance from a 'company-qualified' central Indian facility or US-Indian subsidiary.

It is nearly impossible to identify the one place among the dozen or so alternatives in Asia to establish a single source of RD&E. It takes too much time to find a single place, and it is doubtful whether the right choice would be made even if a consensus process were to be used. The institutions and organizations that lose out in the selection process would certainly be irritated, and it most definitely would not mean that they were loser institutions/organizations. What we are talking about is something even more precious than just the refinement of others' existing plans. To fit into the structure now being implemented at the new Asian GLNs, a company's missing capabilities must intersect with the possible Asian competencies.

What should you do? Identify where, in your organization, you have specific knowledge of specific places and specific persons in Asia and identify the passion and connections to Asia that can link with the research and engineering programmes underway, as well as with new ones being initiated, using the process described.

Invest the same equivalent resources in Asian GLNs as in US GLNs – but, first, match the work with missing capabilities, needs and competencies. Asian GLNs are not meant to be simply low-cost engineering support, or software generation, or call centre management centres – all of which can also be done very cost-effectively outside the USA in many locations. For GM, it is the *intellectual equity* (not intellectual property or intellectual capital) that is co-located with GM business and manufacturing units in Asia that must be captured and leveraged, not simply low overheads. Therefore, we believe that those who want to call the GLN and its processes the art of offshoring have missed the point. The model, we submit, is one of in-sourcing intellectual equity, not intellectual property or jobs.

However, we have observed very positive potential and current developments amongst a few leading multinational corporations in the area of jobs creation. Jobs are created, at least for GM in their Shanghai joint venture SGM, for the local, not foreign, nationals. The employment packages are quite different from those used in the USA, and for very specific reasons.

Elements of the employment packages that are common with those in the USA are fair wage rates, healthcare and company investment plans. The attributes that are different are the holistic family or socioeconomic focus identified by assistance in housing with provisions for accessibility to transport to and from the workplace, accessibility to education for the employee's family members, and an implemented approach to work–life balance that includes the employee's extended family.

THE ROLE OF EDUCATION AND TRAINING IN A SHIFTING ECONOMY

The premise contained in the previous paragraphs outlines the evolution of the roles of paper versus people over the past twenty or so years as the enablers of technology transfer. It is clear that the patents of old are not of the same 'value' as the people that carry the knowledge or the equity attached to the contents of the patent. However, as the shifting tide of global economies drives greater competitiveness among industries, productivity rates of the individual, which incidentally have risen drastically over the past five years, precede also the necessity for a different kind of workforce to maintain the momentum of global knowledge transfer.

Three areas that equal the strengthening of economic growth and new jobs in the USA are promotion of worldwide trade, improving education and training, and fostering investment and innovation (BRT, 2004). Of the three areas mentioned, we would like to elaborate on the role of education and training in our shifting global economy.

As cited in the aforementioned BRT publication, 'those workers who are the most vulnerable to the shifting employment tide are those with only a high school education or less. The average US worker today with only a high school education makes the same real wage as the worker twenty-five years ago' (BRT, 2004, p.19). What this means is that the workers of tomorrow, in order to compete with the ever-expanding workforce, must have a college degree in order to be prepared for shifting requirements across a very broad spectrum of jobs, including many job niches that are so entrepreneurial that they are not on anyone's radar screen today. Therefore, it behoves the kindergarten-twelfth grade (k-12; average ages 4 to 18) systems and the universities of today and tomorrow to prepare their students in a very different way than they have in the past. The difference rests primarily in the teacher's ability to convey the entrepreneurial spirit of creativity, culture and passion into their students' approach to tackling areas of technology, engineering and the hard sciences.

An interesting article was published in the February 2004 issue of *Wired Magazine*, titled 'The new face of the silicon age: how India became the capital of the computing revolution' (Pink, 2004). Pink's article quotes a worker in India as stating, 'Don't you think we are helping the US economy by doing work here? It frees up Americans to do other things so the economy can grow.'

The same *Wired Magazine* published another article titled, 'The eagle is grounded: while America works to protect intellectual property, everyone else is innovating' (Goetz, 2004). In the article, Goetz states that:

> ...*rather than adapting to new economics, American industry is suffocating under over regulation and protectionism. Hence, in the face of new technologies and competition, the US is toughening patent and copyright protections, but if it is not careful, the US will drive its intellectual property offshore into a shadow world that is replete with piracy and rogue states.*
>
> (Goetz, 2004, pp. 23–24)

Indeed, if the USA is not careful, it will find itself spending too much money on what was done rather than what can be done, and the byline of Mr Goetz's article will become all too true in the very near future.

Our observations of the shift in the role of intellectual property that has occurred over the past twenty or so years can best be described illustratively as a bathtub: once full of water (for instance, intellectual content in the form of patent disclosures), with its plug now pulled. Information today, thanks to the Internet and the ever-present Google search engine, has accelerated the use and abuse of information such that its intellectual content, based on careful analysis and synthesis of the information, is now obsolete in a matter of hours, regardless of intellectual property patenting. Therefore, it is the management, not of the patent, but of the people and their intellectual content or (equity) that we have found to be the factor that accelerates the transfer of ideas, innovation and technology globally and at the speed of light – or, at least, at the speed of an Internet connection.

Our view is as follows. If the USA is to keep up with the rapid pace of innovation (known also as change), it must quickly adapt its knowledge conveyance process (also known as k-12, colleges and universities) towards a knowledge-plus-innovation conveyance process in order to produce students with the skills appropriate for today as much as for the future.

Conclusion

We believe that it is unwise to evaluate technology and innovation through the lens of the relatively young Western eyes of educational processes. Historically, Western science is, 'new hypothesis-driven'. It has served the first generation of engineering design and development in the West very well over the past 200 years. Starting from the 'new physics' of the 1700s, based primarily in electronics and mechanics theory, linear, deductive, falsifiable and experimentally-based advances have incrementally improved product quality and, until recently, productivity in manufacturing.

On the other hand, in Asia the 3000-year-old 'to copy is to honour' philosophy of acquiring invention has developed into what we have described in this chapter as examples of how new knowledge frequently comes from non-linear, inductive, discontinuous and experiential processes.

Hundreds of functional brain-imaging experiments for example, over the past several years have shown that first language learned, language actually used during experiments that test understanding of abstract concepts, country of primary education and country of scientific training and experience are dependent variables that result in different brain area usage and pathways.

Certainly, the 'improvements' in cost quality, and timeliness of industrial manufacturing product development is incremental and linear. With the exception of major and visionary attempts to reinvent automotive structural platforms (for example, the AUTOnomy skateboard[3]) and power trains (for instance, fuel cells in place of internal combustion) essentially all productivity improvements and cost-benefits have been linear and deductive to this point. Asian education philosophy has been seen to shift during the past three decades towards the 'honourable copying' of Western educational processes. It should be no surprise that this has led to the very sort of intellectual equity that characterized the development of Western science and engineering. Asian science and technology now rivals that of the West. Therefore, based on what we have discovered, we believe that *global technology transfer is more about a willingness to learn than it is to distribute new knowledge*.

References

BRT (Business Roundtable) (2004), *Securing Growth and Jobs –Improving US Prosperity in a Worldwide Economy*, Business Roundtable Publications, Washington, DC.

Christensen, C.M. (1997), *The Innovator's Dilemma*, Harvard Business School Press, Berkeley, CA.

Friedman, T. (2004), 'What goes around', *New York Times*, 26 February, p. 27, s. a, col. 6.

Goetz, T. (2004), 'The eagle is grounded: while America works to protect intellectual property, everyone else is innovating', *Wired Magazine*, February, pp. 23–24.

Kristoff, N. (2004), 'Watching the jobs go by', *New York Times*, 11 February, p. 29, s. a, col. 6.

Pink, D.H. (2004), 'The new face of the silicon age: how India became the capital of the computing revolution', *Wired Magazine*, February, pp. 94–103, p.138.

Rai, S. (2004), 'Indians fearing repercussions of U.S. technology outsourcing', *New York Times*, 9 February, p. 4, s. c, col. 1.

Stone, B. (2004), 'Should I stay or should I go?', *Newsweek*, 19 April, pp. 27–8.

---

3   The AUTOnomy was GM's first fuel-cell concept vehicle and was launched at the North American International Auto Show in January 2001. The most unique attribute of the vehicle was its chassis, which was nicknamed the 'skateboard'. The skateboard chassis operated in a similar way to a computer docking station by offering ultimate flexibility in vehicle body design that could 'dock' into the chassis. For further information see: www.sciam.com/article.cfm?articleID=00034FE5-BA99-1D80-90FB809EC5880000&pageNumber=1&catID=4.

7 The Relationship between Corporate Competitiveness Strategy, Innovation, Increased Efficiency, Productivity Growth and Outsourcing*

Almas Heshmati and Kyösti Pietola

Within the industrial production arena, there exists an extensive literature, both empirical and theoretical, that covers growth, productivity, efficiency and competition at different levels of aggregation. In recent years production research, as well as technology outsourcing, has expanded. The empirical evidence on the latter is very often based on aggregate country- or industry-level data, originating from industrial countries. While growth and competitiveness issues have mainly been applicable to country studies (Barro and Sala-i-Martin, 1995), the productivity and efficiency studies are mainly micro-oriented (Bartelsman and Doms, 2000; Coelli *et al.*, 1998; Fried *et al.*, 1993; Hulten, 2000; Kumbhakar and Lovell, 2000). The latter issues are frequently used in performance studies heavily concentrated on the agriculture and manufacturing sectors and services. The growing importance of the service sector has induced increasing concern about its performance. In recent years the methods have intensively been used in the evaluation performance of private and public services foremost in provision of healthcare and education (see Balk, 1998; Berndt *et al.*, 1992; Griliches, 1992; Griliches and Mairesse, 1993; Heshmati, 2003; Solow, 1992).

Despite the comprehensive literature on the issues of growth, productivity, efficiency and competition on each subject separately, very little can be found on their linkages and causal relationships. This chapter contributes to the literature by empirically investigating such multidimensional causal relationships among the above variables, and thus attempts to fill the gap by investigating the relationship between corporate competitiveness strategy, efficiency, productivity growth, innovation and outsourcing. Performance is measured in several ways at the firm level. First, it is based on technical efficiency, defined as capacity to produce maximum possible output from a given set of inputs and technology (Aigner *et al.*, 1977; Battese and Coelli, 1995). Second, it is based on growth defined as factor productivity changes in output over time (Good *et al.*, 1997; Kumbhakar *et al.*, 1999). Third, innovation activities are measured based on innovation input and innovation outputs (Crépon *et al.*, 1998; Lööf and Heshmati, 2004). Finally, competitiveness is based on a set of factors important to the firms'

---

*   The authors would like to thank Dr Hans Lööf for providing the innovation data.

competitive strategy (Nayyar, 1993). Outsourcing is used to describe all the subcontracting relationships between firms, and we follow the substitution- and abstention-based definitions of outsourcing as a starting point (for example, Egger and Falkinger, 2003; Fixler and Siegel, 1999; Gilley and Rasheed, 2000).

We do not intend to provide a comprehensive review of the voluminous literature on each subject, but seek instead to overview briefly recent contributions to, and developments of, the literature on the causal relationship between these performance indicators and outsourcing. The main focus is on the empirical analysis of the above relationship at the micro level based on unique innovation survey data. The main contribution of this chapter is thus its focus on the causal relationship between performance and outsourcing. First, recent developments of research on the above relationship are reviewed. Second, information on the sets of each performance indicators is transformed into single indices. Third, given appropriate measures of outsourcing and performance indicators, the causal relationships between the five variables of interest are established. Finally, given the direction of causality, the implications of the findings for estimation of the relationship, its interpretations and guidelines for future research are discussed.

The remainder of the chapter is organized as follows. The second section introduces the concepts of competitiveness, various performance measures, innovation and outsourcing and their theoretical linkage. In the third section we describe the innovation data used in the empirical analysis. The fourth section outlines the methods used to empirically measure the above indicators. Specification of the model is discussed in the fifth section. The empirical results concerning the relationship between the indicators are discussed in the sixth section in which we also present a possible extension of the current approach to improve the consistency and usefulness of the techniques used to study causal relationships between our indicators. The final section summarizes the findings.

Review of the literature

OUTSOURCING

Industrial, communication and technological development have resulted in major changes in the ways in which products and services are produced and distributed. As a measure to improve efficiency firms allocate their resources to activities for which they enjoy comparative advantage, while increasingly outsourcing other activities to external suppliers. Outsourcing is expected to reduce production cost relative to internal production because outside suppliers benefit from economies of scale, smoother production schedules and centralization of expertise (Anderson and Weitz, 1986; Chalos, 1995; Roodhooft and Warlop, 1999; Williamson, 1989). However, the choice between internal or external production requires other considerations than pure production cost differences. For instance, according to the transaction cost economics, outsourcing is desirable only when the cost of asset-specific investments is lower than the production cost advantage. Outsourcing makes previous investments a sunk cost to the firms. Arnold (2000), in studying the design and management of outsourcing, finds that the transaction cost and core competencies approach complement each other. The decision to invest in internal knowledge or to consume external knowledge is affected by a multiplicity of factors. Gavious and Rabinowitz (2003), in determining optimal knowledge outsourcing policy, find that the lower the ability to develop internal knowledge, the more favourable external knowledge becomes.

Barthelemy (2003), in analysing the hard side (the contract) and the soft side (the trust in the relationship with information technology (IT) outsourcing management), shows that both factors are key to the success of outsourcing. Egger and Falkinger (2003), in examining the distributional effects of international outsourcing, find that the interplay of the cost-saving and substitution effects determines the nature of the outsourcing equilibrium and its distributional consequences. Despite the internationalization of outsourcing and its frequent utilization by multinational companies, in an international survey of outsourcing contracts Kakabadse and Kakabadse (2002) find differences in behaviour between European and US companies. The American companies are identified as pursuing more value-added sourcing strategies, while Europeans are more focused on gaining economies of scale through outsourcing.

In discussing globalization the focus has been on increased trade in goods and services and mobility of labour and financial assets. A new phenomenon is the role of advances in technology and reduced cost of services in the fragmentation of vertically integrated production processes into separate segments entering international trade. Declining prices of international services, knowledge of potential suppliers and awareness of legal systems increase the role played by separate and smaller firms connected only by the rules of the international marketplace (Jones and Kierzkowski, 2000). Grossman and Helpman (2002b) investigated the extent of outsourcing and of direct foreign investment in an industry in which producers need specialized components that can be produced by suppliers across national markets. In such situations relationship-specific investments are required and contracts are imperfect, and a consideration of how various cost factors affect the organization of industry production is needed as well (see Grossman and Helpman, 2002a).

The trend in outsourcing activities during recent decades has been globally and continuously increasing. These activities are an attempt to enhance competitiveness and efficiency of firms within countries and across borders. Despite the remarkable increase in outsourcing at the national and international levels, empirical studies of the subject are still rare. Previous research is mainly theoretical in nature, and the conclusions drawn are not always supported by empirical evidence. Feenstra (1998) finds an increasing trend towards the integration of the global economy through trade, but also disintegration in production processes. Holmström and Roberts (1998) analysed the boundaries of firms, with their focus on the investment incentives, and provided examples of how agency issues can affect those boundaries.

The measurement of outsourcing has been neglected in the literature, and there is disagreement about how it is defined. Gilley and Rasheed (2000) examine the definition of outsourcing in prior research and identify three definitions in the management literature. One definition sees outsourcing as the contribution in the physical and human resources by external vendors to the IT infrastructure in the user organization (Loh and Venkatraman, 1992). Another has it as those products supplied to multinational firms by independent suppliers (Kotabe, 1992). The third definition of outsourcing concentrates on the reliance on external sources for value-adding activities (Lei and Hitt, 1995). Gilley and Rasheed (2000) conclude that outsourcing is not simply a purchasing decision, but represents the decision to reject the internalization of activities. They propose that outsourcing may arise in two ways: through the substitution of external purchases for internal activities, and through abstention when firm purchases goods and services that have not been completed in-house in the past. Temporary help supply (THS) employment has increased dramatically in recent years as a more flexible work arrangement to avoid the costly adjustment of labour to changes in economic conditions, and may be one way of measuring outsourcing.

Outsourcing and productivity growth

Outsourcing can be related to the production of intermediate goods or to the hiring of temporary labour. According to a two-sector model, during recent decades the service sector has grown much faster than the goods sector with negative impacts on economic growth (Baumol, 1967; Baumol et al., 1985). In this model, manufacturing is the progressive and technologically advanced sector, while the service sector is stagnant. The negative effect is due to the high labour intensity in the service sector and its low incentives to introduce technological change. However, technology that is specific for use in the service sector is advancing and eliminating previous gaps.

There are a number of studies that focus on explaining the difference in productivity growth rates in the two sectors, particularly in terms of the effects of outsourcing on manufacturing performance. Abraham and Taylor (1996) found that firms contract out services with the objectives of smoothing production cycles, benefiting from specialization and realizing potential labour cost savings. Siegel and Griliches (1992), in reviewing selected services, find weak evidence that outsourcing leads to an overstatement of manufacturing productivity growth. Estevão and Lach (1999) estimate the extent to which the manufacturing sector is outsourcing labour from the service sector by hiring THS workers. Their results show an increasing intensity in the use of THS, which explains the flatness of manufacturing employment and results in an overstatement of productivity growth. Ten Raa and Wolff (1996) found a positive association between outsourcing and productivity growth in the goods sector.

More recently Fixler and Siegel (1999) focused on the internal generation, the buy or outsourcing decision for selected services, and the effects of outsourcing on manufacturing and productivity growth of services. The decision to outsource is modelled for a manufacturing firm consisting of two separate divisions. One unit produces the output and the other provides support services. In the short run, the capital stock of the two divisions is fixed, but labour is the variable factor of production and mobile across sectors. The wage rate is assumed to grow at the same rate as productivity and is lower in the service division. The output of the service division is assumed to be a linear function of the manufacturing output. The firm maximizes profit with respect to output quantity and output price. The propensity of the firm to outsource is a function of the difference between the marginal cost of the external service market and the marginal cost of in-house production. A firm will outsource if the marginal cost of internal production is higher (see Inman, 1985). Jacobson, Lalonde and Sullivan (1993), in their analysis of the wages following a shift of workers from manufacturing to services, found that wages declined and that outsourcing not only resulted in a shift of labour, but also increased the productivity differential between manufacturing and services.

Fixler and Siegel (1999) present five testable hypotheses in their empirical results:

- Increasing wages lead to active outsourcing.
- There is a positive correlation between productivity and outsourcing.
- Output increases as a consequence of increased demand.
- Lower service productivity growth is due to high labour-intensive service production.
- An adjustment in production function leads to an increase in service productivity.

Their investigation into the productivity growth of service and manufacturing industries in the USA yielded results that are consistent with the hypothesis indicating the following:

- A positive and significant correlation exists between wage growth and growth in outsourcing in manufacturing industries.
- A positive correlation exists between growth in manufacturing productivity and the rate of outsourcing.
- Within the service industry, growth in real output is positively correlated with manufacturing outsourcing.
- A fall in service productivity due to high labour intensity is insignificant.
- An adjustment of production functions leads to an acceleration in productivity growth in the service industry.

These results should, however, be interpreted with caution due to the lack of prices in the service sector and possible measurement errors.

A selection of applications

We have already listed findings from several important applications of outsourcing. A number of case studies (for example, Dritna, 1994; Lacity *et al.*, 1996) suggest that decision makers generally overestimate the production cost advantages of outsourcing and underestimate the role of transaction costs. For instance, Roodhooft and Warlop (1999) investigate the inherent sunk cost aspects of outsourcing decisions. The hypothesis is that the intention to outsource activities is lower in the presence of asset specificity and decisions are biased towards internal production. In an application studying the internal or external production of patients' meals, Roodhooft and Warlop show that accounting for asset specificity and sunk costs factors strongly and negatively affected managers' decisions on outsourcing.

The effect of outsourcing on changes in relative employment is an important issue. At an aggregate level, Feenstra and Hanson (1996) argue that outsourcing, defined as the share of import of intermediate inputs in the total purchased materials by domestic firms, has contributed to an increase in the relative demand for skilled labour in the USA. The firms' response to import competition was to outsource non-skilled intensive activities abroad. Their study found that outsourcing could account for 31–51 per cent of the increase in the relative demand for skilled labour in US manufacturing. Falk and Koebel (2000) examined the effects of outsourcing services and imported materials on the demand for labour in German manufacturing, with the results showing little effects on demand for unskilled labour. The shift in demand towards skilled labour can be explained by capital-skill complementarity and skill-biased technological change. The increased trend is found, instead, to be more a consequence of output growth than of input substitution. Egger and Egger (2001) studied the effect of cross-border sourcing and outward processing in the EU manufacturing sector on skill intensity in production. The effect of outward processing in the importing industries was ambiguous, while the effect on the skill ratio when outward processing took place in exporting industries was negative.

The advantages of contracting out the production of goods and services to a firm with competitive advantages in terms of reliability, quality and cost are emphasized by Perry (1997). Using evidence from food processing companies, Young and Macneil (2000) focus on managerial reasons for implementing outsourcing. They find that the motives are to improve strategic focus, to achieve numerical functional flexibility, to change the organizational structure and to intensify the work effort. The issue of the structure of inter-firm cooperative outsourcing ventures is explored by Suarez-Villa (1998). De Kok (2000) considers outsourcing as a measure to allocate capacity: excess capacity needs are not postponed to the future but are instead outsourced. Benson (1999), using Australian manufacturing data, evaluates the effects of outsourcing on the freed-up human and capital resources that allow increased flexibility in both labour deployment and firm performance.

Outsourcing, wages and innovation

Sharpe (1997) argues that outsourcing arose as a means of reducing the adjustment costs of responding to economic changes – that is, to technological innovation, changing customer preferences, and other shifts in supply and demand, all of which affect the labour market and its functions. It has been argued that, in the USA, outsourcing has caused the wages of less skilled workers to fall in relation to those of more skilled workers, causing wage inequality (Feenstra and Hanson, 1995, 1996). Using manufacturing data from the period 1971–1990 Feenstra and Hanson show that outsourcing has contributed to an increase in relative demand for skilled labour. In their 1999 study the same authors find that outsourcing and high-technology capital explain 35 per cent and 15 per cent of the relative wages of US non-production workers. Anderton and Brenton (1999) investigate textile and non-electrical machinery and find that imports from low-wage countries have contributed significantly to the decline in the wage–cost share and relative employment of less skilled labour in the UK. Haskel (1999) found that the skill premium rose by around 13 per cent in UK manufacturing during the 1980s. The introduction of computers into the production of goods and services, growth in small firms, the growing practice of contracting out and the fall in unionization explains 50, 13, 8 and 15 per cent of the rise, respectively.

A few recent studies, however, do not find strong linkages between outsourcing and wages. Falk and Koebel (2000), studying West German manufacturing industries, examine how the outsourcing of services and imported materials affect the demand for different skill classes. Their results show little effect on labour demand for unskilled labour, with outsourcing functioning as a consequence of output growth rather than input substitution. Egger et al. (2001), analysing the effects of increasing outsourcing production from Austrian manufacturing to the Eastern transition countries, find that outsourcing improves the domestic growth in total factor productivity growth. The growth is possibly higher for high-skill and more capital-intensive industries. In the presence of perfect factor markets, wages would be lower (higher) for low-skilled (high-skilled) labour as a result of outsourcing. In an analysis of the relationship between outsourcing human resource activities – namely, training and payroll – and firm performance, Gilley et al. (2003), using manufacturing data, find that both training and payroll outsourcing have implications for firm performance.

The issues of innovation and the wage effects of international outsourcing have also been investigated by Glass and Saggi (2001). They find that reductions in the costs of adopting technologies for production in low-wage countries, increases in production taxes in high-wage countries, and increases in production subsidies or subsidies to adopt technologies in low-wage countries are the main forces explaining an increase in international outsourcing. In addition, they find that outsourcing lowers the marginal cost of production, increases profit and creates greater incentives for innovations. The standardization of production technologies has contributed to the increasing outsourcing of innovation activities.

Ulset (1996), using three models from transaction cost economics and property rights theory, explores the boundary between internal and external research and development (R&D) projects and the mechanism of contracting out activities. The boundary is explained by four control incentive variables – that is, the sunk cost potentials, governance mechanisms, technical novelty in the R&D work and the expected resale value of the final outputs. He used R&D projects from the Norwegian information technology industry for the empirical analysis, and his results supported both the boundary hypothesis and three of the four control incentive hypotheses. Howells (1999a) also discusses the process of externalizing R&D and technical activity that has previously been undertaken internally. The analysis highlights the technological and behavioural changes and their implications for the conduct of the R&D function. The key elements in shaping outsourcing contracts are: increasing flexibility in the R&D function, increasing standardization and automation, technological change in R&D, new players in the contract research and technology market, and the internationalization of such markets. The growth of the external sourcing of R&D by firms has contributed to the evolution of new research and technical markets, which has implications for the national systems of innovation (Howells, 1999b).

Competitive strategy

The measurement of competitive strategy is important in strategic management. Porter (1980) defined three generic competitive strategies: cost leadership, differentiation and focus. Nayyar (1993) reviewed studies measuring Porter's competitive strategies to capture differences in which firms emphasize various competitive dimensions. Although firms offer a multiple of products within an industry and a different competitive strategy is used for each product, the focus has often been on the measurement of competitive strategy at the business level rather than specific products within a business. A disaggregation of product lines is found to be important in the examination of product level as well as product portfolio strategies.

In an attempt to overcome the above limitation of the literature Nayyar empirically identified the appropriate level to measure competitive strategies and determine whether cost-leadership and differentiation strategies are mutually exclusive. The empirical results were based on responses to a questionnaire containing items to measure competitive strategy on large numbers of products and businesses, which were subjected to a principal component analysis. The results pointed to the multidimensionality of each competitive strategy and suggested that cost-leadership and differentiation strategies are mutually exclusive when measured at the product level. No evidence supporting the existence of combined competitive strategy at the product level was found. Nayyar concluded that indication of combined strategies in previous research might have been influenced by the data collected at the business level. Sensitivity analyses suggest that business-level measures are not good indicators of product-level competitive strategies. In addition to greater attention to product level analysis, one should account better for product portfolio heterogeneity held by firms across businesses.

As mentioned previously, outsourcing is primarily a search for labour cost savings and an optimal choice between inside and outside production. The top five reasons for outsourcing based on a large survey of companies were identified by Deavers (1997) as:

1. to improve company focus;
2. to gain access to world-class capabilities;

3.   to accelerate benefits from re-engineering;
4.   to share risks; and
5.   to free resources for other purposes.

However, Chen *et al.* (2003) show that trade liberalization may create incentive for strategic international outsourcing arising from multi-market interactions among firms. Unlike the outsourcing motivated by cost savings, strategic outsourcing can have a collusive effect and raise prices in both the intermediate-good and final-good markets. Quelin and Duhamel (2003) view outsourcing as a choice that lies in the corporate policy, not just business strategy. They review different elements characterizing strategic outsourcing, examine motives and risks associated with outsourcing and provide key points in the implementation of strategic outsourcing operations. Given the risk of losing competencies, outsourcing can be a choice that helps corporations to gain a competitive advantage and ensure future growth.

In reviewing the characteristics of outsourcing strategies Gilley and Rasheed (2000) propose two types of generic outsourcing: peripheral and core outsourcing. The first type occurs when firms acquire less strategically relevant peripheral activities from an external supplier, while the second type occurs when firms acquire activities that are considered highly important to long-run success. The distinction between the two types is firm-specific. Gilley and Rasheed expected peripheral outsourcing intensity to have a positive effect on firm performance, with core outsourcing generating a negative effect. However, regression results from analysing the influence of outsourcing intensity on financial, innovation and stakeholder performance did not support the above hypothesis. The results suggested that firms pursuing more intense outsourcing strategies do not experience significant direct overall performance impacts. However, outsourcing might have effects on the performance of individual functional areas in which it occurs, and the effect can vary with differing levels of environmental dynamism.

The results from a number of large surveys suggest that outsourcing is seen more as a corporate competitiveness strategy that leads to major improvements in company performance and that the outcome is not just a search for low wages (see Deavers, 1997). Shy and Stenbacka (2003) analyse how firms use their design of organizational production mode as a strategic instrument, and demonstrate that introducing competition into input-producing industry does not reduce efficiency (by the non-exploitation of the economies of scale). Sharpe (1997) finds that outsourcing as a management tool addresses organizational competitiveness in an efficient way by moving towards business strategies based on core competencies and outsourcing other non-core activities and services.

Product and process innovation

The link between innovation and performance at the firm level has received great attention in a number of studies. These have resulted in interesting findings regarding expected effects, the data and methods used, as well as their benefits and limitations. Cohen and Klepper (1996) and Klette and Kortum (2001) present a list of stylized facts on the relationship between firm size, R&D effort, productivity and growth. Empirical findings indicate a positive relationship between R&D activity and the level of productivity (see Cohen and Klepper, 1996; Crépon, Duguet and Mairesse, 1998; Griliches, 1992, 1995; Hall and Mairesse, 1995; Klette and Kortum, 2001; Lööf and Heshmati, 2002 for the link between innovation and productivity).

In a survey of econometric studies of R&D and productivity at the firm level, Mairesse and Sassenou (1991) document widely varying estimates of the contribution of R&D to productivity. The variations are mainly observed across data samples, model specifications and in relation to different estimation methods. Mairesse and Sassenou (1991) suggest a number of improvements to the measurement of R&D productivity impacts. These are: the improvement of existing databases and measurement of variables, to gain a better understanding of the diversity of the situations of individual firms and their evolution over time, and to the data-type related puzzling differences in the estimates of R&D elasticity in the productivity equation. Hall and Mairesse (1995) perform sensitivity analysis to identify causes and to quantify the degree of heterogeneity in results. Their results suggest that more information on the history of firms' R&D expenditures helps to improve the reliability of the estimates of R&D elasticity.

Crépon et al. (1998) introduced a four-equation (investment decision, innovation input, innovation output and productivity growth) knowledge production function model, which includes three relationships between: innovation output and productivity; investment in research and innovation output; and the research investment and its determinants. Lööf and Heshmati (2002, 2004) investigated the sensitivity of the estimated relationship between innovativeness and firm performance in a multidimensional framework, with regard to different types of model, estimation methods, measures of performance, subpopulations of industries, different data sources, and different specifications of innovation. The results suggest the presence of heterogeneity in effects in several dimensions.

PRODUCTIVE EFFICIENCY

In empirical studies, production functions have been traditionally described as average functions to estimate the mean output rather than the maximum output conditional on the underlying technologies. However, the maximum possible output is relevant in measuring the performance of firms. Farrell (1957) provides a definition of frontier production function that embodies maximality. The frontier is used to measure the efficiency of production units by comparing observed and potential outputs. Potential output is obtained using best-practice technology from a given vector of inputs.

The literature on the estimation of frontier functions to measure efficiency of firms has been developed in different directions. The different approaches to production, cost and profit frontiers are used to estimate the components of economic efficiency – that is, technical and allocative efficiencies. The former is a measure of possible reduction in inputs to produce a given level of output or, alternatively, a potential increase in output for a given level of input and technology, while the latter is a measure of the possible reduction in the cost of using the correct input proportions to produce a given level of output.

Frontier functions can be classified according to the way in which the frontier is specified and estimated. The classification might be based on the parametric/non-parametric, deterministic/stochastic and cross-section/panel data specifications of the frontier functions. Several researchers (Greene, 1997; Heshmati, 2003; Kalirajan and Shand, 1999; Kumbhakar and Lovell, 2000; Schmidt, 1986) present overviews of the concept, modelling, estimation of models and methods to make efficiency comparisons. They also survey some of the empirical applications of frontier functions. This section focuses on the parametric stochastic production frontiers. The stochastic production frontier model for a cross-sectional case introduced by Aigner et al. (1977) is defined as:

(1) $\ln Y_i = \beta_0 + \sum_j \beta_j \ln X_{jit} + \varepsilon_i,$ $\varepsilon_i = v_i - u_i$

where ln Y_i is logarithm of output of firm i, ln X is a vector of logarithm of J inputs, and β is a vector of unknown parameters to be estimated. The error term ε_i is composed of two components: a symmetric random component $(v_i \neq 0)$ and a one-sided component $(u_i \geq 0)$, representing technical inefficiency. The model can be estimated by corrected ordinary least square, methods of moments, generalized least square or maximum likelihood methods. The random component is assumed to be independently and identically normally distributed, while the inefficiency component is assumed to be distributed as either exponential, half-normal, truncated normal or gamma. In Battese and Coelli (1995) u_i is obtained by truncation at zero of the $N(\mu_i, \sigma^2)$ distribution:

(2) $\mu_i = \delta_0 + \sum_{j=1} \delta_j Z_{ji}$

where Z is a determinant of inefficiency. The estimated model gives an aggregate fitted value of the two components. Measures of technical inefficiency require decomposition of the error term. Jondrow *et al.* (1982) have suggested a decomposition method to obtain point estimates of $\hat{u}$ using the mean or mode of the conditional distribution of $E(u_i \mid v_i - u_i)$. A firm-specific rate of technical efficiency, $0 \leq TE_i \leq 1$, is then obtained as:

(3) $TE_i = \exp(-\hat{u}_i)$

where the value 1 indicates full efficiency. We cannot infer about the significance of the point efficiency estimates. Neither do we have any information about the statistical significance of the various elasticities and scale effects generated if a flexible functional form is applied. Horrace and Schmidt (1996), Hjalmarsson *et al.* (1996), and Battese *et al.* (2000) used the delta method to construct confidence intervals for individual points or some aggregate means of efficiency and input elasticities of interest.

Applications to the manufacturing sector

The efficiency of resource use, using the stochastic frontier approach, has been investigated for manufacturing industries in different countries. For example, Caves and Barton (1990) investigate efficiency in US manufacturing industries, while Caves (1992) reviews studies that replicated the US investigation on the manufacturing sectors of Japan, Korea, UK, Australia and Canada. These studies are heterogeneous in nature and consider the methodology, its strengths and limitations, the time patterns of efficiency changes, determinants of efficiency and their consistency across countries. The empirical results show that efficiency measures are sensitive to the choice of estimation method, distributional assumptions, functional forms, data levels and data samples. Bottasso and Sembenelli (2001) investigate whether ownership affects efficiency, using Italian manufacturing firms. The results show strong evidence that, in large organizations, the identity of the ultimate owner matters. Privatization brings efficiency gains.

Applications to service sector

Most of the efficiency applications to service sector are based on the non-parametric approach or data envelopment analysis (DEA). Fried, Lovell and Schmidt (1993), Coelli, Rao and Battese (1998) and Cooper and Lovell (2000) present reviews of the recent developments in the area. The DEA method has the advantage of being easily applicable to cases with multiple outputs.

The disadvantage is that it does not take random factors into account. All deviations from the frontier are labelled as production inefficiencies. Frontier functions have been applied to various parts of the public- and private-sector services, such as banking, healthcare, education, social security services and public utilities. The results of a selection of applications are presented below.

Healthcare is one area where frontier techniques have been used frequently to measure the performance of clinics and hospitals. For examples of such applications and the usefulness of the methodology as a tool for health economics, see Newhouse (1994) and Zuckerman et al. (1994). Recently Rosko (2001) examined the impact of managed care and other environmental factors on hospital efficiency in the USA. Inefficiency in production of healthcare declined over time, mainly due to health maintenance organization penetration and industry concentration.

Education is another area where performance evaluation has been intensive, with Hanushek (1986) and Hanushek and Taylor (1990) reviewing the methodology used with an emphasis on production and efficiency aspects. Heshmati and Kumbhakar (1997) study the efficiency of Swedish municipalities in the production of primary and secondary schools by estimating stochastic frontier cost and production functions. A number of quality indicators and municipality characteristics are included to explain efficiency differentials across municipalities in the provision of school services. Färe et al. (2001) introduce a decomposition of the Malmquist productivity index into a quality-augmented productivity index and an aggregate quality component index. The method is applied to Swedish primary and secondary school data (Färe et al., 2006). Heshmati (2002b) adjusts output measures of schooling for quality differences using both parametric and non-parametric approaches.

Bjurek et al. (1990) analyse the productive efficiency of local insurance offices using both parametric and non-parametric deterministic frontiers. Kumbhakar and Hjalmarsson (1995) analyse the labour-use efficiency in Swedish social insurance offices based on the same data, but using a parametric frontier production function. Empirical results show substantial variations in labour-use efficiency. Most of the offices were of suboptimal size. Kumbhakar and Hjalmarsson (1998) analyse productive efficiency in Swedish retail electricity distribution using hedonic outputs and a labour input requirement function approach. They examined whether ownership has any systematic impact on the efficiency of distributors. Empirical results show that privately-owned companies are relatively more efficient and that there is evidence of scale economies.

Frontier is a common method for performance analysis in banking. There has been much research interest in the topics of efficiency in banking. For a comprehensive survey of studies that apply frontier efficiency analysis to financial institutions in 21 countries, see Berger and Humphrey (1997). Battese et al. (2000) analyse the impact of the deregulation of the Swedish banking industry and the consequent banking crisis on productive efficiency in the industry. A stochastic frontier model is used to estimate the labour-use requirement function and technical efficiency of banks. Banks were found to be slow in adjusting their labour input. Kumbhakar et al. (2002) investigate the dynamic adjustment process in using labour to its desired level in Swedish banks. Productivity growth is defined in terms of a shift in the desired level of labour use and the catch-up factor, defined as the ratio of actual to desired level of labour.

PRODUCTIVITY GROWTH

Production function is a crucial tool in analysing returns to scale, technical change and productivity growth. Productivity change has a strong influence on organization and incentives in manufacturing and services. It has also major impacts on regulatory structures, privatization and deregulations. Measurement of productivity is often based on the ratio of some function of outputs (Y_m) to some function of inputs (X_j) where the subscripts m and j denote types of outputs and inputs. In cases with single or aggregate output, partial or single-factor productivity (PFP) are computed as:

(4) $PFP_j = Y / X_j.$

PFP can be misleading because productivity is negatively related to factor intensity and changes in shares of production factors. In order to account for changes in input combinations, a total factor productivity (TFP) index is defined as the ratio of (aggregate) output to the weighted sum of production inputs:

(5) $TFP = Y / \sum_j \alpha_j X_j.$

The TFP can be measured as changes over time or relative to other firms in a single period. Here, the changes are compared to some reference time or firm as:

(6) $TFP_{t,t-1} = (Y_{it} / X_{it})/(Y_{it-1}/X_{it-1})$ and $TFP_{i,j} = (Y_i / X_i)/(Y_j / X_j).$

The first measure is credited to Tinbergen (1942), which has been modified by Solow (1956, 1957), Kendrick (1961) and others. The productivity growth, (TFP), over two points in time (0 and 1) (see also recent survey by Good, Nadiri and Sickles, 1997) is measured as:

(7) $\dot{TFP} = \Delta TFP / TFP = [((Y_1 / Y_0) / (\sum_j w_j X_{j1} / \sum_j w_j X_{j0}) -1]$
$$= [(Y_1 / Y_0) / (\sum_j \alpha_j (X_{j1} / X_{j0})]$$

where $\Delta TFP = TFP_{t+1} - TFP_t$ is change in TFP, w is input price, α_j is the expenditure share for inputs j and 0 is the reference time period. TFP growth can be decomposed into technical change and scale components.

Diewert (1981) classified the various measures of technical change into four groups: (i) econometric estimation of production and cost functions; (ii) Divisia indices; (iii) exact index numbers; and (iv) non-parametric methods using linear programming. Here, we focus on the first approach, but also discuss the Divisia index. In the econometric approach, technical change has been represented generally by a simple time trend. The rate of technical change is calculated as the percentage of change in production or cost over time. In flexible functional forms (Christensen et al., 1973), the simple time trend has been modified to include time squared and interactions between time and the other explanatory variables. Access to panel data allows for a richer specification of technical change. Time trend representation of the rate of technical change is quite restrictive, it is smoothly changing and does not capture switching in productivity growth. In order to overcome these limitations a general index of technical change was introduced by Baltagi and Griffin (1988),[1] where the time trend is replaced by a vector of time dummies. To conserve space, in the following only the econometric and Divisia approaches are discussed. Let the production function be characterized by:

(8) $Y = f(X, t)$

---

1   Other applications of the General Index model of technical change are found in Baltagi et al. (1995), Kumbhakar and Heshmati (1996), Kumbhakar et al. (1999) and Kumbhakar et al. (2000).

where Y is output, X is a vector of J input variables, and t is a time trend variable. Taking the total differential of (5) we get:

(9) $$\dot{Y} = \sum_j (f_j X_j / Y) \dot{X}_j + (f_t / Y)$$

where a dot indicates growth rate and f_j is the marginal product of the jth input. The relationship can be rewritten as:

(10) $$\dot{Y} - \sum_j S_j \dot{X}_j = (RTS - 1) \sum_j S_j \dot{X}_j + (f_t / Y)$$

where S_j is the cost share of input j and RTS is returns to scale. The left-hand side is the Divisia index of total factor productivity growth:

(11) $$T\dot{F}P = \dot{Y} - \sum_j S_j \dot{X}_j$$

where only the growth rates in inputs and outputs and the cost shares are required for the calculation of the TFP growth index. Constant returns to scale are assumed. The TFP growth estimates can be obtained by estimating a production function and allowing for variable returns to scale. The TFP growth can be decomposed into technical change (TC), and returns to scale (RTS) components (as well as input and scale biases components, see Kumbhakar *et al.*,1999):

(12) $$T\dot{F}P = TC + (RTS - 1) \sum_j \beta_j \dot{X}_j$$

where β is a vector of parameter estimates. A positive (negative) rate of TC in production (cost) functions indicates technical progress, which is manifested by a positive (negative) shift in the production (cost) function over time. For other decompositions, including effects of non-marginal cost pricing, see Balk (1998).

Assuming that firms minimize their cost for given output quantity, input prices and technology, following Kumbhakar *et al.* (2000) in a cost function approach $C = g(y, w, t)$, the TFP growth rate is written as:

(13) $$T\dot{F}P = -TC + (1 - RTS^{-1})\dot{Y}.$$

Selected TFP applications in manufacturing industries

Nordhaus (2001) in measuring productivity growth examined the welfare–theoretic basis for measuring productivity growth. The productivity growth is then decomposed into three aggregate components: the pure productivity effect, the effect of changing shares of industries over time, and the effect of changing shares of employment on aggregate productivity. These three components are equivalents of pure scale augmenting and non-neutral components of technical change. Nordhaus shows which component is to be included in the welfare-oriented measure of productivity growth, and how this is done.

In general, the components of TFP growth discussed above are constant across firms/industries and over time. The time trend approach is generalized by Baltagi *et al.* (1995), Kumbhakar *et al.* (1999) and Kumbhakar *et al.* (2000) to incorporate firm-specific and time-specific components of TFP growth. In addition, Heshmati and Nafar (1998) account for autocorrelation and heteroscedasticity as well. These generalizations are illustrated with applications to firm-level data. Good, Nadiri and Sickles (1997) discuss incorporating the issues of capacity utilization and dynamics, and Nadiri and Prucha (1999) discuss the Divisia index number and the recent advances in the econometric modelling to estimate dynamic factor demand models. They review the use of such models in applied work and show, in a Monte Carlo study, how sensitive the results are to the incorporation of characteristics of the production process and model misspecification.

Crépon *et al.* (1998) examine the relationship between research, innovation and productivity in French manufacturing with emphasis on the issues of selection bias, simultaneity bias, specification and estimation. They find that simultaneity and selectivity tend to bias the results if it is not controlled for in the estimation. Lööf and Heshmati (2002, 2004) applied a modified version of the model to Swedish innovation data. The results show the presence of a positive relationship between research and innovation, and between innovation and productivity. The estimated relationship is sensitive to the model specification, estimation methods, measures of performance, subsamples, type of innovation and data sources. Arranz-Aperte and Heshmati (2004) investigate factors determining the individual employee's and firm's participation in profit-sharing schemes using Finnish manufacturing data. They find weak evidence of a relationship between performance of firms and employment of profit-sharing schemes at the industrial sector level.

As with innovation, exit and entry may affect the productivity of firms. Campbell (1997) studied the entry and exit of US manufacturing plants over the business. Shocks to the embodied technological change are considered significant sources of economic fluctuations. Empirical results suggest a positive relationship between entry rate and output and total factor productivity growth. Improvements in embodied technological change induce the exit of obsolete plants, the entry of plants with new technology, and increased output and productivity growth.

In another paper, Hulten (2000) explains the origins of growth accounting and productivity methods. He discusses the importance of TFP in the process of economic growth and the controversy about measurement methods and underlying assumptions. A critical point is that TFP is estimated as a residual that measures our ignorance, possibly measurement errors, and unmeasured gains in product quality and environmental costs of growth. Bartelsman and Doms (2000) present another excellent review of research using longitudinal microdata in industrialized countries. The research is divided into two groups: those measuring productivity changes and those examining factors causing growth.

Selected TFP applications in service industries

Griliches (1992) and Solow (1992), in assessing productivity in the service sector, reached the conclusion that services and goods are not that different after all, and that productivity analysis raises similar difficulties in both sectors. In addition to the applications studied above that focus on manufacturing, a brief overview of research in the area of service sector productivity will be provided below. The service industries investigated are quite diverse, although financial, education and healthcare services are overrepresented. Most analyses are performed at the micro level and are often based on panel data. The focus is on performance, the impact of organizational changes on the performance of firms, scale effects, different measurement approaches used, different estimation methods – by accounting attributes of inputs, outputs and production techniques – and other firm characteristics.

Mairesse and Kremp (1993) consider performance across eight privately provided services. The analysis is based on a large sample of small and medium-sized French firms. The focus is on dispersion, heterogeneity, changes in performance and on assessing the contribution of capital and labour to the performance of firms. Industry effects are found to be strongly related to productivity and profitability levels, and the heterogeneity variables play a minor role in explaining the dispersion in performance. The importance of measurement errors in variables and the lack of information on various characteristics of firms are emphasized. Triplett and Bosworth (1999) analyse whether services play an important role in the slowdown of labour productivity in the US non-farm sector. Results suggest that productivity improvements in services are harder to achieve than in goods-producing industries. This view is supported by Mulder (1999) who compared the labour productivity of the services in Brazil, Mexico and the USA. The results suggest that labour productivity grew more slowly in services than in other sectors of the economy. De Melo *et al.* (1999), in their analysis of the evolution of service sector growth in Brazil, found that growth in the service sector is the result of a lack of urban employment rather than the demand for services. For other applications analysing productivity in hospitals and pharmacies, see Färe *et al.* (1989, 1995) and Heshmati (2002a).

The community innovation survey data

The data used here are collected within the framework of the second European Community Innovation Survey (CIS).[2] It is considered to be a good proxy of the complicated process that transforms innovation investments into growth. The empirical results are based on Swedish CIS data covering 1996–98. Summary statistics of the data are presented in Table 7.1, with Lööf and Heshmati (2002) providing additional detailed information.

INNOVATION INVESTMENTS

Innovative investment is broken down into seven different categories. The traditional innovation input measure, labelled as internal R&D, corresponds to 1.5 per cent of total sales, while all seven categories together correspond to 3.9 per cent of the total sales. Nearly 62 per cent of all firms made investment in some innovative activities in 1998. The investment strategy is broadly divided into investment in product and process innovations. The product innovation is further divided into five innovations activities related to: opening up of new markets, improved product quality, replacement of phased-out products, extension of the product range, and fulfilment of regulations and standards. The process innovation involves measures aimed at reducing labour costs, material consumption, environmental damages and energy consumption, and improving production flexibility. Each of the above strategies is further divided according to moderate and strong degrees of importance. Among the product innovations, extension of the range of products and the opening up of new markets are found to be of moderate and strong importance, respectively. In the case of process innovations, improving product flexibility and reducing labour costs exhibit moderate and strong levels of importance, respectively. In general, the degree of importance is much higher for the sample of innovative firms.

---

2   Recently the OECD, Eurostat and several other national and international organizations have developed and standardized the methodology and information collected by innovation surveys. For the first time, innovation surveys that are internationally comparable have been completed by all EU and some non-member countries. The questionnaire and methodology in these surveys are based largely on the Oslo manual (OECD/Eurostat, 1997). The manual proposes guidelines for the collection and interpretation of innovation data.

Table 7.1   Summary statistics of the merged CIS and register data sets (N = 1694)

Variable	Mean	Standard Deviation	Minimum	Maximum
Basic-level variables				
Employees CIS data 1998-12-31	130.445	217.499	20.000	1857
Employees CIS data 1996-12-31	128.035	224.955	20.000	2110
No of employees register data	130.759	226.521	20.000	2870
Turnover 1998	232649.601	515673.729	7721.000	8335900
Turnover 1996	208410.415	494618.103	5922.000	10237400
Value added 1998	74742.996	160602.962	4772.000	2173271
Value added 1996	65334.751	147080.140	3000.000	2237378
Export value 1998	75935.354	293438.030	.000	4808539
Export value 1996	65584.067	258037.777	.000	3596703
Material assets	82295.672	408368.915	4.000	8298362
Dependent variables				
Growth in turnover	17.514	34.292	−65.002	279.607
Growth in value added	22.073	41.040	−68.736	295.437
Innovative	.616	.486	.000	1.000
Innovation input	6251.059	35516.832	.000	999999
Innovation output	35896.454	140246.679	.000	2880000
Explanatory variables				
Labour productivity	1677.524	1686.935	200.215	17324.125
Profitability/employ	42.733	122.508	−654.881	2283.243
Capital stock intensity	554.569	1782.830	.071	39008.160
Capital flow intensity	101.458	257.479	.000	6493.086
R&D intensity	9.212	40.769	.000	670.968
Debt/equity ratio	61.483	21.535	−42.591	138.591
Capital-intensive	.071	.257	.000	1.000
Knowledge-intensive	.305	.461	.000	1.000
Labour-intensive	.286	.452	.000	1.000
Others-intensive	.338	.473	.000	1.000
Manufacturing sector	.664	.472	.000	1.000
Service sector	.280	.449	.000	1.000
Product innovation	.507	.500	.000	1.000
Process innovation	.279	.449	.000	1.000
Radical innovation	.507	.500	.000	1.000
Incremental innovation	.279	.449	.000	1.000
Other innovation	.441	.497	.000	1.000
Size of firm	1.655	.678	1.000	3.000
Export share of value added	.779	1.904	.000	57.017
Growth in employment	8.608	27.726	−74.359	285.714
Growth in capital	21.406	57.896	−99.747	299.277
Growth in export	46.847	340.292	−100.000	8010.204
Various composite indices				
Outsourcing hired employee	1.277	6.204	.000	136.674
Outsourcing expenditure share	23.911	33.348	.000	99.000
Efficiency level	.834	.146	.537	1.000

Table 7.1   *Continued*

PC index hampered project	–.000	1.000	–6.675	.501
PC index hampering factors	–.000	1.000	–.456	7.705
PC index strategy innovation	–.000	1.000	–1.287	2.135
PC index sources product innovation	–.000	1.000	–1.188	1.373
PC index sources process innovation	000	1.000	–.811	1.444
PC index importance of cooperation	.000	1.000	–.900	1.697
PC index location of cooperation	.000	1.000	–.562	11.455

INNOVATION OUTPUT

The CIS survey contains several alternative measures of innovation output. We define a firm innovative if it has positive innovation input and positive innovation sales. There are three categories of innovation sales:

1. products technologically new for the firm but not new for the market, partly or totally developed by the firm, and introduced on the market during the previous three years;
2. products that have been technologically improved; and
3. products that are technologically new both for the firm and for the market.

Here, we use the sum of the first two categories as incremental measure of innovations and compare this measure with the third category which is classified as radical innovations.

PRODUCTIVITY GROWTH

Depending on data availability, the performance of firms can be measured in different ways. We have looked at three measures of performance: growth in turnover, value added and employment. They also show similar growth patterns. However, there is a large difference in growth rates between innovator and non-innovator firms when mean values are used and when size, capital intensity, human capital, R&D and so on are not controlled for.

TREATMENT OF EXTREME OBSERVATIONS

A number of restrictions are imposed on the final data. First, we removed all observations for which value added or employment was zero or missing. Second, we excluded any observation for which the growth in value added or labour productivity for 1996–98 was more than 300 per cent. Finally, observations for which the growth in labour productivity was less than 75 per cent were also excluded. These exclusions eliminated the influence of observations outside the above ranges of expansion and contraction on the estimation results.

CHARACTERISTICS OF THE SWEDISH CIS DATA

Table 7.1 presents some statistics for the variables included in the CIS data and model on the relationship between innovation and performance. The data contain information about the firm's strategy on innovations. The most important objectives of product innovations are the opening up of new markets and improvements in product quality. Reducing labour costs and material consumption dominates among the most important objectives of the innovative sample. Customers and sources in the dominating enterprise are the most important sources of knowledge for innovation. Domestic customers and supplier universities are the most common cooperative partners in innovation activities. There exists intra-firm cooperation on innovation. Domestic cooperation is the dominant form.

Several factors negatively affect innovation, and these are grouped into projects delayed, abolished or hampered at the start. Lack of qualified personnel and organizational rigidities were identified as the two most important factors delaying innovation. The presence of risks and the lack of qualified personnel were the most important factors in abolishing innovation projects. High risks and costs dominate the causes of innovation projects failing to start at all. Among factors hampering innovation, a delay in projects because of a lack of qualified personnel and organizational rigidities are the most important.

THE CAUSAL RELATIONSHIPS AMONG THE VARIABLES

The framework used here is based on a Cobb–Douglas production function explaining variation in firm output by a number of standard input variables and a R&D investment variable. The relation is written as:

$$(14) \qquad \ln Q_i = \beta_0 + \sum_j \beta_j \ln X_{ji} + \beta_{RD} \ln R \& D_i + \varepsilon_i$$

where ln denotes logarithm, i indicates firm, Q is output produced, and X is a J vector of standard inputs (such as labour, capital, material and energy). The β_j is the elasticity of output with respect to a vector of inputs, β_{RD} is the elasticity of output with respect to changes in R&D, and ε is a random error term.

A limitation of the above relationship is that it only measures the relationship between R&D and output. It neglects a link labelled by Pakes and Griliches (1984) as the knowledge production function, defined as the production of commercially valuable knowledge or innovation output. In order to overcome the above limitation, Pakes and Griliches suggest an alternative production function model corresponding to a three-equation relationship including: innovation input, innovation output and productivity equations (see Griliches, 1990). In order to correct for undesirable properties of selectivity and simultaneity biases and account for the complexity of innovation process, Crépon et al. (1998) specified a modified version of the above model consisting of four equations. In the innovation literature the latter model is referred to as the CDM model, referring to the authors, Crépon, Duguet and Mairesse.

The basic econometric problems addressed in the CDM are selectivity (see Verbeck, 2000) and simultaneity biases. The objective is to consistently estimate the causal effect of innovation investment on innovation output and the causal effect of innovation output on productivity. The first equation is a selectivity equation, modelled as a probit, where the dependent variable is a latent innovation decision variable. The remaining three equations correspond to those of the Pakes and Griliches model. When only the innovation sample is used in standard regression analysis, selectivity problem may bias the results. Innovation input and innovation output appear as explanatory variables in the innovation output and productivity equations. Because of the endogeneity of these variables, we cannot assume that the explanatory variables and the disturbances are uncorrelated. As a result, an ordinary least square regression applied to the above relation will be biased and inconsistent. To overcome the endogeneity problem, CDM suggests estimation using a reduced form of the model. Here we use a simpler multi-step estimation approach.

The system consists of four equations. The first two equations representing innovativeness and innovation inputs are estimated separately as a generalized Tobit model in which observations on both innovative and non-innovative firms are included. The last two equations are estimated as a system using the three-stages least-squares (3SLS) method (see Greene, 2000). The endogenous innovation output variable is limited to an innovative sample with a strictly positive innovation output. The four-equation model is written as:

$$(15) \qquad IN^*_i = \beta^1_0 + \sum_n \beta^1_n \ln X^1_{ni} + \beta_{OUTS1} OUTS1_i + \varepsilon^1_i$$

$$(16) \qquad \ln II_i = \beta^2_0 + \sum_m \beta^2_m \ln X^2_{mi} + \varepsilon^2_i$$

$$(17) \qquad \ln IO_i = \beta^3_0 + \sum_l \beta^3_l \ln X^3_{li} + \beta_{RD} II_i + \beta_{MR} MR_i + \beta_{EFF} EFF_i + \beta_Q \ln Q_i$$
$$\qquad\qquad + \beta_{COM} COMP_i + \beta_{OUTS2} OUTS2_i + \varepsilon^3_i$$

$$(18) \qquad \ln Q_i = \beta^4_0 + \sum_j \beta^4_j \ln X^4_{ji} + \beta_{IO} IO_i + \beta_{EFF} EFF_i + \beta_{OUTS1} OUTS1_i + \varepsilon^4_i$$

where IN^* is a latent innovation decision variable; the observable counterpart $IN = 1$ when $IN^* > 0$ if the firm is engaged in innovation, otherwise zero; II represents innovation input; IO innovation output; Q productivity; and MR inverted Mill's ratio introduced to correct for possible selection bias. X are explanatory variables including employment, physical capital, human capital and various indicators; EFF, $COMP$, $OUTS1$ and $OUTS2$ are variables representing productive efficiency, competitiveness and outsourcing, respectively; and the β : s are unknown parameters to be estimated. $OUTS1$ is based on hiring temporary labour, while $OUTS2$ is purchase of external innovation-related services.

Starting with the first two equations, β^1 and β^2 are vectors of unknown parameters to be estimated reflecting the impact of certain factors on the probability of being engaged in R&D and other innovation investments, and on the actual level of these investments. The β^3 is the estimated parameter associated with the level of innovation output, while β^4 is associated with the determinants of productivity growth.

Equations 15 and 16 are estimated jointly in a generalized Tobit model. The ε^1 and ε^2 are random error terms with mean zero and constant variances and are not correlated with explanatory variables, but correlated with each other. From the generalized Tobit model, estimates of II and MR are obtained and used as explanatory variables in equation 16. Equations 17 and 18 are then estimated based on sample with positive innovation input and outputs. One problem with the production function approach is that some of the explanatory variables are often determined jointly with the dependent ones. For example, the innovation input (II) is endogenous in the innovation output equation (17), and innovation output (IO) is endogenous in the productivity equation (18). In order to derive a consistent estimator, we account for simultaneity by relying on the instrumental variable approach. The instruments consist of variables not correlated with the model error terms, but correlated with the endogenous variables. Furthermore, in addition to the simplification of the estimation procedure, splitting the four equations into two parts not only allows for within-part correlation, but also for limited between-part correlation among the error terms facilitated through the inclusion of the MR in the second part. Our approach is thus an intermediate approach compared to the Pakes and Griliches (1984) model, which neglects correlations, and the Crépon et al. (1998) approach, which allows for full correlation among the four equations.

Specification of the model

In using cross-sectional data in the context of innovation, we observe R&D or innovation investment for a single year only. We must assume therefore that the level of investments in year t can be used as a proxy for long-term R&D investment. This presumes that firms do not experience major fluctuations in their R&D investments behaviour. There is evidence that R&D expenditures are highly correlated from one year to another (Griliches, 1988).

The dependent variables include log innovation input per employee, II in equation (16), log innovation sales per employee, IO in equation (17) and log productivity, Q in equation (18). Productivity can be defined in different ways based on value added, turnover, employment or profit, and expressed in levels or growth rates. Here it is measured as the growth rate in turnover between 1996 and 1998 – that is, $\log(\text{fvarde}_{it}) - \log(\text{fvarde}_{i,t-1})$ where t and $t\text{-}1$ indicate 1998 and 1996, respectively.

We now present the specifications of the four equations of the model. The determinants of innovation input labelled as the x^1 vector consist of growth in employment, profitability, capital stock intensity, capital and knowledge-intensive technologies, firm size and industrial-sector dummy variables. The profitability and capital stock intensity variables are measured per employee and expressed in logarithmic forms.

The x^2 variables in the selection equation consist of hired temporary supply labour, profitability, capital investment intensity, indebtedness, export share of turnover, capital and knowledge-intensive technologies, firm size classes and industrial-sector dummy variables. The investment intensity and profitability are expressed per employee and measured in logarithmic forms. The size variables are based on the number of employees. The reference groups include the small-size and industrial sector 1.

The determinants of innovation output labelled as the x^3 vector consist of predicted value of innovation input, inverted Mill's ratio, predicted value of firm performance, logarithm of R&D intensity, growth in employment, purchase of innovation-related outsourcing services, efficiency in production, firm size and industrial-sector dummy variables. The predicted innovation input and Mill's ratio variables are based on results obtained from the first two equations. In addition, the set of variables includes a number of composite indices obtained by using principal component analysis. These include indices of hampered project and hampering factors, sources of product and process innovations, competitive strategy, the importance of innovation cooperation and the importance of location of innovation cooperation partners.

The x^4 vector entering the productivity equation contains information on predicted value of innovation output, the temporary hired share of labour, efficiency in production, R&D intensity, capital investment intensity, capital stock intensity, profitability, indebtedness, size and industrial-sector dummy variables. The R&D, profitability, investment and capital intensity variables are expressed in logarithmic forms.

Empirical results

Empirical results in this chapter are based on the Swedish CIS survey described earlier. It is a cross-sectional survey focusing on 1998 data, and expanded with additional information on employment and output in 1996. The total number of observations used in the estimation steps is 1694. A number of economic variables used in the regression analysis are obtained from the firms' balance sheets, originated from register data. A complete summary of data is given in Table 7.1. For comparison purposes the final sample of firms can be further divided into a number of subsamples of manufacturing, services: innovative (radical, incremental, product and processes) and non-innovative.

SPECIFICATION TESTS

A number of models and estimation methods are involved in generating the results. To obtain our efficiency scores we specify a frontier production function, estimated using the maximum likelihood method. The production function, where the dependent variable is defined as value added, is specified in terms of capital and labour inputs. In addition, we control for heterogeneity by including dummy variables indicating which sector firms belong to and their size based on the number of employees. Furthermore, a number of determinants of inefficiency are incorporated to explain variations in inefficiency among the sample firms. Likelihood ratio tests indicate the presence of inefficiency in production and that the determinants of inefficiency should be included in the efficiency effects model specification.

We have used two different (specific-specific and general) measures of outsourcing to study the effects of outsourcing on efficiency in production, innovativeness, innovation outputs and productivity growth of firms. However, due to a lack of detailed information about firm-level characteristics we avoided identifying determinants of outsourcing and modelling outsourcing decisions of firms.

For the specification of the innovative Tobit model estimated by the maximum likelihood method, availability of data and the relationship between the explanatory variables, and their expected relationship to the decision of innovation investment, as well as individual variables significance levels determined the final model specification. Here instead of a Heckman two-step procedure[3] we used a one-step generalized Tobit model with selection effect.

As previously discussed, the remaining models of innovation output and productivity growth are estimated jointly as a system using the three-stages least-squares (3SLS) estimation method. The sample is restricted to only innovative firms but accounts for selection effects. Many of the innovation activities, obstacles, cooperations and strategy indicators were formulated as complex questions in the questionnaires. In order to avoid large number of dummy variables, we estimated a number of composite indices using principal component analysis (see Table 7.2). These composite indices are then used in the final stage of the model as determinants of the performance of firms.

EFFICIENCY RESULTS

The frontier production function model was specified as a function capital and specific inputs and estimated using maximum likelihood method. The parameter estimates are given in Table 7.3. In the estimation we control for heterogeneity of firms by controlling for the industrial sector that firms belong to. In addition, a number of determinants of inefficiency are identified and their impacts on firms' efficiency quantified. The first two coefficients are elasticity of output with respect to capital and specific inputs. The specific elasticity is much higher (.88) than the capital elasticity (.10). They are significantly different from zero and sum up to .98, interpreted as decreasing returns to scale, but not statistically different from a constant returns to scale. Four of the six sector dummy coefficients are statistically different from zero, indicating the presence of significant industrial-sector heterogeneity in the data.

---

3   Probit to estimate the decision of innovation investment and a standard regression model of determinants of level of innovation investment.

Table 7.2   Maximum likelihood parameter estimates of the frontier production function

Parameters	Coefficient	Standard error	t-ratio
Production function part			
Intercept	5.8637	.1237	47.3784
Log capital	.1025	.0078	13.1160
Log labour	.8800	.0294	67.9984
Sni2	.0811	.0335	2.4213
Sni3	.0706	.0396	1.7837
Sni4	.2742	.0566	4.8404
Sni5	.0799	.0751	1.0647
Sni6	−.2623	.0671	−3.9054
Sni7	.0241	.0650	.3716
Efficiency effects part			
Medium size	−.0160	.0130	−1.2330
Large size	−.1064	.0179	−5.9164
Investment intensity	−.0233	.0040	−5.7274
Profitability	−.0679	.0066	−10.1560
Indebtedness	.0002	.0004	.5858
Outsourcing labour	−.0043	.0010	−4.1723
Export share	.0033	.0051	.6389
R&D intensity	−.0455	.0050	−9.0423
Capital-intensive firm	.5157	.0622	8.2883
Knowledge-intensive firm	.5416	.0500	10.8134
Labour-intensive firm	.6017	.0575	10.4610
Sigma-squared	.0920	.0034	26.9235
Gamma	.0362	.0054	6.6574
Log likelihood function		−357.4846	
LR-test of the one-sided error		380.2175	
Number of iterations		53	
Number of cross-sections		1694	
Mean efficiency		.8335	

There is an increasingly negative relationship between inefficiency in production and size of firm. Profitability and investment intensity per employee, outsourcing defined as share of temporary hired specific and R&D investment intensity enhance efficiency in production. We expected high levels of indebtedness and export orientation to increase efficiency in production, but these were found to be statistically insignificant. Industries with capital knowledge and specific intensive production technologies are found to be technically less effective than industries with average production factor intensity.

Table 7.3   Results of principal component analysis (N = 1694)

	Eigenvalues of the Correlation Matrix			
	Eigenvalue	**Difference**	**Proportion**	**Cumulative**
Factors hampering innovation projects				
Prin1	1.8008	1.1490	.6003	.6003
Prin2	.6517	.1044	.2173	.8175
Prin3	.5473		.1825	1.0000
Summary	−.0000	1.0000	−6.6750	.5010
Factors hampering innovation				
Prin1	2.3846	1.0818	.2168	.2168
Prin2	1.3028	.2500	.1184	.3352
Prin3	1.0527		.0957	.4309
Summary	−.0000	1.0000	−.4560	7.7050
Strategy of innovation				
Prin1	6.4851	5.8436	.7206	.7206
Prin2	.6414	.2509	.0713	.7918
Prin3	.3905		.0434	.8352
Summary	−.000	1.0000	−1.2870	2.1350
Sources of product innovation				
Prin1	12.3648	12.0627	.8832	.8832
Prin2	.3021	.0045	.0216	.9048
Prin3	.2975		.0213	.9260
Summary	−.0000	1.0000	−1.1880	1.3730
Sources of process innovation				
Prin1	13.7644	13.7232	.9832	.9832
Prin2	.0411	.0093	.0029	.9861
Prin3	.0318		.0023	.9884
Summary	.0000	1.0000	−.8110	1.4440
Importance of cooperation				
Prin1	7.7157	7.3549	.8573	.8573
Prin2	.3607	.0788	.0401	.8974
Prin3	.2819		.0313	.9287
Summary	.0000	1.0000	−.9000	1.6970
Location of cooperation				
Prin1	8.9216	4.9553	.1439	.1439
Prin2	3.9662	.3583	.0640	.2079
Prin3	3.6078		.0582	.2661
Summary	.0000	1.0000	−.5620	11.4550

Note: Prin1, Prin2 and Prin3 are the first, second and the third principal components,
Summary = mean, standard deviation, minimum and maximum values respectively.

The mean technical efficiency is .834, indicating that, on average, there is a potential that, for a given level of inputs and production technology, the firms could produce 16.4 per cent more output by using the best-practice production technology. Efficiency in production is positively correlated with innovations input, innovations output, productivity growth and temporarily hired labour (see Table 7.4), with significant differences between efficiency levels and industrial sector. Industrial sectors 1–3 are much less effective than industrial sectors 4–7. Larger firms and firms with radical innovation are more efficient than small and less innovative

Table 7.4 Correlations of the dependent and independent variables (N = 1694)

Dependent variables	1	2	3	4	5	6
1 Innovative input	–					
2 Innovative output	.3149***					
3 Growth in value added	-.0454	.1212***				
4 Outsourcing hired employees	.0298	.0628**	.0546*			
5 Outsourcing exp. share2	.1420***	.1232***	.0277	.0680**	–	
6 Efficiency level	.0900***	.1298***	.1727***	.1095***	-.0145	–

Independent variables	1	2	3	4	5	6	7
1 Pcindex hampered project	–						
2 Pcindex hampered factors	-.5271***						
3 Pcindex sources prod. innov.	-.2748***	.2970***					
4 Pcindex sources proc. innov.	-.1863***	.2315***	.4301***				
5 Pcindex strategy innovation	-.2681***	.2801***	.7503***	.4830***			
6 Pcindex importance of coop.	-.2393***	.2663***	.5576***	.4070***	.5768***		
7 Pcindex location of coop.	-.2144***	.3326***	.3414***	.3152***	.2799***	.5111***	–

Notes: *** $p < .001$; ** $p < .01$; * $p < .05$.

firms (see Table 7.5). The higher efficiency of firms with average input factor intensity is an indication of complementarity of capital, knowledge and labour in production.

PRODUCTIVITY RESULTS

Since we have no access to a cross-section of time-series data, it was not possible to decompose the total factor productivity growth into its underlying technical change and scale components. Furthermore, the returns to scale obtained from the estimation of a production function was found not to deviate from a constant returns to scale. Therefore, we use the growth rate in turnover and value added during 1996–98 to proxy productivity growth, although the latter, which is based on the register data, is found to be more reliable than the former, which is obtained from the survey data. The regression analysis is based on a value-added definition of growth. The different growth variables by various characteristics are presented in Table 7.5.

Growth in employment varies by industrial sector. Employment did not grow in sectors 1 and 4, while sectors 3 and 5–7 grew by 20–22 per cent between 1996 and 1998. The corresponding growth in capital was in the interval 16 per cent to 36 per cent. Growth rates in turnover and value added differ somewhat, but the patterns are similar among the industrial sectors. Growth in value added is higher in general and it is the highest among sectors 3 and 5–7. The medium-sized firms, followed by large firms, experienced much higher growth in turnover and value added than small firms. Productivity growth is much higher for the knowledge-intensive firms compared with capital- and labour-intensive firms, but the rate of productivity growth is the highest amongst firms with average factor intensity. Productivity growth is positively related to the innovativeness, innovation output, temporary hired skilled labour and efficiency in production, but it is negatively correlated with innovation input (see Table 7.4).

OUTSOURCING RESULTS

For the estimations we have used two measures of outsourcing. One is based on hired labour defined as the ratio of temporary hired labour to the total labour force in1998, labelled as *OUTS1*. A second measure is based on the expenditure to develop new or significantly improved product and processes in 1998, labelled as *OUTS2*. It is measured as the sum of expenditure shares associated with the purchase of external R&D services, including acquisition of machinery, knowledge, training and market introduction of innovations.

The average share of temporary hired employees is 1.3 per cent, while the expenditure share of outsourcing is 23.9 per cent, with larger relative dispersion in the former. The two measures are correlated at a very low rate, only .068. The hired labour measure is positively correlated with innovation output and growth in value added and efficiency, while the expenditure measure is positively correlated with both innovations input and output but not with growth in value added or efficiency in production (see Table 7.4).

The industries differ by degree of outsourcing. As mentioned earlier, the outsourcing of products, services and processes is more intensive than hiring labour on a temporary basis. The expenditure share of outsourcing is an increasing function of the size of firm. Large firms outsource 33.4 per cent of total expenditure for their innovation activities; the corresponding share for small firms is only 19.1 per cent. Knowledge-intensive firms' share of outsourcing is highest among firms. Outsourcing is also found to be positively associated with the degree of innovativeness. More details are shown in Table 7.5.

102 Global Outsourcing Strategies

Table 7.5 Mean scores of variables by firm characteristics

Characteristics	Growth variables				Stock intensity	Flow intensity	Debt/ equity	Export share	Innovation input	Innovation output
	Value added	Turnover	Employment	Capital						
Industrial sector										
sni1	66732	278881	132	61362	339	71	57.28	.73	2046	20511
sni2	76693	228431	134	76956	346	84	59.52	1.07	7389	33628
sni3	63999	195437	135	26473	185	53	61.54	1.00	9186	40602
sni4	166952	400210	128	582657	5015	610	56.28	.02	4812	31016
sni5	52863	457944	99	10382	116	47	66.16	.58	5173	143132
sni6	45316	166540	98	50062	511	104	66.38	.39	2205	14164
sni7	77249	155368	149	10302	65	32	67.39	.28	6103	28080
Size of firm										
Small	17563	53141	33	18013	542	107	61.42	.62	1302	6155
Medium	57499	186544	106	58541	557	96	61.24	.85	3911	36451
Large	362760	1107875	604	421843	594	100	62.63	1.14	34237	151359
Factor intensity										
Capital	187637	591004	258	307908	644	130	51.58	1.58	19996	67785
Knowledge	64033	187387	128	27150	200	53	61.28	1.04	8262	39610
Labour	53096	180173	110	41574	338	85	59.85	.84	2541	18413
Others	79049	242766	123	119200	1038	153	65.12	.32	4691	40636
Type of innovation										
Incremental	51625	182254	94	47175	549	121	60.48	.80	3903	33859
Others	55409	168357	97	76554	715	123	61.97	.54	1113	0
Radical	93924	293722	163	90887	416	81	61.16	.98	10959	67321
Sample										
M	74743	232650	130	82296	555	101	61.48	.78	6251	35896
SD	100603	515674	217	408369	1783	257	21.53	1.90	35517	140247

Table 7.5 *Continued*

Mean growth of variables by firm characteristics

Characteristics	Productivity	Employment	Capital	Turnover	Value added	Export	Profitabilty	R&D intensity	Product innovation	Process innovation
Industrial sector										
Sni1	1879	-.18	15.69	6.80	9.93	25.92	31	3	.52	.24
Sni2	1459	4.57	22.63	13.56	18.38	56.85	45	10	.51	.29
Sni3	1329	10.92	20.38	22.50	25.25	80.06	30	21	.66	.30
Sni4	3271	.49	13.68	6.14	11.96	-.45	126	3	.28	.24
Sni5	3800	21.78	35.75	25.54	29.58	51.30	66	2	.64	.31
Sni6	1749	13.35	25.14	20.97	26.19	12.37	23	1	.26	.17
Sni7	1135	20.30	16.96	31.56	37.29	35.93	29	10	.56	.32
Size of firm										
Small	1595	5.78	20.64	15.37	17.79	52.15	39	0	.43	.23
Medium	1720	11.86	23.13	19.80	26.96	42.54	45	11	.53	.31
Large	1851	8.06	18.24	17.74	21.34	41.45	50	37	.72	.37
Factor intensity										
Capital	2141	-.11	25.19	12.11	14.19	38.11	89	14	.56	.35
Knowledge	1294	8.07	22.85	17.71	20.37	93.12	38	19	.59	.32
Labour	1515	3.73	18.92	11.97	17.67	25.70	30	3	.50	.25
Others	2064	15.04	21.41	23.15	28.98	24.79	48	5	.43	.26
Type of innovation										
Incremental	1840	7.90	23.73	18.83	23.09	100.72	51	5	.00	1.00
Others	1638	7.07	20.04	14.57	19.01	45.38	37	2	.00	.00
Radical	1695	10.02	22.36	19.94	24.63	42.60	47	16	1.00	.45
Sample										
M	1678	8.61	21.41	17.51	22.07	46.85	43	9	.51	.28
SD	1687	27.73	57.90	34.29	41.04	340.29	123	41	.50	.45

Table 7.5 *Continued*

Mean composite indices by firm characteristics

Characteristics	Hired labour	Expenditure share	Pcindex hampered factors	Pcindex hampered project	Source product	Source process	Strategy	Pcindex importance of cooperation	Pcindex location of cooperation	Efficiency level
Industrial sector										
Sni1	.64	24.96	.083	-.082	-.095	.004	-.109	-.171	-.050	.712
Sni2	1.10	25.20	-.006	.007	.019	.064	.015	.049	.049	.763
Sni3	.90	30.88	-.030	.024	.227	.133	.224	.246	.177	.763
Sni4	.59	20.86	.065	-.031	-.265	.057	-.146	-.034	-.103	.990
Sni5	.53	21.33	-.036	-.002	.239	-.011	.213	.032	.071	.987
Sni6	1.82	10.31	.150	-.173	-.455	-.444	-.506	-.406	-.287	.983
Sni7	2.88	24.47	-.138	.158	.141	-.029	.167	.000	-.082	.984
Size of firm										
Small	1.37	19.14	.109	-.103	-.157	-.179	-.138	-.167	-.189	.817
Medium	1.16	26.50	-.039	.005	.085	.093	.080	.090	.031	.832
Large	1.36	33.42	-.290	.389	.316	.373	.256	.335	.634	.907
Factor intensity										
Capital	1.59	24.55	-.254	.195	.089	.217	.148	.140	.214	.848
Knowledge	1.12	28.72	-.026	.046	.119	.070	.082	.139	.143	.777
Labour	.71	24.59	.088	-.096	-.035	.041	-.021	-.038	-.057	.711
Others	1.83	18.87	.002	-.002	-.096	-.143	-.087	-.123	-.126	.985
Type of innovation										
Incremental	2.34	34.13	-.009	-.056	.603	.375	.682	.426	-.065	.837
Radical	1.55	38.48	-.257	.275	.698	.367	.542	.439	.366	.840
Others	.84	5.95	.297	-.309	-.874	-.467	-.704	-.554	-.413	.826
Sample										
M	1.28	23.91	.000	.000	.000	.000	.000	.000	.000	.834
SD	6.20	33.35	1.000	1.000	1.000	1.000	1.000	1.000	1.000	.146

COMPETITIVENESS RESULTS

Principal component (PC) or factor analysis (FA) can be used in the computation of composite competitiveness indices. In this chapter we adopt the PC approach.[4] Given a dataset with p numeric variables, at most p principal components can be computed; each is a linear combination of the original variables with coefficients equal to the eigenvectors of the correlation of the covariance matrix. PC analysis can be viewed as a way of uncovering approximate linear dependencies among variables.[5]

The competitiveness index indicates the level and state of competitiveness among firms. If necessary, the index can be broken down into different underlying components. Breaking down the index into major components offers possibilities of identifying key sources of competitiveness. The breakdown of the index can be based on canonical correlation, looking at the correlation relationship between two or more sets of variables. As shown later, the indices can be used to study the causal relationship between competitive strategy, innovativeness, efficiency and productivity growth at the firm level.

The competitiveness strategy index in this study is constructed on the basis of a question about the importance of ten different factors on the competitiveness of firms' products and processes. These include: prices, quality, production flexibility, delivery, originality, brand value, design, uniqueness, knowledge intensity among others. The scale of importance is: very important, important, less important, and not relevant. Using the combination of the ten factors and four scales a composite competitiveness strategy index was created. The resulting index, based on the first principal component, is reported in Table 7.2.

Because of the way in which the scale of importance is numbered, the higher the index the less important is the strategic importance of the factors. Strategy is thus negatively correlated with hampered project and positively correlated with hampering factors, sources of product and process innovation, their importance and location (Table 7.4). The sectors differ by strategy. The index level is increasing function of size of firm. It is highest for capital- and knowledge-intensive and innovative firms (Table 7.5).

OTHER INNOVATION INDICES

In addition to the competitiveness strategy index described above, six other composite indices are computed using the principal component (PC) analysis. These are: factors hampering innovation, hampered innovation projects, sources of product innovations, sources of process innovations, importance of cooperation partners, and geographic location of cooperation partners. The questionnaire was constructed such that high values of the indices have a negative relationship to the performance of firms. The results from PC analysis, together with a summary of the indices, are found in Table 7.2.

Only in two cases – factors hampering innovation (.431) and location of cooperation partners (.266) – are the eigenvalues of the first three principal components larger than 1. However, in those two cases, the share of variance explained (given in parentheses) is relatively low. In the remaining five index cases, only the first principal component eigenvalue

---

4   A PC procedure produces standardized or unstandardized PC scores. An FA performs PC and common FA to produce component scores or common factor scores. FA produces the same results as PC except that scoring coefficients from FA are normalized to give PC scores with unit variance. For a discussion of each method's advantages over the other, see SAS/STAT User's Guide (SAS Institute, 1993).
5   This method gives a least-square solution by minimizing the sum of all the squared residuals, measured as distances from the point to the (first) principal axis. In the least-squares case the vertical distance to the fitted line is minimized.

exceeds 1. The share of the variance, listed in ascending order, are: factors hampering innovation projects (.600), strategy of innovation (.721), importance of cooperation (.857), sources of product innovation (.883), sources of process innovation (.983).

All indices are normalized to mean zero and variance 1. The range and distribution of the individual indices vary among the indices. The source of variations in patterns is dependent on the underlying variables. The location of innovation partners, followed by hampering factors indices, shows the highest variations, while sources of product and process innovations show the lowest.

Correlation coefficients among the composite indices are presented in Table 7.4. A high value of the hampered project, which indicates the success of the project, is negatively correlated with hampering factors, where a higher value of index indicates strength of the negative factors. The hampered projects index is negatively correlated with the remaining indices, but the size of correlation coefficients are small. The sources of product and process innovations are positively correlated among themselves and with all other indices, except hampered projects. The strategy index is highly correlated (.75) with sources of product innovation. The importance of cooperation partners and their location are positively correlated (.51). Cooperation on innovation with a different partner is important for strategy and the success of innovation activities. The same is true with location of partners, but at a lower level of importance. The sources of the product innovations index are highly correlated with the strategy of innovation and the importance of cooperation partners (.56). The latter two are highly correlated as well (.58). These high degrees of correlation might cause multicollinearity and subsequent problems of separation of their effects.

Mean composite indices by firm characteristics are reported in Table 7.5. The industrial sectors differ by index levels. The largest values are, in almost all index cases, associated with sector 6 and the lowest to sector 2. There is a clear pattern in the relationship between the level of the indices and the size of firms. With the exception of hampering factors, the indices are a positive function of the size of firms. Firms with capital- and labour-intensive production technologies show much higher index levels than those with labour or average factor intensity in production. The same positive relationships hold for firms with radical and incremental innovations compared to those without innovation.

THE CAUSAL INNOVATION–PRODUCTIVITY RELATIONSHIPS

In this section we present the results from the empirical analysis of the causal relationship between knowledge capital and performance indicators at the firm level. Up-to-date econometrics techniques accounting for selection and simultaneity biases are applied to Swedish innovation survey data. The results support a positive relationship between investment in innovation and productivity growth at the firm level.

The decisions to make investments in innovation are estimated jointly in a generalized Tobit model with selection effects by the maximum likelihood method (see Table 7.6). Using the parameter estimates from the generalized Tobit model, the Mill's ratio correcting for the effects of sample selection bias and predicted innovation input are computed and introduced in the innovation output equation. The innovation output equation is then jointly estimated, together with the productivity equation, using the three-stages least-squares estimation method (see Table 7.7). The estimation is based on innovative firms. A firm is classified as innovative if both innovation input and innovation outputs are positive. A total of 871 firms or 51.4 per cent of the sample of 1694 firms are classified as innovative.

Table 7.6   Generalized Tobit model estimation of innovativeness and innovation input

	Coefficient	Standard error	z	P|z|	[95% confidence interval]	
Innovation input equation						
Outsourcing hired employee	.0026	.0075	.34	.732	−.0121	.0173
Lprofit	.0367	.0323	1.14	.256	−.0266	.1000
Linvint.	.1893	.0466	4.06	.000	.0980	.2806
Debt/equity ratio	.0035	.0030	1.16	.247	−.0024	.0093
Export share of value added	.1024	.0227	4.52	.000	.0579	.1468
Capital-intensive	.4206	.2360	1.78	.075	−.0420	.8831
Knowledge-intensive	.5051	.1597	3.16	.002	.1922	.8180
Size2	.9528	.1276	7.47	.000	.7028	1.2028
Size3	2.4217	.2061	11.75	.000	2.0176	2.8256
Sni2	.3506	.2244	1.56	.118	−.0891	.7905
Sni3	.3390	.2541	1.33	.182	−.1589	.8370
Sni4	−.1227	.3597	−.34	.733	−.8277	.5823
Sni5	.6593	.3036	2.17	.030	.0642	1.2544
Sni6	.1236	.3325	.37	.710	−.5280	.7753
Sni7	1.0050	.2429	4.14	.000	.5289	1.4811
Constant	4.8560	.4944	9.82	.000	3.8869	5.8249
Innovation decision equation						
Growth in employment	.0018	.0012	1.49	.136	−.0005	.0040
Lprofit	.0333	.0164	2.03	.042	.0011	.0654
Lcapint	.0340	.0300	1.13	.257	−.0248	.0928
Capital-intensive	.1560	.1407	1.11	.268	−.1197	.4317
Knowledge-intensive	.2385	.0908	2.63	.009	.0605	.4163
Size2	.2302	.0670	3.44	.001	.0989	.3614
Size3	.6518	.1088	5.99	.000	.4385	.8650
Sni2	−.0839	.1285	−.65	.514	−.3358	.1680
Sni3	.2435	.1521	1.60	.109	−.0545	.5415
Sni4	−.5465	.1898	−2.88	.004	−.9185	−.1744
Sni5	.1390	.1832	.76	.448	−.2200	.4979
Sni6	−.6366	.1491	−4.27	.000	−.9288	−.3443
Sni7	.1575	.1492	1.06	.291	−.1348	.4498
Constant	−.4175	.1967	−2.12	.034	−.8029	−.0320
Athrho	.1802	.2277	.79	.429	−.2660	.6263
Lnsigma	.4460	.0341	13.07	.000	.3790	.5128
Rho	.1782	.2204			−.2599	.5555
Sigma	1.5620	.0533			1.4609	1.6701
Lambda	.2784	.3511			−.4097	.9666

LR test of indep. eqns. (rho = 0): chi2(1) = .39, Prob chi2 = .5338

Heckman selection model	Number of obs	= 1694
(regression model with sample selection)	Censored obs	= 823
	Uncensored obs	= 871
	Wald chi2(15)	= 230.5100
Log likelihood = −2716.6540	Prob chi2	= .0000

Investment in innovation

The LR test of independence of the two equations containing the generalized Tobit model does not reject the null hypothesis ($H_0 : \rho = 0$), suggesting that it is not necessary that the two equations are estimated jointly. The coefficient associated with selection is also insignificant, indicating no selection on firms that are very likely to be engaged in innovation activities. The estimation results from the two equations are presented on Table 7.6. In order to identify the parameters of interest, the two equations differ in specification by a number of variables, including outsourcing, growth in employment, investment and capital stock intensity and export shares.

The estimation results show that profitability is a major determinant of innovation investment indicating the importance of internal financial sources. Knowledge intensity and size of firm are two other factors positively affecting a decision to invest in innovation. Growth in employment, capital-intensive production technology and capital investment were found to be insignificant. Sectors 4 and 6 have a lower propensity than sector 1 to invest in innovation.

We expected increased outsourcing, defined as the share of temporary hired labour, to enhance investment in innovation. However, this variable was found to be insignificant. Profitability affects the decision to invest but not as much as the level of investment. Indebtedness also turned out to be insignificant. The large firms probably do not have significant liquidity constraints. They are indifferent in their choices between internal and external sources of finance and have the possibility of combining the two sources. General investment intensity, export share and capital- and knowledge-intensive production technologies positively affect the level of investment in innovation activities. The level of investment in innovations is a positive and increasing function of the size of the firms. Industrial sectors 5 and 7 differ in investment level from the reference sector 1.

The innovation output equation

The system of innovation output and productivity equations was estimated when productivity is defined in growth rate and based on the value added. The 3SLS estimation results are presented in Table 7.7. Since this step of the estimation is based on only innovative firms which might have different probability of innovative activities compared to non-innovative firms, a selection variable was included to correct for possible sample selection bias. The coefficient of Mill's ratio was found to be insignificant, indicating that selectivity is not a major problem. However, it is quite important that one takes into account selection bias by using the generalized Tobit model in the first step. An insignificant Mill's ratio coefficient should not preclude the first step of the estimation procedure.

The model performance in form measured as R^2 for the innovation output equation is .42. Innovation output depends largely on the innovations input. The estimation results from the innovation output equation indicates that a 1 per cent increase in investment in innovative activities per employee increases the innovation sales by nearly .57 per cent. The feedback effect on innovation output from the productivity growth is positive and statistically highly significant. R&D investment intensity positively affects innovation output. Unlike the sources of product innovation, the sources of process innovation have a positive impact on innovation output. Competitive strategy factors are found to be important for the innovation sales. The level of innovation sales is an increasing function of the size of firms. Surprisingly,

Table 7.7   3SLS estimation of the innovation output and productivity growth equations

Innovation output equation: Robust						
linnovoutput	Coefficient	Standard error	t-ratio	P|t|	[95% confidence interval]	
pgy	2.6549	.9195	2.89	.004	.8501	4.4596
plinnovinput	.5577	.2193	2.54	.011	.1272	.9880
millsrat	−.3203	1.1431	−.28	.779	−2.5640	1.9234
lfouint	.1275	.0507	2.51	.012	.0278	.2271
gemploy	−.0088	.0056	−1.57	.117	−.0198	.0022
outsource2	.0007	.0013	.54	.591	−.0019	.0033
efficiency	−1.4328	.8516	−1.68	.093	−3.1042	.2386
hamper1	−.0307	.0618	−.50	.619	−.1519	.0905
hamper2	.0802	.0515	1.56	.120	−.0209	.1813
sourceprod	.0611	.1054	.58	.562	−.1457	.2679
sourceproc	.1408	.0504	2.79	.005	.0418	.2397
strategy	−.2805	.0968	−2.90	.004	−.4704	−.0904
importance	−.0032	.0585	−.05	.957	−.1180	.1117
location	.0788	.0501	1.57	.116	−.0195	.1772
size2	.3625	.1928	1.88	.060	−.0159	.7408
size3	.9770	.4506	2.17	.030	.0924	1.8614
sni2	−.4534	.1986	−2.28	.023	−.8431	−.0637
sni3	−.2971	.2669	−1.11	.266	−.8209	.2268
sni4	−.0543	.5838	−.09	.926	−1.2001	1.0916
sni5	.8804	.3309	2.66	.008	.2309	1.5298
sni6	.5060	.7554	.67	.503	−.9765	1.9886
sni7	−.3141	.3066	−1.02	.306	−.9157	.2876
constant	6.5162	2.3779	2.74	.006	1.8490	11.1834

Productivity growth equation: Robust						
gy	Coefficient	Standard error	t	Pt	[95% confidence interval]	
plinnovoutput	.1146	.0384	2.99	.003	.0393	.1899
outsource1	−.0013	.0022	−.57	.566	−.0056	.0030
efficiency	.6434	.2375	2.71	.007	.1772	1.1095
lfouint	−.0536	.0115	−4.66	.000	−.0762	−.0309
linvint	.0363	.0132	2.75	.006	.0104	.0622
lcapint	−.0493	.0168	−2.94	.003	−.0821	−.0163
lprofit	.0020	.0124	.16	.875	−.0224	.0263
deratio	.0021	.0008	2.74	.006	.0005	.0035
size2	−.0387	.0490	−.79	.430	−.1348	.0574
size3	−.2918	.1071	−2.73	.007	−.5019	−.0816
sni2	.0407	.0350	1.16	.245	−.0280	.1094
sni3	.0320	.0423	.76	.450	−.0511	.1150
sni4	−.0680	.0809	−.84	.400	−.2267	.0906
sni5	−.2246	.0955	−2.35	.019	−.4120	−.0370
sni6	−.1274	.0930	−1.37	.171	−.3100	.0551
sni7	−.0653	.0823	−.79	.428	−.2268	.0961
constant	−1.3846	.3402	−4.07	.000	−2.0522	−.7169

IV (3SLS) regression with robust standard Errors, No of obs = 871

Innovation output equation			Productivity growth equation		
Chi2	=	673.6500	Chi2		= 307.6800
Prob	=	.0000	Prob		= 0000
R-squared	=	.4239	R-squared		= 2815
Root MSE		= 1.2037	Root	MSE	= .2815

the hampered projects, hampering factors, growth in employment, importance of cooperation and cooperators' location did not turn out to have significant effects on innovation sales. The negative and weakly significant coefficient of efficiency indicates a negative relationship between efficiency in production and innovation sales. Sector 5 is identified as the sector with the highest innovation sales.

The productivity growth equation

The resulting coefficient of determination R^2 is .19. Most of the selected determinants are found to be significantly different from zero. The coefficient of the key variable – predicted innovation output – is positive. The positive and significant coefficients of productivity and innovation output equations indicate the presence of a two-way positive causal relationship between innovation output and productivity growth among the innovative firms and that the two equations must be estimated as a system of equations. Production efficiency, investment intensity and indebtedness increase productivity, while R&D intensity, capital intensity, and size decrease productivity growth. The latter is consistent with empirical evidence regarding the relationship between growth and size (Jovanovic, 1982). As with innovation output, the degree of heterogeneity in productivity growth by industrial sector is much lower compared to the case of innovation input.

Previous empirical results based on CIS data suggest that the results are sensitive with respect to: the measurement of the dependent variables, industrial sector, estimation methods, data sources, sample of firms and degrees of innovation (see Lööf and Heshmati, 2002, 2004). A systematic sensitivity analysis accounting for the above differences is outside the scope of this study. The data with rich information on organization, strategy and innovation activities, together with the use of advanced estimation method accounting for both simultaneity and sample selection bias, are indications of a successful empirical illustration of the relationship between the key variables.

Summary and conclusions

In this chapter we summarized the methods used and empirical results obtained from studies of the link between corporate competitive strategy, efficiency, outsourcing, innovation and productivity growth at the firm level. After identifying the limitations of previously used methods, the new methods were discussed with a view to dealing with the issues of sample selection and simultaneity biases in innovation studies. Finally, a version of the new econometrics method was applied to unique Swedish firm-level data.

The empirical results from estimation of a stochastic frontier production function suggest that such a function is an adequate representation of production relationship. Firms are found to be relatively efficient, although output can be increased by using best-practice technology. Efficiency in production is positively correlated with innovation input, innovation output and productivity growth. Industrial sectors are heterogeneous in efficiency patterns. The return to scale is close to constant returns to scale, indicating, on average, optimal scale in production. There is a positive association between size of firm, profitability, investment, outsourcing and efficiency in production.

Due to the cross-sectional nature of the data and constant returns to scale it was not possible to estimate the rate of technical change and total factor productivity growth. However, simple growth rates in employment, turnover and value added were computed. The growth in employment, turnover and value added differ in levels, and the pattern is heterogeneous by industrial sectors, size of firms and innovativeness. Growth in value added is positively correlated with innovation output, outsourcing, and efficiency in production. The outsourcing share of innovation expenditure is higher than the temporary hired share of labour. The two outsourcing variables differ by size of firm, factor intensity and innovativeness.

It is rather difficult to represent corporate competitiveness strategy in a proper and simple way. The competitive strategy variables have a quite complicated structure, causing a severe multicollinearity problem. A simple composite, competitive strategy index was estimated using principal component analysis and this indicates the level and state of competitiveness among the firms. In addition, we used six other composite indices, including factors hampering innovation, hampered innovation projects, sources of product and process innovations, importance and location of cooperation partners in innovation. A composite index is preferred to sets of dummy variables in regression analysis. However, a single index has the disadvantage of mixing the individual factor effects. The composite indices are used to test their causal relationships with key innovations and growth variables.

We identified a number of determinants of decisions to invest in innovation activities, how much to invest, innovation output and productivity growth. The systems of four equations were estimated in a multi-step estimation procedure, using a combination of generalized Tobit and simultaneous equation systems accounting for both sample selection and simultaneity biases. The results suggest that the approach used is appropriate for such case studies. Internal financial sources, knowledge-intensive production technology and size of firms are major determinants of investment in innovations. Industrial sectors differ in their propensity to invest in innovation. General investment intensity, export share and capital- and knowledge-intensive technologies, and size of firms positively affect the level of investment in innovation.

Variation in innovation output is, to a large extent, explained by variations in innovation input. The feedback effect from productivity growth on innovation output is also found to be positive. R&D intensity, sources of innovation, competitive strategy and the size of firm have positive impacts on innovation output. Production efficiency has a negative but weakly significant effect on innovation output. The interactive positive and significant coefficients of innovation output and productivity equations indicate the presence of a two-way causal relationship between innovation output and productivity growth among innovative firms. Production efficiency, investment intensity and indebtedness increase productivity growth, while R&D intensity, capital intensity and firm size decrease productivity growth. The above results are sensitive, however, to the choice of measures of dependent variables, estimation methods and degree of innovativeness. Despite the limitations of the data, we find the illustration useful in shedding light on the complex relationship between the five key variables.

References

Abraham, K. and Taylor, T. (1996), 'Firms' use of outside contractors: theory and evidence', *Journal of Labor Economics*, vol. 14, pp. 394–424.

Aigner, D., Lovell, C.A.K. and Schmidt, P. (1977), 'Formulation and estimation of stochastic frontier production function models', *Journal of Econometrics*, vol. 6, pp. 21–37.

Anderson, J. and Weitz, B. (1986), 'Make-or-buy decisions: vertical integration and marketing productivity', *Sloan Management Review*, Spring, pp. 3–19.

Anderton, B. and Brenton, P. (1999), 'Outsourcing and low-skilled workers in the UK', *Bulletin of Economic Research*, vol. 51, no. 4, pp. 267–85.

Arnold, U. (2000), 'New dimensions of outsourcing: a combination of transaction cost economics and the core competencies concept', *European Journal of Purchasing & Supply Management*, vol.6, pp. 23–29.

Arranz-Aperte, L. and Heshmati, A. (2004), 'Determinants of profit sharing in the Finnish corporate sector', *Indian Economic Review*, vol. 39, no. 1, pp. 55–79.

Balk, B. (1998), *Industrial Price, Quality, and Productivity Indices. The Micro-Economic Theory and Applications*, Kluwer Academic, Boston, MA.

Baltagi, B.H. and Griffin, J.M. (1988), 'A general index of technical change', *Journal of Political Economy*, vol. 96 no. 1, pp. 20–21.

Baltagi, B.H., Griffin, J.M. and Rich, D.P. (1995), 'The measurement of firm-specific indexes of technical change', *The Review of Economics and Statistics*, vol. LXXVII, pp. 654–63.

Barro, R.J. and Sala-i-Martin, X. (1995), *Economic Growth*, McGraw-Hill Inc., New York.

Barthelemy, J. (2003), 'The hard and soft sides of IT outsourcing management', *European Management Journal*, vol. 21, no. 5, pp. 539–48.

Bartelsman, E.J, and Doms, M. (2000), 'Understanding productivity: lessons from longitudinal microdata', *Journal of Economic Literature*, vol. 38, no. 3, pp. 569–84.

Battese, G.E. and Coelli, T.J. (1995), 'A model for technical inefficiency effects in a stochastic frontier production function for panel data', *Empirical Economics*, vol. 20, pp. 325–32.

Battese, G.E., Heshmati, A. and Hjalmarsson, L. (2000), 'Efficiency of labour use in the Swedish banking industry: a stochastic frontier approach', *Empirical Economics*, vol. 25, pp. 623–40.

Baumol, W.J. (1967), 'Macroeconomics of unbalanced growth: the anatomy of urban crisis', *American Economic Review*, vol. 57, pp. 415–26.

Baumol, W.J., Blackman, A.B. and Wolff, E.N. (1985), 'Unbalanced growth revisited: asymptotic stagnancy and new evidence', *American Economic Review*, vol. 75, pp. 806–17.

Benson, J. (1999), 'Outsourcing, organisational performance and employee commitment', *Economic and Labour Relations Review*, vol. 10, no. 1, pp. 1–21.

Berger, A.N. and Humphrey, D.B. (1997), 'Efficiency of financial institutions: international survey and directions for future research', *European Journal of Operational Research*, vol. 98, pp. 175–212.

Berndt, E.R., Englund, P. and Hjalmarsson, L. (eds) (1992), 'Proceedings of a symposium on productivity concepts and measurement problems: welfare, quality and productivity in the service industries', *The Scandinavian Journal of Economics*, vol. 94, Supplement.

Bjurek, H., Hjalmarsson, L. and Førsund, F.R. (1990), 'Deterministic parametric and nonparametric estimation of efficiency in service production', *Journal of Econometrics*, vol. 46, pp. 213–27.

Bottasso, A. and Sembenelli, A. (2001), 'Does ownership affect firms' efficiency? Panel data evidence on Italy', unpublished manuscript, University of Genova.

Campbell, J.R. (1997), 'Entry, exit, embodied technology, and business cycles', NBER Working Paper, no. 5955.

Caves, R.E. (ed.) (1992), *Industrial Efficiency in Six Nations*, MIT Press, Cambridge, MA.

Caves, R.E. and Barton, D.R. (1990), *Efficiency in U.S. Manufacturing Industries*, MIT Press, Cambridge, MA.

Chalos, P. (1995), 'Costing, control, and strategic analysis in outsourcing decisions', *Journal of Cost Management*, Winter, pp. 31–37.

Chen, Y., Ishikawa, J. and Yu, Z. (2003), 'Trade liberalization and strategic outsourcing', *Journal of International Economics*, vol. 63, no. 2, pp.419–36.

Christensen, L.R., Jorgenson, D.W. and Lau, L.J. (1973), 'Transcendental logarithmic production frontiers', *The Review of Economics and Statistics*, vol. 55, pp. 28–45.

Coelli, T.J., Rao, D.S.P. and Battese, G.E. (1998), *An Introduction to Efficiency and Productivity Analysis*, Kluwer Academic Publishers, Boston, MA.

Cohen, W. and Klepper, S. (1996), 'A reprise of size and R&D', *The Economic Journal*, vol. 106, pp. 925–51.

Cooper, W.W. and Lovell, C.A.K. (2000), 'New approaches to measures of efficiency in DEA: an introduction', *Journal of Productivity Analysis*, vol. 13, no.2, 91–92.

Crépon, B., Duguet, E. and Mairesse, J. (1998), 'Research, innovation, and productivity: an econometric analysis at the firm level', NBER Working Paper, no. 6696.

Deavers, K.L. (1997), 'Outsourcing: a corporate competitiveness strategy, not a search for low wages', *Journal of Labor Research*, vol. 18, no. 4, 503–19.

De Kok, T.G. (2000), 'Capacity allocation and outsourcing in a process industry', *International Journal of Production Economics*, vol. 68, pp. 229–39.

De Melo, P.H., Rocha, F., Ferraz, G., Dweck, R. and Di Sabbato, A. (1999), 'Service sector growth in Brazil', unpublished manuscript, University of Federal Fluminense.

Diewert, W.E. (1981), 'The theory of total factor productivity measurement in regulated industries', in T.G. Cowing and R.E. Stevenson (eds), *Productivity Measurement in Regulated Industries*, Academic Press, New York.

Dritna, R.E. (1994), 'The outsourcing decision', *Management Accounting*, March, pp. 56–62.

Egger, H. and Egger, P. (2001), 'Cross-border sourcing and outward processing in EU manufacturing', *North American Journal of Economics and Finance*, vol. 12, pp. 243–56.

Egger, H. and Falkinger, J. (2003), 'The distributional effects of international outsourcing in a 2x2 production model', *North American Journal of Economics and Finance*, vol. 14, pp. 189–06.

Egger P., Pfaffermayr, M. and Wolfmayr-Schnitzer, Y. (2001), 'The international fragmentation of Austrian manufacturing: the effects of outsourcing on productivity and wages', *North American Journal of Economics and Finance*, vol. 12, pp. 257–72.

Estevão, M. and Lach, L. (1999), 'Measuring temporary labor outsourcing in U.S. manufacturing', NBER Working Paper, no. 7421.

Falk, M. and Koebel, B. (2000), *Outsourcing of Services, Imported Materials, and the Demand for Heterogeneous Labour: An Application of a Generalized Box-Cox Function*, Centre for European Economic Research (ZEW) Discussion Paper no. 2000:51, Mannheim.

Färe, R., Førsund, F.R., Grosskopf, S., Hays, K. and Heshmati, A. (2001), 'A note on decomposing the Malmquist productivity index by means of subvector homotheticity', *Economic Theory*, vol. 17, no. 1, pp. 239–45.

Färe, R., Førsund, F.R., Grosskopf, S., Hays, K. and Heshmati, A., (2006), 'Productivity and quality in Swedish schools', *Quality Assurance in Education*, vol. 14, no 1, pp. 21–36.

Färe, R., Grosskopf, S., Lindgren, B. and Roos, P. (1989), *Productivity Development in Swedish Hospitals: A Malmquist Output Index Approach*, Discussion paper 1989:9, Department of Economics, Southern Illinois University, Carbondale, IL.

Färe, R.. Grosskopf, S. and Roos, P. (1995), 'Productivity and quality changes in Swedish pharmacies', *The International Journal of Production Economics*, vol. 39, pp. 137–44.

Farrell, M.J. (1957), 'The measurement of productive efficiency', *Journal of the Royal Statistical Society*, Series A, vol. 120, pp. 253–90.

Feenstra, R.C. (1998), 'Integration of trade and disintegration of production in the global economy', *Journal of Economic Perspectives*, vol. 12, no. 4, pp. 31–50.

Feenstra, R.C. and Hanson, G.H. (1995), 'Foreign investment, outsourcing and relative wages', NBER Working Paper, no. 5121.

Feenstra, R.C. and Hanson, G.H. (1996), 'Globalization, outsourcing, and wage inequality', *American Economic Review*, vol. 86, no. 2, pp. 240–45.

Feenstra, R.C. and Hanson, G.H. (1999), 'The impact of outsourcing and high-technology capital on wages: estimates for the United States', 1979–1990, *Quarterly Journal of Economics*, vol. 114, no. 3, pp. 907–40.

Fixler, D.J. and Siegel, D. (1999), 'Outsourcing and productivity growth in services', *Structural Change and Economic Dynamics*, vol. 10, pp. 177–94.

Fried, H.O., Lovell, C.A.K. and Schmidt, S.S. (eds) (1993), *The Measurement of Productive Efficiency: Techniques and Applications*, Oxford University Press, Oxford.

Gavious, A. and Rabinowitz, G. (2003), 'Optimal knowledge outsourcing model', *Omega: The International Journal of Management Science*, vol. 31, pp. 451–57.

Gilley, K.M. and Rasheed, A. (2000), 'Making more by doing less: an analysis of outsourcing and its effects on firm performance', *Journal of Management*, vol. 26, no. 4, pp. 763–90.

Gilley, K.M., Greer, C.R. and Rasheed, A.A. (2003), 'Human resource outsourcing and organizational performance in manufacturing firms', *Journal of Business Research*, vol. 57, no. 3, pp. 232–40.

Glass, A.J. and Saggi, K. (2001), 'Innovation and wage effects of international outsourcing', *European Economic Review*, vol. 45, no. 1, pp. 67–86.

Good, D.H., Nadiri, M.I. and Sickles, R.C. (1997), 'Index number and factor demand approaches to the estimation of productivity', in M.H. Pesaran and P. Schmidt (eds), *Handbook of Applied Econometrics. Volume II: Microeconometrics*, Blackwell Publishers, Oxford, pp. 14–80.

Greene, W.H. (1997), 'Frontier production functions', in M.H. Pesaran and P. Schmidt (eds), *Handbook of Applied Econometrics. Volume II: Microeconometrics*, Blackwell Publishers, Oxford, pp. 81–166.

Greene, W.H. (2000), *Econometric Analysis* (4th edn), Prentice Hall International, Inc., New Jersey.

Griliches, Z. (1988), 'Hedonic price indexes and the measurement of capital and productivity: some historical reflections', NBER Working Paper, no. 2634.

Griliches, Z. (1990), 'Patent statistics as economic indicators: a survey', *Journal of Economic Literature*, vol. 28, no.4, pp. 1661–707.

Griliches, Z. (1992), 'Introduction', in Z. Griliches (ed.), *Output Measurement in the Service Sector*, NBER and University of Chicago Press, Chicago, IL, pp. 1–22.

Griliches, Z. (1995), 'R&D and productivity: Econometric results and measurement issues,' in P. Stonemann ed. *Handbook of the Economics of Innovation and Technological Change*, Oxford, UK and Cambridge, MA: Basil Blackwell, pp. 52–89.

Griliches, Z. and Mairesse, J. (1993), 'Introduction', *The Journal of Productivity Analysis*, vol. 4, pp. 5–8.

Grossman, G. and Helpman, E. (2002a), 'Outsourcing in a global economy', NBER Working Paper 2002:8728.

Grossman, G. and Helpman, E. (2002b), 'Outsourcing versus FDI in industry equilibrium', NBER Working Paper 2002:9300.

Hall, B.M. and Mairesse, J. (1995), 'Exploring the relationship between R&D and productivity in French manufacturing firms', *Journal of Econometrics*, vol. 65, pp. 263–93.

Hanushek, E.A. (1986), 'The economics of schooling: production and efficiency in public schools', *Journal of Economic Literature*, vol. 24, pp. 1141–77.

Hanushek, E.A. and Taylor, L.L. (1990), 'Alternative assessments of the performance of schools: measurement of state variations in achievement', *The Journal of Human Resources*, vol. 25, pp. 179–201.

Haskel, J. (1999), 'Small firms, contracting-out, computers and wage inequality: evidence from UK manufacturing', *Economica*, vol. 66, pp. 1–21.

Heshmati, A. (2002a), 'Productivity measurement in Swedish departments of gynecology and obstetrics', *Structural Change and Economic Dynamics*, vol. 13, no. 3, pp. 315–36.

Heshmati, A. (2002b), 'Quality adjusted measures of services in public schools', *European Journal of Operational Research*, vol. 136, no. 3, pp. 655–70.

Heshmati, A. (2003), 'Productivity growth, efficiency and outsourcing in manufacturing and service industries', *Journal of Economic Surveys*, vol. 17, no. 1, pp. 79–112.

Heshmati, A. and Kumbhakar, S.C. (1997), 'Efficiency of the primary and secondary schools in Sweden', *Scandinavian Journal of Educational Research*, vol. 41, no. 1, pp. 33–51.

Heshmati, A. and Nafar, N. (1998), 'A production analysis of the manufacturing industries in Iran', *Technological Forecasting and Social Change*, vol. 59, pp. 183–96.

Hjalmarsson, L., Kumbhakar, S.C. and Heshmati, A. (1996), 'DEA, DFA and SFA: a comparison', *Journal of Productivity Analysis*, vol. 7, nos 2–3, pp. 303–27.

Holmström, B. and Roberts, J. (1998), 'The boundaries of the firm revisited', *Journal of Economic Perspectives*, vol. 12, no. 4, pp. 73–94.

Horrace, W.C. and Schmidt, P. (1996), 'Confidence statements for efficiency estimates from stochastic frontier models', *Journal of Productivity Analysis*, vol. 7, nos 2–3, pp. 257–82.

Howells, J. (1999a), 'Research and technology outsourcing', *Technology Analysis & Strategic Management*, vol. 11, no. 1, pp. 17–29.

Howells, J. (1999b), 'Research and technology outsourcing and innovation systems: an explanatory analysis', *Industry and Innovation*, vol. 6, no. 1, pp. 111–29.

Hulten, C.R. (2000), 'Total factor productivity: a short bibliography', NBER Working Paper, no. 7471.

Inman, R.P. (1985), 'Introduction and overview', in R.P. Inman (ed.), *Managing the Service Economy: Prospects and Problems*, Cambridge University Press, Cambridge, pp. 1–24.

Jacobson, L., Lalonde, R. and Sullivan, D. (1993), 'Earnings losses of displaced workers', *American Economic Review*, vol. 83, no. 3, pp. 685–709.

Jondrow, J., Lovell, C.A.K., Materov, I.S. and Schmidt, P. (1982), 'On the estimation of technical inefficiency in the stochastic frontier production function model', *Journal of Econometrics*, vol. 19, pp. 233–38.

Jones, R.W. and Kierzkowski, H. (2000), *A Framework for Fragmentation*, Tinbergen Institute Discussion Paper TI 2000-056/2.

Jovanovic, B. (1982), 'Selection and the evolution of industry', *Econometrica*, vol. 50, no. 3, pp. 649–70.

Kakabadse, A. and Kakabadse, N. (2002), 'Trends in outsourcing: contrasting USA and Europe', *European Management Journal*, vol. 20, no. 2, pp. 189–98.

Kalirajan, K.P. and Shand, R.T. (1999), 'Frontier production functions and technical efficiency measures', *Journal of Economic Surveys*, vol. 13, no. 2, pp. 149–72.

Kendrick, J.W. (1961), *Productivity Trends in the United States*, Princeton University Press, Princeton, NJ.

Klette, J. and Kortum, S. (2001), 'Innovating firms: evidence and theory', Working Paper presented at a workshop on Innovation, Technological Change and Growth in Knowledge Based and Service Intensive Economies, Stockholm, December.

Kotabe, M. (1992), *Global Sourcing Strategy: R&D, Manufacturing, and Marketing Interfaces*, Quorum, New York.

Kumbhakar, S.C. and Hjalmarsson, L. (1995), 'Labour-use efficiency in Swedish social insurance offices', *Journal of Applied Econometrics*, vol. 10, pp. 33–47.

Kumbhakar, S.C. and Hjalmarsson, L. (1998), 'Relative performance of public and private ownership under yardstick competition: electricity retail distribution', *European Economic Review*, vol. 42, pp. 97–122.

Kumbhakar, S.C. and Heshmati, A. (1996), 'Technical change and total factor productivity growth in Swedish manufacturing industries', *Econometric Reviews*, vol. 15, no. 3, pp. 275–98.

Kumbhakar, S.C. and Lovell, C.A.K. (2000), *Stochastic Frontier Analysis*, Cambridge University Press, Cambridge.

Kumbhakar, S.C., Heshmati, A. and Hjalmarsson, L. (1999), 'Parametric approaches to productivity measurement: a comparison among alternative models', *Scandinavian Journal of Economics*, vol. 101, no. 3, pp. 405–24.

Kumbhakar, S.C., Heshmati, A. and Hjalmarsson, L. (2002), 'How fast do banks adjust? A dynamic model of labor-use with an application to Swedish banks', *Journal of Productivity Analysis*, vol. 18, no. 1, pp. 79–102.

Kumbhakar, S.C., Nakamura, S. and Heshmati, A, (2000), 'Estimation of firm-specific technological bias, technical change and total factor productivity growth: a dual approach', *Econometric Reviews*, vol. 19, no. 4, pp. 493–515.

Lacity, M.C., Willcocks, L.P. and Feeny, D.F. (1996), 'The value of selective IT outsourcing', *Sloan Management Review*, Spring, pp. 13–25.

Lei, D. and Hitt, M. (1995), 'Strategic restructuring and outsourcing: the effect of mergers and acquisitions and LBOs on building firm skills and capabilities', *Journal of Management*, vol. 21, no. 5, pp. 835–59.

Loh, L. and Venkatraman, N. (1992), 'Determinants of information technology outsourcing: a cross-sectional analysis', *Journal of Management Information Systems*, vol. 9, no. 1, pp. 7–24.

Lööf, H. and Heshmati, A. (2002), 'Knowledge capital and performance heterogeneity: a firm-level innovation study', *International Journal of Production Economics*, vol. 76, no. 1, pp. 61–85.

Lööf, H. and Heshmati, A. (2004), 'On the relationship between innovation and performance: a sensitivity analysis', *Economics of Innovation and New Technology*, vol. 15, nos 4–5, pp. 317–44.

Mairesse, J. and Kremp, E. (1993), 'A look at productivity at the firm level in eight French service industries', *The Journal of Productivity Analysis*, vol. 4, pp. 211–34.

Mairesse, J. and Sessanou, M. (1991), 'R&D and productivity: a survey of econometric studies at the firm level', *Science-Technology, Industry Review*, vol. 8, OECD, Paris, pp. 9–43,.

Mulder, N. (1999), 'The economic performance of the service sector in Brazil, Mexico and the USA', unpublished manuscript, Centre for International Economics, French Planning Agency (CEPII).

Nadiri, M.I. and Prucha, I.R. (1999), 'Dynamic factor demand models and productivity analysis', NBER Working Paper, no. 7079.

Nayyar, P.R. (1993), 'On the measurement of competitive strategy: evidence from a large multiproduct U.S. firm', Academy *of Management Journal*, vol. 36, pp. 1652–669.

Newhouse, J. (1994), 'Frontier estimation: how useful a tool for health economics?', *Journal of Health Economics*, vol. 13, pp. 317–22.

Nordhaus, W.D. (2001), 'Alternative methods for measuring productivity growth', NBER Working Paper, no. 8095.

OECD/Eurostat (1997), *Oslo Manual: Proposed Guidelines for Collecting and Interpreting Technological Innovation Data*, OECD/Eurostat, Paris.

Pakes, A. and Griliches, Z. (1984), 'Patents and the R&D at the firm level: a first look', in Z. Griliches (ed.), *R&D, Patents and Productivity*, Chicago University Press, Chicago, pp. 390–409.

Perry, C.R. (1997), 'Outsourcing and union power', *Journal of Labor Research*, vol. 18, no. 4, pp. 521–34.

Porter, M.E. (1980), *Competitive Strategy*, Free Press, New York.

Quelin, B. and Duhamel, F. (2003), 'Bringing together strategic outsourcing and corporate strategy: outsourcing motives and risks', *European Management Journal*, vol. 21, no. 5, pp. 647–61.

Roodhooft, F. and Warlop, L. (1999), 'On the role of sunk costs and asset specificity in outsourcing decisions: a research note', *Accounting, Organization and Society*, vol. 24, pp. 363–69.

Rosko, M.D. (2001), 'Cost efficiency of US hospitals: a stochastic frontier approach', *Health Economics*, vol. 10, no. 6, pp. 539–51.

SAS Institute (1993), *SAS/STAT User's Guide*, SAS Institute Inc., Cary, NC.

Schmidt, P. (1986), 'Frontier production functions, including comments', *Econometric Reviews*, vol. 4, no. 2, pp. 289–355.

Sharpe, M. (1997), 'Outsourcing, organizational competitiveness, and work', *Journal of Labor Research*, vol. 18, no. 4, pp. 535–549.

Shy, O. and Stenbacka, R. (2003), 'Strategic outsourcing', *Journal of Economic Behavior & Organization*, vol. 50, pp. 203–24.

Siegel, D and Griliches, Z. (1992), 'Purchased services, outsourcing, computers, and productivity in manufacturing', in Z. Griliches (ed.), *Output Measurement in Service Sector*, University of Chicago Press, Chicago, IL, pp. 429–58.

Solow, R.M. (1956), 'A contribution to the theory of economic growth', *Quarterly Journal of Economics*, vol. 70, no. 1, pp. 65–94.

Solow, R.M. (1957), 'Technical change and the aggregate production function', *Review of Economics and Statistics*, vol. 39, pp. 312–20.

Solow, R.M. (1992), 'Introduction', *The Scandinavian Journal of Economics*, vol. 94, Supplement, pp. 5–7.

Suarez-Villa, L. (1998), 'The structure of cooperation: downscaling, outsourcing and the networked alliance', *Small Business Economics*, vol. 10, no. 1, pp. 5–16.

Ten Raa, T. and Wolff, E.N. (1996), *Outsourcing of Services and the Productivity Recovery in US Manufacturing in the 1980s*, Center for Economic Research Discussion Paper, Tilburg University, September.

Tinbergen, J. (1942), 'Zur Theorie der langfristigen Wirtschaftsentwicklung', *Weltwirtschaftliches Archiv*, vol. 55, pp. 511–49.Triplett, J. and Bosworth, B. (1999), 'Productivity in the service sector', unpublished manuscript.

Ulset, S. (1996), 'R&D outsourcing and contractual governance: an empirical study of commercial R&D projects', *Journal of Economic Behavior & Organization*, vol. 30, no. 1, pp. 63–82.

Verbeck, M. (2000), *A Guide to Modern Econometrics*, John Wiley & Sons Ltd, Chichester.

Williamson, O.E. (1989), 'Transaction cost economics', in R. Schmalensee and R.D. Willig (eds), *Handbook of Industrial Organization*, vol. 1, Elsevier, Amsterdam, pp. 136–81.

Young, S. and Macneil, J. (2000), 'When performance fails to meet expectations: managers' objectives for outsourcing', *Economic and Labour Relations Review*, vol. 11, no. 1, pp. 136–68.

Zuckerman, S., Hadley, J. and Iezzoni, L. (1994), 'Measuring hospital efficiency with frontier cost functions', *Journal of Health Economics*, vol. 13, pp. 255–80.

8 Outsourcing: The Employee Perspective
Mike Dodsworth and Mike Constable

When the outsourcing decision is made, most of the attention focuses on the cost savings it promises and the efficiency it will create – from the corporate vantage point. Looking from another angle, we have investigated outsourcing from the employee's point of view, exploring the issues that surface when the outsourcing decision goes into effect. For example, what potential change scenarios do employees face, and what impact do these have on them? What regulatory protection do affected employees have? How can companies ensure employees remain committed and productive during the transition process?

In addition, results from a Capgemini survey of cross-industry employee attitudes towards outsourcing reveal some interesting insights into employee perceptions. Over 200 supervisors and junior managers from UK companies were interviewed to gain their perspectives on outsourcing and being outsourced. The survey was designed to identify employees' concerns and questions about the outsourcing process. For instance, how aware of outsourcing and its nuances is the typical employee? What perceptions of upsides and downsides do employees share? What level of knowledge do they have about their rights in the outsourcing situation? What key questions should they be asking when the outsourcing decision is made?

We believe that answers to these questions and others like them will help employers and employees alike understand and respond more effectively when the outsourcing decision is made. We start with an overview of four scenarios to which employees may be subjected during an outsourcing process.

Four scenarios

As Figure 8.1 illustrates, when a company decides to outsource an employee's function (information technology (IT), for example), that company's employees usually face one of four scenarios based on the role they are expected to play, and whether or not they must transfer employment to the outsourcer. Each of these scenarios is described below.

SCENARIO 1: EMPLOYEES ARE RETRAINED AND ASSIGNED OTHER ROLES IN THE CURRENT COMPANY.

Full-time employees suffer minimal disruption in this case, because they retain their current terms, conditions, and culture, and develop new skills through retraining (temporary contracts, however, are usually terminated). This option is feasible when the number of affected employees is small, but for a larger group, which is more often the case, it is not a practical solution for most companies. Where employees are retained, it is most likely that their skills

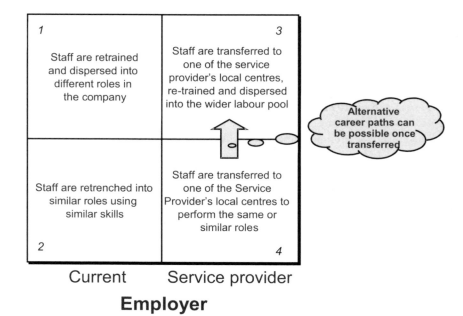

Figure 8.1 Four employee outsourcing scenarios

are not specific to the department being outsourced. Certain groups – secretarial assistants – can easily transfer their skills to another part of the client organization.

SCENARIO 2: EMPLOYEES ARE MOVED TO OTHER AREAS IN THE CURRENT COMPANY REQUIRING THEIR CURRENT SKILLS.

Employees obviously face the least disruption in this scenario, but it is an unlikely one. When a function is outsourced, demand for similar skills elsewhere in the company is usually not high. Many employers do, however, try to retain critical organizational knowledge and skills by selecting a few candidates for this outcome. Staff with critical organizational knowledge and skills, such as business analysts, are often retained by the client organization to keep the strategic direction of the function close to the business, and also to manage the contract. In the case of an IT outsource, keeping key staff who use the same business language as the users of the system helps translate business requirements into technical specifications.

SCENARIO 3: EMPLOYEES ARE TRANSFERRED TO THE OUTSOURCER, RETRAINED, AND MOVED INTO OTHER PARTS OF THE BUSINESS.

This is a disruptive scenario for employees. It is rarely seen, and few outsourcers can manage a large influx of personnel who must be retrained for other tasks. It is most likely to be adopted where service improvements are achieved through consolidation and economies of scale, and the valuable specialist skills that are no longer required are transferred to another part of the outsourcer, to the benefit of other clients.

It can be argued also that the Transfer of Undertakings (Protection of Employment) Regulations 1981 (TUPE) should not apply in this case – after all, two of the legal justifications for TUPE to apply are where the current role continues unchanged after the transfer and the knowledge and skills of the individuals transferred represent intangible assets. In the case of a transformational outsource, where the current service will ultimately be replaced by a new service, then this scenario can occur, with retraining staggered over a period of time.

When this scenario does occur in the UK, the transferred employees retain their current employment contracts under TUPE (see Figure 8.2). Depending on the outsourcer's site locations, employees may have to relocate, but the disruption and cost associated with moving home means that this rarely happens. The vast majority of transfers involve a change of work location, and the home-to-office journey time then becomes the cause of concern. On the upside, employees remain employed and have the opportunity to learn new skills and be exposed to a broader range of career choices.

Success here depends on matching human resources (HR) grades between the two companies. Where employees are accurately graded, their transition is easier emotionally, and they will be better positioned to contribute to the outsourcer's business. As no two companies have matching structures and the associated competencies can be significantly different, the most effective solution is often to leave staff 'ungraded' in the early days post-transfer. This 'parks' the issue while the outsourcer sees what their new staff can do in practice and how they adjust before correctly grading them.

SCENARIO 4: EMPLOYEES ARE TRANSFERRED TO THE OUTSOURCER TO PERFORM THE SAME OR SIMILAR ROLE.

Less disruptive than the previous alternative, this is the most typical scenario for outsourcing agreements and is the focus of this chapter. Employees are transferred into the service provider's company under protected transfer, and retain their employment status, terms and conditions. They simply continue their employment contracts with the outsourcer from the point of transfer, although there may have to be changes for things that cannot be replicated by the new employer.

Much depends on the outsourcer's location and how it delivers its service. To succeed with this approach, outsourcers must be offering service delivery within the transferring employees'

Protection of employee rights – TUPE

The UK Transfer of Undertakings (Protection of Employment) Regulations 1981 (TUPE) were originally introduced to implement the EC Acquired Rights Directive, adopted in 1977. Designed to protect both the employer and employee during business transfers, it provides a legal framework to ensure that both parties are treated and act fairly.

For an employee who transfers to a new employer, TUPE protects the employee's employment contract. The employee transfers on the same terms and conditions that existed prior to the transfer, including such elements as pay and annual leave. It also ensures that the employee's service with the former employer is fully recognized. Any collective agreements made by a recognized union on behalf of the employee remain intact also.

For the employer, this forms a set of rules for employee transfer. However, it does not bypass the need to negotiate staff terms and conditions with the outsourcer, or the possibility of recrimination from transferred employees.

The primary exclusions from TUPE protection are terms that relate to an occupational pension scheme. A recognized union or workers council negotiates these terms.

Figure 8.2 Overview of the protection of employee rights – TUPE

commuting range. The real problems arise when the outsourcer needs the transferred employees to commute a long way or has a very different corporate culture.

On the plus side, outsourcing companies usually deliver their services to several client companies over a wide area, and transferred employees join a diverse labour pool where their skills and experience can be used effectively by their new employer – initially delivering a managed service to their previous employer. In many cases, employees who transfer find themselves in a more advantageous position than they enjoyed at their previous firm. In our survey, 51 per cent of the respondents thought that outsourcing would increase their career opportunities. Success stories abound of transferred people developing excellent careers in their new surroundings. The outsourcer, by the nature of its business, has a high proportion of staff who have joined them through TUPE, and who are well represented at senior management level.

A STRESSFUL EXPERIENCE

Whatever outsourcing scenario plays out, employees obviously face a period of uncertainty about their future. Trade unions have highlighted employee anxiety and resistance during periods of change. Particularly when employees feel the threat of redundancy, or are asked to change employers or relocate their homes, management should expect them to have anxious moments.

Nearly 70 per cent of our survey respondents cited job security as their primary concern during the outsourcing process. With this in mind, effectively managed outsourcing projects ensure that affected employees are not kept guessing, but instead are informed regularly through a well-planned programme of information-sharing – even bad news is better than uncertainty!

The timing, and type of communication, must be consistent with the decision-making process and corporate culture. When organizations are evaluating outsourcing options, but have not yet made a commitment, they risk unsettling their staff by sharing their thoughts too early. Once the strategic decision to outsource has been taken, many companies make an initial announcement, coupled with advice about employment protection legislation. One resource that is available for employees is the Transfer of Undertakings (Protection of Employment) Regulations 1981 (TUPE), which are designed to safeguard employment.[1] See Figure 8.2 for an overview.

If staff are likely to find out about the deal – perhaps the contract is going through a public sector procurement process – the decision to communicate is likely to be taken earlier than for companies which decide that, until the contract is signed, it is not a done deal, and therefore too early to let their staff know.

REDUNDANCY

Redundancy is the worst-case outcome for both employer and employee. Employers and suppliers are required to use economic, technical or organizational reasons to justify headcount reductions as part of an outsource – redundancies resulting simply from outsourcing are not allowed under TUPE. From an economic perspective, furthermore, upfront redundancy costs can scuttle the early cost savings that outsourcing promises.

In the UK both full-time and fixed-term contract staff made redundant are protected by TUPE, which provides the legal framework that ensures redundancies are performed fairly. Employees must be given due notice to prepare, and unions and workers' councils must be consulted as necessary to negotiate exit terms and packages. In our survey, however, fewer than

---

1   For further information about TUPE, visit www.businesslink.gov.uk.

30 per cent said they would seek trade union advice in the outsourcing situation, primarily because, once staff understand their legal status, they have confidence that TUPE protects their rights. Instead of turning to trade unions, transferring staff list such alternatives as 'my boss', 'a solicitor', and 'the new employer'.

IMPLICATIONS FOR DIFFERENT EMPLOYEE TYPES

Employees within any one organization can include full-time staff, fixed-term contractors, and various types of temporary contractor. In business transfers, fixed-term contractors and permanent employees are eligible for transfer under protected employment. Although TUPE protects their employment status, terms and conditions, it does not cover pensions.

The results from our survey revealed that 44 per cent of respondents had not heard of TUPE and had no idea what their rights were in an outsourcing situation. However, 52 per cent of the private-sector respondents were aware that being outsourced would affect their pensions.

Temporary contractors are not protected in transfers unless specified in their contracts. Most transfer situations involve some contract staff, and many service providers renew temporary contracts for a set period to avoid losing key knowledge and to ensure uninterrupted service levels. At the end of this period, they are offered either a contract renewal or a permanent position. Otherwise, their contracts are terminated in accordance with their specific contract terms.

Employee transfers: best practice

Outsourcers with a good track record of retaining staff who transfer design programmes to ensure that the process of moving staff into their company is rational, legal and fair; they recognize that maintaining employee morale and motivation is essential to their enterprises' success in the marketplace. Because employees feel vulnerable, these comprehensive communication and involvement programmes ensure that employees feel they are part of the transition process and are receiving active management support. More than 75 per cent of respondents to our survey said that they wanted to discuss the possible impact of a planned outsourcing with their employer.

Communications programmes provide the information, personal contact and reassurance employees need to minimize anxiety and preserve service levels during the change process. Figure 8.3 illustrates a programme designed to engage employees throughout the transition. At critical times, it offers regular, unambiguous and informative information. Both group and one-on-one meetings provide safeguard against anxiety, low morale and resignations.

These programmes aim to prevent disruption by reassuring employees, updating them continuously on progress, involving them and their representatives in the process, answering questions and seeking feedback. Providing clear information on individual employment rights, the transfer process, the new employer's policies, and the way ahead for the transferring employees is the best way of ensuring that employees remain motivated during the transition process.

KEY MESSAGES

Key messages that must be delivered to employees include:

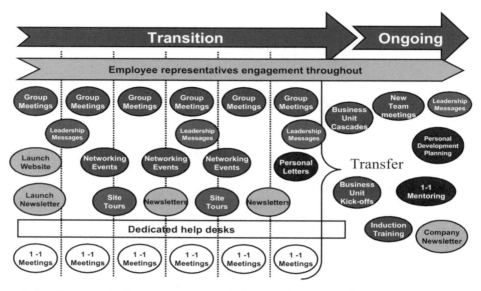

Figure 8.3 Communication programmes during employee transfer

- *Information about the outsourcer:* Background information is provided in phases during the pre-transfer transition to explain the position of the transferred employees in the new company, career and training opportunities, and effects on terms and conditions, including pensions and any relocation necessary.
- *Information about the transfer:* This includes the scope of the business transfer, how the transfer will work and when it will begin, what the service from the outsourcer involves, and addresses such questions as 'Is it the same as what we were delivering?' and 'Will it evolve?'.
- The current employer and outsourcer need also to take affirmative action in participative activities that give employees the information that they need in order to remain calm and confident – for example:
  - *Meetings*: one-on-one meetings, personal development planning, one-on-one mentoring
  - *Events*: networking events and roadshows, induction training, site tours of the outsourcing provider's premises
  - *Reference Information* newsletters and websites.

Presentations delivered at various employee sites – often called roadshows – are a good way of introducing the new company to transferring employees. The transfer process can be explained carefully and demystified. Knowing what lies ahead helps employees cope with the inevitable stress of change. This is helped by a transition period – the time between announcement of transfer and transfer itself – which is not unduly drawn out. Allowing for a three-month transition in the final contract negotiations helps contain the feelings of uncertainty, which begin to resurface over a longer period.

As we found in our survey, respondents see the availability of one-to-one discussions with management of the incoming employer as essential. Aside from making transferring employees comfortable with the changes, it also gives the transition team the opportunity to identify and understand the local issues important to employees, seek their views on the way forward, and establish individual employees' aspirations and career aims with their new employer.

Given our survey finding that few understand the ramifications of a transfer on their pensions, seminars explaining available pension options will help employees feel more reassured. Visits to the new employer's premises to sample daily working life and meet new colleagues, many of whom will have been through the TUPE process themselves, is also valuable for creating a more positive environment. In addition, arranging formal consultations with employee representatives, including trade unions, will smooth the transition and reassure all involved that the transfer is a positive step.

Review and summary: answering six key questions

Most of the respondents we surveyed were aware of outsourcing, and many had even experienced it directly in the past. Yet nearly one-quarter had little knowledge of the concept or its ramifications. In any case, stress is inevitable during periods of change, and the best defence lies in solid information about what is going to happen, when, and with what personal impact on the individual employee.

We found, however, that affected employees often did not know what questions to ask. As a brief guide to help employees understand how an outsourcing transfer will affect them personally, and also by way of review, we have developed the following six key questions and answers.

1. *What will happen to my terms and conditions?* Under protected transfer (TUPE), terms and conditions will remain the same or equivalent with the new employer. If something cannot be replicated, it will be bought out. Whilst not specifically required by the legislation, the ongoing package is required to be broadly comparable in value. Where terms and conditions do change with the new employer, it usually occurs after a period of time with an *offer* to change to the outsourcers' own standard terms and conditions, and such offers are not enforced against individuals' wishes. Pensions are not protected under TUPE and are therefore something that workers' councils or unions may negotiate on behalf of employees. This is often a contentious area, and proposed changes to the TUPE regulations will mean that enhanced protection will be available once the new legislation is introduced.

2. *What support networks are available for people who join the company through the outsourcing route?* The best outsourcing companies, who have lengthy experience and below-average staff attrition rates, have well-established support networks and professional human resources teams that induct and manage new employees into the company. The communications and involvement processes used during transition ensure that all transferees are fully informed and have the opportunity to express concerns both during and after transfer.

3. *What career opportunities will be open to me?* Outsourcing organizations typically offer career and skill development programmes, as well as individual career counselling. Many transferred employees find that their career opportunities increase significantly after transfer.

4. *What learning and development opportunities will be on offer to me?* To grow, outsourcing businesses need to add a continuous stream of new skills, knowledge, and experience. Most are committed to comprehensive employee development programmes, and set aside several training days each year for each employee's personal and professional development.

5. *How will the transfer happen?* It is usually a staged process. First, employees receive both group and one-on-one information about the reasons for the outsource, the outsourcing company, and what it means for employees. This reassures the employees about their future and protects also morale and productivity.

   Next, employees visit their future office, meet future colleagues, get to know their new employer, and get an introduction to their new working environment. Then the physical move takes place. This is sometimes phased in a few employees at a time prior to the transfer deadline to ensure smooth, uninterrupted service.

6. *Are there any differences in the way you treat people who join the company as a result of an outsourcing deal?* Leading outsourcing companies do not distinguish between existing employees and those being transferred. It is in their best interest to create open and collaborative environments that promote well-motivated and highly productive staff. They regularly survey their employees to measure staff satisfaction, and publish open action plans.

Summary

Implementing an effective outsourcing solution is not easy. Employees will inevitably feel anxious and threatened by the changes it implies. Yet when handled properly – by demystifying the process through clearly articulated information all along the way – a well-executed outsourcing effort can pay dividends both to the companies involved and to the employees transferred to their new place of work.

Appendix: outsourcing attitude survey

In April 2003, Capgemini commissioned a cross-industry survey of 212 UK-based employees, seeking their perceptions of outsourcing and being outsourced. It was designed to identify employees' concerns and questions about the outsourcing process.

KEY FINDINGS

- Awareness of the outsourcing concept is high; employees understand its main benefits for the organization and why it is an option employers often choose.
- Most respondents appreciate the potential benefits of outsourcing for themselves personally, with factors such as better career opportunities, higher pay, better working conditions, better training and development facilities, and an enhanced CV being frequently cited.
- Most respondents perceive a potential downside to outsourcing in terms of reduced job and pension security, increased workload and stress, and a change of employment location.
- Respondents had a limited understanding of their legal rights when faced with the prospect of being outsourced, and many were unsure about where to look for information and advice.

The above conclusions emerged from the following quantitative findings.

Awareness

- About 74 per cent of respondents (rising to 76 per cent for those in the public sector) were aware of the concept of outsourcing.
- 27 per cent of respondents in the private sector had personal experience of outsourcing, but this figure is much higher for certain sectors, for example:
  - professional services: 47 per cent
  - financial services: 43 per cent
  - IT/telecoms: 40 per cent.

Perceived benefits

- 51 per cent felt that outsourcing would improve their career opportunities.
- 43 per cent of private-sector respondents viewed outsourcing as a chance to work alongside recognized experts in a leading company.
- 35 per cent of public-sector respondents viewed higher pay as a significant transfer benefit, and 56 per cent said that it would enhance their CVs.

Perceived downside

- Over 67 per cent of respondents in the private sector believed that outsourcing would reduce their job security.
- 52 per cent of private-sector respondents said that being outsourced would lead to a loss of pension rights.
- More than a third of total respondents thought that their workload would increase, and 39 per cent believed that outsourcing would create increased stress in their workplace.

Miscellaneous

- More than 44 per cent of respondents had never heard of TUPE (Transfer of Undertakings, (Protection of Employment) Regulations) and had no idea of their legal rights in relation to outsourcing.
- Fewer than 30 per cent said they would seek trade union advice if faced with being outsourced.
- Nearly half the respondents disagreed with the idea that trade unions should oppose all outsourcing deals on principle.
- Over 75 per cent of private-sector employees and over 80 per cent of public-sector employees said that they wanted to discuss the possible impacts of planned outsourcing directly with their current employer.

9 *Outsourcing for a Competitive Advantage: The Human Resource Dimensions*

John Benson

Firms are faced with a number of strategic choices. One of the key decisions is whether required components or services are best developed internally or purchased from the market. This 'make or buy decision' (Miles and Snow, 1984) has been used to evaluate the relative efficiency of internal and external production, and more recently to consider whether the firm should train and develop its staff or gain the required skills from the external labour market. When firms decide to buy in the required skills they are faced with a further choice: to gain the required skills directly from the external labour market or to outsource that activity to market-based agents.

Although the management literature portrays outsourcing as a recent development, it is not new, for firms have been outsourcing some of their activities, under a variety of labels, since the early 1900s (Cappelli, 1995; Chandler, 1964; Quinlan, 1998). These activities were not generally, however, part of the firm's core competencies and usually made a low contribution to the value chain. Core competencies were not usually outsourced because delegating such activities to an outside party was seen as a threat to the firm's competitive advantage (Bettis, Bradley and Hamel, 1992). The success of many Japanese manufacturing companies has, however, demonstrated that a competitive advantage can be achieved through strategic outsourcing arrangements (Nishiguchi, 1994). Moreover, these firms have outsourced some of the traditionally perceived core competencies, such as product design, software development and distribution.

Western firms are increasingly recognizing that their current organizational arrangements of vertical integration may no longer be suitable for their key competencies (Goldman, Nagel and Preiss, 1995). Significant advantages, such as lower costs, faster product development and improved quality can result from market-based relationships (Stalk, 1988). This has led to an increasing number of firms using market or quasi-market arrangements to develop core competencies and capabilities (Priore and Sabel, 1984; Miles and Snow, 1992). As a consequence, what may have been once considered as core competencies with higher value are now being outsourced. Management, it appears, are taking a more strategic approach to outsourcing, and this may explain why surveys have found that outsourcing has become an area of key interest to senior management (Grindley, 1994).

Despite these developments, Bettis *et al.*, (1992, p. 7) warned that 'a whole series of incremental outsourcing decisions, taken individually, may make economic sense, but collectively they may represent also the surrender of the business's capability to compete'. Moreover, little attention has been paid to the human resource dimensions of outsourcing. The search for efficiency and flexibility in the pursuit of improved competitiveness may leave employees disaffected and contract workers uncommitted. These are important issues as disaffected and uncommitted workers have been shown to have higher absenteeism (Angle and Perry, 1981; Sagie, 1998), higher turnover (Jaros, 1997; Michaels and Spector, 1982; Muller and Price, 1990; Porter *et al.*, 1974; Williams and Hazer, 1986), lower motivation and involvement (Farrell and Rusbult, 1981; Somech and Bogler, 2002; Stumpf and Hartman, 1984), poorer job performance (Angle and Perry, 1981; Mowday *et al.*, 1979; Steers, 1977), lower acceptance of change (Brewer and Hensher, 1998; Iverson, 1996), reduced organizational citizen behaviour (Mathieu and Zajac, 1990; Schappe, 1998), and lower corporate ethical values (Valentine, Godkin and Lucero, 2002). It is these human resource issues that are the focus of this chapter. Drawing on research that I have conducted over the past ten years, the chapter will explore the impact of outsourcing on labour flexibility, productivity and employee commitment. The chapter begins with a discussion of the reasons why firms outsource.

The outsourcing decision

In deciding what to outsource, firms could utilize a number of theoretical approaches. The first of these is transaction cost economics where market transactions and internal production are seen as distinct alternatives, and which allows a comparative measure of efficiency to be generated. A second approach is human capital theory, which suggests that enterprises should only develop their human resources when the investment in training can be recouped by improved productivity. A third approach is what has been termed the resource-based view of the enterprise where it is argued that core competencies or unique attributes should be developed internally while all other activities should be outsourced.

Lepak and Snell (1999) argued that the common theme across these three approaches is the value attached to human resources, and the uniqueness of those resources. Using these two dimensions they developed a fourfold typology of employment strategies. For unique and valuable skills the appropriate strategy is internal development. This would involve extensive skill-building and training programmes. In contrast, common and low-value skills are most appropriately gained through the contracting-out process. High–value, but not unique, human resources can be obtained through recruitment, while unique but low-value human resources can be best obtained through some form of alliance.

Outsourcing is thus seen as the most appropriate strategy, either directly or through alliances, where low-value skills are involved. In contrast, high-value skills are best seen as being achieved through recruitment or development. Such strategies, however, neglect the context in which any resourcing decision is made. The recruitment and development of human resources rests on a long-term strategy, which in many firms may be unrealistic due to product life cycle or the lack of appropriate staff who can provide the necessary training. As a consequence, it may be necessary, or more appropriate and cost-effective, to buy in these resources. In these cases firms can gain the advantages of scale efficiencies as well as being able to access the latest technology and knowledge.

For many firms, however, reducing costs appears to be the driving force for outsourcing (McCune, 1993; Plunkett, 1991; Rees and Fielder, 1992; Sharpe, 1997; Tully, 1993). For example, Plunkett (1991, p. 8) reported that outsourcing is usually implemented to save money rather than forming part of any coherent strategy, while Strassman (1995, p. 2) concluded that, for most companies, 'strategy is not driving outsourcing' but rather 'they're in financial trouble'. Notwithstanding, cost minimization may represent a strategic approach to management if the activities outsourced require only low-value skills as this 'frees companies to direct scarce capital to where they hold a competitive advantage' (Tully, 1993, p. 52). If, however, high-value skills are outsourced then, in the long term, this may lead to a loss of core competencies and may contribute 'little to building the people-embodied skills that are necessary to sustain product leadership' (Prahalad and Hamel, 1990, p. 84). In either case, the effectiveness of the outsourcing strategy may be severely reduced if it results in lower employee morale and commitment, and resistance to change.

To test the above arguments, data from a number of studies will be evaluated (Benson and Ieronimo, 1996; Benson, 1998; Benson and Littler, 2002). These studies will be referred to as S1, S2 and S3. The first of these studies (S1) involved detailed case studies of four Australian manufacturing companies that had outsourced their maintenance activities (Benson and Ieronimo, 1996). The four companies were involved in tobacco (Tabac-Co), dairy products (Food-Co), paper products (Paper-Co) and brewing (Beer-Co). Employee numbers were 1800, 304, 323, and 417 respectively and, prior to outsourcing, all the companies had three maintenance unions on site, with the exception of Tabac-Co where six unions were present. Maintenance work was examined as it requires high skill levels and is a key link between technology and production. In all the companies the decision to outsource was underpinned by multiple reasons (see Table 9.1). All four companies wanted to reduce labour costs, and three of the four companies wanted to increase labour flexibility and to improve industrial relations. In this latter case this was hoped to be achieved by a reduction in demarcation disputes over who should do what work and a relaxation of restrictions on hours of work, overtime availability and the tasks undertaken. Only in one case did outsourcing represent a long-term strategic approach by focusing on core competencies.

The findings of the four case studies were confirmed in a survey of 26 Australian manufacturing companies (S2) [1] (see Benson and Ieronimo, 1996). Fifteen companies (57.7 per cent) had outsourced maintenance work. The reasons why these companies had outsourced this activity are given in Table 9.2. The most common reason cited was to improve maintenance service. Yet, while a poor maintenance service may reflect the ethos and composition of the particular group of workers, it may also indicate poor management practices, inadequate supervision and insufficient training. In this latter case, outsourcing will have little impact on

Table 9.1   Reasons for outsourcing maintenance work (S1: case studies)

	Tabac-Co	**Food-Co**	**Paper-Co**	**Beer-Co**
Reason	**Involvement of companies**			
Concentrate on core activities	✓			
Labour flexibility	✓		✓	✓
Reduce operating costs	✓	✓	✓	✓
Improve labour productivity		✓		
Improve industrial relations		✓	✓	✓

Source: Benson and Ieronimo (1996, p. 67).

---

1   Eighty-five manufacturing companies were surveyed in 1994. Twenty-six companies responded for a response rate of 31 per cent. These companies employed an average of 2200 employees and most had annual sales exceeding $200 million.

Table 9.2 Reasons for outsourcing maintenance work (S2: Survey of manufacturing companies, n = 15)

Reason	n	%
Improve maintenance Service	14	93.3
Costs		
Reduce labour costs	14	93.3
Reduce employee numbers	8	53.3
Flexibility		
Supplement capacity	12	80.0
Act as a change catalyst	6	40.0
Increase range of skills	5	33.3
Lower union influence	8	53.3
Improve industrial relations	4	26.6
Concentrate on core competencies	3	20.0

Source: Benson and Ieronimo (1996, pp. 64–65).

the quality of the service. A large percentage of companies indicated also that the objectives of cost reduction and improved labour flexibility were driving outsourcing. Improved labour flexibility, according to respondents, would be achieved by supplementing capacity, acting as a change agent, gaining additional skills, and improving industrial relations and reducing the influence of unions. Only three of the firms surveyed indicated that outsourcing was part of a wider strategy to concentrate on core competencies.

The finding that outsourcing is used by most companies as a cost reduction method suggests that companies that outsource may have similar objectives to companies that engage in other forms of restructuring such as downsizing. Do companies see these actions as alternatives or do they engage in outsourcing for more strategic reasons? To answer this question, data from a survey of 649 Australian companies (S3) that had decreased employee numbers by outsourcing or downsizing were examined (Benson and Littler, 2002). These data were part of a survey of 4500 Australian companies that resulted in a 30 per cent response rate (1222 companies). A subset of this dataset (*n*=649), representing only organizations that had downsized as a result of restructuring in the past two years, was used in this analysis. About half of this group of companies had increased their level of outsourcing. This group will form the basis for the statistics reported in this chapter and will be compared to the remaining group that had experienced a workforce reduction via other restructuring approaches. The results confirmed the findings of Benson and Ieronimo (1996), and, as reported in Tables 9.1 and 9.2, those companies that had increased outsourcing had primarily done so to reduce labour costs and improve labour productivity and flexibility. Results from this large survey (S3) are presented in Table 9.3. The findings showed that reduced labour costs and improved labour flexibility were statistically significant when compared to companies that had reduced employment levels by

Table 9.3 Objectives underpinning a company's increased level of outsourcing (% of companies, S3)

Objective	Choices of companies (%)		
	Not an objective	Minor objective	Major objective
Reduce labour costs	5.4	29.6	64.9
Improve labour productivity	9.8	24.6	65.6
Improve labour flexibility	16.9	30.1	53.1
Improve decision making	32.4	34.1	33.5
Improve customer service	24.1	26.9	49.0
Increase job enrichment	43.4	37.9	18.8
Improve internal communications	50.4	32.0	17.6

Note: n = 341 to 368 depending upon the objective.
Source: Benson and Littler (2002, p. 25).

other means. Clearly, the search for flexibility and reduced costs has become a major objective for management and underpinned the outsourcing decision.

Human resource dimensions of outsourcing

The findings outlined above confirm the results of a range of studies reported in the literature and suggest that management often use outsourcing as a reactive, short-term costcutting approach to achieve the required flexibility (Boyer, 1988; Rojot, 1989). The value attached to human resources and the uniqueness of those resources appeared to play little part in the outsourcing decision. This raises a number of human resource management issues, such as the impact on labour flexibility, productivity and employee commitment.

The four case-study companies presented in Table 9.1 sought to reduce costs by outsourcing, and, as shown in Table 9.4, this was achieved by a decrease in the maintenance workforce. However, the redundancy payments and the increased cost per worker meant that it would take two years before they would realize the cost advantage. With the reduced maintenance workforce, all companies reported an increase in labour productivity (see Table 9.4). For three of the companies, productivity was substantially higher. Yet this finding must be placed in the context of a declining level of service (Food-Co, Beer-Co) and/or a higher level of machine downtime in the three companies where data were available (Food-Co, Paper-Co, Beer-Co). Part of the increase in productivity may be related also to the lack of preventive maintenance being carried out. This less measurable and more long-term aspect of maintenance work led to some confusion between the company management and the service provider as to whether this formed part of the maintenance contract. As Lacity and Willcocks (1996) found with IT outsourcing, costly disputes can arise, even where a contract exists, as ambiguities, failure to identify full costs, fluctuations in business volume, and changes in technology are often not foreseen at the time of the agreement.

Table 9.4   Human resource dimensions of outsourcing (S1: case studies)

Dimension	Tabac-Co	Food-Co	Paper-Co	Beer-Co
	Involvement of companies			
Labour productivity	Much higher	Little higher	Much higher	Much higher
Workforce reduction (%)	22	34	47	51
Level of service	Same	Lower	Higher	Lower
Machine downtime	Not available	Higher	Higher	Higher
Industrial relations	Improved	Improved	Improved	Improved
Absenteeism	Same	Higher	Lower	Not available
Labour turnover	Higher	Lower	Higher	Higher
Commitment Level*	3.53 (0.90)	3.26 (0.85)	2.87 (0.38)	3.77 (0.62)

* Mean scores on a five-point scale. Standard deviations are provided in parentheses.
Source: Benson and Ieronimo (1996, p. 70) and unpublished figures from Benson (1998).

The case-study companies reported also that the other key objectives of outsourcing were to improve labour flexibility and industrial relations (see Table 9.1). Improved industrial relations was achieved by a reduction in the number of unions representing maintenance workers, which in turn led to a reduction in demarcation and work restriction disputes (tasks and overtime restrictions) and the opportunity to improve flexibility by integrating maintenance and production tasks. Production supervisors became responsible for maintenance work activities, except where this involved technical issues. These gains, however, must be considered alongside the possible negative impacts of outsourcing on other company employees. Absenteeism among remaining company employees increased in one of the companies (Food-Co), although this may have been caused by the high level of overtime worked in that company. On the other hand, the high levels of overtime available in this company may partially explain why labour turnover was lower after outsourcing. Labour turnover, among remaining employees, increased in the other three companies where outsourcing had created among employees a sense of insecurity and a concern that other areas of the company activities might be outsourced as well. The speed with which outsourcing had taken place, without any consultation with maintenance workers, contributed to this concern. The inability of the maintenance workers' unions to resist such a change further consolidated this perception.

The lower level of service that resulted in two companies (Food-Co, Beer-Co) and the higher machine downtime in all companies where data were available suggests that the organizational commitment of contract workers to their host employer might be lower than that of the employees they had replaced. On the other hand, notwithstanding that the commitment of those workers who lost their jobs through outsourcing could not be measured, in three of the four case-study companies the mean value of contract workers' commitment [2] to their host

---

2   Organizational commitment refers to the 'strength of an individual's identification with and involvement in a particular organization' (Porter *et al.*, 1974, p. 604) and was measured by the nine-item version of Porter's organizational commitment index (Porter *et al.*, 1974; Mowday *et al.*, 1979). Responses were on a five-point Likert scale ranging from 'strongly agree' to 'strongly disagree'. Commitment scores were the averaged responses to the items. Higher scores indicate higher levels of commitment. The reliability of commitment to the host employer was 0.91 (Cronbach, 1951).

employer was equal to, or higher than, that of other workers reported in the literature (Deery *et al.*, 1994; Deery *et al.*, 1995; Iverson *et al.*, 1995; Pearce, 1993). The mean values of the scores on a five-point scale were 3.07, 3.28, 3.04 and 3.37 respectively. It appears that outsourcing may have led to an improvement in the commitment of the maintenance workforce. The one company with low organizational commitment (Paper-Co, see Table 9.4) was the one that had been outsourcing this function the longest. This supports the findings of Kessler *et al.* (1999) that commitment rises slightly over the first 18 months following outsourcing. As outsourcing maintenance work was a recent event in the other three companies, it is possible that, over a longer time period, commitment may decline among the contract workers. However, an alternative explanation for the low level of contractor commitment and higher labour turnover among regular employees in Paper-Co was that this company had also restructured its production processes, which had led to both contractors and employees expressing concern about work processes.

Benson (1998) also found that the commitment of contract workers was higher towards the host company than towards their employer. More importantly, different factors influenced the two forms of commitment. Stress and perceived level of resources were significant factors in determining commitment to employer, while role ambiguity was an important determinant of commitment to the host company. Supervisor support was, however, important to both forms of commitment. With maintenance workers now reporting to the production supervisors in all four companies, the potential for conflict over assigned roles is high. If this conflict is accompanied by less supervisor support, then commitment, over the long term, will fall.

Similar findings were found in the study of the 649 Australian companies (Benson and Littler, 2002). Respondents were asked to rate the success of their stated outsourcing objectives, as outlined in Table 9.3, and the ensuing results are presented in Table 9.5 below. The most significant results were that about half of the respondents reported that costs had been reduced and labour productivity improved due to outsourcing. These objectives were, however, equally likely to be achieved by companies that had reduced the number of employees by other forms of restructuring, such as downsizing. There appears, therefore, little unique benefit to be gained by undertaking outsourcing compared to other forms of restructuring. Given some of the possible employee problems associated with outsourcing (see Table 9.4) the pursuit of this strategy may prove to be costly and undesirable.

The case studies indicated that outsourcing has had some unanticipated human resource consequences which were not taken into consideration in the decision-making process. Are these possible impacts recognized by management and are they more likely to occur with outsourcing than other forms of restructuring? To explore these issues, managers from the 649 companies were asked to assess the effect on employees of increased outsourcing (Benson and Littler, 2002). Although some level of systematic bias may be evidenced in these responses,[3] the results indicated a high level of concern about the negative impact of outsourcing and restructuring. Employee morale, commitment, motivation and job satisfaction were reported to have decreased where increased outsourcing had occurred. Promotional opportunities had declined also, while job responsibilities had increased. Nearly three-quarters of managers had increased concerns about employee job security. Results are presented in Table 9.6. In the cases of employee commitment, job satisfaction, promotional opportunities and job responsibilities, the perceived effects were more significant for employees where outsourcing had taken place compared to those companies that had restructured in other ways.

---

[3]   Although it would be expected that managers would understate, rather than overstate, the problems associated with outsourcing.

Table 9.5 Achievement of companies that increased their level of outsourcing (% of companies, S3)

	Level of achievement (%)		
	None	Minor	Major
Objective			
Reduced labour costs	5.7	42.1	52.2
Improved labour productivity	10.5	42.4	47.2
Improved labour flexibility	15.1	46.3	38.6
Improved decision making	30.3	46.8	22.9
Improved customer service	26.5	42.0	31.5
Increased job enrichment	43.3	40.5	16.3
Improved internal communications	44.5	39.1	16.4

Note: Only organizations that increased their level of outsourcing are considered in this table; n = 326 to 368 depending upon the objective.
Source: Benson and Littler (2002, p. 25).

Table 9.6 The impact of outsourcing on employees in companies that increased their level of outsourcing (% of companies, S3)

	Impact of outsourcing		
Work experiences	Decreased	No change	Increased
Morale	55.9	21.8	22.3
Commitment	45.0	32.4	22.6
Motivation	43.4	29.8	26.9
Job satisfaction	44.0	36.7	19.4
Promotional opportunities	43.4	26.4	30.2
Job responsibilities	1.6	6.8	91.6
Concern about job security	8.7	16.5	74.8

Note: n = 346 to 369 depending on the issue.
Source: Benson and Littler (2002, p. 26).

Discussion

The decision to make or buy the required human resources underpins outsourcing. The buy or outsourcing decision will, however, depend on a variety of factors, including whether the required skills are available in the external labour market. In the analysis presented above companies sought to achieve multiple objectives by outsourcing. This finding provides support for the claim by Abraham and Taylor, (1996, p. 417) that 'the picture of employers' motives for contracting out is rather more complex than that given in the typical popular account'. The desire for an improved service, reduced costs, improved labour flexibility and increased productivity seemed to be the key driving forces for outsourcing. Yet, what characterized the case studies and surveys explored in this chapter were the range of other reasons that contributed to the decision to outsource a key function such as maintenance work. One of these reasons was the improved industrial relations that would probably occur from having fewer unions on site. This, management hoped, would lead to fewer industrial disputes over who does what work and to the ability to bring maintenance work under the control of production supervisors.

While all of these objectives are important to firms operating in a competitive global marketplace, they do not reveal a strategic approach to outsourcing. Few companies mentioned the desire to concentrate on core competencies, and where this was the case it appeared to be a secondary consideration. Moreover, there was little evidence that the decision to outsource was based on an assessment of the value or uniqueness of human resources (Lepak and Snell, 1999). The activities outsourced included relatively unskilled and peripheral functions such as cleaning and catering, but included also high-skill activities such as maintenance work, transportation and training. Clearly more than low-skill functions are outsourced. This is best illustrated by the fact that most of the Australian companies surveyed had outsourced, or were planning to outsource, the maintenance activity. This stood in stark contrast to the approach adopted by Japanese companies revealed in a survey administered to Japanese manufacturing plants operating in Australia. According to respondents, outsourcing maintenance work would reduce the synergy that had developed between production and maintenance workers and would have a negative impact on the team approach to productivity and quality issues, problem solving and productivity[4] (Benson and Ieronimo, 1996, p. 65).

The findings reported in this chapter reveal the present state of outsourcing in many Western companies. Decisions to outsource were rarely based on long-term strategy aiming at improving competitiveness as a result of a focus on core competencies. Rather, for many firms it was a way of solving short-term financial, flexibility and industrial relations problems. This extended to the selection of outsourcing providers which revealed an 'antagonistic bargaining' approach rather than the 'synergistic problem-solving' approach adopted by many Japanese companies (Nishiguchi, 1994, p. 5). In other words, cost minimization was driving the choice of outsourcing providers where tasks were clearly delineated and were managed though legal contracts. Little evidence existed that either the company or the provider perceived their relationship as one of sharing of risks between two companies in a long-term strategic alliance. Certainly, this appeared to be the case as human resource issues, such as training, may arise. These issues were seen as problems outside of the formal contract for services and were matters with which the employer needs to deal. Moreover, little consideration was given to the potential conflict that could arise between the provider and the client caused by cost pressures that may, in the long term, compromise service quality (Lacity and Willcocks, 1996, p. 14).

Conclusion

The case studies and surveys considered in this chapter revealed a short-term, operational approach to outsourcing that was primarily aimed at improving service, reducing costs, improving labour flexibility and rectifying existing industrial relations problems. Outsourcing

---

4   This finding came from a survey of 36 Japanese manufacturing companies operating in Australia. Responses were received from 16 companies. After allowing for four questionnaires that were returned unopened, this represented a response rate of 50 per cent.

was, however, less likely to result in an improved service, and often had a detrimental impact on the remaining employees. As a consequence, much of the possible strategic value of outsourcing that could have created a competitive advantage was lost. How, then, should management approach outsourcing so as to avoid these problems? First, it must take a more strategic, long-term view of outsourcing in terms of the activities to be outsourced. Outsourcing should only be considered where a clear case can be made that it will contribute to the firm's key objectives. Other objectives, including reducing costs and improving labour flexibility, may be better achieved by different forms of restructuring, such as downsizing. Second, where a decision has been made to outsource, management will need to develop key alliances with appropriate providers and extend the partnership beyond contractual forms of obligation. Finally, management will need to be more inclusive in the outsourcing process. Employees, and other affected parties, need to be involved in the decision-making process from its inception. Consultation with, and the involvement of, employees may alleviate many of the employee problems identified in this chapter. A failure to learn these lessons will almost certainly mean that outsourcing will be a short-term remedy for a long-term problem.

References

Abraham, K.G. and Taylor, S.K. (1996), 'Firms' use of outside contractors: theory and evidence', *Journal of Labor Economics*, vol. 14, no. 3, pp. 394–424.

Angle, H. and Perry, J. (1981), 'An empirical assessment of organizational commitment and organizational effectiveness', *Administrative Science Quarterly*, 26 March, pp. 1–14.

Benson, J. (1998), 'Dual commitment: contract workers in Australian manufacturing organizations', *Journal of Management Studies*, vol. 35, no. 3, pp. 355–75.

Benson, J. and Ieronimo, N. (1996), 'Outsourcing decisions: evidence from Australia-based enterprises', *International Labour Review*, vol. 135, no. 1, pp. 59–73.

Benson, J. and Littler, C. (2002), 'Outsourcing and workforce reductions: an empirical study of Australian organisations', *Asia Pacific Business Review*, vol. 8, no. 3, pp. 16–30.

Bettis, R., Bradley, S. and Hamel, G. (1992), 'Outsourcing and industrial decline', *Academy of Management Executive*, vol. 6, no. 1, pp. 7–22.

Boyer, R. (ed.) (1988), *The Search for Labour Market Flexibility*, Clarendon Press, Oxford.

Brewer, A. and Hensher, D. (1998), 'The importance of organisational commitment in managing change: experience of the NSW private bus industry', *Logistic & Transport Review*, vol. 34, no. 2, pp. 117–30.

Cappelli, P. (1995), 'Rethinking employment', *British Journal of Industrial Relations*, vol. 33, no. 4, pp. 563–602.

Chandler, M. (1964), *Management Rights and Union Interests*, McGraw-Hill, New York.

Cronbach, L.J. (1951), 'Coefficient alpha and the internal structure of the tests', *Psychometrika*, vol. 16, pp. 297–334.

Deery, S., Erwin, P. and Iverson, R. (1995), 'Union management co-operation, dual allegiance and organisational performance', Working Paper, no. 89, Department of Management and Industrial Relations, University of Melbourne, Australia.

Deery, S., Iverson, R. and Erwin, P. (1994), 'Predicting organisational and union commitment: the effect of industrial relations climate', *British Journal of Industrial Relations*, vol. 32, no. 4, pp. 581–97.

Farrell, D. and Rusbult, C. (1981), 'Exchange variables as predictors of job satisfaction, job commitment and turnover: the impact of rewards, costs, alternatives and investments', *Organizational Behavior and Human Performance*, vol. 28, no. 1, pp. 78–95.

Goldman, S., Nagel, R. and Preiss, K. (1995), *Agile Competitors and Virtual Organisations*, Van Nostrand & Reinhold, New York.

Grindley, K. (1994), *Price Waterhouse Annual IT Review*, Price Waterhouse, London.

Iverson, R. (1996), 'Employee acceptance of organizational change: the role of organizational commitment', *The International Journal of Human Resource Management*, vol. 7, no. 1, pp. 122–49.

Iverson, R., McLeod, C. and Erwin, P. (1995), 'Employee commitment and trust: implications for effective marketing', Working Paper, no. 92, Department of Management and Industrial Relations, University of Melbourne, Australia.

Jaros, S. (1997), 'An assessment of Meyer and Allen's 1991 three-component model of organizational commitment and turnover intentions', *Journal of Vocational Behavior*, vol. 513, pp. 319–37.

Kessler, I., Coyle-Shapiro, J. and Purcell, J. (1999), 'Outsourcing and the employee perspective', *Human Resource Management Journal*, vol. 9, no.2, pp. 5–19.

Lacity, M. and Willcocks, L. (1996), *Best Practice in Information Technology Sourcing*, The Oxford Executive Research Briefings, Templeton College, Oxford.

Lepak, D. and Snell, S. (1999), 'The human resource architecture: toward a theory of human capital allocation and development', *Academy of Management Review*, vol. 24, no.1, pp. 31–8.

McCune, J. (1993), 'Thin is in', *Small Business Reports*, May, pp. 30–40.

Mathieu, J. and Zajac, D. (1990), 'A review and meta-analysis of the antecedents, correlates and consequences of organizational commitment', *Psychological Bulletin*, vol. 108, no. 2, pp. 171–94.

Michaels, C. and Spector, P. (1982), 'Causes of employee turnover: a test of the Mobley, Griffeth, Hand and Meglino Model', *Journal of Applied Psychology*, vol. 67, no. 1, pp. 53–59.

Miles, R. and Snow, C. (1984), 'Designing strategic human resource systems', *Organizational Dynamics*, vol. 13, pp. 36–52.

Miles, R. and Snow, C. (1992), 'Causes of failure in network organizations', *California Management Review*, Summer, pp. 53–72.

Mowday, R., Steers, R. and Porter, L. (1979), 'The measurement of organizational commitment', *Journal of Vocational Behavior*, vol. 14, no. 2, pp. 224–47.

Muller, C. and Price, J. (1990), 'Economic, psychological and sociological determinants of voluntary turnover', *Journal of Behavioral Economics*, vol. 9, pp. 321–35.

Nishiguchi, T. (1994), *Strategic Industrial Sourcing: The Japanese Advantage*, Oxford University Press, New York.

Pearce, J.L. (1993), 'Toward an organizational behavior of laborers: their psychological effects on employee co-workers', *Academy of Management Journal*, vol. 36, pp. 1082–96.

Plunkett, S. (1991), 'Outsourcing: A new way to save', *Business Review Weekly*, 1 November, pp. 8–10, 14.

Porter, L., Steers, R., Mowday, R. and Boulian, P. (1974), 'Organisational commitment, job satisfaction, and turnover among psychiatric technicians', *Journal of Applied Psychology*, vol. 59, no. 5, pp. 603–09.

Prahalad, C. and Hamel, G. (1990), 'The core competence of the corporation', *Harvard Business Review*, vol. 11, no. 3, pp. 79–91.

Priore, M. and Sabel C. (1984), *The Second Industrial Divide: Possibilities for Prosperity*, Basic Books, New York.

Quinlan, M. (1998), 'Labour market restructuring in industrialised societies: an overview', *The Economic and Labour Relations Review*, vol. 9, no. 1, pp. 1–30.

Rees, G. and Fielder, S. (1992), 'The services economy, subcontracting and the new employment relations: contract catering and cleaning', *Work, Employment & Society*, vol. 63, pp. 347–68.

Rojot, J. (1989), 'National experiences in labour market flexibility', in OECD (ed.), *Labour Market Flexibility: Trends in Enterprises*, Organization for Economic Cooperation and Development, Paris, pp. 37–60.

Sagie, A. (1998), 'Employee absenteeism, organizational commitment, and job satisfaction: another look', *Journal of Vocational Behavior*, vol. 52, no. 2, pp. 156–71.

Schappe, S. (1998), 'The influence of job satisfaction, organizational commitment and fairness perceptions on organizational citizenship behavior', *Journal of Psychology*, vol. 132, no. 3, pp. 277–90.

Sharpe, M. (1997), 'Outsourcing, organizational competitiveness, and work', *Journal of Labor Research*, vol. 18, no. 4, pp. 535–49.

Somech, A. and Bogler, R. (2002), 'Antecedents and consequences of teacher organizational and professional commitment', *Educational Administration Quarterly*, vol. 38, no. 4, pp. 555–77.

Stalk, G. (1988), 'Time – the next source of competitive advantage', *Harvard Business Review*, vol. 9, no. 4, pp. 41–51.

Steers, R. (1977), 'Antecedents and outcomes of organizational commitment', *Administrative Science Quarterly*, vol. 22, March, pp. 46–56.

Strassman, P. (1995), 'Outsourcing: a game for losers', *Computerworld*, 21 August, pp. 1–3.

Stumpf, S. and Hartman, K. (1984), 'Individual exploration to organizational commitment or withdrawal', *Academy of Management Journal*, vol. 27, no. 2, pp. 308–29.

Tully, S. (1993), 'The modular corporation', *Fortune*, 8 February, pp. 106–15.

Valentine, S., Godkin, L. and Lucero, M. (2002), 'Ethical context, organizational commitment, and person-organization fit', *Journal of Business Ethics*, vol. 41, pp. 349–60.

Williams, L. and Hazer, J. (1986), 'Antecedents and consequences of satisfaction and commitment in turnover models: a re-analysis using latent variable structural equation methods', *Journal of Applied Psychology*, vol. 71, no. 2, pp. 219–31.

3 *The Long-Term Effects of Outsourcing as an Organization-Driven Process*

Part 3 highlights the ways in which outsourcing has impacted on the workplace, and the changes that will continue to occur within the workplace, due to the dynamic nature of the process. The different dimensions covered in this section concern the overall functioning of the organization, especially in terms of outsourcing's influence on the financial and policy processes.

Robert Stehrer starts the section with a chapter that explores the effects of outsourcing on international trade flows. He focuses on international trade theory and notes that outsourcing is one of the highest growing components in international trade flows. Although his research is limited to the manufacturing sector only, the results show that there are both country and industry differences within outsourcing activities.

Small and medium-sized enterprises (SMEs) tend not to generate an excessive amount of research within the context of outsourcing. However, it is one area that can benefit from more research. David Brown and Nigel Lockett, in Chapter 11, present the findings of studies that examine the usefulness of outsourcing to SMEs and the hindrances that may limit their engagement in such activities. Their research focuses in particular on e-business applications and the value that these types of applications could generate for SMEs wishing to engage in global expansion.

Chapter 12 by Andreas Knabe and Bertrand Koebel delves into the economic rationale for outsourcing activities, especially the impact that outsourcing has on wages and employment. They observe outsourcing at both firm and international level and find some support for the ability of outsourcing to increase wage inequality and decrease labour demand. However, they caution against the total acceptance of these findings due to the differences between measurement and theory.

The direct and indirect influences of outsourcing on trade unions are areas investigated by Valeria Pulignano in Chapter 13. She notes the effects that outsourcing has had on a firm's structure and the resulting ways in which trade unions have dealt, or attempted to deal, with the subsequent changes. In particular, she highlights the adjustments that were necessary within the trade union structure as a consequence of outsourcing. The chapter also provides evidence from the automobile industry on the trade unions' attempt to negotiate and maintain an element of control on the outcomes of an outsourcing process. She ends by noting the limitations of unions in influencing outsourcing outcomes.

The final chapter in Part 3 explores the economic and behavioural aspects of outsourcing on accounting practices. Ahmad Juma'h, the author, uses transaction cost theory, agency theory and signalling theory as aids in understanding the process. He outlines the reasons why companies outsource and the effects that these have on accounting practices. In his conclusion he notes that, as announcements of outsourcing are not compulsory, it can lead to a gap in market efficiency, and that more consistent reporting could lead to a better assessment of the risk facing a firm and of its performance.

10 Outsourcing Activities in the World Economy[1]

Robert Stehrer

Outsourcing is gaining increasing importance in shaping production and trade patterns, as well as relationships, across firms in different countries in the globalizing world. On the basis of various studies, which are examined below in further detail, it can be concluded that outsourcing is one of the highest growing components in international trade flows. In this chapter we shall shed some light on this component of trade from the perspective of international trade theory and on the basis of empirical evidence considering mainly measurement issues and long-term trends. In the literature a number of different terms have been used to capture this phenomenon. In general, outsourcing activities are understood to be the manufacture of inputs to a production process (or a part of this process) in other locations (firms or plants), especially in other countries. Alternatively, and more generally, outsourcing may be viewed as a production activity, previously undertaken within a firm or plant, which was then switched outside the firm or plant. The term 'outsourcing' is a compound expression from 'outside resource using'. However, a number of other terms have been used: Jones and Kierzkowski (1990) use the term 'fragmentation' to describe the 'splitting of production processes into separate parts that can be done in different locations, including different countries'. Other terms used for this phenomenon are delocalization (Leamer, 1996), internationalization (Grossman and Helpman, 1999), multistage production (Dixit and Grossman, 1982), slicing up the value chain (Krugman, 1996), disintegration (Feenstra, 1998), subcontracting, vertical specialization (Hummels, Rapoport and Yi, 1998), intra-mediate trade (Antweiler and Trefler, 2002), intra-product specialization (Arndt, 1997) and splintering (Bhagwati, 1984). Outsourcing must be distinguished from other forms of international integration, mainly from trade and (horizontal and vertical) foreign direct investment although in parts of the literature the distinction is not clear. Finally, offshoring is a term mainly used for the outsourcing of service activities.

Let us start with some illustrative examples that emphasize the importance of this kind of world integration. The annual report of the World Trade Organization (WTO, 1998) presents one such example: the production of a particular car manufactured by one of the large US automobile companies involved no fewer than nine countries in some aspect of production, marketing and selling. Thirty per cent of the car's value goes to Korea for assembly, 17.5 per cent to Japan for components and advanced technology, 7.5 per cent to Germany for design, 4 per cent to Taiwan and Singapore for minor parts, 2.5 per cent to the UK for advertising and marketing services, and 1.5 per cent to Ireland and Barbados for data processing. This means that only 37 per cent of the production value of this 'American' car is generated in the USA (WTO, 1998, p. 36).

1   Research was financed by the 'Jubiläumsfonds der österreichischen Nationalbank (OENB)' within the project 'Stylised Facts of Foreign Direct Investment and Their Implications on Economic Development', Project No. 10214.

There are other examples also: Tempest (1996) notes that the raw materials for a Barbie doll are obtained from Taiwan and Japan. The dolls are assembled in low-cost locations like Indonesia, Malaysia and China, which also supply the cotton cloth for dresses. The export value of $2 to the USA covers 35 per cent for labour and 65 per cent for raw materials. The majority of value added is from US activities and includes mainly transportation, marketing, wholesaling and retailing. The location of workers is another example. To produce its range of shoes and clothing Nike employs about 75 000 workers in Asia, who work mainly in factories that have contractual arrangements with the company. As a comparison, Nike has, on average, 2500 employees in the USA (Tisdale, 1994).

These examples show that the level of outsourcing can be quite high and can take different forms. The World Bank (1997) estimated that the share of affiliate output of multinational corporations in world output was at about 7.5 per cent of world gross domestic product (GDP) and about 20 per cent of world manufacturing output in 1995. Yeats (2001) calculated the share of components and parts in world exports and concluded that global production sharing amounted to about 30 per cent of world trade in manufacturing. Furthermore, this type of trade is growing significantly faster than trade in finished products. These figures do not include trade in services for which similar trends can be observed. In terms of number of firms, the *World Investment Report 1996* figures show that there are more than 39 000 parent firms and 279 000 foreign affiliates worldwide. The value added of these affiliates accounted for about 6 per cent of world GDP in 1991: this means that it had more than tripled from the beginning of the 1980s.

These examples illustrate that outsourcing activities are an important component, and account for an increasing share, of total world trade. Its increasing importance can be attributed to the reduction of tariff and non-tariff trade barriers and improvements and cost reductions in communications and transportation technologies, which in this sense are 'distance-reducing'.

In this chapter we focus mainly on studies showing trends and characteristic features in terms of industry and firm structure for the outsourcing phenomenon. In the next section we provide an overview of studies focusing on the trends in and the extent of outsourcing in recent decades, and also discuss measurement issues. In the third section we review how the literature on outsourcing and other forms of international integration – mainly foreign direct investment and trade structures – are related. In the fourth section we look at studies using firm-level data. These are compared to the industry-level studies but also give some information on the characteristics of firms that are engaged in outsourcing activities. Here we mainly focus on company characteristics and not on company motives for outsourcing or the effects of outsourcing activities on productivity or profitability. Conclusions are presented in the final section. The studies reviewed in this chapter are only of empirical nature and do not give an overview of theoretical approaches. A large number of contributions in this field – empirically and theoretically – analyse the question on the effects of outsourcing on labour markets and especially on the different effects on skilled and unskilled workers. Again, this topic is not covered here. Finally, the main emphasis here is put on the manufacturing sector and not on outsourcing activities of services.

Outsourcing: measurement and trends

There is no single measure to capture the phenomenon of outsourcing as a range of firms' activities. In this section the most common measures of outsourcing, which are used in the literature are reviewed. Irwin (1996) suggested an examination of the composition of trade using 'end-use' categories and showed that, in the period from 1889 to 1990, merchandise exports as a share of tradables output rose from about 15 per cent to more than 30 per cent whereas merchandise exports as a share of GDP rose from about 6 per cent to about 7 per cent (with a decline in this ratio in the first half of the twentieth century). The largest increase occurred in the 1970s and 1980s. Furthermore, this increase was mainly in manufacturing which saw an increasing share in the composition of US trade, in contrast to agricultural goods and raw materials which fell. Looking at end-use categories of US trade (that is, consumer goods, industrial materials and capital goods) it can be seen that the share in intermediate inputs, measured as the share of capital goods (which include machinery, components and so on), generally rose, whereas it fell for industrial (raw) materials and remained almost stable for consumer goods.

Feenstra (1998) using a similar method to Irwin (1996), but differentiating between more end-use categories, finds that US trade shifted away from foods, feeds and beverages and industrial supplies and materials which, together, accounted for more than 90 per cent of imports in 1925 and 1950. The import share of these categories fell to less than 25 per cent in 1995. Similarly, the export share fell from 1925 to 1995 from 80 to about 30 per cent. On the other hand, the import share of capital goods except automobiles (which includes, for example, all electrical parts and components except finished consumer goods) increased from about 10 per cent in 1925 to about 60 per cent in 1995, and the export share rose from about 15 per cent to more than 50 per cent. The import and export shares of consumer goods (except automobiles) also increased, but less dramatically and with a more value-added component (for example, for advertising, marketing and product design) realized in the USA. Finally, the export and import share of automotive vehicles and parts nowadays amounts to about 11 and 19 per cent respectively from almost zero in 1925.

Another way of measuring outsourcing is by calculating the amount of imported intermediate inputs within each industry. This information is collected in some countries when input–output tables are constructed. Audet (1996) presents numbers for the ratio of imported to domestic intermediate inputs for six OECD countries for the textile, apparel and footwear industry (summarized in Table 10.1). As Table 10.1 illustrates, this ratio was rising in all six countries from the 1970s to the 1990s, which again confirms the increasing importance of the globalization of production. Furthermore, in the cross-country dimension there is a tendency for larger countries to show a lower ratio.

Table 10.1   Ratio of imported to domestic intermediate inputs for textiles, apparels and footwear

Country	Early 1970s (%)	Mid/late 1970s (%)	Mid-1980s (%)
Canada	41	50	60
France	15	26	42
Germany	n.a.	49	64
Japan	3	6	9
United Kingdom	19	33	48
United States	7	6	13

Source: Audet (1996, Table 8.18).

These results of the growing importance of outsourcing for these industries are confirmed also by more detailed industry-level studies; for the apparel industry see, for example, Jones (1995) for the USA and Gereffi (1999) for Europe, and for the footwear industry see Yoffie and Gomes-Casseres (1994).

Campa and Goldberg (1997) use a time series analysis to assess the imported input share in production by using input–output tables and industry-by-industry import shares for four countries (Canada, Japan, United Kingdom and the USA). Their general findings are that external orientation has increased considerably over recent decades (with the exception of Japan). In addition, the relative ranking of industries with respect to the measures of outward orientation has been very stable over time and the industries with high export orientation are the same across countries. On the other hand, rankings of industrial import shares and imported input shares are not highly correlated across countries. The calculations reported in Campa and Goldberg (1997) with respect to imported inputs are presented for total manufacturing and some sectors (chemical and allied products, non-electrical industrial machinery, electrical equipment and machinery, and transportation equipment in Table 10.2 (for more detailed figures involving about 20 industries see Campa and Goldberg, 1997).

Table 10.2 Share of imported to total intermediate inputs (%)

Country	1974	1984	1993
All manufacturing industries			
Canada	15.9	14.4	20.2
Japan	8.2	7.3	4.1
United Kingdom	13.4	19.0	21.6
United States	4.1	6.2	8.2
Chemical and allied products			
Canada	9.0	8.8	15.1
Japan	5.2	4.8	2.6
United Kingdom	13.1	20.6	22.5
United States	3.0	4.5	6.3
Industrial machinery (non-electrical)			
Canada	17.7	21.9	26.6
Japan	2.1	1.9	1.8
United Kingdom	16.1	24.9	31.3
United States	4.1	7.2	11.0
Electrical equipment and machinery			
Canada	13.2	17.1	30.9
Japan	3.1	3.4	2.9
United Kingdom	14.9	23.6	34.6
United States	4.5	6.7	11.6
Transportation equipment			
Canada	29.1	37.0	49.7
Japan	1.8	2.4	2.8
United Kingdom	14.3	25.0	32.2
United States	6.4	10.7	15.7

Note: US figures are for 1975, 1985, and 1995.
Source: Campa and Goldberg (1997) and Feenstra (1998).

One can see from Table 10.2 that this measure for 'outsourcing' increases for all countries and in all industries with the notable exception of Japan. For total manufacturing Canada and the UK have the highest share of imported to total intermediate inputs. This is also the common pattern in each of the four industry types. With respect to similarities across industries, Campa and Goldberg (1997) present rank correlations showing that the USA and the UK have the highest correlations, which became stronger over time. The Canadian industry rankings were negatively correlated in the 1970s but have changed to positive correlations since then, whereas Japan's rankings have increasingly negatively correlated relationships with the US and UK rankings. Feenstra and Hanson (1997) multiply the purchases of each type of input by the economy-wide import share for that input. This is summed up over all inputs within each industry in order to arrive at an estimate of imported inputs. For total US manufacturing industries they found that imported inputs increased from 5.7 per cent in 1972 to 13.9 per cent in 1990, which confirms the conclusions above, that reliance on imported intermediate inputs has increased for the USA.

Other studies that portray the increasing importance of outsourcing are Hummels, Rapoport and Yi (1998) and Hummels, Ishi and Yi (2001), where the phenomenon is called 'vertical specialization' and defined as the amount of imported inputs embodied in goods that are exported. Using four case studies, the investigations show that this vertical specialization increased dramatically during the 1980s and 1990s. Using input–output tables the authors then calculated estimates of vertical-specialization-based trade for ten OECD countries and find that whereas horizontal trade still accounts for most of the trade, vertical-specialization-based trade gains in significance and amounts to 14.5 per cent of all trade in these ten countries (an increase of about 20 per cent from the late 1960s). The authors also find a strong statistical relationship between the increasing share of vertical specialization and the share of total trade in GDP, implying that outsourcing activities show higher growth rates than trade. As in the Campa and Goldberg (1997) study, vertical trade was found to increase in relation to total trade in all countries, with the exception of Japan. Furthermore, the cross-country variation – already mentioned above – is confirmed for this larger sample of countries. Countries with the lowest share of vertical trade are Japan, the USA and Australia (with only about 7 per cent of vertical trade in total trade); at the other extreme is the Netherlands with a share of almost 37 per cent in 1986.

This result suggests that larger countries engage relatively less in vertical trade. Because of economics of scale large countries find it easier to retain more stages of production than smaller countries. The industries with the highest shares of vertical trade in total trade are motor vehicles, shipbuilding, aircraft, industrial chemicals, non-ferrous metals and petroleum and coke products. The industries with the lowest shares are agriculture, mining, wood products and paper products. However, it is emphasized also that there are large differences across countries with respect to the importance of vertical trade across industries. For example, in the Australian motor vehicle industry only 4.5 per cent of trade is vertical, whereas in the same industry in Canada it is close to 50 per cent. Finally, it is shown that the industries that principally account for overall export growth are also the industries that account for growth in vertical trade. This means that there is also a tight link between growth in world trade and growth in vertical trade.

Fontagné et al. (1997) compare two different methods that can be used to identify trade in intermediate products. The first uses input–output tables (see the studies discussed above); the other is based on international trade statistics. It is argued that the first approach is inadequate if the aim is to study the competitive positions or the intra- and inter-industry nature of trade in intermediate goods. In this study the input–output approach is replaced by the reconstruction of data on trade flows. This entails the aggregation of a very detailed nomenclature (5000 products) on the basis of assumed use: (i) primary products, (ii) processed products, (iii) parts and (iv) finished products. Intermediate products comprise the first three groups; the fourth group is intended for final use – that is, investment or consumption. Detailed analysis of trade flows shows that about 11 per cent can be classified as 'primary', 27 per cent as 'processed', about 17 per cent as 'parts' and 45 per cent as final goods. Thus more than one half of trade (almost 55 per cent) represents trade in intermediate goods. Table 10.3 presents similar figures by industry for 1992.

In this table the industries are ranked according to the share of intermediate goods trade. Within intermediate goods trade, chemicals, mining and quarrying, metals, and electrical and electronics count for most of intermediate goods trade (more than 50 per cent). Fontagné *et al.* (1997) apply this method to study the structure of comparative advantages of the European Union. Yeats (2001) uses a similar method based on SITC revision 2 data for machinery and transport equipment industries. All these studies show that at least 30 per cent of total world trade in these products are due to global production sharing which is growing also at a faster pace than trade of other (finished) products. For a study on Eastern European countries see Kaminski and Ng (2001).

In summary, all these different measures and studies indicate that the amount of outsourcing has increased substantially over the last few decades, although there are quite large country differences with respect to levels of the importance of outsourcing activities and trends (for example, outsourcing is becoming less important for Japan). In addition there are quite large country differences with respect to sectoral reliance on imported intermediate inputs.

Foreign direct investment, trade and outsourcing activities

Although the studies summarized above confirm the rising importance of outsourcing, other factors may have to be taken into account. Kleinert (2003) proposes three hypotheses to explain the growing trade in intermediate goods: namely, outsourcing, the increasing importance of multinational enterprise (MNE) networks, and global sourcing. The first hypothesis, outsourcing, suggests that increases in imported inputs are related to growing *outward* foreign direct investment (FDI) stocks of firms in the industrialized countries as parts of production are relocated. In contrast, the MNE network hypothesis argues that increasing imports of inputs relate to a growing *inward* FDI stock as trade intensity is increasing between MNEs' affiliates in foreign countries and companies in the home country. The third hypothesis, global sourcing, suggests that companies buy intermediate inputs in locations with the best conditions (for example, the lowest costs) that should not be related to outward or inward FDI stocks. Using a cross-sectional framework for OECD countries and time series data for Germany, Kleinert (2003) tests these hypotheses. The general findings are that the increasing importance of MNE networks has the strongest support. Evidence for the importance of outsourcing or global sourcing is much weaker, allowing the conclusion that global sourcing is not the dominant force behind the increases in imported intermediate inputs.

Another study by Bardan and Jaffee (2004) focuses on the relationship between intra-firm trade and multinationals. They use US data to study the importance of intra-firm trade in explaining the increasing trade in intermediate inputs. Their results show the increasing

Table 10.3 Intermediate goods trade by industry (1992)

	Primary	Processed	Parts	Intermediates	Final	Total industry
	(i)	(ii)	(iii)	(i)+(ii)+(iii)	(iv)	(i)+(ii)+(iii)+(iv)
Chemicals	0.0	8.8	0.5	9.3	2.4	11.7
Mining and quarrying	7.3	0.8	.	8.1	0.0	8.1
Metals	0.3	6.2	0.4	6.8	0.5	7.3
Electrical and electronics	.	1.1	5.7	6.7	7.0	13.8
Wood and paper	0.2	3.3	1.1	4.7	0.9	5.5
Mechanical engineering	.	0.1	3.3	3.4	6.8	10.2
Cars and HGVs	.	.	3.3	3.3	6.6	9.9
Agriculture	2.7	0.0	.	2.7	1.2	3.9
Coking and refining	0.0	2.5	.	2.5	0	2.5
Textiles	0.1	1.9	0.1	2.1	5.8	7.8
Other transport equipment	.	0.0	1.8	1.8	3.4	5.2
Data processing	.	.	1.7	1.7	3.2	4.9
Agri-food industries	0.3	1.1	.	1.4	4.3	5.7
Miscellaneous	0.0	0.9	0.0	0.9	2.6	3.5
Stage total	10.9	26.7	17.8	55.4	44.6	100.0

Source: Fontagné et al. (1997); own calculations.

importance of intra-firm imports in the 1990s in comparison to the period before during which most US intermediate imports were attributable to arms' length trade. In addition to the intra-firm trade variables, standard gravity variables are also found to be important in explaining trade in intermediate inputs. The authors present estimates for high-tech intermediate imports (mainly computers and electronic products) only. For this subgroup, distance was not a contributing factor, whereas intra-firm trade was the key determinant. This suggests that foreign outsourcing is especially important for MNEs in high-tech industries. In their sample on US firms, two thirds of all imports of high-tech intermediate inputs into the USA are made by MNEs. Similar findings of the complementarities between FDI and trade can be found in some other studies: see for example, Graham, (2004) who analyses this topic for the USA and Japan; Urata (1995) who studies the electronics industry in East Asia, Brainard (1995a, 1995b); Blomström, Lipsey and Kulchyck (1988) on Swedish firms; and, finally, Buigues and Jacquemin (1994) who focus on US and Japanese direct investment in the European Union. All of these studies find that FDI and trade (exports) are complements rather than substitutes.

There are few studies that focus on the relationship between trade structures and outsourcing activities. Simone (2003) empirically studies this issue for France, Japan and the USA based on a general equilibrium framework. He concludes that these three countries show quite different profiles with respect to outsourcing activities: for example, the production structure in France is most affected by the fragmentation of production in contrast to Japan, which is scarcely vertically specializing at all. The USA sits somewhere in between and is thus used as a benchmark case in the econometric analysis. Controlling for other variables (for example, size, relative endowments, R&D expenditures and so on.) the empirical analysis reveals that the vertical specialization variable shows a small positive effect on the relative exports of France versus the USA. For Japan, Simone (2003) finds a negative coefficient for the effects of vertical specialization on exports. Thus it can be concluded that the impact of fragmentation on trade patterns is not one-way and depends on other structural characteristics – a conclusion consistent with other studies based on statistical analysis of trade flows.

Firm-level studies

All the studies reviewed above were structured at the industry level. Studies using firm-level data to analyse structures and effects of international outsourcing are rather scarce. Here, we focus on those studies that distinguish between domestic and foreign outsourcing. Studies have focused on firm characteristics (for example, Abraham and Taylor, 1996) and on the effects of firms' productivity and profitability (see Görzig and Stephan, 2002, and Görg and Hanley, 2003 for the Irish electronics sector, and Swenson, 2000 for US firms). The latter two studies find that outsourcing generally raises the return per employee but that the effect on profitability is ambiguous.

Tomiura (2004) uses micro-data from 118 300 Japanese firms in all manufacturing industries and distinguishes foreign from domestic outsourcing, including all firm sizes without thresholds. In this sample only about 2 per cent of firms are outsourcing internationally and half of the firms are outsourcing at the national level (but see the industry-level results for Japan above). Firms that undertake foreign outsourcing are substantially larger in terms of numbers of employees and sales than firms engaged only in domestic outsourcing or firms that do not outsource at all. This can be explained by the fixed costs of searching and contracting. This result is in line with the finding by Abraham and Taylor (1996) that it is mainly firms in metropolitan areas that are outsourcing, which, in their view, supports the economies of scale hypothesis. Furthermore, Tomiura (2004) finds that firms with higher labour productivity and higher human capital to labour ratios, per employee R&D or per employee use of computers tend to be more engaged in foreign outsourcing. These results are consistent with the hypothesis that the motivation driving outsourcing is saving costs or that higher technological capability or managerial skills are required. In a more sophisticated econometric framework it is shown that higher productivity, use of computers and lower capital to labour and human capital to labour ratios are positively related to foreign outsourcing activities. The latter result favours the interpretation that outsourcing of labour-intensive products is more attractive. The firm size variable has a negative coefficient, which suggests that foreign outsourcing does not rise proportionally with firm size. While outsourcing is positively related to firm size when descriptive analysis is used, Tomiura (2004) uses a selection equation specification and finds that the intensity of foreign outsourcing relative to firm size increases under-proportionally if the firm has decided to outsource to foreign countries. Kimura (2001) provides another example of a study using micro-data of Japanese firms.

Kurz (2004) uses data from the US Census of Manufacturers in 1987 and 1992 that differentiate between outsourcers and non-outsourcing establishments and between firms and plants. The largest outsourcing industries are printing and publishing, petroleum and coal, apparel and leather products, primary metal industries, and food and tobacco (the ranking changes between 1987 and 1992). These findings are similar to those of Feenstra and Hanson (1996, 1998) and Campa and Goldberg (1997) already discussed above. The differences between firm- and plant-level characteristics show that the most important difference between outsourcers and non-outsourcers is in total employment and shipments, for which outsourcers show higher values. Furthermore, these differences are larger at the firm than at the plant level. At the firm level, large differences also exist for shipments, capital, investment and value added per worker (these results are similar to Bernard and Jensen 1999, where differences between exporters and non-exporters are studied). In addition, outsourcing firms are more skill-intensive.

These descriptive results are confirmed using more sophisticated econometric methods. Wages are generally higher in outsourcing establishments, although this is not the case for the wages of production workers, which is in line with the hypothesis that most likely labour-intensive stages of production are outsourced. Further findings from Kurz's 2004 study are that productivity is higher amongst outsourcers even after controlling for industry affiliation, plant size and location and that firm-level productivity growth is higher. This result does not hold at the plant level. Some of these results are confirmed by other studies using more aggregate data but nonetheless based on survey data. For example, Mora (2004) studies data on Spanish manufacturing industries at the three-digit NACE level (93 sectors) for a more recent period, 1993–2002, which are based on the Industrial Companies Survey. Sectors with higher labour costs per employee are outsourcing more. Furthermore, sectors with a lower average size of firms are, on average, outsourcing more than sectors with larger firms.

Conclusions

In this chapter we reviewed empirical studies which focus on measurement, size and trends of outsourcing activities in international economics, but restricted attention to the manufacturing sectors only. International outsourcing was one of the strongest components of international integration in recent decades, although the size of this component depends on measurement and definitions. However, there are large differences across countries (larger countries tend to have lower outsourcing activities) and across industries. Furthermore there are quite large country differences with respect to sectoral reliance on imported intermediate inputs. When looking at the relationship between foreign direct investment activities and outsourcing most studies conclude that these are complements rather than substitutes.

The relationship between trade structures and outsourcing – which is commonly seen as two-way – is ambiguous. Firm-level studies on outsourcing more or less confirm the findings of the industry-level studies with respect to sectoral characteristics. Here some firm characteristics of outsourcing firms are summarized also. Other issues such as, for example, the effects of outsourcing on labour markets and performance of outsourcing firms and theoretical contributions have not been summarized here.

References

Abraham, K.G. and Taylor, S.K. (1996), 'Firms' use of outside contractors: theory and evidence', *Journal of Labor Economics*, vol. 14, pp. 394–424.

Antweiler, W. and Trefler, D. (2002), 'Increasing returns and all that: a view from trade', *American Economic Review*, vol. 92, no. 1, pp. 93–119.

Arndt, S.W. (1997), 'Globalization and the open economy', *The North American Journal of Economics and Finance*, vol. 8, no. 1, pp. 71–79.

Arndt, S.W. and Kierzkowski, H. (2001), *Fragmentation: New Production Patterns in the World Economy*, Oxford University Press, Oxford.

Audet, D. (1996), 'Globalisation in the clothing industry', in OECD, *Globalisation of Industry: Overview and Sector Reports*, OECD, Paris, pp. 323–55.

Bardan, A.D. and Jaffee, D. (2004), 'On intra-firm trade and multinationals: foreign outsourcing and offshoring in manufacturing', Working Paper, University of Berkeley.

Bernard, A.B. and Jensen, B. (1999), 'Exceptional exporter performance: cause, effect, or both?', *Journal of International Economics*, vol. 47, pp. 1–25.

Bhagwati, J.N. (1984), 'Splintering and disembodiment of services and developing nations', *The World Economy*, vol. 7, June, pp. 133–43.

Blomström, M., Lipsey, R.E. and Kulchyck, K. (1988), 'US and Swedish direct investment and exports', in R. Baldwin (ed.), *Trade Policy Issues and Empirical Analysis*, University of Chicago Press, Chicago.

Brainard, S.L. (1995a), 'An empirical assessment of the proximity-concentration tradeoff between multinational sales and trade', NBER Working Paper No. 4580.

Brainard, S.L. (1995b), 'An empirical assessment of the factor proportions explanation of multinational sales', NBER Working Paper No. 4583.

Buigues, P. and Jacquemin, A. (1994), 'Foreign direct investment and exports to the European community', in M. Mason and D. Encarnation (eds), *Does Ownership Matter? Japanese Multinationals in Europe*, Oxford University Press, Oxford and New York.

Campa, J. and Goldberg, L.S. (1997), 'The evolving external orientation of manufacturing industries: evidence from four countries', NBER Working Paper no. 5919.

Dixit, A.K. and Grossman, G.M. (1982), 'Trade and protection with multistage production', *Review of Economic Studies*, vol. 59, pp. 583–94.

Feenstra, R.C. (1998), 'Integration of trade and disintegration of production in the global economy', *Journal of Economic Perspectives*, vol. 12, Fall, pp. 31–50.

Feenstra, R. and Hanson, G. (1996), 'Globalization, outsourcing and wage inequality', National Bureau of Economic Research, Working Paper 5424.

Feenstra, R.C. and Hanson, G.H. (1997), 'Foreign direct investment and relative wages: Evidence from Mexico's Maquiladoras,' *Journal of International Economics*, vol. 42, 371–93.

Feenstra, R.C. and Hanson, G.H. (1999), 'The impact of outsourcing and high-technology capital on wages: estimates for the United States 1979–1999', *Quarterly Journal of Economics*, vol. 114, no. 3, pp. 907–40.

Fontagné, L., Freudenberg, M. and Ünal-Kesenci, D. (1997), *Statistical Analysis of EC Trade in Intermediate Products*, EuroStat Statistical Document, Luxembourg.

Gereffi, G. (1999), 'International trade and industrial upgrading in the apparel commodity chain', *Journal of International Economics*, vol. 48, no. 1, pp. 37–70.

Görg, H. and Hanley, A. (2005), 'International outsourcing and productivity: evidence from the Irish electronics industry', *The North American Journal of Economics*, vol. 16, no. 2, pp. 225–69.

Görzig B. and Stephan, A. (2002), 'Outsourcing and firm-level performance', Discussion Paper No. 309, DIW, Berlin.

Graham, E.M. (2004), 'On the relationship among direct investment and international trade in the manufacturing sector: empirical results for the United States and Japan', Institute for International Economics, at: www.ap.harvard.edu/mainsite/papers/recoop/graham/graham.html.

Grossman, G.M. and Helpman, E. (1999), 'The internationalisation of economic activity', National Science Foundation.

Hummels, D., Ishi, J. and Yi, K-M. (2001), 'The nature and growth of vertical specialization in world trade', *Journal of International Economics*, vol. 54, no. 1, pp. 75–96.

Hummels, D., Rapoport, D. and Yi, K-M. (1998), 'Vertical specialization and the changing nature of world trade', *Federal Reserve Bank of New York Economic Policy Review*, June, pp. 79–99.

Irwin, D. (1996), 'The United States in a new world economy? A century's perspective', *American Economic Review*, May, vol. 86, no. 2, pp. 41–51.

Jones, J. (1995), 'Forces behind restructuring in U.S. apparel retailing and its effect on the U.S. apparel industry', *Industry, Trade and Technology Review*, March, pp. 23–27.

Jones, R.W. and Kierzkowski, H. (1990), 'The role of services in production and international trade: a theoretical framework', in R.W. Jones and A.O. Krueger (eds), *The Political Economy of International Trade: Essays in Honor of Robert E. Baldwin*, Basil Blackwell, Oxford, pp. 31–48.

Kaminski, B. and Ng, F. (2001), *Trade and Production Fragmentation: Central European Economies in EU Networks of Production and Marketing*, The World Bank, Washington DC.

Kimura, F. (2001), 'Fragmentation, internationalisation, and interfirm linkages: evidence from the micro data of Japanese manufacturing firms; in L.K. Cheng and H. Kierzkowski (eds), *Global Production and Trade in East Asia*, Kluwer Academic Publishers, Boston, MA.

Kleinert, J. (2003), 'Growing trade in intermediate goods: outsourcing, global sourcing and increasing importance of MNE networks', *Review of International Economics*, Vol. 11, no. 3, pp. 464–82.

Krugman, P.R. (1996), 'Does third world growth hurt first world prosperity?', *Harvard Business Review*, vol. 72, pp. 113–21.

Kurz, C.J. (2004), 'Outstanding outsourcers: a firm and plant-level analysis of production sharing', Working Paper, University of Michigan.

Leamer, E.E. (1996), 'The effects of trade in services, technology transfer and delocalisation on local and global income inequality', *Asia-Pacific Economic Review*, vol. 2, April, pp. 44–60.

Mora, C.D. (2004), 'Trends and pattern of outsourcing in Spanish industry: a comparative sectoral perspective', paper presented at the 6th European Trade Study Group Conference, Nottingham, September.

Simone, G. (2003), 'The effects of international fragmentation of production on trade patterns: an empirical assessment, Working Paper, University of Turin.

Swenson, D.L. (2000), 'Firm outsourcing decisions: evidence from U.S. foreign trade zones', Economic Inquiry, vol. 38, no. 2, pp. 175–89.

Tempest, R. (1996), 'Barbie and the world economy', *Los Angeles Times*, 22 September, sections A1 and A12.

Tisdale, S. (1994), 'Shoe and tell', *The New Republic*, 12 September, pp. 10–11.

Tomiura, E. (2004), 'Foreign outsourcing and firm-level characteristics: evidence from Japanese manufacturers', Discussion Paper Series d04-64, Institute of Economic Research, Hitotsubashi University.

Urata, S. (1995), 'Emerging patterns of production and foreign trade in electronic products in East Asia: an examination of a role played by foreign direct investment', paper presented at the Competing Production Networks in Asia: Host Country Perspective Conference, Asia Foundation, San Francisco, California, 27–28 April.

World Bank (1997), *Global Economic Prospects and the Developing Countries*, World Bank, Washington, DC.

World Investment Report 1996, at: www.unctad.org/en/docs/wir96ove.en.pdf.

WTO (1998), *Annual Report 1998*, at: www.wto.org/english/res_e/booksp_e/anrep_e/anre98_e.pdf.

Yeats, A.J. (2001), 'Just how big is global production sharing?', in S.W. Arndt and H. Kierzkowski (eds), *Fragmentation: New Production Patterns in the World Economy*, Oxford University Press, Oxford.

Yoffie, D.B. and Gomes-Casseres, B. (1994), *International Trade and Competition*, McGraw-Hill, New York.

11 SMEs' Ability to Go Global: The Relevance of Aggregation and Critical E-Applications in Outsourcing
David H. Brown and Nigel J. Lockett

The economic scale and importance of small and medium-sized enterprises (SMEs) is often underestimated. Within the European Union (EU) there are over 18 million SMEs generating 67 per cent of employment and 59 per cent of total GDP (Coridos, 2002). Typically, over 98 per cent of all the enterprises have fewer than 250 employees – the upper threshold for SMEs. This small-firm dependency is mirrored in the USA, and even more so in Asia. With such an important role in the creation of national wealth, it is not surprising that governments are concerned with developments that could affect this sector's performance. One such development is the slow engagement by SMEs in e-business, particularly in the more complex collaborative applications, such as supply chain management and customer relationship management. Recent studies suggest that this adoption is proving more problematic than anticipated.

> ... the government target of having 1 million businesses trading online by 2002 will be missed ... the study has found a slowdown in the uptake of ICTs, and for micro and small businesses there has been a clear reverse.
>
> (DTI, 2002, p. 6)

It is against this background of the low engagement of SMEs in e-business that this chapter investigates the potential for critical e-aggregation applications, defined as 'an e-business application, promoted by a trusted third party, who engages a significant number of SMEs by addressing an important shared business concern within an aggregation'. These specialized e-business applications represent an emerging form of selective outsourcing (Ward and Peppard, 2002) that is of particular relevance to SMEs and their ability to compete in increasingly competitive and global markets.

In writing this chapter the conventional approach of critically examining and interpreting current SME e-business practice was not possible. The reasons are twofold. First, although virtually all SMEs are Internet–connected, the number engaged in advanced applications is too small. Second, the theory related to SME outsourcing *per se* is limited. For these reasons the chapter is research-focused and based on very recent work by ourselves, using multiple methodologies, including qualitative case studies, quantitative surveys, participant observation and context monitoring. The research suggests that selective outsourcing to access critical e-aggregation applications can facilitate the e-business engagement of SMEs. There are three key findings that are explored in detail within the chapter. Together they provide some insight for SMEs into both the rationale for selective outsourcing and the particular form that this outsourcing might take locally and globally. Although this research was UK based, benchmarking studies have shown that the engagement in e-business by SMEs in Europe, the USA, Asia and Australasia follows a similar pattern (DTI, 2002).

The research was framed in three ways. First, it recognized that the relative failure of SMEs to engage in e-business was not simply down to the SMEs themselves. Rather, it anticipated that the perspective of the service providers would be crucial, and hence user and provider viewpoints were deliberately incorporated into the research. Second, the research assumed that an important factor in the decision of SMEs to engage in e-business was their perception of the complexity, relevance and accessibility of the e-business functions – hence the significance of 'critical e-applications' as a concept. Third, and from an explicit provider perspective, the research took as axiomatic that service providers would only be interested in profitable business models and that this would necessitate some form of SME aggregation. Finally, within this framework, the supporting literature, which provides the interpretation for the various findings, draws on both praxis and three areas of theory, namely information technology (IT) adoption by SMEs, inter-organizational networks (IONs) and e-business models.

Reflecting the above, the chapter is divided into four further sections: e-business and complexity; the context for outsourcing of e-business applications by SMEs; some key findings from a UK investigation; and, finally contributions to theory and global practice for SMEs.

E-business, complexity and application service providers (ASPs)

Before exploring the potential of e-business outsourcing for SMEs it is necessary to clarify terms. This is especially important when the area is so new. Until very recently e-commerce and e-business were used interchangeably, but increased understanding of the role of e-networks for consumers, industry partners and internal business processes have led to a common view. E-commerce can be seen as transaction-focused, whereas e-business is transaction-, process- and collaboration-focused and can be defined as 'the use of electronic communication networks to transact, process and collaborate in business markets'. Hence e-business incorporates e-commerce (Brown and Lockett, 2004). For the purposes of this chapter the use of e-business applications by SMEs, which ordinarily would be 'hosted', is taken to be a form of selective outsourcing.

The recent and rapid emergence of e-business applications has been primarily the result of the availability of a low-cost, ubiquitous electronic communication network – the Internet. Using this technology, telecommunication, technology and service companies have emerged or evolved to provide a range of e-business services. Typically these are known as application service providers (ASPs) that:

> ... *provide a contractual service offering to deploy, host, manage and rent access to an application from a centrally managed facility, responsible for either directly or indirectly providing all the specific activities and expertise aimed at managing a software application or set of applications.*

> (Gillian *et al.*, 1999)

In order to appreciate the full spectrum of outsourcing offered by ASPs we need to classify e-business applications, as there are significant differences between e-mail and e-marketplace applications in terms of both complexity and added value. Overall, the superficial reporting of high levels of connectivity by SMEs in many countries does little to encourage critical analysis of the apparent lack of engagement in higher complexity e-business applications. The International Data Corporation used application complexity to segment the ASP market, and this forms an initial basis for a proposed classification (see Table 11.1). Importantly this classification of application complexity stresses the roles of collaboration and interaction as key features of e-business applications and recognizes the resultant increase in complexity. In the context of this research, application complexity incorporates both technical and organizational factors – for example, both the security technologies underpinning virtual private networks used in higher-complexity hosted applications and the perceived commercial risk from storing sensitive client information in third-party data centres. Thus application complexity provides a meaningful framework in which to consider, compare and analyse e-business engagement.

The context for outsourcing e-business applications by SMEs

Ward and Peppard (2002) place application service provision within the context of outsourcing strategies and, in particular, its role in selective outsourcing. They note that 'ASPs primarily target SMEs that cannot afford their own IS functions' (2002, p. 574), but conclude that customers remain to be convinced. The value proposition for ASPs is still emerging, but benefits can be significant and the adoption decision requires consideration of multiple factors (see Tables 11.2 and 11.3).

Kern *et al.* (2002) explored the strategic outsourcing nature of ASPs through the use of a contingency model, which incorporated resource dependency, resource-based transaction cost and agency theory, and argued that there were many similarities with more traditional IT outsourcing. Currie and Seltsikas (2001) noted the similarity between IT outsourcing and applications service provision as well, but also noted that SMEs had little experience of outsourcing. Interestingly their study stated that, of the 424 ASPs reviewed, over 45 per cent

Table 11.1 Classification of e-business application complexity

Proposed classification		Examples	Complexity
Communication	COM	E-Mail, web access	Very Low
Marketing	MAR	Website	Low
Productivity	PRO	Microsoft Office, intranet	Low
E-commerce	E-C	Buying & selling online	Medium
Collaborative	COL	Extranet	Medium
Enterprise	ENT	Financials, sales force automation, vertical applications	High
Marketplace	M-P	E-Marketplaces	High
Collaborative enterprise	C-E	Supply chain management, customer relationship management	Very High
Collaborative platform	C-P	Emerging platforms	Very High

Source: Lockett and Brown (2001).

Table 11.2 Potential user benefits of application service provision

Benefit	Description
Reducing TCO	The total cost of ownership can reduce by between 30% and 60% over purchasing and managing hardware and software.
More predictable costs	The rental business model transfers the financial risk of software and hardware to the ASP.
Flexibility	Contracts are typically one-year, with minimal exit fees. Generally able to change services used.
Quicker deployment	Significant reduction in the overall implementation time of IOS into productive operation.
Reduction in complexity	The ASP manages the IT infrastructure themselves. Organizations buy a service rather than software application.

Source: Ward and Peppard (2002).

Table 11.3 Factors for consideration when selecting an ASP

Failsafe back-up servers to ensure 24x7x365	Set-up templates to speed implementation
Automatic load-balancing to ensure accessibility	Simple set-up for new users
Highly configurable application-level security	User statistics by application
Offline data back-up scheduling	Automatic up/download from application
Service-level agreement to ensure performance	E-mail delivery of alerts and reports
Secure access to application servers	Online FAQs, manuals and training courses
Support for EDI	Online support via e-mail and real-time chat

Source: Ward and Peppard (2002).

failed over the four years of the investigation and that only 42 per cent had survived in their original form, with the remainder being the subject of mergers and acquisitions. Patnayakuni and Seth (2001) similarly described ASPs as a new model of IT outsourcing and proposed an adoption model which incorporated social exchange theory, particularly concerning power and trust. The comparison of the traditional IT outsourcing and ASP models highlighted the differences in the target clients, namely large organizations with their own IT departments and, initially, SMEs with low IT expertise respectively. Interestingly, the recent trend for larger organizations to adopt the ASP model was identified. Clearly there are differences between IT outsourcing and the ASP model in terms of user, provider, delivery and functionality, but the extensive research on IT outsourcing has much to contribute to this emerging field, not least in the strategic nature of this decision regardless of company size (Kern *et al.*, 2002; Willcocks *et al.*, 2000; Willcocks and Lacity, 1998).

Key findings from a UK investigation

The research on which this chapter is based is part of a wider ongoing programme investigating the engagement of SMEs in e-business. The key findings presented here draw primarily from a survey instrument and case study investigation, both of which are described briefly. First, the quantitative data was obtained from questionnaire surveys of adopters (users) and non-adopters (non-users). In this context 'users' are defined as enterprises using e-aggregation applications within the aggregation cases and 'non-users' are defined as enterprises within the wider aggregation not using e-aggregation applications. The two samples of users and non-users were independent of each other. In both samples the number of responses was greater than 30 (that is, 43 for users and 104 for non-users). In this situation the parametric independent samples t-test could be applied and this demonstrates statistically important differences between the two samples. The t-test was applied to a number of variables anticipated to highlight differences (see Tables 11.4 and 11.5). Second, the choice of case study as a research method was central to the design and interpretation of this research. Identification of suitable data sources was undertaken in 2000 and 2002, with the field investigations carried out between 2000 and 2003. Interview data collection took the form of semi-structured interviews with mostly senior managers in 26 organizations, which included a range of community and enterprise intermediaries. The semi-structured interviews covered: the context for e-business engagement and SMEs, including: special factors and personal experience; the evidence and nature of aggregation, including governance, intermediary roles and actual or future actors; provider business models, including strategy, structure, processes, revenues, legal issues and technology. The interviews showed considerable internal consistency, suggesting that the sample numbers were representative. Where possible, additional data, marketing material, technical briefs and websites were collected in order to supplement interview data and achieve a triangulation of data sources. Qualitative data analysis was undertaken in parallel to the data collection. The units of analysis were individual organizations in each case. The overall method of data collection and analysis was rooted in the concept of embedded case design as suggested by Yin (1994). This necessitated a methodical, systematic approach to the multiple site investigations. There were three main findings, as described below:

EVIDENCE OF HIGHER LEVELS OF SELECTIVE OUTSOURCING BY SMEs IN AGGREGATIONS

There are significantly higher levels of e-business engagement (selective outsourcing) by users of e-aggregation applications in the four aggregations surveyed compared with non-users in the wider aggregations and two European studies (see Figure 11.1). This is true at all levels of complexity. This is hardly surprising for web access (very low complexity) and e-aggregation application (high complexity) as these are self-selecting requirements for the user sample. However, engagement in low-, medium- and very high-complexity applications was also significantly higher when compared with both non-users in the wider aggregation and the secondary data. The use of IT generally was greater in users, with 74 per cent of employees using computers daily compared with 45 per cent in non-users. The conclusions are threefold. First, there are aggregations of SMEs that have significant levels of engagement in higher-complexity e-business applications – that is, the industry-specific e-applications, or (critical) e-aggregation applications. Second, the users of e-aggregations applications have significantly

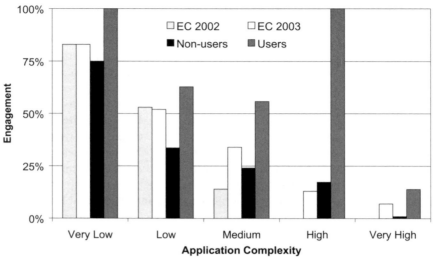

Figure 11.1   Selective outsourcing by SMEs

higher levels of engagement in other e-business applications than non-users. Third, non-users in the wider UK sample are not markedly different from the European SMEs.

This latter finding is reassuring in that the aggregations selected as part of the authors' research do not appear to be intrinsically different from SMEs generally. It emerges also from the survey that there are several statistically significant differences between users of e-aggregation applications and non-users in the wider aggregation. Compared to non-users, users of the e-aggregation applications are generally more knowledgeable and experienced on e-business, are more willing to believe that e-business can deliver efficiencies and new ways of doing business, are more influenced by sales, marketing and innovation factors, and, finally, are less concerned by cost and benefit issues. In respect of security, both users and non-users felt that this was an important barrier to adoption. Tables 11.4 and 11.5 summarize the position.

In conclusion, both the secondary European studies and the non-user survey indicate high levels of connectivity and usage of very low-complexity applications, such as e-mail and web browsers, amongst SMEs in the UK, Europe and North America. One recent study concluded that SME connectivity was static or declining (Oftel, 2003) and another that connectivity was no longer a barrier to e-business engagement (EC, 2003). This suggests that most SMEs appeared comfortable with e-mail and web access (lower complexity). However as application complexity increased, levels of engagement declined significantly, indicating that SMEs are tentative with the use of the Internet for online buying and selling (medium complexity), but had little or no engagement in the high- or very high-complexity applications, such as e-marketplaces, supply chains or inter-organizational collaborative networks. In direct contrast to these studies, our surveys have provided evidence that SMEs' engagement in complex e-business applications through critical e-aggregation applications, discussed in the next section, is a significant development, and that such SMEs had significantly higher levels of engagement in other e-business applications.

EMERGENCE OF CRITICAL E-AGGREGATION APPLICATIONS

All 12 community intermediaries (for example, trade associations) and the eight vertical application service providers (VSPs), a type of enterprise intermediary, confirmed the

Table 11.4 Statistically significant differences between non-users and users

		Degrees of freedom	Critical Value (%) 5.0%, 2.5%, 1.0%	t-test
Attitude to e-business	*	100	1.660, 1.984, 2.364	4.694
Knowledge and experience of e-business	*	85	1.663, 1.988, 2.371	3.612
E-business allows you to do same activities more efficiently?	*	100	1.660, 1.984, 2.364	4.855
E-business allows you to develop new ways of doing business?	*	95	1.661, 1.985, 2.366	2.285
What has helped or encouraged you to use e-business applications (enablers)?				
i) Sales and marketing	*	100	1.660, 1.984, 2.364	1.864
ii) Operational		100	1.660, 1.984, 2.364	0.466
iii) Innovation	*	100	1.660, 1.984, 2.364	4.642
iv) External		100	1.660, 1.984, 2.364	0.564
What is discouraging you from further use of e-business applications (barriers)?				
i) Security		100	1.660, 1.984, 2.364	1.193
ii) Cost and benefits	*	100	1.660, 1.984, 2.364	5.130
iii) Infrastructure and services		100	1.660, 1.984, 2.364	0.711
iv) Information and education	*	100	1.660, 1.984, 2.364	3.870

Table 11.5 Arithmetic mean of perceived benefits

	DTI 2002	Non-users	Users
What has helped or encouraged you to use e-business applications (enablers)?			
i) Sales and marketing	3.35	3.56	3.89
ii) Operational	3.38	3.71	3.64
iii) Innovation	3.45	3.27	4.04
iv) External	–	2.98	3.07
What is discouraging you from further use of e-business applications (barriers)?			
i) Security	3.43	3.71	3.52
ii) Cost and benefits	2.80	3.55	2.86
iii) Infrastructure and services	3.06	3.25	3.14
iv) Information and education	2.65	3.30	2.68

* indicates a significant difference (greater that 0.05 or 5%).

importance of SME-focused applications that attempted to address particular needs of SMEs within aggregations. In the four aggregations where both intermediary types were interviewed the interaction between the community intermediary and VSP was stated to be a very important factor in achieving the engagement of users. This continuous interaction between the two intermediary types helped to identify business needs and the resultant modifications to the e-aggregation applications in order to benefit the users. The manager of one VSP stated that:

> ... working with them [the trade association] has been critical to us developing an application that meets the user's needs. It has given us a competitive advantage and a better product.

Early examples of e-aggregation applications developed in this collaborative way and confirmed through the interviews include: advertising artwork management, for artwork agencies in regional newspapers; and project management, for the construction industry.

In the main, these e-aggregation applications were relatively new and in the early stages of development but already they appeared to be successful if measured by the level of uptake. For example, the artwork management application provider reported that the recruitment of users had been exponential and that 'more than 60 per cent of potential users, small artwork agencies, had registered'. In the case of the project management application there were high levels of engagement by contractors and future building contracts would only be awarded to contractors using the e-aggregation application.

All eight of the VSPs supplying applications had identified what they believed to be an unmet business need of SMEs in a specific business market. Two of the five providers interviewed took the lead and developed the e-aggregation applications without a guaranteed market for the product. However, they had identified community intermediaries early in the application's development and sought to establish collaborative arrangements that mitigated the risk. The three remaining service providers developed the applications in response to the business needs identified by the community intermediary, but even here there was no guarantee of adoption by the aggregation of SMEs. This depended on the perceived effectiveness of the application, which could vary within the aggregation, and on cost.

All eight VSPs could be characterized as offering a new functionality that was valued by aggregation members, was developed by interaction with community intermediaries and used a 'one-to-many' business model. In the user survey 85 per cent confirmed this provision of new functionality. On this basis these e-aggregation applications can be seen as 'critical' in terms of both functionality and perceived importance. *The innovative nature of these 'critical e-aggregation applications' was the single most important factor for using the application in the aggregation cases.* For example, in the case of the project management application, SME contractors (users) benefited from access to the project plan and opportunities for increased sales. The lead client provided support to use this project management application, which hosted over 500 projects covering £1.6 billion worth of assets and resulted in 100 000 user log-ins per month. In contrast, the four horizontal enterprise intermediaries offered applications to SMEs that aimed to meet standard business functions, such as accounting and material control. Although these could be customized to meet local needs, the providers were explicitly not attempting to produce innovative applications requiring deep industry knowledge.

These critical e-aggregation applications emerged, at the instigation of both community and enterprise intermediaries, in order to address a perceived business need within aggregations dominated by SMEs. Most users confirmed that the provision of this new functionality was important to their business. The main three drivers for engaging in these e-aggregation applications were: (i) managing upgrades to the applications; (ii) the need to reduce costs; and (iii) the reduced working life of applications. The three main benefits were: (i) speed of deployment; (ii) reduced costs; and (iii) improved quality of service to customers. Interestingly 75 per cent of users had no internal IT specialist.

THE ROLES AND MECHANISMS FOR INTERMEDIARIES IN FACILITATING OUTSOURCING?

In this empirical research all 26 data sources confirmed the importance of trust within the formation and development of SME aggregations engaged in e-business. Some of the community intermediaries noted that the emergence of new and unknown online intermediaries addressing aggregations added to the confusion many SMEs felt regarding e-business. Many community and enterprise intermediaries recognized that existing trusted offline relationships, be they a lead company in a business network or a trade association, could be important in recruiting SMEs to online services. Trade associations, in particular, identified a new role for themselves as a sponsor or facilitator, rather than as a direct provider of e-business services. In their view this situation derived from the SMEs' view of them as trusted third parties that could be relied on to act in their interests. One general secretary of a trade association stated that:

> ... our members are finding it increasingly difficult to know which provider (e-marketplace) to use and are wanting us to endorse products. We are organizing a special event at our next general meeting to discuss this with members... I cannot see how it could be cost-effective for us to develop our own [e-marketplace].

This new role was genuinely emergent – none of the trade associations (not involved in e-aggregation applications) had foreseen the possibility that this new role could have very significant strategic implications. Not surprisingly, all VSPs specifically identified the role of the community intermediary as being important in the recruitment of users to their applications, based on their trusted relationship within the aggregations. The nature of this relationship varied from simple provision as in the case of the advertising artwork service provider to active joint initiatives as in the case of the field management application.

The trusted third parties in the aggregation cases exhibited several clear differences from those not involved in e-aggregation applications. Firstly they deliberately worked with service providers (enterprise intermediaries) to appreciate the business needs within the aggregation and develop e-aggregation applications to meet these needs. Secondly they were aware of the accumulation of valuable information about the aggregation resulting from interaction with the e-aggregation application and thirdly they participated in activities that attempted to increase e-aggregation application engagement of SMEs in the aggregation. These activities included (i) shaping users' perceptions, (ii) identifying and introducing the innovation to intact sub-groups within the aggregations, (iii) promoting (targeting) it to and through key actors, and (iv) providing incentives to early adopters. These critical mass building activities were evident, to a greater or lesser extent, in all of the aggregation cases.

In addition to the contribution made by the community intermediaries to the development of specific applications and to facilitating access to the SMEs, they had two further roles that derived directly from their trusted third party status: first, as negotiators of the fees charged either directly to users or themselves; and, second, as negotiators for the service-level agreement (SLA) with the service providers. For example, the lead client of a construction consortium for new retail stores negotiated and paid the service provider fees for the project management application to be used by the designated network of contractors and subcontractors. Similarly, the newspaper trade association paid the service fees for advertising agencies submitting artwork via the artwork management application. In each of these cases the perceived or actual benefits of more effective project management and the ease of use resulting in increased advertising respectively were sufficient to provide the services with no direct charge to users.

In nearly all instances both the community and enterprise intermediaries indicated that the SMEs appeared to rely heavily on the community intermediaries as the trusted third party to approve and hold the SLA with the service provider. Clearly, the role of trusted third parties goes beyond simply negotiating fees and SLAs with service providers. They hold unique positions, based on resilient trust, within business sectors often gained over many years and across many aspects of trading relationships. This research highlights their importance in the engagement of SMEs in e-business applications.

In conclusion, the role of trusted third parties, acting as community intermediaries, appears to be critical to the adoption of e-aggregation applications provided by VSPs acting as enterprise intermediaries. These trusted third parties worked with service providers to identify the business needs of users within the aggregations and to develop applications to meet these. Importantly there was strong and compelling evidence that trusted third parties used existing relationships based on mutual trust to facilitate the negotiation of fees and SLAs. This negotiating role seemed to be particularly valued because of the confusion felt by SMEs as result of the rapidly changing technological environment and emergence of new unknown intermediaries.

Contributions to theory and global practice for SMEs

This recent work has helped to identify the business benefits to SMEs from adopting e-business applications and the special role of aggregation in facilitating engagement. Theoretically, the work adds to the framework of concepts that help interpret more generally the issues of engagement by SMEs. It makes specific contributions to the theory supporting the interpretative framework constructed from the review of: (i) SMEs' adoption of IT; (ii) inter-organizational networks (IONs) and inter-organizational information systems (IOS); and (iii) e-business models and intermediaries. Each of these is discussed briefly below.

First, in relation to other work on ICT adoption specific to SMEs (for example, Blili and Raymond, 1993; Levy et al., 2001; Mehrtens et al., 2001) the emphasis is on such factors as strategic logic, implementation enablers and organization-specific factors – all viewed from a user perspective. This work has been influential, but application complexity per se is not singled out. In this investigation, however, the findings emphasize that, in the experience of the providers, perceived application complexity is crucial to SMEs and that these organizations would not proceed to adopt high-complexity applications without substantial support.

Second, the research findings in respect of aggregation as a means of helping SMEs develop their e-business capability can be reflected on theoretically in several ways. In terms of the rationale for inter-organizational network (ION) formation there have been significant research contributions (for example, Ebers, 1997; Miles and Snow, 1986; Oliver, 1990). The research contributes to the important theoretical area of IONs by the development of taxonomy of aggregations (see Figure 11.2). This embodies two notions. One is that the concept of aggregation is best conceived as a meta-concept and that there are different types of aggregation. The other is that the dimensions of structure and integration can distinguish these different types. This highlights the importance of existing groupings or aggregations, consisting predominantly of SMEs.

Third, there are some observations on the theory of e-business models and, in particular, intermediaries. The value of conceptualizing the different roles in the form of the eTrust Platform (Figure 11.3) has already been highlighted. In the small but growing literature on e-business

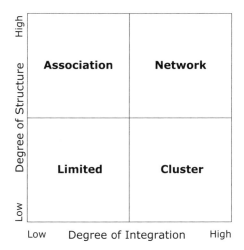

Source: Brown and Lockett (2004)

Figure 11.2 Taxonomy of aggregations for SMEs

models (for example, Earle and Keen, 2000; Tapscott *et al.*, 2000; Timmers, 2000) there is considerable emphasis on the opportunities for disintermediation and reintermediation. In terms of theory, even before any empirical data were interpreted, the research has confirmed the usefulness of the eTrust Platform conceptualization (Figure 11.3) as a means of framing the discussion with the different types of organization involved.

In terms of praxis, the findings are unequivocal with respect to how the service providers are organized. In the context of large enterprises the 'one-to-one' marketing business model is viable for both vertical (that is, sector-specific) and horizontal (that is, generic) business applications. Enterprise resource planning (ERP), from either a specialist or generic provider, serves as a good example. In this instance, the implementation of this complex application will generate further demands on financial and human capital as the requirements of customization, integration and ongoing support are recognized, and these demands can normally be met by large enterprises. In the setting of SMEs, whilst it is economic to provide higher e-business applications on a 'one-to-many' basis, the cost of marketing and supporting on a 'one-to-one' basis appears to be larger than the potential return. This is clearly not the case for lower-complexity applications, such as e-mail. It would be possible to conclude that, as SMEs become more aware of the advantages of higher-complexity e-business applications, adoption rates would increase, but this was not borne out by the statistics. The clear evidence from all of the community and enterprise intermediaries interviewed was that the aggregation model is likely to be the most viable means of engaging SMEs. By confirming this provider perspective the research adds to our understanding of the likely mechanisms for engaging SMEs in complex e-business applications that are both desirable and economically feasible.

For the individual SME the question of whether or not to adopt e-business applications specific to their sector is too simplistic. In reality, such applications would generally not be available from providers for the reasons previously given. It is the actual, or likely, existence of an 'organized' aggregation (that is, a network, association or cluster in terms of the taxonomy of aggregations) that underwrites the providers' interest. Once an aggregation has formed, then the relevance for individual SMEs of a range of factors, such as common interests, resource efficiencies and stability, governs whether or not to participate in the network. Their decision

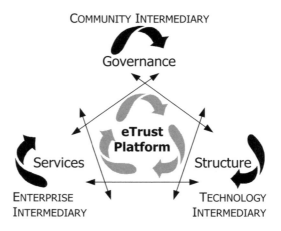

Figure 11.3 eTrust Platform (developed from Brown and Lockett, 2001)

is greatly supported by the mitigation of risk that involvement in a collaborative arrangement offers (Contractor and Lorange, 1988).

Conclusion

So, in summary, what are the implications for SMEs with global ambitions? The outsourcing of hosted simple web catalogue-type applications is clearly already available. Also accessible are the generic applications, such as accounting ledgers from the horizontal ASPs. However, for the larger and more complex applications, especially the collaborative B2B applications such as supply chain and customer relationship activities, the reality is much more difficult. Both international statistics and empirical work has signalled the low uptake by SMEs. Success globally is likely to be little different from success at a regional or national level. The evidence for the latter is that the key to engaging significant numbers of SMEs in the more complex e-business lies in industry-specific applications that can be delivered by providers on an economic basis. In turn, this suggests aggregations of SMEs, supported by community intermediaries, such as a trade association. Hence the role of these intermediaries is likely to prove strategic. As the trusted third party, they would occupy a governance role and be able to provide or facilitate the technical and commercial interface between ASPs and SMEs. It is this facilitation that, in the end, will empower SMEs to extend their international trade through effective e-business support.

References

Blili, S. and Raymond, L. (1993), 'Information technology: threats and opportunities for small and medium-sized enterprises', *International Journal of Information Management,* vol. 13, no. 6, pp. 439–48.

Brown, D.H. and Lockett, N, (2001), 'Engaging SMEs in e-business: the role of intermediaries within eClusters', *EM: Electronic Markets,* vol. 11, no. 1, pp. 52–58.

Brown, D.H. and Lockett, N. (2004), 'The potential of critical applications for engaging SMEs in e-business', *European Journal of Information Systems,* vol. 13, no. 1, pp. 21–34.

Contractor, F. and Lorange, P. (1988), *Cooperative Strategies in International Business,* Lexington Books, Lexington, MA.

Coridos (2002), at http://www.cordis.lu/euroabstracts/en/home.html (accessed October 2002).

Currie, W. and Seltsikas, P. (2001), 'Exploring the supply-side of IT outsourcing: evaluating the emerging role of application service providers', *European Journal of Information Systems*, vol. 10, no. 3, pp. 123–34.

DTI (2002), *Business into the Information Age: International Benchmarking Study 2002*, Department of Trade and Industry, 6366, London.

Earle, N. and Keen, P. (2000), *From .com to .profit: Inventing Business Models that Deliver Value and Profit*, Jossey-Bass, San Francisco, CA.

Ebers, M. (1997), *The Formation of Inter-Organisational Networks*, Oxford University Press, Oxford.

EC (2002), *Benchmarking National and Regional E Business Policies – Stage 1 – Synthesis Report, 7 February 2002*, European Commission, Brussels.

EC (2003), *The European E-business Report 2002/03 edition*, European Commission, Brussels.

Gillian, C., Graham, S., Levitt, M., McArthur, J., Murray, S., Turner, V., Villars, R. and McCarthy Whalen, M. (1999), *The ASPs' Impact on the IT Industry*, An ICS-Wide Opinion, Bulletin, IDC (International Data Corporation).

Kern, T., Kreijer, J. and Willcocks, L. (2002), 'Exploring ASP as sourcing strategy: theoretical perspectives, propositions for practice', *Journal of Strategic Information Systems*, vol. 11, no. 2, pp. 153–77.

Levy, M., Powell, P. and Yetton, P. (2001), 'SMEs: aligning IS and the strategic context', *Journal of Information Technology*, vol. 16, no. 1, pp. 133–44.

Lockett, N. and Brown, D.H. (2001), 'A framework for the engagement of SMEs in e-business', *Proceedings of the Americas Conference on Information Systems*, Boston, MA, pp. 656–62.

Mehrtens, J., Cragg, P. and Mills, A. (2001), 'A model of Internet adoption by SMEs', *Journal of Information and Management*, vol. 39, no. 3, pp. 165–76.

Miles, R. and Snow, C. (1986), 'Organisations: new concepts for new forms', *California Management Review*, vol. 28, no. 2, pp. 62–73.

Oftel (2003), *Business Use of Internet Oftel Small and Medium Business Survey: Q12 February 2003*, Office of Telecommunications, London.

Oliver, C. (1990), 'Determinants of interorganisational relationships: integration and future directions', *Academy of Management Review*, vol. 15, no. 2, pp. 241–65.

Patnayakuni, R. and Seth, N. (2001), 'Incorporating a social perspective to the adoption of application service provider model', *Proceedings of the Americas Conference on Information Systems*, Boston, MA, pp. 1848–50.

Tapscott, D., Ticoll, D. and Lowe, A. (2000), *Digital Capital: Harnessing the Power of the Business Web*, Nicholas Brealey, London.

Timmers, P. (2000), *Electronic Commerce: Strategies and Models for Business to Business Trading*, John Wiley and Sons, Chichester.

Ward, J. and Peppard, J. (2002), *Strategic Planning for Information Systems* (3rd edn), Wiley and Sons, Chichester.

Willcocks, L. and Lacity, M. (1998), *Strategic Sourcing of Information Systems: Perspective and Practices*, John Wiley and Sons, London.

Willcocks, L., Sauer, C. and associates (2000), *Moving to E-Business*, Random House, London.

Yin, R. (1994), *Case Study Research: Design and Methods*, Sage Publications, Beverley Hills, CA.

12 *The Economic Rationale and Labour Market Effects of Outsourcing: A Survey*

Andreas Knabe and Bertrand Koebel

The growing importance of outsourcing activities has given rise to an important economic literature on its impact on jobs, wages, efficiency and economic competitiveness. The purpose of this chapter is to present the economic rationale for outsourcing activities and to document the empirical evidence on the impact of outsourcing on wages and employment. Its focus will be both on the outsourcing decision at the firm level (domestic outsourcing) and on international outsourcing.

To analyse the economic rationale for domestic outsourcing, we will apply the theory of the firm as a theory of vertical *dis*integration. In this sense, outsourcing is understood as the split-up of two elements in the production chain which were formerly organized in one firm into two separate firms. By analysing why certain production processes were integrated in a firm in the first place, one understands also why firms decide to return to pure market exchange – that is, why they outsource. We will also present some empirical findings about the determinants and effects of firm-level outsourcing.

The other main focus of this chapter is on international outsourcing defined as substitution of production activities made within the firm by purchases of intermediate inputs from foreign firms. Whereas usual macroeconomic approaches deal with the formation and allocation of value added, they neglect, by construction, the role of intermediate material inputs and consider only imports and exports of *final* products. Recent contributions have explicitly considered intermediate material inputs in the production decision process in order to better understand the driving forces of outsourcing.

The common denominator of most contributions is the principle of maximization under constraints. The purpose of cost reduction or profit maximization not only determines the optimal amount of outsourcing but also the optimal labour demand, as well as the substitution possibilities between outsourcing and labour inputs.

In a closed economy the impact of outsourcing on total employment is quantitatively not very important since it mainly reallocates jobs from one firm to others. By contrast, in an open economy international reallocation may hurt employment in some countries. Since economists are mainly interested in the aggregate outcome of outsourcing, we focus on international outsourcing in this chapter.

In order to reach this objective, it is important to consider the specificities of labour markets, which are quite different across countries. Whereas in countries where unemployment has risen over recent decades researchers study the impact of outsourcing on unemployment and the demand for labour, in countries where the disparity in wages increased researchers mainly investigate the relationship between outsourcing and wages. Both aspects will be surveyed in this chapter.

Economic theories of outsourcing

The following two subsections will discuss various theoretic approaches to explaining the outsourcing phenomenon. In the first part, insights from the theory of industrial organization about firms' vertical structure will be reviewed and applied to the outsourcing decision. The main emphasis will be on problems of asset specificity, incomplete contracts and the hold-up problem. In the second part, international outsourcing will be discussed.

OUTSOURCING AT THE FIRM LEVEL

It is one of the central questions in economic theory, especially in the theory of industrial organization, why some productive activities are organized within firms, while others are conducted by market exchange between firms. In answering this question, traditionally the emphasis of economics was not so much on the question of outsourcing as on why firms 'insource' activities in the first place. In principle, all transactions necessary in the various stages of production could be undertaken using the spot-market or short-term contractual relations. In such an economic system, the production of any good would be conducted by the market interaction of atomistic production units, and thus everything would be 'outsourced'. The simple reason why we do not observe such extreme forms of market exchange in real-life economies is that market transactions are not costless. To avoid such transaction costs, some portions of the production process are withdrawn from short-term market exchanges and are instead governed by long-term relations, which are called 'firms'. Starting with Coase (1937), the existence of non-market modes of production has spurred the development of the 'theory of vertical integration', which is at the same time a theory of outsourcing.[1] Once one recognizes why firms as an integrated mode of production exist, one can understand why firms decide to vertical *dis*integrate – that is, why they outsource.

The driving force of vertical integration is transaction costs. A firm's procurement of inputs from independent suppliers is not costless – contracts have to be written, business conditions have to be negotiated, the quality of inputs has to be monitored and so on. Of course, in-house production is not costless either since it creates problems of workforce training, monitoring and motivation. Therefore, transaction cost assessments are comparative by nature. However, two phenomena clearly shift the balance in favour of in-house production: asset specificity and uncertainty with respect to the future.

Many business transactions involve investments that are specific. Such specificity can arise because suppliers must design equipment specific to the buyer's order (a car-component supplier produces parts that can only be used in a particular car maker's models), because a buyer promotes or sells a final product before an intermediate good is delivered (promoting a concert in a particular concert hall), or because users of raw materials invest in machinery that only works with this special kind of input (a power plant that can only combust a specific type of coal – see Tirole (1988, p. 21)). Other types of specificity are site specificity and firm-specific human capital (Williamson, 1975). By locating close to a potential buyer or seller, firms can

---

1   Perry (1989) gives a detailed overview of the theory of vertical integration. A shorter treatment can be found in Williamson (1996).

obtain a cost advantage specific to this site. A worker obtains firm-specific human capital by investing in training that increases his or her productivity only with the technology applied in one particular firm.

Making specific investments fundamentally transforms the relations of two firms. After a specific investment has been made, it becomes a sunk cost – that is, its next-best alternative use yields a much lower pay-off compared to the use for which it is specific. Asset specificity creates a lock-in effect: the part of the profits exceeding the pay-off from alternative uses can only be achieved if the business relation with the respective partner is continued. Since this part of profits is what exceeds the profits that the two firms could make with outside partners, it is an 'appropriable quasi-rent' (Klein *et al.*, 1978). No market forces can prevent either of the two firms from trying to appropriate these rents, and the division will be determined by the two firms' bargaining in a bilateral monopoly.

If contracts could be written before specific investments are undertaken, this would not cause a problem. The division of the quasi-rents would be determined *ex ante* in a way that gives the right investment incentives to the party making the specific investment, and the investment decisions could be made in an efficient way, maximizing the joint profit of the two firms. The problem is, however, that contracts governing business relations are generally incomplete. Economic environments are complex and uncertain, so it is impossible to design contracts that account for all possible contingencies. This is because contingencies are either not foreseeable at the contract date or there are too many to include them in the contract. In other cases, contracts might not be enforceable because contingencies are not observable by third parties – for example, courts. With incomplete contracts, each firm will try to act opportunistically and appropriate the quasi-rent after the investment is sunk. Anticipating that it might not be able to reap all the benefits from its investment, each firm will not invest efficiently in the specific asset *ex ante*. This inability to precommit leads to underinvestment and less than maximum joint profit. This is the so-called 'hold-up' problem.

The failure to maximize joint profits indicates that both parties prefer organizational modes in which they cannot be held up. One way of solving the problem is to integrate both firms, which eliminates the hold-up problem. An integrated firm has no incentive to opportunistically appropriate quasi-rents and will thus undertake the efficient level of investment.

Of course, integration is costly, too. Larger firms have more difficulties monitoring employees or identifying the productivity of single workers or departments, resulting in attenuated incentives. Also, large institutions are typically associated with higher bureaucratic distortions and costs. Thus, a simple cost–benefit analysis looks like this: the benefits of integration are that the specific asset is accumulated at the efficient level and joint profits are maximized. The costs are the institutional difficulties of managing a large organization. By comparing the two, the optimal pattern of integration for each firm can be derived.

The theory of vertical integration predicts that firms integrate if their relationship is dominated by specific investments. Conversely, this theory would predict that outsourcing should occur if the degree of asset specificity declines. Such a decline could occur under various circumstances. For example, it will often occur in growing industries. An industry in its early stages of development will typically comprise a small number of firms at each point in the value chain, producing specialized products. In such a value chain, each firm faces specificity with respect to both its inputs and its output. Therefore, one would expect to see a large level of integration in such a value chain. As the industry grows, more firms enter each point of the value chain such that upstream and downstream firms can avoid being held up more easily by reverting to firms producing similar products. Moreover, other industries might discover how to make use of the value chain's various products. In this process, the level of asset specificity is declining continually. Since the hold-up problem ceases to be important, but firms face bureaucracy costs if they stay integrated, the optimal reaction is clear: firms disintegrate and outsource parts of their production.

The divestiture of a monopoly can cause also downstream outsourcing. If an intermediate good is specific because its supplier is a monopoly, the resulting hold-up problem and underinvestment could cause the monopoly to integrate with the downstream firms. If the intermediate monopoly is divested into a number of smaller, but fully integrated firms, these new firms will not stay integrated since the initial reason to integrate has vanished.

Abstracting from the particular problems of asset specificity and incomplete contracts, other models have been developed that illuminate part of the reasons why under specific circumstances firms might optimally decide to (dis)integrate.

A line of literature emphasizes the role of demand fluctuations on vertical integration. Perry (1984) analyses a two-stage production chain in which there exists exogenous random net demand on the market for an intermediate good. This causes the price of the input good to fluctuate. Since profit functions are convex in the output price, sellers prefer to 'ride the highs and lows of the market' instead of trading at the expected price; buyers prefer the same because cost functions are concave in input prices (cf. Oi, 1961). Perry (1984) assumes that integration saves transactions costs; by integrating, however, firms withdraw from the intermediate good market and forego the benefits of demand fluctuations. If transaction costs savings exceed the benefits from 'riding the market', some firms will integrate. This will strengthen the influence of the exogenous demand component and make prices more volatile, thus raising the benefits from non-integration. Equilibrium will occur at some intermediate level of integration, where the two effects exactly balance. The model provides an explanation for the observation that seemingly identical firms opt for different outsourcing strategies.

De Kok (2000) offers a production-theoretic model of outsourcing that incorporates also fluctuating demand. A firm has to fix its productive capacity before knowing the exact demand for its product. If demand exceeds the predetermined capacity, the firm has two choices: it can either postpone serving the excess demand or it can serve the excess demand by hiring the productive capacity of other firms (outsourcing). It is assumed that outsourcing is more costly than serving demand by the firm's own capacity (if not, all capacity would be outsourced). In the model, optimality rules are derived which determine the optimal fixed capacity and the decision when to postpone service and when to use outsourcing. Intuitively, a higher interest rate favours outsourcing as postponing becomes more costly. Higher volatility of demand favours outsourcing as it becomes more likely that fixed capacity lies idle.

Generally, outsourcing means that buyers and sellers have to search for suitable trading partners. Grossman and Helpman (2002) take this as a starting point to develop a matching model of outsourcing. Their model is able to explain cross-regional differences in outsourcing by 'market thickness'. If there are increasing returns to scale in matching, 'thicker' markets (more buyers and sellers) reduce search costs and thus induce more outsourcing. Certain other developments might have had an influence on the efficiency of the search technology – for example, IT services might have made finding business partners easier and thus have accelerated outsourcing. More densely populated areas, or more closely networked economic environments in general, should see higher levels of outsourcing.

Outsourcing might serve also as a second-best reply to the non-integrability of specific factors. In the model of Lyons and Sekkat (1991), two firms suffer from a possible hold-up problem due to the specificity of the good traded between them. Although the two firms can integrate and thus eliminate this problem, both are still subject to the potentially opportunistic behaviour of labour unions. Unions are input suppliers that firms cannot integrate. Outsourcing might be a way of alleviating union power, even at the cost of hold-up behaviour. As the theory of the second-best predicts, some distortions might be desirable if they help alleviate an unavoidable distortion. Outsourcing can decrease the power of unions, either because they have to negotiate with separate firms (and thus cannot utilize the complementarities of labour in the two stages of production; cf. Horn and Wolinsky (1988)), or because production is sourced out to a non-unionized firm. Even though part of the profits has to be given to the subcontracting firm (opportunistic hold-up bargaining), less has to be given to the union. Lyons and Sekkat (1991) show that, under certain conditions, the latter effect dominates and that outsourcing can increase the firm's profits.

Various institutional and legal reasons can also affect the outsourcing decision. To just mention one, employment protection legislation decreases the discretionary power of management to adjust a firm's employment level at will. Since contracts made with input suppliers are typically not subject to employment protection, firms can circumvent such restrictions by outsourcing. For example, the subsequent adoption of the unjust dismissal doctrine by various US states has significantly spurred the rise of temporary help services, which provide a convenient way of outsourcing employees (Autor, 2003).

INTERNATIONAL OUTSOURCING

The outsourcing phenomenon affects the production structure not only between different firms, but also between different regions and countries. The rising integration of world markets is associated with a disintegration/delocalization of the production process. The main causes for this development can clearly be found in trade liberalization and lower transportation costs.

By 'international outsourcing', we mean an outsourcing process whose driving force is not differences between single firms, but differences between entire countries. Such international outsourcing takes place because countries differ in their factor prices, mainly in their wage levels, which encourages firms to move production to these countries in order to reduce their production costs.[2] This phenomenon has caught the interest of trade economists, who have applied conventional models of international trade to explain the surge in international outsourcing. These studies' principal interest is on the impact of trade on employment and wages, mainly of low-skilled workers in industrialized economies.

The majority of the literature applies the Heckscher–Ohlin trade model (also known as the factor proportions theory). Highly simplified, the model's reasoning is this: let two countries be endowed with skilled and unskilled labour in different proportions – that is, let one country be skill-abundant while the other is skill-scarce. In autarky, wages are determined by the proportions of the different types of labour in the respective country alone: in other words, in a skill-abundant nation, unskilled labour will receive a (relatively) high wage because it is (relatively) scarce, and vice versa in a nation with a relatively unskilled labour force. However, if the two nations can trade and are able to exchange their goods, unskilled labour becomes less scarce in the skill-abundant nation because it can 'import' unskilled labour embodied in the goods imported from the skill-scarce nation. Thus, although factors of production might be immobile, trade makes them indirectly mobile via the goods in which their labour is embodied. For the skill-abundant country, this process causes the wage gap between skilled

---

2   This type of international outsourcing is often referred to as 'offshore sourcing' or 'offshoring'.

and unskilled labour to widen, while the opposite happens in the skill-scarce country. Under certain conditions, the equilibrium outcome predicts that the same wage structure prevails across the world (factor price equalization). It should be noted that the factor proportions theory is not undisputed. Some restrictive assumptions are needed to reach the extreme result of complete factor price equalization: identical technology and tastes, absence of scale effects, and incomplete specialization (which means that all countries produce at least some amount of all traded goods).

In recent years, a number of models have been developed that relate the Heckscher–Ohlin model to international outsourcing. These models weaken the rigid assumptions necessary for complete factor price equalization by explicitly accounting for the specialization of trading countries, increasing returns to scale or transportation costs. Moreover, they also model trade in intermediate goods, which is closer to the notion of outsourcing than trade only in final goods.

Building on a Heckscher–Ohlin model, Feenstra and Hanson (1996a,b) assume that one final good is produced with a large number of intermediate goods. Factor endowments are allowed to differ sufficiently between different countries: in other words, factor prices do not converge completely, and countries specialize in the production of certain intermediate goods. If one region is well endowed with skilled labour, whereas the other region is abundant in unskilled labour, there will be a critical level of skill intensity in the production of intermediate goods that divides the production structure of the two regions. Outsourcing is understood as foreign investments – that is, the movement of the capital necessary for production of a certain fragment. If capital flows from the skill-intensive to the less skill-intensive region, the dividing critical level of skill intensity decreases, such that products at the lower end of the skill-intensity scale are outsourced from the skill-abundant to the skill-scarce region, where they appear at the high end of skill intensity. Through this shift, outsourcing increases the skill intensity and reduces the relative demand for unskilled workers in *both* countries. Thus, the assertion that outsourcing to less developed countries hurts low-skilled workers in industrialized countries is supported by the theory, but it does not mean that the reverse has to hold in the insourcing country.

Other models predict that outsourcing can also alleviate the problem of diverging wages. While Feenstra and Hanson (1996) focus on the factor bias of outsourcing, Arndt (1997, 1999) emphasizes the possible sector bias of outsourcing by allowing for more than one final good. Using a standard model of trade, he looks at small, open economies in which the prices of final goods are determined on world markets. If an industry can reduce production costs by sourcing out a single fragment of its final product, it gains competitiveness and will expand production. The benefits will accrue to the factor that is intensively used in the remaining fragments of the final good compared to the rest of the economy. If, for example, a textile producer (on average not skill-intensive) sources out the least skill-intensive fragment of shirt production, saves costs and gains a competitive advantage on the world market, this will benefit unskilled labour in its home country. Generally, the outsourcing of production fragments has different effects depending on the factor intensities of the final product. Thus, there is no clear effect of outsourcing on the labour demand for unskilled workers in industrialized countries.

Deardorff (2001a) also considers a Heckscher–Ohlin model with different final and intermediate goods. If trade in final goods were sufficient to equalize factor prices and disintegration was costly, no outsourcing would occur. Therefore, outsourcing can only arise in a situation in which factor prices differ initially (for example, due to complete specialization in final goods). Since the production of any final good might comprise fragments that are intensive in the country's scarce – that is, expensive – factor, these fragments can be sourced out profitably. Such outsourcing allows production to become more diversified and, if it enlarges the sets of feasible factor uses enough to accommodate endowment differences across countries, can lead to factor price equalization.[3]

Since Heckscher–Ohlin models often yield ambiguous results, Kohler (2001) applies a specific factors model to analyse outsourcing. Capital is assumed to be sector-specific, while labour can easily switch between sectors. If outsourcing takes place through foreign direct investment (FDI), capital goods specific to the outsourced sector move physically to another country. If such outsourcing is driven by low foreign wages, it unambiguously depresses the domestic wage. As capital leaves the economy, workers have to switch to other sectors where the additional labour supply depresses the wage. Obviously, this happens independently of the factor intensity of the outsourced component. The case looks somewhat different if capital cannot leave the economy – that is, outsourcing takes place through arm's-length transactions between the two countries. Since the total factor endowment stays constant in each country, the factor-intensity of the outsourced component is decisive for factor prices. If a fragment is sourced out which is more capital (labour)-intensive than the domestic average, the demand for labour rises (falls) and wages increase (decrease).

This quick glance at the theory has shown that it is conditioned by restrictive assumptions and often leads to ambiguous results. It is therefore difficult to draw clear and generally applicable predictions about the labour market effects of outsourcing. For domestic outsourcing, the theory tends to predict rising (aggregate) labour demand. If firms disintegrate because the main reason for their integration – asset specificity – has ceased to exist, they can save the administrative costs of integration and reduce their (combined) production costs. Outsourcing lowers the combined production costs of both the outsourcing and outsourced firm and thus increases the productivity of an economy. Thus, its effects are analogous to technological progress. If this cost reduction is passed on to consumers through lower prices, this will create additional demand either for the final good of the two firms or for other firms' products. In a competitive labour market, labour demand will increase to serve the additional demand, even if not in the same firm. The stimulated aggregate labour demand can be observed in higher wages, higher employment or a combination of both.

Things are, of course, somewhat different if outsourcing does not increase the firm's (technical) productivity, but is mainly aimed at weakening union power. In this case, the explicit goal of such a policy is to reduce wages in the firm. If it is successful, one should observe falling wages in the firm, while employment possibly increases.

The labour market effects of international outsourcing are theoretically ambiguous as well. First of all, firms might outsource internationally for the same reasons as they could domestically, and we would not expect to see any different effects from it. This effect should prevail mainly in outsourcing activities between economically similar countries. If outsourcing is motivated by international differences in factor prices, trade theory generally predicts that a country's scarce factor loses if the production of a good that is intensive in this scarce factor is outsourced. This means that labour, especially unskilled labour, is mainly hurt by international outsourcing to less capital/skill-rich countries. In some cases, however, the opposite might be true – for example, if a labour-intensive industry becomes internationally more competitive

---

3   On the other hand, if outsourcing does not cause factor prices to converge completely, one cannot conclude that outsourcing a single fragment does at least cause partial convergence. In fact, Deardorff (2001b) shows, in a follow-up study, that outsourcing of single fragments might also lead to a divergence of factor prices.

by sourcing out part of its production, it might raise the demand for labour in the capital-abundant country.

Review of empirical studies

Since the theoretical ambiguities do not allow us to draw clear conclusions, we will have to consider empirical investigations that might help us determine which effects dominate in real-world economies. This section gives an overview of such empirical studies.

THE IMPACT OF OUTSOURCING AT THE FIRM LEVEL

Despite the recent interest in the subject, very few studies have attempted to examine outsourcing at the firm level. One of the few exceptions is Abraham and Taylor (1996), who attempt to empirically support different hypotheses about firms' reasons for outsourcing: first, outsourcing saves wage and benefit costs; second, subcontracting can help smooth the workload of the regular workforce; and, third, outside suppliers might make use of economies of scale. The authors use data from the US Industry Wage Survey (IWS), which contain specific information on the subcontracting behaviour of 2700 firms between 1979 and 1987. The study finds that firms with a high wage level (approximated by the average wage paid to workers in a certain skill category) outsource significantly more low-skilled jobs (for example, janitorial services) to decrease their wage bill. On the other hand, low-wage firms are found to outsource high-skilled services, such as accounting. It is surprising that this effect occurs also in non-unionized firms, as one could expect that such firms are able to adjust their wages to those of potential subcontracting firms. Abraham and Taylor explain this phenomenon by equity considerations: since high dispersion of wages inside the firm would harm the work climate, businesses tend to outsource activities, which fit least in their general wage structure. Moreover, there is no effect of unionization (besides their impact on wages): even though union work rules function like higher labour costs and encourage outsourcing, stronger unions often influence management decisions and can prevent jobs from being outsourced. Cyclical product demand does not necessarily cause more outsourcing. As Abraham and Taylor find, anti-cyclical tasks (for example, janitorial and machine maintenance services) are less often subcontracted, as the regular workforce can complete these tasks in off-peak periods. Furthermore, firms in metropolitan areas are found to outsource more, which supports the 'economies of scale in matching' hypothesis.

Besides the determinants of firms' outsourcing decision, its effects on productivity and profitability have been examined empirically also. A number of case studies (Dritna, 1994; Lacity et al., 1996) have found that managers typically overestimate the benefits of outsourcing and underestimate the associated transactions costs. The opposite result is obtained by Roodhooft and Warlop (1999), who conduct a field experiment with managers of healthcare organizations. They find that managers are quite aware of the transactions costs associated with asset specificity. Moreover, their experimental results show that managers exhibit a sunk costs bias in outsourcing decisions. Instead of only taking into account future profits, the mere fact that investments for in-house production have been undertaken in the past causes managers to abstain from outsourcing. Here, the conservatism of managers results in an underengagement in outsourcing.

Which of these effects is more important has to be determined at a more aggregate level. Görzig and Stephan (2002), using data on 43 000 German manufacturing firms over the period from 1992 to 2000, find that outsourcing generally raises firms' efficiency, as measured by the return per employee. However, the effect on profitability is ambiguous. While increasing material inputs relative to labour costs typically results in better firms' performances, the outsourcing of services leads to lower profit margins. The authors presume that the difference is caused by the easy observability of product quality in competitive material input markets as opposed to the market for services where quality is much harder to monitor. Görzig and Stephan (2002) take these findings as evidence that firms have overengaged in the outsourcing of service jobs. Görg and Hanley (2003) obtained similar results in their study of the Irish electronics sector.

INTERNATIONAL OUTSOURCING AND ITS IMPACT ON THE LABOUR MARKET

Contrary to the relative scarceness of firm-level studies, empirical research on international outsourcing has taken off strongly since the 1990s. These contributions attempt to identify the causes of the growing gap between skilled and unskilled labour, either manifested in wage inequality or in unemployment. One important difficulty lays in disentangling the impact of international trade and the impact of technological progress.

   The common denominator of recent analyses is the estimation of the impact of outsourcing on *heterogeneous* labour qualifications. We try to present a selective, but representative, survey of the literature by grouping the contributions into three topics: (i) those studying the effect of outsourcing on wages; (ii) those quantifying the impact of outsourcing on labour demand (for given wages); and (iii) the 'equilibrium' approach estimating the total impact of outsourcing on labour input. Figure 12.1 sketches the three types of transmission from imports to labour demand and wages. Labour supply, represented by the upward sloping curve L^s , is not affected by outsourcing, but labour demand L^d shifts downwards when outsourcing increases from O_1 to O_2, so that, for the initial wage level, fewer workers are now needed in the outsourcing production unit (this explains the transition from point A to B – see arrow (ii)). When wages adjust in response to excess labour supply, the increase in outsourcing translates into a negative impact on wages (see arrow (i)). This decrease in wages stimulates employment, which shifts from point B to point C. This conjugated adjustment in wages and employment leads to the new equilibrium point C and the shift from A to C characterises the 'equilibrium' approaches to outsourcing.

   Aggregating labour demands over all production units gives the impact of outsourcing on the whole economy. Since outsourcing also creates jobs in the subcontracting firms, only delocalization to foreign firms is expected to exert a significant negative impact on aggregate (national) labour demand. Recent empirical studies not only try to measure shifts in labour demand and wages due to outsourcing, but also compare these impacts for different qualification levels or educational attainments of workers. Whereas studies in the early 1990s considered the impact of total imports on wage and employment, Feenstra and Hanson (1996a) recommend distinguishing imports according to their purpose (final consumption versus intermediate material inputs) and note that only intermediate material inputs can be considered as reflecting outsourcing.

The impact of outsourcing on wages

Assuming that wages are market-clearing, as it is the case in Figure 12.1 (points A and C), shifts in labour demand due to outsourcing translate into shifts in wages. The economic literature

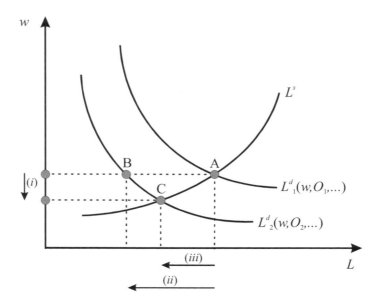

Figure 12.1   The impact of outsourcing on labour demand and wages

on the impact of outsourcing on wages distinguishes between the impact of outsourcing on the *average* wage and on wage *dispersion*. Wolff (2000) reviews this literature for the USA. Other empirical contributions on wages, employment and trade are overviewed in Table 12.1, distinguishing the data (period and country), and results, and will be discussed hereafter. Most of the contributions regress the wages (or log wages) of different individuals on a variable reflecting outsourcing (for example, trade or imports) and several other variables having an impact on wages (education, experience, gender and so on). This method allows the identification of the impact of outsourcing on wages (see arrow (i) on Figure 12.1).

To summarize the literature overviewed on wages, there is evidence for a rather small but significant impact of trade and outsourcing on both the wage level and wage inequality. Borjas *et al.* (1997) for instance attribute a maximum of 11 per cent of the growth in the wage differential between skill groups in the US to rising imports.

The impact of outsourcing on employment

The impact of outsourcing (or imports of intermediate inputs) on labour demand is usually estimated from a complete system of input demands comprising labour demand functions for different qualifications.

Morrison-Paul and Siegel (2001) examine 450 US manufacturing industries from 1958 to 1989, using a dynamic cost function model and more detailed measures of labour composition and technical change. Their findings support the hypothesis that outsourcing has negatively affected the employment of low-skilled workers, but the authors do not find significant evidence for effects on high-skilled employment. These empirical findings are in line with those of Berman *et al.* (1994), who also find that the impact of trade on labour demand is limited.

Table 12.1 Overview of studies assessing the impact of outsourcing on wages, employment and trade

	Authors	Data	Empirical results	Comments
Wages	Borjas and Ramey (1994)	Time series data, USA, 1964–91	Imports (of durable goods) increase wage inequality.	Few tests for the adequate choice of alternative explanatory variable.
	Borjas, Freeman and Katz (1997)	Three-digit manufacturing data for the USA, 1980, 1990 and 1995	A simulation suggests that trade widens wage inequality, but explains only 4–11 % of the observed increase in relative (skilled/unskilled) wages. The impact of immigration on relative wages is bigger.	In their model, relative wages depend on relative supply of skilled and unskilled workers, whose changes can be split into immigration and trade contributions. It is necessary to calculate the labour skill intensity embodied in imports and exports.
	Geishecker and Görg (2004)	Matched workers/industry panel data, Germany, 1991–2000	A 1% increase in outsourcing is found to decrease the wages of less skilled workers by about 7% and to increase wages of more skilled workers by about 3% (the latter effect is not always statistically significant).	The outsourcing variable is either defined as the output share of imported intermediate inputs or as the output share of imported intermediate input from the same industry abroad.
	Taylor (2002)	Cohorts of individuals, UK, 1973–94	Some evidence is found that the wages of more educated workers are less affected by globalization than those of less educated workers. Technology has a larger impact on wages than trade.	Globalization proxies the share of imports in value added. The author controls for education and occupation.
Employment	Anderton and Brenton (1999)	Panel of 11 four-digit sectors (textile and non-electrical manufacturing), UK, 1970–86	About 33% of the rise in the employment share of high-skilled workers can be explained by imports from low-wage countries.	Total imports are taken as the proxy variable for reflecting outsourcing. Domestic intermediate inputs, which are expected to be substitutes to imports, are not considered in the analysis.
	Falk and Koebel (2002)	Panel of 26 two-digit German manufacturing industries for the period 1978–90	For a given output, imported material inputs and labour are not substitutes. Domestic and imported materials are substitutes.	The outsourcing and import decision is a function of the input prices and output level.

Table 12.1 *Continued*

	Morrison-Paul and Siegel (2001)	Panel of 450 four-digit US manufacturing industries for the period 1958–89	Trade and outsourcing are found to decrease low-skilled demand. Trade is found to stimulate the demand for high-skilled workers. However, these variables explain less than 6% of the observed shift in employment.	Trade is measured as the ratio of imports to output. Outsourcing is defined as purchased services by manufacturing industries. The determinants of the amount of trade and outsourcing are not studied.
	Yan (2004)	Panel of 84 manufacturing industries, Canada, 1981–96	An increase of the share of imports by 1 % leads to an increase in the relative employment of skilled labour by 4.2%. This impact is greater for low-skilled than for high-skilled industries.	Outsourcing is measured as the share of imported intermediate inputs in value added. The determinants of outsourcing are not studied.
Trade	Egger and Egger (2003)	Panel of 20 Austrian two-digit industries, 1990–98	A 1% increase of imports from Central and Eastern European countries increases the high to low skill labour ratio by about 0.08–0.12%.	The determinants of relative wages are not investigated, but their endogeneity is taken into account when explaining relative employment. The authors also evaluate the impact of the variables that influence imports.
	Feenstra and Hanson (1999)	Panel of 447 four-digit US manufacturing industries, 1972–90	Outsourcing has no impact in the 1972–79 period and accounts for 11–15% of the increase in the wage share of non-production workers over the 1979–90 period.	The explained variable is the share of non-production wages to the wage bill. It turns out that it is difficult to say something about employment and wages separately.
	Harrigan (1998)	Time series for the US economy, 1967–95	Changes in factor supply and final good prices explain the growing wage differential between skilled and unskilled labour. The import price has a small impact on equilibrium wages and relative wages.	Labour supply is assumed to be independent from the wage (it is vertical in Figure 12.1). The impact of foreign prices on domestic product prices (which are shown to affect wages) is not considered.
	Revenga (1992)	38 three-digit US manufacturing industries, 1977–87	When import prices rise by 1%, employment increases by 0.24–0.39% and wages increase by 0.04–0.09%. Estimates are mostly, but not always, statistically significantly different from zero.	Industry-specific labour markets, which are in equilibrium. The author considers the price of imports p_{im}, which is crude proxy for international outsourcing (because imports include final consumption goods as well as intermediate inputs).

Studies show that, the UK, unlike the USA, has a higher import share from other industrialized countries and a relatively low share of imports from developing countries. Consequently, one would expect total trading in intermediate goods to have a lower impact on the skill structure of employment. This is exactly what Anderton and Brenton (1999) find: total import penetration has not significantly affected low-skilled employment. However, when separately examining imports from low-wage countries, the coefficient of import penetration is statistically significant. For example, in the textiles industry up to 33 per cent of the rise in the employment share of high-skilled workers can be explained by imports from low-wage countries. Their results stand in contrast to those found for the UK by Machin and van Reenen (1998) who did not find a significant impact of imports on the skill structure of labour demand. Such empirical contradictions, which are rather frequent, show that the estimates of the shift in labour demand function often are not robust. Better data, but also more specification tests, should help to improve our knowledge about the size of the foreign outsourcing impact on labour demand.

The equilibrium impact of trade

Instead of measuring shifts in employment for given wages, 'equilibrium' approaches of the labour market also take the wage adjustment implied by increased outsourcing into account in order to assess its labour market consequences. In terms of Figure 12.1, the equilibrium impact of trade is represented by the shift *(iii)* from A to C. From a theoretical viewpoint, the implied wage change compensates the initial negative impact of outsourcing on labour demand. Under some regularity conditions on the labour supply and demand functions, Diewert (1981), for example, has shown that that the shift from A to C (when wages adjust) is smaller than the distance between A and B (obtained at given wages). This result can be directly seen on Figure 12.1.

Equilibrium approaches recognize that wages are endogenous, which often requires the use of instrumental variables techniques for empirical investigation. Now, it becomes necessary to model both the labour demand and supply functions simultaneously, or to consider the labour demand function together with the wage formation. The model can either then be estimated from its structural form or from its 'reduced form'. Revenga (1992) followed this last route and found that, in the USA, changes in the import price have a large impact on employment and a more limited impact on wages. Hakura (1997) obtained a similar result using US data for the period 1980–90. However, the empirical results are not often statistically significant in this latter study.

One drawback of these studies is that they focus on employment and do not explicitly consider the different qualifications of workers. This question has been tackled by Harrigan (1998) and Harrigan and Balaban (1999), who investigate the impact of trade on different qualifications of US workers. However, they find no evidence for a significant impact of trade on wages and relative wages. Such an empirical finding is, however, not consensual. Using more detailed data for US manufacturing sectors, and defining the outsourcing very precisely, Feenstra and Hanson (1999) find that outsourcing explains 11–15 per cent of the increase in the wage share of non-production workers.

For European countries, there are but a few contributions adopting the equilibrium approach.

Conclusion

In this chapter, we have identified the economic rationale for outsourcing and have examined its labour market effects. In our analysis, we distinguish between domestic outsourcing (a firm spins off a fragment of its production process into a separate firm) and international outsourcing (a firm makes use of international differences in factor prices and 'offshores' parts of its production).

As we have argued, domestic outsourcing is more a return to the rule than an exceptional phenomenon in a market economy. Only under circumstances that inhibit market forces to work frictionless might the non-market mode of production inside one firm be economically desirable. In our view, one of the most important inhibitions of markets is asset specificity and the resulting hold-up problem. However, as industries grow and economies globalize, business relations tend to become less specific, thereby reducing the need for integrated firms. Then, outsourcing occurs as firms return to their most efficient mode of production as separate economic entities.

International outsourcing occurs when firms make use of international differences in factor prices. Most trade models, based on the ideas of the Heckscher–Ohlin model, predict that this will cause factor price equalization. While the whole economy gains, its relatively scarce factor loses. This can be seen as a theoretical explanation for the widening gap between wages and/or employment rates of high-skilled and low-skilled workers in industrialized countries. However, there are also reservations to this simple logic. For example, if a production fragment is sourced out to save costs and make the remaining production more profitable, this might well benefit the low-skilled if the remaining fragments are also intensive in low-skilled labour.

From an empirical point of view, several studies confirm that outsourcing contributes to increasing wage inequality and decreasing labour demand. However, the size of this impact is not robustly estimated. As outsourcing is difficult to measure, it should not be surprising that the estimation of its impact is somewhat imprecise. A further reason for the high variability of the results is the difficulty to combine equilibrium models and disaggregate economic data. On the one hand, some contributions rely on aggregate data in order to be consistent with economic 'equilibrium theory', but neglect useful information contained in micro-data. On the other hand, studies using disaggregate data often are not able to identify the aggregate equilibrium impact of outsourcing, because these are not defined at a disaggregate level. This may provide an explanation for why studies using macroeconomic and disaggregate data often find quantitatively different results.

Beyond these approaches, it seems possible to develop macroeconomic studies that rely on microeconomic data. To us, this seems to be a promising approach for future research, which could yield more reliable results on the impact of outsourcing on labour demand.

References

Abraham, K. and Taylor S. (1996), 'Firms' use of outside contractors: theory and evidence', *Journal of Labor Economics*, vol. 14, no. 3, pp. 394–424.

Anderton, B. and Brenton, P. (1999), 'Outsourcing and low-skilled workers in the UK', *Bulletin of Economic Research*, vol. 51, no. 4, pp. 267–85.

Arndt, S. (1997), 'Globalization and the open economy', *North American Journal of Economics and Finance*, vol. 8, pp. 71–79.

Arndt, S. (1999), 'Globalization and economic development', *The Journal of International Trade and Economic Development*, vol. 8, pp. 309–18.

Autor, D. (2003), 'Outsourcing at will: the contribution of unjust dismissal doctrine to the growth of employment outsourcing', *Journal of Labor Economics*, vol. 21, no. 1, pp. 1–42.

Berman, E., Bound, J. and Griliches, Z. (1994), 'Changes in demand for skilled labor within US manufacturing: evidence from the annual survey of manufactures', *Quarterly Journal of Economics*, vol. 109, no. 2, pp. 367–97.

Borjas, G.J. and Ramey, V.A. (1994), 'Rising wage inequality in the United States: causes and consequences', *American Economic Review*, vol. 84, pp. 17–22.

Borjas, G.J., Freeman, R. and Katz, L. (1992), 'On the labor market effect of immigration and trade', in G. Borjas and R. Freeman (eds), *Immigration and the Workforce: Economic Consequences for the United States and Source Areas*, Chicago University Press, Chicago.

Borjas, G., Freeman, R.B. and Katz, L.F. (1997), 'How much do immigration and trade affect labor market outcomes', *Brookings Papers on Economic Activity*, vol.1, pp. 1–90.

Coase, R.H. (1937), 'The theory of the firm', *Economica*, vol. 4, pp. 386–405.

Deardorff, A. (2001a), 'Fragmentation in simple trade models', *North American Journal of Economics and Finance*, vol. 12, pp. 121–37.

Deardorff, A. (2001b), 'Fragmentation across cones', in S. Arndt and H. Kierzkowski (eds), *Fragmentation: New Production Patterns in the World Economy*, Oxford University Press, Oxford, pp. 35–51.

De Kok, T. (2000), 'Capacity allocation and outsourcing in a process industry', *International Journal of Production Economics*, vol. 68, pp. 229–39.

Diewert, W.E. (1981), 'The elasticity of derived net supply and a generalized Le Chatelier principle', *Review of Economic Studies*, vol. 48, pp. 63–80.

Dritna, R. (1994), 'The outsourcing decision', *Management Accounting*, March, pp. 56–62.

Egger, H. and Egger, P. (2003), 'Outsourcing and skill-specific employment in a small economy: Austria and the fall of the iron curtain', *Oxford Economic Papers*, vol. 55, pp. 625–43.

Falk, M. and Koebel, B.M. (2002), 'Outsourcing, imports and labour demand', *Scandinavian Journal of Economics*, vol. 104, pp. 567–86.

Feenstra, R. and Hanson, G. (1996a), 'Foreign investment, outsourcing and relative wages', in R. Feenstra, G. Grossman and D. Irwin (eds), *The Political Economy of Trade Policy: Papers in Honor of Jagdish Bhagwati*, MIT Press, Cambridge, MA, pp. 89–127.

Feenstra, R. and Hanson, G. (1996b), 'Globalization, outsourcing and wage inequality', *American Economic Review*, vol. 86, pp. 240–45.

Feenstra, R. and Hanson, G. (1999), 'The impact of outsourcing and high-technology capital on wages: estimates for the United States, 1979–1990', *Quarterly Journal of Economics*, vol. 114, no. 3, pp. 907–40.

Geishecker, I. and Görg, H. (2004), 'Winners and losers: fragmentation, trade and wages revisited', IZA Discussion Paper No. 982, Bonn.

Görg, H. and Hanley, A. (2003), 'Does outsourcing increase profitability?', Nottingham University Business School, Economics Division, Working Paper Series No. 01/2003.

Görzig, B. and Stephan, A. (2002), 'Outsourcing and firm-level performance', DIW Discussion Paper No. 309, Berlin.

Grossman, G. and Helpman, E. (2002), 'Integration versus outsourcing', *Quarterly Journal of Economics*, vol. 117, no. 1, pp. 85–120.

Hakura, D. (1997), 'The impact of trade prices on employment and wages in the United States', Working Paper 97/16, International Monetary Fund, Washington.

Harrigan, J. (1998), 'International trade and American wages in general equilibrium, 1967–1995', NBER Working Paper 6609, National Bureau of Economic Research, Inc.

Harrigan J. and Balaban, R. (1999), 'U.S. wages in general equilibrium: the effects of prices, technology, and factor supplies, 1963–1991', NBER Working Paper 6981, National Bureau of Economic Research, Inc.

Horn, H. and Wolinsky, A. (1988), 'Worker substitutability and patterns of unionisation', *Economic Journal*, vol. 98, June, pp. 484–97.

Klein, B., Crawford, R. and Alchian, A. (1978), 'Vertical integration, appropriable rents, and the competitive contracting process', *Journal of Law and Economics*, vol. 21, October, pp. 297–326.

Kohler, W. (2001), 'A specific-factors view on outsourcing', *North American Journal of Economics and Finance*, vol. 12, no. 1, pp. 31–54.

Lacity, M., Willcocks, L. and Feeny, D. (1996), 'The value of selective IT outsourcing', *Sloan Management Review*, Spring, pp. 13–25.

Lyons, B. and Sekkat, K. (1991), 'Strategic bargaining and vertical separation', *Journal of Industrial Economics*, pp. 577–93.

Machin S. and van Reenen, J. (1998), 'Technology and changes in skill structure: evidence from seven OECD countries', *The Quarterly Journal of Economics* vol. 113, pp. 1215–44.

Morrison-Paul, C. and Siegel, D. (2001), 'The impacts of technology, trade and outsourcing on employment and labor composition', *Scandinavian Journal of Economics*, vol. 103, no. 2, pp. 241–64.

Oi, W. (1961), 'The desirability of price instability under perfect competition', *Econometrica*, vol. 29, pp. 58–64.

Perry, M.K. (1984), 'Vertical equilibrium in a competitive input market', *International Journal of Industrial Organization*, vol. 2, pp. 159–70.

Perry, M.K. (1989), 'Vertical integration: determinants and effects', in R. Schmalensee and R. Willig (eds), *Handbook of Industrial Organization*, Vol. 1, Elsevier, Amsterdam, pp. 183–255.

Revenga, A.L. (1992), 'Exporting jobs? The impact of import competition on employment and wages in US manufacturing', *Quarterly Journal of Economics*, vol. 107, pp. 255–84.

Roodhoft, F. and Warlop, L. (1999), 'On the role of sunk costs and asset specificity in outsourcing decisions: a research note', *Accounting, Organizations and Society*, vol. 24, pp. 363–69.

Taylor, K. (2002), 'The impact of technology and trade upon the returns to education and occupation', *Applied Economics*, vol. 34, pp. 1371–77.

Tirole, J. (1988), *The Theory of Industrial Organization*, MIT Press, Cambridge, MA.

Williamson, O.E. (1975), *Markets and Hierarchies: Analysis and Antitrust Implications*, Free Press, New York.

Williamson, O.E. (1996), 'Vertical integration', in J. Eatwell and R. Palgrave (eds), *The New Palgrave: A Dictionary of Economics*, Vol. 4, Macmillan, London, pp. 807–12.

Wolff, E.N. (2000), 'Trade and inequality: a review of the literature', US Trade Deficit Review Commission.

Yan, B. (2004), 'Demand for skills in Canada: the role of foreign outsourcing and information-communication technology', mimeo, Statistics Canada.

13 Transforming Organizations: An Analysis of Outsourcing and its Effects on Trade Unions

Valeria Pulignano

The purpose of this chapter is to explore the effects of outsourcing strategies on the collective structures of union representation and bargaining arrangements, which are the main pillars of strength of trade union organizations. It is clear that outsourcing of both peripheral and core tasks has influenced firms' performance as well as played a significant role within debates on the changing world of employment and on the structure and the nature of employee relations. Previous work on companies' externalization practices has sought to place outsourcing within the context of labour utilization strategies adopted by management (Atkinson, 1987). More specifically, in line with management's objective to achieve 'economy of scope', outsourcing has ushered in a new regime of precarious employment and trade union absence. This was the result of the externalization of simple tasks to small non-union firms in order to search for 'numerical flexibility' (Rannie, 1989).

During the 1990s some of the managerial literature stressed the use of outsourcing as a 'strategic choice' for management. Accordingly, firms may increase their performance by focusing more narrowly on the things they do better (Quinn, 1992). Thus, the focus is on the achievement of 'economy of specialization' by enterprises interested in enhancing competitive advantage rather than 'economy of scope', which would only impinge on the reduction of costs. Hence, in the most competitive export-oriented product markets, including labour-intensive industries, only a small proportion of the value of the product is still produced in-house. Yet, the number of companies in manufacturing, banking and the service sectors responsible for coordinating diverse suppliers, has increasingly assumed an important role as a result of company advantages in terms of both improvement of firms' financial performance and enhancement of the level of cost-effectiveness, especially within the high-technology industry (Bettis et al., 1992).

Despite the dramatic rise and change in the nature of outsourcing, few empirical investigations into the implications for trade unions' representation rights and their bargaining power have been conducted. Instead, studies have emphasized the current changes in industrial organization in order to reflect firms' trajectories within a specific local context as the result of the advantages which they could potentially derive from changes in their sourcing relationships with suppliers (Lung et al., 1999). Thus, the theoretical debate has focused on exploring the implications outsourcing entails for the organization (Bonazzi and Antonelli, 2003) and the perceptions and attitude of the outsourced employees (Kessler et al., 1999; Logan et al. 2004). The analysis on the social effects of outsourcing for organized labour remains, therefore, limited to previous research, which most notably emphasizes a critical view of trade unions. This reflects unions' weak engagement at the planning stage of the outsourcing strategy because of the pressure on terms and conditions of employment, which governs the conventional image of contracting out. In short, both employers and governments have traditionally attempted to reduce the labour costs of the internal production unit by avoiding unionized labour while outsourcing to small and medium-sized firms (Saundry and Turnbull, 1999).

Conversely, economic integration and logistic coordination between companies and suppliers are the main features characterizing contemporary outsourcing. It often involves the restructuring of the organization in accordance with a process of redefining production activities between what is understood to be the 'core' activity, on one hand, and those activities that are considered to be 'subcontractable' on the other hand. Generally speaking, outsourcing primarily involves great pressure to achieve a higher level of company performance while specializing those tasks for the creation of a structure of networked enterprises. This is combined with the reduction of costs and the deregulation of working conditions traditionally associated with the rise of contracting out.

Due to the change in the nature of outsourcing, it becomes crucial to investigate the extent to which the new internal reorganization of activities leads to a major restructuring not only of employment, but also of trade unions' systems of representation and intervention within both the main company and the suppliers. In other words, we need to discuss the extent to which trade unions are involved in the planning stage of contemporary outsourcing. To what extent can trade unions recapture the initiative while pursuing compromise agreements with employers on strategic outsourcing? What are the processes, preconditions and factors that may increase or limit such capacity? Although the answer to the question of whether there is still space for union action in a framework of outsourcing is probably tricky, the identification of factors facilitating and inhibiting the extent to which trade unions are able to operate as effectively in an outsourced environment is, nonetheless, of general relevance.

In the following sections we first clarify the concept of outsourcing in the light of the evolution it has experienced in recent years. First, we provide a brief overview of strategic outsourcing followed by a critical and detailed analysis of the impact of outsourcing decisions and initiatives on union structure and organization, representation and collective bargaining. By drawing on the literature on outsourcing we attempt to generate some ideas and to conjecture about which factors affect the labour unions' ability to fit into the new scheme of working practices, as well as indicate union responses. In the third section relevant examples are drawn from the automobile industry in the European metalworking sector, and the extent of unions' ability to engage in the outsourcing process by negotiating with management on its social effects is discussed. In the conclusions we critically reflect on the factors that may enhance or reduce the efficacy of trade unions' response to outsourcing.

From 'make or buy' to strategic outsourcing

Greaver defines outsourcing as 'the act of transferring some of a company's recurring internal activities and decision rights to outside providers' (1999, p. 3). This definition of outsourcing is very broad and includes virtually any good or service that an organization procures from outside firms. Transferring some of the company's activities to outside parties in accordance to 'make or buy', is a principle that management has traditionally used to reduce costs while ensuring the quality of the goods and services produced. The latter has been achieved through maintaining internally the highest level of value of the product in accordance to the principle of vertical integration. This has led to 'economy of scope'. However, defining outsourcing simply in terms of procurement activities and 'economy of scope' does not capture the true strategic nature of the activity. Management researchers and practitioners have demonstrated that outsourcing is not simply a purchasing or 'make or buy' decision. All firms decide to purchase elements of their operations, but outsourcing seems to represent the fundamental decision to reject the internalization of an activity because of the 'competitive advantages' (costs advantages, increase in organizational commitment and organization's core competencies, spread of the risk) that it generates. In this way Quinn and Hilmer (1994) consider outsourcing as a highly strategic decision that has the potential to cause ripple effects throughout the entire organization. Hence strategic outsourcing concerns the company's ability to create 'value' within its own organization – that is, to individuate along the value chain of the product those areas that best represent its customers' interests and thereby to develop them while strategically emphasizing the company's 'core competencies' (Prahalad and Hamel, 1990). Strategic outsourcing, therefore, reduces a firm's involvement in successive stages of production, the latter often being outsourced to outside suppliers. As such, it may be viewed as vertical disintegration, with an aim to minimize the costs of investment and enhance the level of specialization by letting enterprises focus on what they do best. This is the result of the firm's strategic decision to reject internalization while selecting what to buy and what to make internally (Gilley and Rasheed, 2000). The benefits that the organization can strategically achieve by making a certain choice will depend on the nature of this choice. Hence strategic outsourcing can be an attractive method of improving the firm's performance in the long term.

In accordance with a rationale of strategic outsourcing firms can often raise barriers to market competitiveness by focusing on the 'core competences'. This explains why, for example, in the aircraft industry companies prefer to invest in the development of the marketing function while concentrating their resources on improving relations with the customer as a competitive advantage. As such, the differentiation of the service, such as the typology of aircraft and the equipment in use, are activities often outsourced to suppliers since they are not considered a long-term competitive advantage for the firm (Pellicelli, 2000; Venkatesan, 1992). Likewise, in the automobile industry, car makers most notably retain the ability to monitor the production process either through assembling the single parts produced by external firms (as does Fiat, for example) or, from the very outset, delivering the assembly of the finished products to external suppliers while keeping 'in-house' strategic functions such as the quality control of the final product (as does Volkswagen, for example). This is typical of the most advanced and recent case of outsourcing in the automobile industry – the introduction of 'modular production' or 'insourcing' by which an organization purchases 'non-core' functions and services from enterprises co-located under the same roof. The new arrangements involve the shifting of main-line assembly jobs to subassembly lines or segments of production where suppliers use their own workforces rather than simply deliver the product through the main assembly line.

Nevertheless, in both outsourcing and insourcing arrangements the main innovation lies in the presence of an 'industrial condominium' or 'consortium', where suppliers are located. As a result, the investment for the establishment of the supply operations (mechanical systems, the supplier production floor, presses), which are next to or inside the main company's location, is normally a joint venture between the company and the suppliers. This syndication of business risk is a novel approach to outsourcing since, in the past, the assembler alone assumed all liability. Moreover, the 'industrial condominium' arrangements also have implications for the key partners in terms of commercial and employment relationships. Previously, the major risk faced by companies involved a fall in demand – a risk that could be offset if they were to agree a contract with a new client. Now, enterprises find themselves in a new situation, one that is singularly lacking in the same degree of flexibility and autonomy – in most cases, their investments tie them to a single client, and this customer has now become their partner. This implies some change in the way in which commercial transactions are carried out as well as changes in the workforce which is now covered by a new contract with the main customer and which therefore has to be solely dedicated to the production of a final product that can be sold to that particular customer. This particularity may well shed some light on the way in which employment relations will be set up under the new procedures of outsourcing. For example, whenever an engine is produced and delivered 'just-in-time', it must be assumed that employees from different enterprises, with diverse employment contracts and a different degree of involvement in the trade unions as well as in employee representation matters, come together and share work experiences.

All this means that, from both the employer's and trade union's perspective, employment and labour issues are very delicate matters when contemporary forms of outsourcing are being established. Obviously, employers will be interested in enhancing organizational and production coordination among the different actors while minimizing any cause of social unrest. Equally, however, employees and their union representatives will welcome the harmonization of wage contracts and working conditions that the experience of outsourcing brings as a consequence of the clustering of geographically different firms. The achievement of such results demands a partial redefinition of the forms of trade union organization, representation and collective bargaining. As the next section will illustrate, the discussion on these issues is part of a broader current debate on changing company structure and its impact on trade union organization.

Changing company structure and its impact on union organization

COMPANY CHANGE CHALLENGES UNION TRADITIONS

Since companies have started to restructure their entire value chain, their boundaries have enlarged, and their strategies have changed. The change has included the direct production of parts that firms consider to be strategic as well as the reorganization of their relationships with suppliers. Of course, this process has varied according to the specific strategy of each firm and the sector. Nevertheless, some common elements can be indicated. The changes introduced have led directly to the restructuring of the supplier firms. Specifically, outsourcing and insourcing have led companies to supply complete sets of parts, units and/or services that involve technological complexity and expertise. Thus, subcontracting firms have undergone the most profound transformation, with a high degree of business concentration and globalization of production, and the adoption of similar production strategies to those of the major customer in order to speed up their rate of performance improvement to meet global competition. Just-in-time systems of delivery have become the most evident factor of transformation, regulating supply relationships in order to foster competitiveness through the achievement of line flexibility and the reduction of in-stock costs. Hence geographical proximity to the customer has to be guaranteed in order to portray beneficial effects on performance. As Sako and Helper (1999) illustrate, changes in the supply chain have led suppliers to become mutually dependent on their customers in terms of investing more in specific assets, participating in product development (co-design), and extending the length of their contractual relationship with the customer.

It is evident that this process has a clear impact on employment matters. Outsourcing has caused a dispersion of the labour force, which is governed by diverse employment conditions. This diversity of conditions is reflected by a more general diversification in the collective agreements covering the employees of the outsourced companies (chemicals, textiles, transport, wood, catering, cleaning and so on). This situation clearly involves a significant change in the patterns of interest aggregation and bargaining activity. Specifically, the dispersion of workers and the general diversification of collective agreements under outsourcing render many traditional forms of union organization inappropriate and almost ineffective. The traditional concept of having only one union per sector and/or company is undermined by the recent structural changes in companies. Historically, trade unions were rooted in the occupational communities of skilled workers or, as Hyman puts it, in 'the relatively undifferentiated work situation of labour in the expanding sectors of mass production' (1994, p. 117). Here he is clearly referring to the prevalent structural form of the country-based trade union movements, marked by the predominance of 'occupational', 'industrial' and 'enterprise' unionism. Unions in many post-war European and non-European countries have grown within a particular occupation ('craft') or sector, and, as such, were considered completely 'inclusive' in terms of representing and recruiting all the workers within that particular industry or occupational category. This form of 'exclusive' unionism reflected the historical and social circumstances of their formation. As Fairbrother and Griffin (2002) argue, for much of the post-war period there was an expansion of mass production and mass consumption, giving rise to arguments about the relationship between trade union structure and forms of mass production associated with Fordism. Generally speaking, Fordist methods of production and work organization encouraged the organization of the trade union movement on a structural basis, relating it to industry or occupational boundaries for reasons most notably concerned with strategies for mobilization and collective action: well-organized sectors facilitated efforts to represent workers' economic and political interests. These patterns of unionism are inevitably reflected in what Hyman indicates as a contrast between unions based on 'narrow membership constituencies', which generally pursue job-related concerns for certain occupational categories of workers, and more broadly-based unions which often 'address a wide range of issues' for wider groups (Hyman, 1994, p. 121).

It is easy to understand that, when manufacturing or service are not the product of one isolated firm, but the result of close relationships between suppliers and customers, usually located in geographical proximity close to each other, the effectiveness of union representation and bargaining is weakened. The new situation requires the establishment of a more articulated trade union around cohesive and coherent interrelationships between workplace and (across) regional levels of organization and activity. In other words, the union's strategy needs to be redirected towards the elaboration of new proposals for organizing activities under the most recent transformations in industry. As indicated, these transformations should include close relationships with diverse suppliers, within different sectors, as a result of the strong dependence of subcontracting companies on the manufacturer's rate of production. The effects on employment conditions and labour activity are fairly visible in these cases and need regulation. More specifically, they require a higher ability to adjust restructuring in respect of industrial and employment relations. This is done by fostering inter-sectoral agreements, setting up protective measures for the ex-workers of the subcontracting company ('clauses') or homogenizing the employment and pay conditions of the subcontracting company's and the contractor's employees,.

Recent research findings, however, illustrate that the effects of outsourcing cannot be approached in an integrated way because of the constraints and the cross-national diversity in the legal and negotiated framework of countries. This diversity reflects the extent to which unions are entitled to receive information and negotiate at the planning stage of the outsourcing strategy. For example, a comparative study conducted by the European Industrial Relations Observatory (EIRO, 2000a) on the metalworking sector in Europe shows that union engagement at the point of transfer of authority depends on the protection offered to the workers by national law, through the establishment of information and consultation rights of the contractor's and subcontractor's works councils. In this respect, Dutch and Swedish laws arguably play a very important role in controlling outsourcing because their legal systems regulate employee participation. Conversely, in countries with deregulated labour relations the extent to which information and consultation are guaranteed depends on the employers' approach within the sector. For example, in the UK, the Engineering Employers' Federation has recognized information rights on multi-level agreements within supply chains. Moreover, the extent to which sector-level agreements can deal with outsourcing by successfully harmonizing the employment conditions across firms depends on the presence of a national system of sectoral collective agreements that includes the participation of workers' representatives. Hence, in Belgium, France, Italy, Spain and Portugal, company-level bargaining seems to be the most practicable level for negotiating employment issues in the case of outsourcing. This is because in these countries the sector-level agreements do not cover participation rights, making it more difficult to avoid a deterioration of working conditions in the contractor company.

This evidence leads to a further, no less important implication – that is, the tendency towards weakened union representation power as a consequence of the dispersion of workers caused by the atomization of companies under outsourcing. Hence trade unions need to reinforce closer cross-sectoral and inter-firm cooperation within (and across) countries, as well as expanding employee structures of representation and bargaining at the company level. The main aim is to overcome the narrow framework of the plant or the company under the implementation of outsourcing so that decision making at the level of the business group can be more easily influenced. Despite these factors, union pluralism still prevails in many countries, as the following section will illustrate. However, trade unions in Europe have proposed solutions to respond to company changes at both central and company-level.

Searching for solutions

In recent years, increasing attention has been paid to the potential strategies for unions to overcome their structural problems resulting from company restructuring. In particular, attention has been concentrated on: restructuring union organization; developing company- and sector-level bargaining to cover subcontractors; and enlarging the structure of worker representation within the supply chain. Challenges arising from the need to develop inter-sectoral and inter-firm solutions under the introduction of outsourcing by companies necessitate a strong union ability to organize along the new trends. This is of vital importance for trade unions, particularly in view of the fact that they have seen a considerable reduction in their traditional membership strength over recent years (Ebbinghaus, 2002).

One of the unions' responses has been to restructure their internal organization via mergers to increase the union concentration within and across the union confederations, across diverse firms, and within (and across) sectors. A unified union confederation is seen to better facilitate efforts to represent the different political and economic interests of the fragmented workforce. Consequently, several unions have planned mergers, amalgamations of medium-sized unions or the absorption of smaller unions by larger ones. Since the late 1980s and early 1990s several union mergers in Europe have taken place, two examples being the Amicus merger in 2002, which brought together the engineering, technicians and managerial British unions MSF and AEEU, and the Ver.di in 2001, which merged the independent German white-collar union DAG, four DGB affiliates and the IG media union), both of which are seen as partly the result of the ongoing structural changes in industry (Undy, 1999). Union mergers bring together diverse sections of the trade union movement – that is, different occupational groups of workers – and therefore represent a breakaway from the traditional occupational separation of trade union structure. Nevertheless, difficulties still persist along the road of trade union integration as an effective response to industrial restructuring. The most notable concern with potential union mergers is that they hamper transnational cooperation at sector- and workplace levels across diverse firms.

Although organizational restructuring offers space for setting up new pillars in respect of bargaining coordination and employees' political voice, it does not provide any supervision of the conditions of the employees who work in the contractor companies. Furthermore, in some cases the outsourced activities may not fall within a defined bargaining framework. Business restructuring often creates new economic sectors (for example, computer maintenance, telemarketing), and the traditional bargaining units begin to correspond less and less to the structures of production. These new sectors tend to be governed only by minimal employment conditions, since they are usually sectors in which it is difficult for trade unions to become established. Thus, it is unlikely that the employment conditions negotiated with the unions in these units are equal to, or surpass, those of the contracting companies. Hence it becomes important to set up mechanisms for equally negotiating the protection of the rights of workers involved in outsourcing.

One first step would be to negotiate inter-sectoral agreements, which provide for the participation of workers' representatives to bargain at company-level agreements aimed at harmonizing the employment conditions of the subcontracting companies' employees. Two considerations are important here. First, the introduction of inter-sectoral agreements usually depends on legislative provisions, which are strongly affected by the country-based level of regulation. Second, the experience of several countries influences the application of the sector agreement in harmonizing employment conditions in cases of outsourcing. However, since, as indicated earlier, country-level harmonization may be problematic, collective bargaining at company level (within sectors) appears to be the most common method used to deal with outsourcing in most countries. Generally speaking, under company-level bargaining the social effects of outsourcing are negotiated by workers' representatives. They regulate the rights of the workers affected by this process in order to avoid increasing numbers of employees working in the same area of activity being governed by different employment conditions. Nevertheless, the possibility of negotiating does not automatically guarantee a good outcome: sometimes it may be poor because it proves impossible to ensure fair working conditions in the contractor company.

Two factors emerge from these results: diversity in the scope of the sectoral agreement between the contracting and the contractor companies, and difficulty in identifying a defined bargaining framework in the location of the outsourced activity. In some European sectors (for example, the metalworking sector in Italy) trade unions at the local level have tried to extend the scope of the sectoral agreement to the outsourced activities irrespective of the nature of the activity of the latter. However, success has been limited because the activity into which workers are classified is determined at the company level. Conversely, in Belgium the trade unions and the employers' organizations have agreed to take action to maintain companies and workers within the metalworking sector as part of the agreement. Likewise, in Germany a new bargaining framework covering pay, working time and other employment conditions has been established for the companies providing services to other companies (EIRO, 1998a).

Despite unions' attempts to overcome the effects of outsourcing through either enlarging the scope of, or setting up, a new framework of bargaining within the sector, difficulties still exist. These mostly concern the extent to which workers' representatives in the subcontracting companies are able to influence the regulation of the working conditions of those who work in the contractor companies. This is due to the weak coordination among the representatives' bodies in the firms involved in outsourcing. Challenges arising from the need to better coordinate bargaining require a reinforcement of both vertical (within the same group of activity) and horizontal (between companies and suppliers) structures of worker representation. These objectives are linked but are not mutually exclusive. They aim at increasing the amount of communication and cooperation between the works councils of the main company and of the supplier companies while reinforcing integration between works councils within the same business group.

Aligning outsourcing with systems of employees' representation and collective bargaining: experiences from the European automobile industry

This section will present some evidence from the European automobile industry regarding trade unions' involvement in regulating the outcomes of outsourcing. Evidence highlights that the way in which unions have responded to outsourcing sometimes seems at odds with certain traditional assumptions underlying the antagonistic labour union approach to company restructuring. As already indicated, this may reflect a stronger union engagement at the planning stage of the outsourcing strategy, with a consequent union involvement in negotiating with management. On the other hand, it may be the result of a defensive union response towards restructuring while trying to redirect the strategy or to moderate its effect on the employees involved. This was the case, for example, in Belgium where in 1998 the workers' representatives at Opel's Antwerp plant negotiated night work and the outsourcing of the materials handling department within the Opel group as a way of avoiding dismissals as the outcome of a big restructuring plan, announced by the company in 1997 (EIRO, 1998b). As a result, Opel created a new company to which it transferred 654 employees who had their employment conditions maintained, since it was agreed to apply the metalworking sector agreement to all employees involved in outsourcing. Although the joint committee for the metalworking industry had reached an agreement to try to maintain the maximum possible number of companies in the sphere of application of the agreement, not all the companies undertaking subcontracted work for the motor manufacturing industry were covered by the metalworkers' agreement. An explanation may be the weak preparation by the Belgian trade unions in elaborating an active response to the company's initial demand for more flexibility. An active response should have included, from the outset, the local union's ability to primarily consider an international option, rather than restrict itself to purely local or regional ones, when considering the company's decisions to move production, in response to the implementation of available strategies to respond to its restructuring plan.

A number of trade unions have found it difficult to advance the various examples of negotiating agreements in directions that would guarantee employment in case of restructuring. This has been a reflection not only of an absence of a fully developed union policy, but also of differences in the extent to which information and consultation rights are regulated at the workplace. It seems that in Germany, France and Italy, for example, using different forms of trade unions has allowed more progress to be made in drawing up proposals and adopting new strategies for coordinating inter-firm structures of employee representation than in Belgium.

More generally, the debate on outsourcing has centred on one major question: how to enlarge the structures of worker representation. In Germany, unions have mainly been concerned about the reinforcement of systems of employees representation (works councils) at the company level while assigning primary responsibility to European-level structures of representation (European works councils or EWCs). This allowed the signing of agreements on the transfer of employees in case of outsourcing. The existence of well-established legal structures for consultation at both company (co-determination) and board level have played an important role while seeking regulation on the social outcomes of restructuring. For example, in 2000 Ford Europe and the management of its component supplier Visteon in Germany signed an agreement with the Ford EWC on the transfer of employees from Ford to Visteon in exchange for a commitment by the management of both companies to guarantee their jobs and maintain their employment conditions such as pay, pensions, length-of-service-related entitlements and other benefits (EIRO, 2000b). Conversely, in Italy and France trade unions were more concerned to reinforce the structures of horizontal representation by strengthening cooperation between the works councils of the main company and the supplier companies. In France the unions have used the law to create inter-company works councils in order to negotiate on the employment conditions of the employees in the supplier companies, whereas in Italy this was mainly the result of a negotiated agreement with management promoting coordination between workers' representative bodies across the diverse suppliers in exchange for industrial peace. The difference in the French case is explained by the higher level of independence the structure of employees representation retains from the unions on the one hand, and the more extensive implementation of flexible management practices (just-in-time) in the Italian than in the French automobile sector on the other hand..

Overall, the experiences from the European motor industry illustrate that in those countries where the outsourcing debate has taken place, the unions' proposal followed paths of pragmatic responses to the outcomes of outsourcing rather than of opposition to it. The maturity of this stance is accompanied by a serious engagement on the part of trade unions in tackling company change at two levels. The first level refers to the acceptance at a supranational sector level of a broad view with regard to outsourcing as part of an ongoing industrial change. This presupposes rejecting technological determinism as a singular superiority of free-market forces, taking into account also political and social processes, aspects like employment, employability and social cohesion, as well as consumer preferences and environmental aspects by both employers' associations and trade unions. Second, at the company level, a redefinition of the structures of representation and collective bargaining is required in order to develop a framework which overcomes the traditional 'sector' and 'company' union structure while opening up vertical and horizontal linkages across firms and within sectors. The mode of operation of some companies in the motor industry illustrates that some progress has been made in Europe in enlarging structures of employee representation and extending the scope of collective bargaining to the supplier firms.

Although all this may demonstrate a serious attempt by national unions to overcome traditional sector- and enterprise-based demarcations, such developments seem to face further difficulties when patterns of global sourcing are taken into consideration. A weak integrated international labour movement becomes politically and strategically ineffective when the production of a single commodity spans many countries, with each nation performing tasks in which it has a cost advantage. Hence the organizational structure of densely networked enterprises (see Porter, 1990) probably represents a further increasingly problematic area for trade union action in the future.

Conclusion

The extent and the dynamic of outsourcing, and the development of trade unions responses to regulate this process at both national and international level, has set the progress and identified problems in the European arena. By drawing evidence from the automobile industry this chapter has illustrated that trade unions in Europe have been mostly concerned about horizontal reinforcement, seeking to create bargaining frameworks for the new economic activities. To achieve this they have used legal provisions to enable them to be engaged at the outset of the outsourcing strategy while creating 'inter-company' works councils through agreement between the works councils or trade unions. At the same time, where this possibility has not been present, the trade unions have negotiated with management the creation of a horizontal structure of worker representation in exchange for social peace at the workplace. At this stage, in the light of the examples reported above, two factors appear as the most conducive of the difficulty involved in generating a framework where bargaining and employee representatives can be coordinated under outsourcing. First, the trade unions' action towards outsourcing is variably formalized and is not always treated as a priority. Second, the cross-national diversity of the legal rules regulating levels and forms of employee consultation and information – especially in the large companies – shapes the extent to which trade unions can effectively engage at the point of transfer of ownership. The degree of union engagement is reflected in their ability to enlarge the structure of employee representation as well as extending the scope of collective bargaining among the employees within the supplier companies. The maturing of these positions, where they exist, reflects a higher proactive union approach to redefine the forms of organization, representation and bargaining under outsourcing. Specifically, it addresses the trade unions' attempt to overcome the traditional concept of 'industrial' and 'enterprise-level' unionism and, thereby, to engage themselves in more effective actions in order to face the social consequences that company change imposes on labour.

However, evidence seems to suggest that the reorganization of relationships between suppliers and its impact on employment is still largely outside the scope of union intervention. Although trade unions have fostered the creation of an inter-firm (sector) structure of workplace representation, 'inter-company' works councils – where they exist – have very few functions and are usually restricted to running joint social activities. Thus, multi-sector structures are necessary in trying to achieve integration and better coordination between members in the different sectors and branches that perform work production or services activities. At this stage, more action at the European level is required. In particular, it seems important to reinforce the European level of bargaining in order to succeed as the trade unions have done when negotiating outsourcing at the group level. Currently, two factors seem to limit the effectiveness of such action. The first factor is the absence, at the European level, of a strong institutional framework concerning the regulation of information and consultation rights which can support the creation of an effective European-based structure of employees' involvement in company decision making. The second factor is the weakness of an international political union cohesion, which can act as a counterbalanced force to those features characterizing company change. This situation has a clear impact on the extent to which collective action can be organized and is thereby able to endure the social effects of restructuring more generally.

References

Atkinson, J. (1987), 'Flexibility or fragmentation? The United Kingdom labour market in the eighties', *Labour and Society*, vol. 12, no. 1, pp. 87–105.

Bettis, R., Bradley, S. and Hamel, G. (1992), 'Outsourcing and industrial decline', *Academy of Management Executive*, vol. 6, no.1, pp. 7–22.

Bonazzi, G. and Antonelli, C. (2003), 'To make or to sell? The case of in-house outsourcing at Fiat-Auto', *Organisation Studies*, vol. 24, no. 4, pp. 575–94.

Ebbinghaus, B. (2002), 'Trade unions' changing role: membership erosion, organisational reform, and social partnership in Europe', *Industrial Relations Journal*, vol. 33, no. 5, pp. 465–83.

EIRO (1998a), 'Provisions on working time accounts in collective agreements' at: www.eiro.eurofound. eu.int/1998/03/feature/be9803229f.html (accessed August 2006).

EIRO (1998b), 'Opel-Belgium: more flexible work organisation reduces redundancies' at: www.eiro. eurofound.eu.int/1998/03/feature/be9803229f.html (accessed August 2006).

EIRO (2000a), 'Outsourcing and industrial relations in motor manufacturing',at: www.eiro.eurofound. eu.int/2000/08/study/tn0008201s.html (accessed August 2006).

EIRO (2000b), 'Ford EWC and management sign pioneering agreement on Visteon employees' at: www. eiro.eurofound.eu.int/2000/04/inbrief/de0004254n.html (accessed August 2006).

Fairbrother, P. and Griffin, G. (2002), *Changing Prospects for Trade Unionism*, Routledge, London.

Gilley, K.M. and Rasheed, A. (2000), 'Making more by doing less: an analysis of outsourcing and its effects on firm performance', *Journal of Management*, vol. 26, no. 4, pp. 763–90.

Greaver, M.F. (1999), *Strategic Outsourcing. A Structured Approach to Outsourcing Decisions and Initiatives*, American Management Association Press, New York.

Hyman, R. (1994), 'Changing trade union identities and strategy', in R. Hyman and A. Ferner (eds), *New Frontiers in European Industrial Relations*, Blackwell, Oxford.

Kessler, I., Shapiro, C. and Purcell, J. (1999), 'Outsourcing and the employee perspective', *Human Resource Management Journal*, vol. 9, no. 2, pp. 5–19.

Logan, M.S., Faught, K. and Ganster, D.C. (2004), 'Outsourcing a satisfied and committed workforce: a trucking industry case study', *International Journal of Human Resource Management*, vol. 15, no. 1, pp. 147–62.

Lung, Y., Salerno, M.S., Zilbovicius, M. and Diaz, V. (1999), 'Flexibility through modularity: experimentations with fractal production in Brazil and in Europe', in Y. Lung, J.J. Chanaron, T. Fujimoto and D. Raff (eds), *Coping with Variety. Flexible Productive Systems for Product Variety in the Auto Industry*, Ashgate, Aldershot, pp. 224–58.

Pellicelli, R. (2000), '"Outsourcing" dal "make or buy" allo "strategic outsourcing"?', *Economia e Direzione delleImpresa*, G. Giapepellichelli Editore, Turin, pp. 178–219.

Porter, M. (1990), *The Competitive Advantage of Nations*, Free Press, New York.

Prahalad, C.K. and Hamel, G. (1990), 'The core competence of the corporation', *Harvard Business Review*, vol. 90, no. 3 (May–June), pp. 79–91.

Quinn, J.B. (1992), *Intelligent Enterprise: A Knowledge and Service Based Paradigm for Industry*, Free Press, New York.

Quinn, J.B. and Hilmer, F.G. (1994), 'Strategic outsourcing', *Sloan Management Review*, vol. 35, no. 4, Summer, pp. 43–55.

Rannie, A. (1989), *Industrial Relations and the Small Firms*, Routledge, London.

Sako, M. and Helper, S. (1999), 'Supplier relations and performance in Europe, Japan and the US: the effect of the voice/exit choice', in Y. Lung, J.J. Chanaron, T. Fujimoto and D.M.G. Raff (eds), *Coping with Variety. Flexible Productive Systems for Product Variety in the Auto Industry*, Ashgate, Aldershot.

Saundry, R. and Turnbull, P. (1999), 'Contractual (in) security, labour regulation and competitive performance in the port transport industry: a contextualised comparison of Britain and Spain', *British Journal of Industrial Relations*, vol. 37, no. 2, pp. 271–94.

Undy, R. (1999), 'The British merger movement: the importance of the "aggressive" unions', *Industrial Relations Journal*, vol. 30, no. 5, pp. 464–81.

Venkatesan, R. (1992), 'Strategic sourcing: to make or not to make', *Harvard Business Review*, vol. 70, no. 6, November–December, pp. 98–107.

14 The Materiality of Outsourcing

Ahmad Hussein Juma'h

Multinational companies are continually seeking innovative methods to compete globally. In the 1980s, top managements were judged on their ability to restructure the corporation and, in the 1990s, on their ability to identify, cultivate and exploit the core competencies (Prahalad and Hamel, 1990). In the 2000s, managers are expected to deal with changes in the times and uncertainties surrounding their companies. To improve efficiency companies seek innovative strategies. One innovative strategy that was exploited in the 1990s was outsourcing. In this chapter transaction cost theory (Coase, 1937; Williamson, 1975), agency theory (Jensen and Meckling, 1976), and signalling theory (Ross, 1973) are used to understand the economic and behavioural aspects of outsourcing and the implications of outsourcing for accounting practices.

Companies outsource some of their activities for short-term motives or strategic motives. Short-term motives include cost reduction, failure to meet the company's standards, obtaining new technologies and skills, and increasing the liquidity of outsourcing companies by selling assets to the outsource contractor. Strategic motives include concentrating on the core business and increasing the efficiency of outsourcing companies through strengthening the company's financial position and increasing market value (Bryce and Useem, 1997; Loh, 1992; Hayes, Hunton and Reck, 2000; Juma'h and Wood, 2003).

Decreasing future investments in assets and activities alters the financial structure of outsourcing companies. Therefore, outsourcing may reduce the issuance of liabilities or capital that would be necessary if outsourced functions were produced in-house. However, direct measurement of the outsourcing effect on companies' assets and liabilities is difficult, and outsourcing in effect creates off-balance sheet items that challenge current accounting practices, particularly if there are new forms of alliances (outsourcing) which are not considered in the outsourcing companies' financial statements.

From the outsourcing contracts that appear in press releases, outsourcing impacts on a number of the outsourcing companies' stakeholders. The main objective of this chapter is to discuss the materiality of outsourcing announcements by UK companies and the consequences of outsourcing on accounting and auditing practices. In the next section, accounting theories, standards and practices that might have applications when accountants are considering outsourcing agreements are discussed. The third section relates to the content of outsourcing announcements that include the outsourcing contract length and value, the size of outsourcing companies, the type of outsourcing functions, transfer of employees, restructuring, the performance of outsourcing companies, and annual reports of outsourcing companies. The fourth section introduces the impact of outsourcing announcements on stock markets. The conclusions are given in the final section.

Accounting theories, standards and practices with respect to outsourcing

Positive accounting theory (Watts and Zimmerman, 1978) is relevant to accountants and auditors with respect to managing, monitoring, and reporting outsourcing agreements. Watts and Zimmerman explain the role of theory and state that 'the objective of accounting theory is to explain and predict accounting practice' (1986, p. 2). Positive accounting theory emerges from agency theory and deals with how accountants or auditors conduct their work and why companies change or adopt accounting techniques. It is distinct from normative accounting theory that deals with what or how companies adopt, or change specific accounting techniques. In this sense, the accountants' consideration and evaluation of outsourcing agreements are important, since these influence the presentation of financial statements and therefore affect the perceptions of the readers of the financial statements. In addition, the degree to which generally accepted accounting principles (GAAPs) are applied to outsourcing in respect of materiality and ongoing core principles are important issues for exploring the consequences of strategic outsourcing on accounting and auditing practices.

UK accounting standards appear to create ways for accountants to incorporate outsourcing agreements in their evaluation of outsourcing companies. Accounting standards include the need to reflect on the substance of transaction, the creation of contingent liabilities, the possibility of onerous contracts, the existence of a restructuring process, the disposal of a segment of business, and the existence of related party transactions. In extreme cases the dependency of an outsourcing company on their suppliers for a core capability might create a basis of ongoing concern issues. Although these accounting standards cover outsourcing contracts, the subjectivity and judgement of accountants are important in considering outsourcing contracts as material or non-material items in the presentation of financial statements.

Financial Report Standard (FRS) 5 (Accounting Standards Board, 1994) is related to reporting the substance of transactions – particularly complex and specialized transactions. For example, the innovative methods of finance that use off-balance sheet items that include leasing or deferred liabilities can enable companies to increase their ability to expand without issuing liabilities or shares. Alliances and strategies adopted by companies, such as outsourcing, may be considered as off-balance sheet items that increase the company's risk. In applying FRS 5 to outsourcing, all the consequences of outsourcing should be considered, such as the disposal of assets against a given payment agreement and contingent liabilities that are created with respect to breaches of the outsourcing contracts.

In the case of information technology (IT) outsourcing, outsourcing providers have an information advantage over outsourcing companies with respect to the software and hardware costs and are also in a price-making position due to the relatively few outsourcing providers in the market. The outsourcing providers may offer cheaper terms in the first year and may buy equipment at above book price and charge particularly attractive rates to the outsourcing company. This means that during the first year outsourcing companies may obtain significant benefits that do not reflect the reality in subsequent years. The failure to note the accurate contract price and not to consider the differences between fair market payments and obligations under the outsourcing agreements may be significant in constituting an onerous contract (FRS 12).

Some companies enter into outsourcing agreements to enable the restructuring of their departments or units. Outsourcing companies have a detailed formal plan to outsource that may affect both outsourced and non-outsourced functions. A significant number of employees are generally transferred to the service supplier. Transaction costs are incurred, the plan is implemented and the resulting outsourcing contracts may receive wide coverage in press releases. Transaction costs that arise from outsourcing agreements are significant, necessary and not associated with ongoing activities. Therefore, the transaction costs (restructuring costs) should be included in the restructuring provision as required by FRS 12. It is apparent that outsourcing agreements have the potential to become onerous contracts and they involve also reorganization or restructuring processes. A possible reason that may be used to leave outsource agreements undeclared in the financial statements is that they may not involve a provision because restructuring costs occur in the accounting year and are simply treated as a period expense rather than a long-term obligation.

There is a possibility that some of the outsourcing contracts involve more than classical contracts in particular relational contracts. Outsourcing to the extent that it involves delegation of strategic control may be equivalent to the influence held by a minority interest. If there are agreements within the outsource contracts dealing with participation in intellectual property development, then gain on equity equivalence may be created. Related party issues arise where any party controls, or can significantly influence, the management or operating policies of the company to the extent that the company may be prevented from fully pursuing its own interests (FRS 8). Therefore, outsourcing may signal issues similar to related parties.

Outsourcing could also influence the presentation of the financial statements and the quality of the operational audit (Barr and Chang, 1993). In the early stages of the outsourcing phenomenon auditors demanded access to the data of outsourcing suppliers to ensure that accrual principles were reflected in these agreements and the level of performance achieved. Friedberg and Yarberry (1991) point out that the level of audit rights depends on the sophistication of the services provided. Audit rights may be important in the negotiation and initial operations of outsourcing contracts in any environment (sophisticated or not), but the longer the contract, the more payments and service delivery conform to trust-based norms rather than strict contract terms. Barr and Chang (1993) state that outsourcing requires the expansion of internal audit services into organizations where such a function was not previously contemplated.

Several limitations affect the judgements and perceptions of the accountants and auditors with respect to outsourcing contracts. The limitations of applying accounting standards for reporting outsourcing contracts include materiality, conservatism, cost–benefit criteria and industry practices. The concept of materiality plays a central role in accounting practices. Accountants must exercise professional judgement in evaluating information and concluding on its materiality. Materiality is dependent on the size of an item relative to the total activity of the entity, the precision with which the item can be estimated, and the nature of the item itself. A crucial factor is whether the materiality of an event is judged on a single transaction or on aggregate transactions. For example, when a company starts contracting one function but subsequently outsources more and more functions, at what stage does materiality become an issue if a company outsources one function this year and another next year and then continues to outsource more functions? Conceivably, it ends up as a financing shell with little operational capability. The absence of material information on outsourcing, therefore, makes the financial statements misleading. However, US, UK and international accounting standards do not explain or provide guidance in distinguishing material information from immaterial information in terms of influencing the reader of the financial statements.

Qualitative characteristics of accounting information are affected by accounting conservatism. Conservatism is a reaction to uncertainty and may mislead the users of the financial statements if it results in understatement of net assets and net income or is in steps that affect the company's risk exposure (for example, outsourcing contingent liabilities to the service supplier). Such arrangements may produce biased financial statements in subsequent years that contradict the basic characteristics of representational faithfulness, neutrality and comparability of financial statements. Also, cost–benefit criteria are the main limitations in accounting practices that arise from a concern that the benefits received from disclosing outsourcing agreements are more than the costs involved in auditing and presenting outsourcing agreements in the financial statements.

The content of outsourcing announcements

Content analysis as a form of text analysis is widely used in social science (Krippendorff, 1980). Krippendorff defines content analysis as 'a research technique for making replicable and valid inferences from data based on their context' (1980, p. 21). These techniques are systematic and apply quantitative description (Berelson, 1971, p. 18) to textual material. Berelson (1971, pp. 18–20) states three general assumptions that are made about content analysis studies. The first assumption is that the inferences concerning the relationship between intent and content can be validly established. Content analysis helps to reveal the purpose, motives and other characteristics of the announcement companies. The second assumption is that the manifest content of the announcement is meaningful, and the third assumption is that content analysis assumes that the quantitative description of the content of outsourcing announcements is meaningful. In other words, the frequency of occurrence of different characteristics within outsourcing announcements is an important variable.

In this chapter, content analysis identifies the patterns and trends of outsourcing announcements by classifying the content characteristics of the announcements and calculating frequencies, averages, the correlation between the occurrence of information types and other statistics. The characteristic features in outsourcing announcements are contract length, contract value, type of activities or functions outsourced, mention of outsourcing drivers, specific benefits attributed to the outsource deal and, finally, the relationship with the outsourcing companies, if declared.

The empirical work in this chapter is concerned with the UK private sector, which, as in the USA, has seen a remarkable growth of outsourcing agreements. This has been accompanied by a rapid process of entity consolidation through merger and acquisition which, all things being equal, would increase the scale of activities of internal provision relative to outsource contractors and is a common factor in the two countries. Also, a large part of growth has been in outsourcing between large-sized companies and has concentrated on information system and/or information technology outsourcing and related functions, such as accounting services and finance. The primary sample for the research was based on outsourcing announcements appearing in newspapers. The primary search for outsourcing announcements involved collecting press announcements by companies that have made, or disclose an intention to make, agreements with service suppliers. The start date for the search was 1989. This was based on the announcement of the ten-year outsourcing contract between Eastman Kodak and IBM to consolidate and operate data centres.

The first outsourcing announcement by an UK company after the 1989 start-date was found in the year 1991. This announcement describes the contract made between British Petroleum (BP) and Arthur Andersen Consulting (*Computer Weekly*, 13 June 1991, p. 72). The year 1991 was established as the first year for outsourcing announcements in the UK within the sample period. The sample consists of UK companies that recorded or publicly announced an outsourcing contract between 1991 and 1997. The delay between the start of the search, 1989, and the first example located, 1991, means that the later distinction between continuing and multiple outsources and one-off outsources is not likely to be invalidated by agreements pre-dating the start of the observation period.

THE SAMPLE COMPOSITION

The sample consists of 100 companies that made 141 announcements of outsourcing agreements and includes both quoted and non-quoted companies, but excludes governmental agencies and other public-sector units on the grounds that there was no financial benchmark data. In the research each outsourcing event is considered as a case study that potentially involves multiple examples (contracts) and numerous levels of analysis (for example, national/global outsourcing, the financial performance of outsourcing and outsource vendor companies). According to Yin (1981, 1984), the distinguishing characteristic of the case-study approach is that it attempts to examine a contemporary phenomenon in its real-life context and is appropriate where the boundaries between phenomenon and context are not clear and multiple sources of information exist.

The sample composition shows that the financial sector accounts for about one-third of the companies involved in outsourcing announcements and that this sector accounts for more than one-third of total outsourcing announcements in the sample. Within the financial sector, businesses can be classified as originating with banks, insurance companies, fund management and other financial companies. The overrepresentation of financial companies, which accounts for around 15 per cent of UK GDP but made 34 per cent of outsource announcements, is consistent with the argument of growth in outsourcing and its potential for the financial services sector (Jennings, 1996). The second sector is the utilities sector that represents 22 per cent of the total outsourcing companies. The industrial, distribution, consumer, business service, leisure, construction and real estate sectors represent the remainder of outsourcing announcements (44 per cent).

THE OUTSOURCING CONTRACT LENGTH AND VALUE

The average (mode, mean or medium) contract length is over five years with a minimum and maximum of two years and 11 years respectively. These contracts are, therefore, long term and, in most cases, are potentially renewable and have penalties for non-completion. The disclosed contract values in the sample range from £0.5 million in the case of the three-year contract between Calor and Hoskyns (*Computing*, 11 June 1992, p. 6) to £900 million in the case of the ten-year contract between British Aerospace (BAe) and Computer Science Corporation (CSC) (RNS, 16 November 1993). From the contract length and value, it seems that some dependency on the service provider is created and there is a possibility of contingent liabilities that may arise from the contract terms.

To evaluate the magnitude of outsourcing contract value in relation to the outsourcing company, the ratios of announced outsourcing contract values to total sales, total assets, and total capital employed are calculated. The relevant data are obtained directly from the outsourcing announcements or from the Data-Stream database. On average, outsourcing contract value represents about 8.5 per cent of total annual sales revenue. If an annual outsourcing payment is determined by dividing the announced outsourcing contract value by the announced contract length, the implied annual outsourcing payment represents approximately 1 per cent of the total sales revenue of outsourcing companies. Outsourcing contract value represents about 7.1 per cent and 14 per cent of total assets and total capital employed, respectively. As a result, it is possible to conclude that many outsourcing agreements involve amounts large enough to be significant to a company's long-term performance.

THE SIZE OF OUTSOURCING COMPANIES

Most of the announcements of outsourcing contracts are attributed to large-sized companies. More than 30 per cent of the FTSE 100 and 43 per cent of the FT 30 share indexes are in the sample. The FTSE 100 represents about 2 per cent of all UK companies listed in the Data-Stream database in 1998 and about 8 per cent of UK companies listed in *Risk Measurement Services*, published by the London Business School in 1998. However, it is possible that smaller firms' deals are underrepresented because they are infrequent or because the press is not focused on them. It is noticeable also that service suppliers who appear less than three times in the sample are normally associated with smaller-sized outsourcing companies.

In attempting to determine the relationship between the size of outsourcing companies and outsource contractors, 52 outsourcing companies with their outsource contractors are considered, based on the availability of outsourcing companies' market value. The natural logarithm of market value (ln (MV)) was calculated as a proxy for the size of outsourcing companies, and outsource contractors were divided into two groups according to their success in obtaining large outsource contracts. Group 1 includes EDS, IBM, CSC, Andersen and KPMG (with ranking 1), and group 2 includes other outsource contractors (with ranking 0). The second group of contractors had three or fewer announcements in total. The results indicate that company size correlated with the important outsource variable with a Pearson correlation of 56 per cent, which is significant at the 1 per cent level.

TYPES OF OUTSOURCING FUNCTIONS

Ninety-one per cent of the total sample announcements indicate the types of outsourcing functions. These include information technology (IT) specialities such as networking, operating maintenance, and data centre and facility management. The outsourcing of these functions independently of other IT functions occurs with a high frequency in the sample. Other IT functions, such as system development and installation, mainframe, IT support and management, and data communication and telecommunication, have a moderate frequency. Other functions such as data provision, international communication and telephone services occurred relatively infrequently in the outsourcing announcements. The infrequent announcements of these functions is possibly an indication of their smaller size and possibly because they relate to homogeneous services that are handled by short-term routine contracts rather than true outsource arrangements.

Other areas identified as forming the basis of outsource agreements include payroll management, which has a high frequency of outsourcing. Billing and credit management, accounting and tax services, cheque processing, strategic consulting and investment administration functions have a moderate frequency. Human resource management, portfolio management, payment management and repair centre operation have a low frequency of occurrence in the sample of outsourcing announcements.

TRANSFER OF EMPLOYEES

Outsourcing announcements mainly involve the transfer of employees (Lacity and Hirschheim, 1993; Lacity et al., 1995, 1996; Sharpe, 1997). The announcement of outsourcing intentions has occasionally precipitated strikes or other action against outsourcing agreements. However, the transfer of undertaking mechanism leaves employees with little negotiating strengths since the service provider preserves existing employees' benefits, and dissenting employees would need to resign and claim constructive dismissal. For example, when Barclays outsourced its data processing to FI (Computer Weekly, 9 September 1993, p.2), Barclaycard's IT director, Rosemary Horwood, said, 'Outsourcing enabled us to release key IT staff with knowledge of our business (engaged on managing process system) to work on strategic systems.' A Banking, Insurance and Finance Union (BIFU) spokesman claimed that Barclays 'hasn't exactly looked hard to find other IT staff within the bank' that might have worked on strategic issues, and BIFU speculated that the move was due to the bank's declared commitment to outsource more of its activities to create 'greater freedom to reduce numbers'.

In the short term, however, the union spokesman said that there was 'no immediate concern that we will lose our jobs', and suggested that Barclays had suffered a damaging strike in 1991 and were anxious to avoid further industrial action. A Barclays' spokesman denied that jobs could be lost. 'The total number of IT staff will actually increase during the programme,' he said. For example, the FI Group has a longstanding relationship with Barclays, providing training and support services. It trained about 30 of the bank's inter-mortgage staff, with its recruitment division, AMP Computer Recruitment, which was awarded preferred supplier status. However, Collins and Millen (1995) found that half the information executives surveyed indicated that outsourcing has a negative impact on employees' morale, thereby supporting the role of outsourcing in creating employees' dissatisfaction.

The outsourcing announcements indicate that, in most outsourcing contracts, companies transfer a significant number of their employees in the affected area to the outsourcing supplier, retaining only a small number of employees to liaise with the contractor. The outsourcing companies may reallocate in turn any remaining surplus employees from the outsourced department into other internal departments. In general, it is expected that there will be some overall reduction in employment.

Outsourcing agreements often have immediate and continuing effects on employment in absolute and relative (to sales) terms. Usually, a significant number of employees are transferred to the service supplier, who then enters into a service contract to provide the service that the employees previously delivered directly. The following are examples of such transfers: 1250 BAe employees were transferred into CSC. (Business Wire, 16 November 1993; RNS, 16 November 1993); British Petroleum outsourcing agreements involved transferring 1400 of its IT staff (Computer Weekly, 1 October 1992, p.1) and around 1100 of the chemical giant, ICI's staff have been transferred to Origin as a result of an outsourcing deal (Computer Weekly, 30 May 1996, p. 4). Other announcements relate to a smaller number of employees: for example, General Accident and Rolls Royce who transferred 250 and 160 respectively (Glasgow Herald, 15 April 1997, p. 20; Birmingham Post, 7 January 1997, p. 22).

Most of the cost management literature and empirical studies of cost structures indicate that employment cost is the second biggest cost variable in manufacturing companies and generally the biggest cost variable in service companies. Through outsourcing, companies generally terminate the continuing direct cost of the resources they have transferred, such as employment cost, other benefits and profit sharing, and may also reduce transaction costs associated with lay-offs where the outsource contractor accepts liabilities for these resources. In addition, they may avoid any investment expenditure (and often other employment) that may be involved in supporting the outsourced activities – for example, they can avoid investment in recruitment and employee training (McFarlan and Nolan, 1995). They may also be able to reduce the personnel support staff previously needed to support the outsourced staff and may dispose of physical assets.

When employment costs decrease by more than the incremental outsourcing contract cost, the net effect will be to increase operating profits. Even if outsource charges leave little direct cost savings, associated savings may still increase profit. Therefore, outsourcing implies an immediate, and a possible continuing, reduction in employee cost, a reduction in employment cost to sales, a reduction in employment cost to value added (greater efficiency), a reduction in capital investment, an increase in absolute profits, and an increase in margin (profit percentage of sales).

The wages to sales (W/S) ratio is used to proxy employment costs to examine the relationship between outsourcing and employment cost. The sample shows a decline, which reflects the declining proportional contribution of wages to value added in the sample companies. W/S is noted as being at a minimum in the outsourcing year. This is consistent with the expectation that outsourcing agreements decrease employment costs almost immediately. In effect the outsourcing announcement is associated (and may be precipitated) by the imminence of staff transfer. Comparing outsourcing companies with the average of UK companies, outsourcing companies incurred less employment cost than the average UK company.

Examining the change in employment cost by change in W/S indicates that employment costs decreased by 1.7 per cent and 2.1 per cent in the outsourcing year and in the subsequent year, respectively. The change is statistically significant at the 5 per cent level in both years. This is consistent with the argument that there is a trade-off between outsourcing payment and reduction in employment costs.

RESTRUCTURING

According to McFarlan and Nolan (1995), companies may initiate outsourcing as a solution to unmanageable, non-productive or otherwise problematic departments. Furthermore, Bettis, Bradley and Hamel (1992), Apte (1991) and McMullen (1990) state that companies outsource as a reaction to financial pressures. Another outsourcing motive is to prepare a company for restructuring. In the case of five of the sample companies, the outsourcing announcement was followed by a major restructuring in the form of acquisition or merger as a follow-up to their outsourcing initiative (see Table 14.1).

There is a possibility that planning to outsource a department results in its operational disposal. This is likely to affect the presentation of the financial statements. In particular, the sale of equipment (computers) increases the cash flow of the outsourcing companies and also has a direct effect on the presentation of the financial statements, especially in terms of liquidity. Moreover, the sale of equipment at book value, as indicated by many outsourcing announcements, may not reflect the fair or market value of the equipment. This may result in inappropriate recording of the transaction or possibly a solution in which over- or undervaluation is balanced by other terms of the agreement.

Table 14.1   Examples of outsourcing announcements followed by major restructuring

Outsourcing			Restructuring	
Company	Contractor	Year	Year	Type
Calor Group	Hoskyns	1992	1997	Acquisition (by SHV Holding NV)
TSB Bank	Hoskyns	1993	1995	Merger (with Lloyds Bank)
	Syncordia	1995		
United Friendly Insurance Plc	Unisys	1996	1996	Merger (with Refuge Assurance Plc to form United Assurance Group plc)
Lucas Industries	CSC	1995	1996	Acquisition (by Lucas Varity)
Mercury Asset Management	Excell	1995	1997	Acquisition (by Merrill Lynch)

THE PERFORMANCE OF OUTSOURCING COMPANIES

It is argued that outsourcing strategy is among a variety of options for increasing efficiency. During the period 1988 to 1992, the operating profit declined for outsourcing companies and for the average of all UK companies. However, the sample showed improvements in operating profits following the year of outsourcing and, on average, the operating profit percentage (OP%) of the sample outsourcing companies is above the OP% of the average of all UK companies. The UK companies' improvement in profitability in the upturn is also below the OP% of the outsourcing companies' sample. Outsourcing, though, is just one option among a range of different options available to companies in the sample to improve performance relative to the benchmark profitability.

On average, the sample shows that OP% declined in the event year in absolute terms and relative to the benchmark for all UK companies. Given that the majority of outsourcing announcements occurred in the period from 1994 to 1996 during which there was an improvement in profitability in UK companies, the decline may reflect the transaction costs associated with the companies' rearranging and reorganizing activities affected by the outsourcing contract. In particular, the transaction costs of negotiating the contract and the liquidation of employment liabilities in the outsourcing year may involve transaction effects that would, in general, be expected to be transitory. The downtrend in OP% is reversed in the year following outsourcing, with companies generally increasing both profit and OP%. The sample shows that the change of OP% (that is, the difference between OP% in the event year and average OP% in three years prior to the event) is negative in the outsourcing year and it becomes positive in following years. By coincidence the OP% benchmark was at a minimum point in the matching year. Therefore, either outsourcing is a response to a general decrease in companies' profitability in the period prior to, and including, the outsourcing contract or else outsourcing involves significant transaction costs in the year in which contracts start. In any event OP% in general seems to be declining prior to outsourcing reaching a low point in the year of outsourcing and beginning to recover in the following year.

In examining the liquidity of outsourcing companies, the quick ratio and cash to current liabilities declined after 1994. This is coincidental with the increasing number of outsourcing contracts in this period. By rearranging data with respect to outsourcing year, it is noted that quick ratio has a minimum point at the outsourcing year, but in the subsequent year it experienced a recovery. Cash to liabilities decreased in the outsourcing year and slightly decreased in the following year. In the three years immediately before the outsourcing year, quick ratio and cash to liabilities showed no notable change. The quick ratio benchmark was at its minimum point in the outsourcing year then increased in the following year, and the quick ratio of outsourcing companies was above the average quick benchmark ratio of all UK companies. The change in liquidity ratios in the outsourcing year is an indication of current resources or current financing being used to cover the one-off set-up costs of outsourcing contracts. In the year subsequent to the outsourcing agreement, liquidity ratios show an increase; this indicates that outsourcing companies, on average, achieve a better liquidity position than in the event year. Again, there is an accounting issue in the sense that the front-end costs of outsourcing are not capitalized.

One opportunity arising in outsourcing is that companies can transfer some elements of R&D cost to the outsource contractor and, indeed, would gain competitive advantage by accessing the research base of skills, experience and scale advantages of the outside contractor. However, only a few companies disclose R&D expenditures in their accounts throughout the sample period. To investigate the relationship between outsourcing and R&D, the subsample of 12 companies that did so was examined. On average, outsourcing companies decreased their R&D expenditure relative to their sales after the event year, confirming a fall in R&D logically associated with the transfer of strategic responsibility for a function to an outsource contractor. This might create dependency between outsourcing companies and outsourcing suppliers, and therefore requires more attention by accountants in evaluating outsourcing companies' profitability and liquidity.

ANNUAL REPORTS OF OUTSOURCING COMPANIES

Four companies from the sample described their outsourcing contracts or their outsourcing strategies in their annual reports. Two companies, MEPC plc and Greenalls Group, described the outsourcing contracts under the section of business review and strategy. MEPC indicated that the outsourcing of property and facilities management activities allow the company to concentrate on those areas which contribute most to its performance – namely, the management of assets, income and major projects (MEPC *Annual Report*, 1997, p. 5). Greenalls described the benefit obtained from the outsourcing of its distribution functions that represent a major cost in the supply chain. The outsourcing agreement is a long-term contract with Wincanton Logistic. The company expects to obtain £1.75 million as annual savings (Greenalls *Annual Report*, 1996, p. 20). Despite considering outsourcing agreements as beneficial and of strategic importance for their business, these two companies discussed the derived benefits from outsourcing in the business review section of annual report, which is not considered as part of the financial statements. Therefore, these companies recognize the importance of outsourcing for their operations, but do not consider that a note in the financial statements is necessary. This is consistent with conservative principle in accounting. A third company, Shell Oil Company, disclosed a joint venture and alliance, under which they outsourced IT services to the new company (TASCO).

An interesting case is British Aerospace (BAe) plc that included a description of some outsourcing agreements under material contracts. The particular event to be considered is BAe's decision to outsource IT to the CSC, announced in 1993. In its 1993 annual report, in the declaration of material contracts, BAe provided the following disclosure.

... an agreement made between (1) the company, (2) CSC Computer Science Limited and (3) computer Science Corporation (jointly 'CSC') and effective on 1 April 1994, by which the Company sold its Information Technology infrastructure assets and activities and its software systems and consultancy business carried on under the name 'BAeCAM' to CSC for the sum of £46.5 million subject to adjustment following the preparation of a completing statement. By an associated agreement made between (1) the company and (2) CSC Aerospace System Inc ('CSC AS') and effective upon the same date, the Company, in consideration of the payment to it of the sum of £34.9 million, awarded to CSC AS a contract to provide to the Company certain IT services described therein upon the terms and conditions therein stated. (BAe, Annual Report, 1993, p. 88)

This disclosure summarizes the relevant issues regarding the outsourcing contract. However, other information, which would have been of assistance to the reader of the financial statements in evaluating the contract, was not given. Helpful details might include: the length of the contract, if the contract is renewable, the penalties for breaching the contract, access to data, and if any legal relationship is created with the service supplier.

The BAe outsourcing contract has similarities with sale–lease-back agreements used in property transactions. In selling the IT assets, transferring staff and accepting an obligation to use these resources on a continuing basis, a very equivalent transaction to a lease/rental agreement is created. Therefore, part of this outsourcing transaction may be equivalent to either a capital lease or to an operating lease. The outsourcing of the IT department also meets the disposal of a segment criterion. Any gain or loss on the sale of IT assets should be classified as 'other gain or loss' in the income statements, and increases in cash flow for the amount received from the proceeds should be declared.

Investors' reactions to outsourcing announcements

It is important to compare investors' reaction to outsourcing announcements with accountants' consideration to evaluate the materiality of outsourcing. The stock market, faced with an outsourcing announcement, may perceive this as an indication of a company's difficulties or interpret it as a signal that outsourcing companies are improving their focus on core businesses to deliver gains in profit and growth. Either way there will be a change in the company's stock price. Therefore, anticipating the impact of outsourcing on a shareholder value must be part of the outsourcing process.

Event studies are a common way of examining the market reaction to outsourcing announcements. Using US data, Peak (1994) found a negative reaction while McLellan (1991), Loh (1992) and Hayes, Hunton and Reck (2000) concluded the opposite. Peak (1994) examined the announcements of the information systems outsourcing of 14 US Fortune-500 companies, using risk measured by implied volatility in stock option prices based on multiple window intervals (45 days before to 45 days after the event day). He found that there was no immediate reaction for financially weak firms, but the data showed subsequently increased volatility, and financially healthy firms exhibited an immediate risk reduction, with the risk residuals quickly rising to levels comparable to the financially weak firms.

Using 30 outsourcing announcements from the period 1985 to 1990, McLellan found substantial positive excess returns on the day of outsourcing announcements but not in a larger event window before or after the announcement. In a sample of 55 US companies Loh applied a ten-day event window (three days before the announcement day and six days after the announcement day). This event window indicated that there was uncertainty about fixing the time when the outsourcing information was to be made available to investors. Hayes, Hunton and Reck (2000), studied 78 outsourcing announcements made in the period 1990 to 1997 and concluded that the abnormal return was greater for smaller than for larger firms.

Using UK data, Juma'h and Wood (2000, 2003) studied the outsourcing announcements in the period 1991 to 1997 and showed that innovative announcements (that is, single or initial announcements that do not include multiple announcements such as re-outsourcing, renewals and frequent announcements) have significant mean cumulative excess returns and that outsourcing information was potentially available in the market before the public announcement was made. Contrary to Hayes, Hunton and Reck, Juma'h and Wood found that the shareholders' reaction was more notable for larger companies than for smaller companies. This is consistent with the interpretation that larger companies have more power in negotiating with service suppliers.

The investors' positive reaction to outsourcing announcements is consistent with the conservative principle in accounting and explains why companies do not present notes in the financial statements. However, accountants should exercise due care and at least consider any negative consequences with respect to outsourcing agreements.

Conclusions

Transaction costs, controlling and monitoring costs are important in outsourcing agreements, particularly during the outsourcing year. These costs affect the outsourcing companies' profitability and liquidity. The outsourcing companies' profitability tended to decrease in the event year but increased in the subsequent year. This captured the initial transaction costs in arranging the contract. The liquidity of outsourcing companies, the quick ratio and cash to current liabilities have minimum values at the outsourcing year, but in the subsequent year these ratios experienced a recovery. In the three years immediately prior to the outsourcing year, these ratios showed no notable change, so the decrease in the outsourcing year is probably a result of the transaction costs that occurred in that year. The change in liquidity ratios indicates that current resources are used to cover the payment of outsourcing contracts, including set-up costs. Subsequent to the year of outsourcing agreements the quick ratio showed an increase which reflects the fact that the cost reduction delivered by the outsource agreement was no longer masked by transaction fees. The sample showed that announced outsourcing companies decreased employment costs and R&D expenditures relative to sales. Outsourcing provides a measurable response that can increase performance by concentrating on the core business and providing a systematic element in re-engineering the value chain of outsourcing companies.

Although there is no evidence of account manipulation, it is probable that outsourcing agreements that shift profits from one period to the next, reduce apparent indebtedness and transfer considerable strategic control and the part it plays in disposal proceedings outside the corporation. Rolls Royce's decision to outsource engine supply to BMW, for example, played a major role in negotiating with potential acquirers of the business. This means that accounting practices can be revised to assist extended corporations in producing information to investors and thereby possibly undermine debt providers and suppliers. Consequently, accountants should be more innovative in conducting their works.

The case-by-case situation that is considered relevant in deciding on the materiality of outsourcing agreements is based on the size of contract, uncertainty of valuation of capital items transferred, the risk profile, costs associated with failure to deliver, and the procedure for dispute resolution. Also, improvements to the existing accounting standards to adequately cover outsourcing agreements include risk profile, contingencies arising from failure in delivering and disputes, and the spreading of costs between periods. If outsourcing payments represent a commitment to outsourcing companies, the inclusion of the amount of any future commitment existing at the balance sheet date may be considered necessary. Where the outsourcing company becomes dependent on an outsource supplier, and huge transaction costs and/or losses may occur if the contract is breached, at least a note showing best estimates of outsourcing payments should be considered. However, most accountants consider the outsourcing contract as a service contract, and the examination of outsourcing annual reports reveals that few disclosures are made with respect to outsourcing in the financial statements. As the overwhelming majority of the sample of outsourcing companies does not include any reference to the outsourcing contracts, this may reflect an industry practice. In fact, outsourcing companies and their auditors may consider outsourcing payments as period expenses and underestimate the risks which arise from outsource contractor failure to deliver the level of outsourcing services or any deviation from arms' length pricing involved in the contract.

Accountants emphasized that existing accounting standards do not adequately cover risk profiles or contingencies resulting from failure to deliver the agreed and implied terms or the possibility of disputes over the obligation of each party. Accessing outsourced function data represents another problem when auditing outsourcing companies, but it is possible to overcome these problems by examining long-term performance and reviewing internal risk management.

Outsourcing appears to be worth the attention of accountants and, in most cases, is a material event. First, the voluntary and unregulated announcements of outsourcing seem to reflect a major gap in market efficiency, which generally requires coordinated and simultaneous announcement through the stock exchange and the media. Second, the ad hoc nature of disclosure in announcements and in subsequent annual reports is questionable. There are no guidelines in terms of mandatory disclosure of details, nature of contract and objective basis of pricing arrangements. Third, the capital structure and risk profile change as a result of outsourcing. Capitalizing that part of an outsource payment related to asset finance would make outsource reporting consistent with lease reporting. Finally, outsourcing redefines the boundary of the firm. The function of the audit based on legal/control definitions will be incapable of capturing the risk and performance characteristics of the extended firm.

References

Accounting Standards Board (1994), *Financial Reporting Standard No. 5: Reporting the Substance of Transactions*, December, ASB, London.

Apte, U. (1991), 'Global outsourcing of information systems and processing services', *The Information Society*, vol. 7, pp. 287–303.

Barr, R.H. Jr and Chang, S.Y. (1993), 'Outsourcing internal audits: a boon or bane?', *Management Auditing Journal*, vol. 8, no. 1, pp. 14–17.

Berelson, B. (1971), *Content Analysis in Communication Research*, Hanfer Publishing Company, New York.

Bettis, R.A., Bradley, S.P. and Hamel, G. (1992), 'Outsourcing and industrial decline', *Academy of Management Executive*, vol. 6, no. 1, pp. 7–22.

Bryce, D.J. and Useem, M. (1997), 'The impact of corporate outsourcing on company value', *European Management Journal*, vol. 16, no. 6, pp. 635–43.

Coase, R.H. (1937), 'The nature of the firm', *Economica*, vol. 4, November, pp. 386–405.

Collins, J.S. and Millen, R.A. (1995), 'Information systems outsourcing by large American industrial firms: choice and impacts', *Information Resources Management Journal*, Winter, vol. 8, no. 1, pp. 5–13.

Friedberg, A.H. and Yarberry, W.A. Jr (1991), 'Audit rights in an outsource environment', *Internal Auditor*, August, pp. 53–59.

Hayes, D.C., Hunton, J.E. and Reck, J.L. (2000), 'Information systems outsourcing announcements: investigating the impact on the market value of contract-granting firms', *Journal of Information Systems*, vol. 14, no. 2, Fall, pp. 109–25.

Jennings, D. (1996), 'Outsourcing opportunity for financial services', *Long Range Planning*, vol. 29, no. 3, pp. 393–404.

Jensen, M.C. and Meckling, W.H. (1976), 'Theory of the firm: managerial behavior, agency costs and ownership structure', *Journal of Financial Economics*, vol. 3, no. 4, pp. 305–60.

Juma'h, A. and Wood, D. (2000), 'Outsourcing implications on companies profitability and liquidity: a sample of UK companies', *Work Study*, vol. 49, no. 7, pp. 265–74.

Juma'h, A. and Wood, D. (2003), 'The price sensitivity of business service outsourcing announcements by UK companies', *International Journal of Information Technology and Decision Making*, vol. 2, no.1, March, pp.161-180.

Krippendorff, K. (1980), *Content Analysis: An Introduction to its Methodology*, Sage, Beverly Hills, CA.

Lacity, M.C. and Hirschheim, R. (1993), 'The information systems outsourcing bandwagon' *Sloan Management Review*, Fall, pp. 73–86.

Lacity, M.C., Willcocks, L.P. and Feeny, D.F. (1995), 'IT outsourcing: maximize flexibility and control', *Harvard Business Review*, May–June, pp. 84–93.

Lacity, M.C., Willcocks, L.P. and Feeny, D.F. (1996), 'The value of selective IT sourcing', *Sloan Management Review*, Spring, pp. 13–25.

Loh, L. (1992), 'The economics and organization of information technology governance', doctoral thesis, Sloan School of Management, MIT.

McFarlan, F.W. and Nolan, R.L. (1995), 'How to manage an IT outsourcing alliance', *Sloan Management Review*, vol. 36, no. 2, Winter, pp. 9–23.

McLellan, K. (1991), 'MIS outsourcing, organizational networks, and competitive advantage', Working paper, School of Business Administration, The University of Western Ontario, London Canada, January.

McMullen, J. (1990), 'New allies: IS and service suppliers', *Datamation*, 1 March, pp. 42–51.

Peak, D.A. (1994), 'The risk and benefits of outsourcing on the information systems function and the firm', doctoral dissertation, University of North Texas 0158.

Prahalad, C.K. and Hamel, G. (1990), 'Core competence of the corporation', *Harvard Business Review*, May–June, pp. 79–91.

Ross, S. (1973), 'The economic theory of agency: the principal's problem', *American Economic Review*, vol. 63, pp. 134–39.

Sharpe, M. (1997), 'Outsourcing, organizational competitiveness, and work', *Journal of Labor Research*, vol. XVIII, no. 4, Fall, pp. 535–49.

Watts, R.L. and Zimmerman, J.L. (1978), 'Towards a positive theory of the determination of accounting standards', *The Accounting Review*, vol. LIII, no. 1, January, pp.112–34.

Watts, R.L. and Zimmerman, J.L. (1979), 'The demand for and supply of accounting theories: the market for excuses', *The Accounting Review*, April, pp. 273–305.

Watts, R.L. and Zimmerman, J.L. (1986), *Positive Accounting Theory*, Prentice-Hall, Englewood Cliffs, NJ.

Williamson, O.E. (1975), *Market and Hierarchies: Analysis and Antitrust Implication*, Free Press, New York.

Williamson, O.E. (1979), 'Transaction-cost economics: the governance of contractual relations', *The Journal of Law and Economics*, pp. 233–61.

Williamson, O.E. (1981), 'The modern corporation: origin, evolution, attributes', *Journal of Economic Literature*, vol. XIX, pp. 1537–68.

Williamson, O.E. (1985), *The economic institutions of capitalism*, The Free Press, NY.

Williamson, O.E. (1986), *Economic Organisation*, Wheatsheaf Books Ltd, Brighton.

Yin, R.K. (1981), 'The case study crisis: some answers', *Administrative Science Quarterly*, vol. 26, pp. 58–65.

Yin, R.K. (1984), *Case Study Research – Design and Methods*, Sage, London and New Delhi.

4 Outsourcing: Legal Issues, Control And Relationships

There are aspects of the outsourcing process that should be firmly established in order to minimize any disruptions that may occur. These can include clarifying clearly any legal concerns, maintaining control when outsourcing occurs or ensuring that the relationship between the outsourcer and outsourcee is manageable to ensure productivity. Part 4 acknowledges that the transfer of departments or specific functions to an outside entity requires the establishment of certain parameters. Legal issues, for example, are key components on which companies should focus to ensure successful relationships between themselves and those to whom they outsource. The five chapters in Part 4 focus on these key concerns.

The opening chapter discusses the outsourcing legal contract. The author, Rachel Burnett, addresses the various components that go into contract negotiation and legally managing the outsourcing process. The chapter is very thorough in describing the many elements, such as contract format, personal data and software, which need to be understood and considered before, during and after services are outsourced from one company to a provider. She emphasizes the benefits that a good contract can achieve, such as allowing both parties to achieve their objectives, while ensuring that any risks are allocated according to each party's obligations. The chapter ends by highlighting that a well-constructed contract can contribute to a successful outsourcing relationship.

In Chapter 16 Chris Lonsdale examines the risks involved in outsourcing. He notes that there are two main risks that may occur during outsourcing, which relate to maintaining competitive advantage and managing supply. He provides three models that companies can use to mitigate these types of risks. These include *the strategic partnership model*, the *balanced contracting model* and the *asymmetric power model*. He outlines each model and their nuances, and notes that the applicability of any particular model depends on the business environment and its capabilities and capacities. Overall, the models do provide options from which practitioners can function.

Dai Davis, in Chapter 17, acknowledges that service-level agreements are necessary in any outsourcing relationship. As service-level agreements state the level of service that should be provided during outsourcing, it is necessary that both parties involved agree on all specifics before the agreement comes into place. Dai outlines the different types of service-level agreements that companies can select to ensure that they have in place the one that is most suited to their needs. These can include for example, the *guaranteed service agreement* or the *guaranteed capacity agreement*. He focuses also on the importance of limitations of liability and notes that it is a component of the outsourcing process that is frequently overlooked. He provides various examples of limitations of liability.

Kathleen Goolsby, in Chapter 18, presents a detailed overview of those critical requirements that are needed to build and sustain an outsourcing relationship that is successful for the parties concerned. She notes that outsourcing relationships need to function from within very dynamic processes, especially as it is the relationship that directs the outcomes between parties. Kathleen proposes, therefore, the concept of a *partnership mentality* that should allow for beneficial outcomes, and defines those factors that constitute it. She concludes the chapter by recommending how best to achieve this state in order to benefit when outsourcing is undertaken.

Part 4 concludes with Alison Smart's chapter, which examines ethical supply chain issues within outsourcing. Ethics has become topical within the last few years due to the various actions of some companies. Alison's chapter is very useful in delineating why ethics is important not only in the overall business environment, but especially when outsourcing occurs. She addresses concepts such as fair trade, social responsibility and codes of conduct, which are meant to encourage more ethical behaviour. Alison concludes the chapter by noting that there are still many issues that need to be determined before deciding exactly what represents ethical or unethical behaviour, but that there are policies available to assist with the process.

15 Legal Aspects of Outsourcing: An Overall Perspective

Rachel Burnett

This chapter discusses the rationale for the outsourcing legal contract in terms of its theoretical philosophy, practical format, the parties to it and its operational management. It also includes its associated requirements of confidentiality and treatment of personal data; and some typical features of its content: human resources; software; management of the ongoing relationship; dispute management; and a transition strategy on contract termination or expiry. Although an English law perspective underlies the discussion, it is largely applicable to outsourcing contracts generally.

As the outsourcing market continues to grow and evolve, many agreements are now being negotiated for second- and third-generation outsourcing. Generally, the contracts have become more useful and relevant as clients and providers, as well as their advisers, gain in experience. However, there are no sophisticated methodologies for the legal practitioner in this area. Legal methodologies are generally in their infancy, in contrast to technical and commercial methodologies, such as outsourcing process models. Legal risk management, referred to later, is a novel approach to legal services, which is not generally espoused.[1] Meanwhile the outsourcing contract lawyer for each party will draft, review and negotiate the terms and conditions in the context of what is legally feasible, reflecting the specific commercial requirements of the lawyer's client (that is, the outsourcing provider or provider's client) and including many details. The advice and document drafting will be pragmatically based on the lawyer's previous legal outsourcing expertise, other outsourcing agreements or contract structures, and checklists.

Specific arrangements may vary widely. Selective outsourcing may involve limited functions or processes contracted out to different service providers. Alternatively, an entire operational function or division of an organization may be the subject of the agreement. The provider's staff may carry out the services at the client's site or at its own facilities. Thus outsourcing may encompass the transfer to the provider of the client's staff and/or associated fixed assets and/or premises used in the provision of the services, with the client buying back the services. This latter kind of wholesale outsourcing is high-value and high-risk. Because of the variety of arrangements, customized for each client's business objectives, and the continuing development of new types of transactions, there is no single form of contract precedent that is consistently applicable.

---

1   Richard Susskind (1996) advocates a proactive approach by lawyers, developing this theme.

The contract as a method of legal risk management

Legal risk management is a business-focused approach for negotiating the legal requirements of outsourcing. Its focus is on awareness, evaluation and management of those risks, which may lead to liability for fault or failure, resultant legal processes and associated effort, losses and costs. A contract is one of the principal mechanisms for managing legal risk. It is a formal method for regulating the commercial relationship of the parties to the contract. A good contract will enable the parties to achieve their commercial objectives by defining the terms of the transaction comprehensively and allocating the risks between the parties, taking account of their respective requirements and obligations, and the scope of the services. It is the lawyer's framework for advising on the outsourcing.

As outsourcing is a long-term relationship, one of the functions of the contract is to provide certainty, so that the requirements specified in it will last through any changes of business circumstances or changes of personnel on either side. It will be legally binding, so that if either party does not meet any of its terms and conditions, the other party will be entitled to enforce it. In any event, the contract will ideally become a source of reference for the parties in continuing to work together and a useful live working document.

The continuing expansion in cross-border deals and offshore outsourcing has implications for the contract. Areas which need close attention in the negotiation of these transactions include the choice of jurisdiction for interpretation, construction and enforcement of the contract; workable principles for dispute management and resolution and, from a European perspective, the processing, transfer and control of personal data.

Contract format

The contract format and contents will be dictated by the scope of the services being outsourced and the client's objectives in outsourcing. For example, costs are often behind the decision taken by the client. The charging provisions can be structured in many different ways and are likely to be features unique to any particular outsourcing agreement. The more comprehensive the services being transferred, the more complicated the charging mechanisms may be. Whether the charges imposed during the life of the contract are as predicted at the outset, and whether savings are achieved, will be affected by the way in which the contract is negotiated and finally worded, as well as by the extent of any changes made to the services during the contract term. The services themselves must be well defined and measurable. The contract must lay down a structure for achieving quality of service by identifying clearly the services to be provided in a form in which their performance may be measured. Service levels are the key to successful outsourcing for both providers and clients, and these are normally documented in separate, but intrinsically linked, service level agreements.

The contract structure and organization should be carefully considered. One method is to include the main legal conditions in the body of the contract and to separate much of the information unique to the relationship into linked appendices or schedules referenced from the main clauses. Special considerations arise for those contracts where there are to be transfers to the provider of premises and equipment, requiring specialist legal advice in respect of taxation, property and corporate issues. These matters will generally be dealt with in a separate business transfer agreement. Staff transfers and other human resources matters may require, in addition, a separate agreement. There may be other associated agreements for discrete functions or services such as disaster recovery. However, the agreements, appendices and schedules will be incorporated to form the overall contract and to operate together.

This method of contract structuring will also assist in its operational management. Certain people will need access to some of the information, such as service levels or change control procedures, but will not need to know other aspects. This will make reference to the appropriate section easier. Linking and detailing the different contractual elements may be complex, especially if the arrangements cover premises and staff and the transfer or licensing of the client's assets, as well as the work involved in agreeing the service levels. It takes time to collate all the information needed for effective drafting, and time for thorough negotiation. Preparation of the contract should begin early.

The parties to the contract

No contract obviates the necessity for each party to assess the other objectively. However sound a contract is, it will not detract from the need for the parties to be well matched. The client must research the provider's financial viability, reliability and experience. The provider should investigate the financial strength of the client. The risk to avoid is that either party might be financially unstable and unlikely to have a long-term future. The provider's interests best lie with those clients whose business areas it understands and to which it can add value. Certain attitudes should be shared, such as those towards working environments, security and treatment of staff. Without this mutual understanding, the provider will find service management difficult to achieve in the environment, and the client's staff, whether interacting with the provider or transferred to the provider, may resent the provider's methods. The cooperation and close working relationships must nevertheless remain at arm's length as, in an outsourcing arrangement, the parties' objectives differ. The provider and the client are independent parties, each with different business goals. The provider needs to be able to do a good job and make a profit. The client is paying to have its functions and activities outsourced efficiently.

Suppliers may promote the cooperative style of their outsourcing relationship by the use of such terms as 'partnership' or 'partnering'. 'Partnership' is not, however, the relationship that either party should be seeking. In legal terms a partnership is defined as a relationship for carrying on a business together with a view to making a profit.[2] It is a 'fiduciary relationship', which arises where there is a special relationship between the parties concerned, legally implying heavy obligations of 'good faith' as a relationship of trust, over and above the obligations applicable to a normal contractual relationship where the parties have different business aims. According to the definition on the website of the Office of Government Commerce[3] a 'partnering' agreement means 'sharing risks and rewards, problems and solutions'. This approach also implies mutual objectives and a kind of relationship that is beyond a normal outsourcing arrangement.

Occasionally, a joint venture is contemplated – a relationship in which a business is formed for a deliberate purpose between two or more parties of whom each takes a share. Here, the provider will offer technical expertise and experience and the client will provide the experience of its business sector, with a view to marketing and selling the combined expertise jointly. However, these forms of outsourcing are rare. For both parties the risk of financial and

---

2 Partnership Act, 1890.
3 www.ogc.gov.uk.

commercial lock-in to the relationship is greater than the customer's risk of dependence on the outsourcing services themselves.

Confidentiality

Confidential information should be expressly protected by contract. Information which one party regards as confidential to its business, and which it simply assumes that it has disclosed in confidence, will not necessarily be protected automatically at law. It will be a question of fact in the circumstances whether damage has been caused by the disclosure. And once the information has been disclosed, it will be too late because the harm will have been done. Therefore confidentiality clauses and non-disclosure agreements are essential to ensure that specifically valuable information will be protected. Written provisions that emphasize what does need to be confidential will in themselves not only act as a deterrent to disclosure, but also focus attention on the methods for achieving confidentiality.

The client's decision to outsource is initially a highly sensitive matter, usually within its own organization and perhaps within its business sector. Information which is not for general circulation may have to be made available. Outsourcing consultants and prospective providers should therefore sign a non-disclosure agreement. Conversely, tenderers will be disclosing their own commercially sensitive information about their business, charges and proposals for the outsourcing, and these should also be treated in confidence by the client.

If the client's business sector is one in which the provider specializes, the provider will be interested in legitimately furthering its knowledge in order to win more work from the client. The client runs the risk that it would be possible for the chosen provider to use information derived from working in the client's business for activities with the client's competitors, in a way that would be unacceptable to the client. At the same time, the provider will also be concerned to protect any of its proprietary information and methodologies employed in the services.

The levels of risk will differ according to the business sector, the individual client and the provider. In general, the client should identify what trade secrets and business information may be at risk from disclosure and take steps to ensure that it is safeguarded in the contract. The provider should negotiate any exceptions to this where it perceives that it would not be reasonable to be prevented from extending its own business. The more distinctively a provision can circumscribe the actual confidentiality requirements, the better the prospects of its efficacy. The contract details themselves may well be confidential to the parties, being so closely connected with their respective business practices and strategies.

Towards the end of the contract term, the client must itself be able to continue to use, or ensure that an alternative provider will be able to use, any of the provider's information, software or proprietary methodologies that have become essential to the services. It may need to obtain a waiver of confidentiality or licence or other permission from the provider in this respect. This should be considered at the time the contract is negotiated, along with other matters relevant to the continuity of services, as further discussed later.

Personal data

Personal data exemplify legal requirements both for confidentiality and for compliance with regulations. Within the European Union (EU), data protection law applies to the use of information that relates to a living, identifiable individual (data subject), and which is processed automatically or is held in a non-automated structured filing system.[4]

Where personal data are dealt with in the outsourcing services, the outsourcing provider will normally be the 'data processor' in that it is holding or processing the personal data only on behalf of the client and in accordance with instructions from the client as 'data controller'; it is not the provider's responsibility as to *how* or *why* the data are processed. The client thus remains responsible for the personal data, and this includes taking responsibility for the actions of the data processor.

The Seventh Principle of the Eight Principles set out in the legislation stipulates that appropriate technical and organizational measures should be taken against the unauthorized or unlawful processing of personal data and against accidental loss or destruction of, or damage to, personal data. The data processor must notify the Information Commissioner of its function in relation to the personal data and comply with this Principle. The client in its role of data controller is required to comply with the Seventh Principle in: choosing a data processor; providing sufficient technical and security guarantees; taking reasonable steps to ensure that appropriate contractual provisions are in place with the data processor, for compliance with the code governing the principles on which the personal data are held, processed and used; and having a written contract with the data processor to cover these aspects. Model contract terms are available for use in this regard. The client as data controller remains ultimately liable for compliance with the Data Protection Principles, which require personal data to be treated properly, fairly and lawfully, ensuring accuracy and adequate security.

Cross-border transfers of personal data outside the European Economic Area (EEA) are restricted under the Eighth Principle. However, if the offshore outsourcing provider is acting solely in the function of data processor under the legislation and the personal data are not being transferred for decisions to be made by the provider about their access or use, but only for processing on behalf of the client as data controller, the client is responsible for compliance, as described above.

However, if the outsourcing provider is to take its own decisions in respect of the personal data – perhaps, for example, if it is providing transformational outsourcing services relating to human resource systems, then the personal data must not be transferred to any country outside the EEA without an 'adequate level of protection' for the data. This means a level of protection which is adequate in all the circumstances, taking account of such matters as: the nature of the personal data; the country to which the data are to be transferred; the purposes for which and the period during which the data are intended to be processed; the law in force in the country in question, its international obligations, any relevant codes of conduct or other rules which are enforceable there; and any security measures taken in respect of the data.

The European Commission can produce a Community Finding that a country's laws do provide this level of protection, and indeed has done so in certain instances, such as Hungary, Switzerland, Canada and Argentina, and the voluntary self-certification 'Safe Harbour' regime in the USA. Alternatively, the data controller who wants to export personal data should obtain

---

4   EU Data Protection Directive 95/46/EC, implemented in the UK by the Data Protection Act 1998 at: www.informationcommissioner.org.uk.

the consent of the data subject and ensure, through contract, that its own legal obligations are also imposed on the foreign recipient of the personal data. There is a set of model clauses approved by the European Commission for transfers of personal data outside the EEA. These clauses may be adopted, or equivalent provisions drafted, for the outsourcing contract. For the transfer of sensitive personal data, additional obligations apply, and the consent of the data subject to the transfer abroad must be expressly obtained.

Human resources

Both the provider and the client need to understand the position of employees affected by the change to outsourcing under their contracts of employment and statutory employment law. In the EU, legislation affecting employees[5] has been implemented into member states' legal systems[6] wherever a commercial business, in whole or in part, is transferred through legal transfer or merger as a going concern. The purpose of the legislation is to safeguard employees' rights.

Case law in EU member states has prescribed that this legislation will generally apply to outsourcing in cases where any staff are transferred, even though this may be only part of a business. Cases decided in the European Court of Justice in relation to this are relevant, as are precedents from national courts. This legislation is more complicated than is immediately apparent. If the legislation applies, all employees who were employed in the relevant part of the client's business immediately before the transfer automatically transfer across to the new provider on at least their then existing terms and conditions. They retain their accrued rights of employment arising from continuous service and from the transfer of their collective rights.

The transferred employees will be deemed, for most purposes, to have been employed by their new employer company since their original start date of employment with the client organization. Dismissals of the outsourced company's employees occurring at the time of transfer for a reason connected with the transfer will be regarded as unfair, unless it can be demonstrated by the employer that they were made because of economic, technological or organizational reasons entailing changes in the workforce. Entitlement to redundancy in the event of dismissal or a claim for unfair dismissal will be determined as though employment had started on the date on which the transferring client company first employed the employee. There is an obligation at the outset to inform and consult any employee of either the new provider or the former employer who may be affected by the transfer.

There is much uncertainty in the applicability of the law in practice. The case law often concerns highly specific situations, the decisions occasionally appear to conflict, and it is sometimes difficult to draw any general conclusions. The law in this area is developing, and specialist and up-to-date employment law advice is essential.

In practice however, it means that the provider must evaluate its risk and the likelihood of any legal claims – for example, for unfair dismissals. The charges will reflect the cost of this risk. The provider will take indemnities in the contract from the client for the potential liabilities. The legislation may also apply on expiry of the outsourcing and on transfer back in-house or to a new third-party provider.

---

5   EU Acquired Rights Directive 77/187/EC.
6   In the UK this is by means of the Transfer of Undertakings (Protection of Employment) Regulations (TUPE) 1981, SI 1981, No 1794.

Software

One major legal issue in outsourcing relates to the intellectual property involved in the services. Two general principles apply in owning and using intellectual property material. The first is that the owner will protect the conditions of use of the material by third parties, so that it may be commercially exploited. Second and conversely, a user must be properly entitled to access and use material that it does not own. In outsourcing, the principal intellectual property will normally be software and databases. Their use will no longer be under the client's direct control, but will be managed by the provider.

The exercise of ascertaining the ownership of the relevant software and databases used by the client, and the current conditions of use permitted to the client prior to the outsourcing, may often take much longer and more effort than anticipated. For software owned by the client, the client will retain ownership and license the provider's use in the outsourcing contract. The actual grant of permission to the provider should cover the purposes of actual use, but go no further.

Following a due diligence exercise to ensure that all relevant third-party software is identified, the outsourcing provider will take over the licences from third-party software licensors, unless it has its own licences for certain commonly used software. Existing licence agreements between the third-party licensor and the client will typically prevent assignment and limit the use of the software. It may involve extensive negotiation with the licensors to get the appropriate permissions for use in outsourcing. The responsibility for this negotiation is likely to lie with the client initially. However, the provider may have sufficient experience to be willing to negotiate with certain third-party software owners.

The third-party licensors often seek extra payment on the basis that the licence to the outsourcing provider is an extension of the original licence. If any licensor tries to impose excessive charges, the use of alternative software may be a possibility either immediately or, more realistically, in the longer term. It may also be open to the client to consider legal action on the grounds of unfair trading or unfair competition. The client may be required to execute any related transfer or novation or new licence agreements for the third-party software as required by the licensors under the terms of the original licence agreements. The provider may take on the responsibility for the payment of ongoing support and upgrade fees, and the implementation of upgrades and enhancements. An indemnity from the provider in the contract may be required against misuse of the third-party software.

In providing the services the provider may use its own proprietary software that is not generally available – for example, for business process re-engineering, system development or for project management. If such software becomes essential in delivering the services, the client must negotiate terms to permit its use beyond any contract termination or expiry. It may be that a copy of the provider's proprietary source code should be held under contract by an escrow agent, as protection for the client in the event of termination or expiry, or for default in providing the services.

Ongoing relationship management

During the course of the outsourcing, continuing liaison between the parties is critical to its success. The client has delegated the management and operation of the services and other functions, but nevertheless remains responsible. It must be constantly assessing that the quality of the service provision is being maintained and the reasonableness of the charges agreed. It will need expertise to do this effectively, either by using existing resources, or creating a new role, or using consultancy services. For both parties, the management representatives should be senior, with sufficient authority to take decisions on behalf of their respective organizations and ensure that these will be implemented. For a large outsourcing, there may be more than one representative on each side, each with defined functions.

To ensure that the formal channels of communication are effective, the contract must set out the details of what is agreed. Such channels of communication will consist mainly of face-to-face meetings and written reports with built-in checkpoints, such as annual contract reviews. The objectives of the meetings should be clearly specified, as different kinds of meetings may be necessary, with different participants. There may be regular operational progress meetings attended by a number of personnel in addition to the management representatives. There may be strategic meetings for the management representatives alone or for other senior managers, individually or as a steering group. The attendees at the less frequent contract meetings may also be specified in the contract.

It is important not only to review service achievements as set out in the reports and statistics, but also to watch out for persistent trends, perhaps in increasing or decreasing volumes or changes in quality, so that if it looks as if there are incipient problems, any consequential actions can be put into effect. The provider should have feedback that either it is providing what is required under the contract or that there is a discrepancy which needs to be sorted out. Proposals by either party for innovations, quality improvement or cost reduction can be followed through.

In the course of the outsourcing, the contract will therefore be used in relation to monitoring, review and for reference, as part of ongoing relationship management. If the communication channels are not contractually defined, the relationship will not be effective either for the supplier to demonstrate its compliance in providing the services or to allow the client to keep overall control. Moreover there will be no means of formally requesting and coordinating changes to the services or the contract processes.

Coordinating change

For outsourcing of any scale or complexity, changes will be required over the term of the contract. Some changes may be built into the contract, such as those for fluctuating volumes, software upgrades or changes to the equipment used. However, other changes will not have been predictable when the requirements were first defined. Indeed, changes to the services may even have been the aim – for instance, where the provider was selected for its skills in business transformation in addition to service delivery. In such cases the provider will need to spend time assessing what needs to be changed as an intrinsic part of the services that it is carrying out under the contract.

A procedure must therefore be detailed in the contract for enabling changes to be agreed and made in a controlled way. Either party may put forward a proposal for varying any of the contracted services, their delivery or management. Any implications affecting service levels, deliverables or any other aspect of the services need to be taken into account. The provider must estimate any changes to the charges as a result. Only at this point, with this information available, can an informed decision be taken as to whether to proceed with the change. If the change is to be made, it should be recorded.

Dispute management

For a complex and detailed business arrangement over a number of years, which is important to both parties, disputes are almost bound to arise. In the normal course of events it is helpful to have various procedures set out in the contract for foreseeable potential disputes. This is another aspect of legal risk management, in an endeavour to help the relationship survive.

An escalation procedure will advance the dispute to senior levels of management representatives from both parties, who do not normally deal with the contract's operation and may be able to be more dispassionate about working through to a mutually acceptable result or compromise than those managers who are closely involved operationally. It is an opportunity to attempt to reach agreement without acrimony and thereby to enable the outsourcing to continue with minimal disturbance. If this fails, the parties may resort to litigation as a formal means of dispute resolution.

The contract may stipulate other approaches as alternatives to litigation in the event of a dispute. The parties may decide that an expert should be consulted for the resolution of technical disputes. Alternative dispute resolution is a methodology growing in popularity; it entails using an independent conciliator or mediator who actively works with representatives of both parties to reach consensus. Arbitration is another formal method of dispute resolution with an impartial adjudicator – or more than one. Like alternative dispute resolution, this is a process which takes place in private but which, like litigation in the UK or USA, is adversarial. It involves a framework of formal rules which may be amended by the parties. Terms can therefore be set out in the contract in respect of venue, rules of evidence and formalities of procedure. The objective of dispute resolution is to solve the problem and to minimize, as far as possible, the effect on the business. Without these provisions in the contract, early confrontation may hinder the continuance of the outsourcing relationship.

Transition management

The outsourcing contract will be for a finite term. Where a long term is agreed, early termination options on notice by either party – for example, five years into an eight-year term, may be built in. However, such flexibility will be at a cost to the client, because the provider will reflect the risk of termination in its charges or may demand a compensation payment if the client gives notice early. On the other hand there are a number of cases where it is the provider who has been able to negotiate an early exit, where for various reasons the contract was not providing the anticipated profits or there were greater difficulties than expected in delivering the services.

When so much care is being expended in selecting a provider and establishing all the terms, carrying out due diligence on the software, agreeing the service levels and, managing staff expectations, it is hard to imagine an end to the arrangements. However, this is also the time to plan and document exit routes. If this is not done, inevitable problems are simply being stored up. The client will have to negotiate under time pressures to access the information to which it should be entitled, when it will not normally be in a strong position. At expiry of the contract the client's options will be: to renew the contract, on the same or on renegotiated terms, to bring the services back in-house (this happens more often than might be envisaged), or to invite tenders for the outsourcing services, which may include an invitation to the current provider. Within the EU, public-sector organizations may be legally obliged to invite tenders, for the first and for subsequent outsourcings, in the interests of competition.

Now, at this point the provider will be in possession and control of much of the information that should be available to the client and to other bidders. The contract must therefore ensure that the provider will supply all that information to enable a proper retendering exercise and thus avoid potential dependence by the client. It may be that the provider will make a charge for the time and effort in doing this, and this should be negotiated at the same time. Specific matters for maintaining service continuity during any transition, in respect of which principles should be set out in the contract, include the issues of software licences, any assets or equipment, premises, and transferable know-how.

One or both parties should be responsible for drawing up a transition plan, in the client's interests, as a programme and checklist of what to do and what to hand over as the contract draws to its close. The sorts of matters it should cover will include details of the means of ensuring continuing provision of the services throughout the transition; plans for communicating with everyone concerned to avoid any detriment to the client's business as a result of the transition; plans for the transfer of personnel engaged in the outsourcing, where legal implications may arise again; details of the relevant software licences and other contracts; issues of ongoing confidentiality of information; and documentation used in delivering the services. It is normally almost impossible to complete this before the contract is in force, but the management representatives should not forget it, as it will be essential when the time comes. The transition plan should also be kept up-to-date.

Conclusion

The risks and concerns for the outsourcing relationship will be addressed and managed in a properly drawn-up and negotiated contract. A clearly articulated and well-organized contract, which is tailored to the unique requirements of the parties and the kinds of outsourcing service to be provided, will help the outsourcing relationship to function effectively. A contract which does not include appropriate details, which is ambiguous or which is not immediately referable to the transaction it should be reflecting is likely to hinder the relationship.

Some legal aspects need to be dealt with only at certain points of the contractual process, such as human resources transfer at the beginning and expiry of the contract, non-disclosure in relation to the invitation to tender, and transition management when the contract is due for renewal or expiry. Other aspects incorporated into the contract are helpful for the ongoing operation of the service provision, such as formal channels of communication or procedures for the management of any disputes that may arise. Lessons can be learned from the experience of professional advisers. To date, high-profile outsourcing disputes in the UK have been settled or arbitrated on confidential terms. New ways of handling the functions being outsourced, of charging, of selective outsourcing and of providing the services mean that contract formats and contents will continue to evolve in order to accommodate developing, and sometimes innovatory, outsourcing business practices.

Reference

Susskind, R. (1996), *The Future of Law*, Clarendon Press, Oxford.

16 Risk Mitigation and Outsourcing: Alternative Models for Managing Supply Risk

Chris Lonsdale

Over the past 15 years or so, outsourcing has become an increasingly prominent feature of the business environment. Whole business functions have been transferred to third-party suppliers, some of them integral to the performance of the organization, like information technology, logistics, manufacturing and procurement. During this time of change, managers have had at their disposal much advice to help them manage the potential supply risks arising out of outsourcing. Out of all this advice, three broad theoretical decision-making models that have dominated the scene can be identified. These are referred to in this chapter as *the strategic partnership model*, *the balanced contracting model* and the *asymmetric power model*. This chapter reviews each of these three models, discussing their implications for outsourcing practice in detail.

Outsourcing and supply risk: key concepts

There are two broad categories of risk that are associated with outsourcing: risks related to the maintenance of competitive advantage and risks related to the management of supply (Quinn and Hilmer, 1994). The two categories need to be analysed sequentially – competitive concerns first. The first category of risk can be analysed with respect to the strategic management literature. For example, the ideas of the resource-based school have been integrated into outsourcing frameworks by many writers, including Quinn and Hilmer (1994), Bettis, Bradley and Hamel (1992) and Venkatesan (1992). Porter (1996) has also interpreted the practice of outsourcing within the context of his competitive strategy framework, although he came to a less positive conclusion about the practice than most resource-based writers.

However, the focus of this chapter is on the second category of risk: that concerning the management of supply. There are a number of managerial concepts that are relevant to this category: asset specificity, switching costs, and uncertainty and information asymmetry. Asset specificity refers to the extent to which the resources used in a transaction can be redeployed for another purpose. Switching costs are those costs associated with the task of transferring responsibility for supply from one supplying firm to another (search costs, contracting and negotiation costs, logistical costs and the costs of inducting a new supplier). Uncertainty, meanwhile, refers to situations where there are either many known alternative outcomes or there are known to be currently unimaginable possibilities. Finally, information asymmetry refers to a situation where one party to a transaction possesses superior relevant information to the other party.

The aim of outsourcing, of course, is to obtain better value for money from a third-party supplier than that which is being delivered by the existing in-house team (without exposing the organization to the risk of losing 'core' activities). The concept of value for money consists of two components: functionality (for example, innovation and quality) and the cost to the buying organization. The extent to which the outsourcing organization will prioritize functionality against cost will depend on the activity that is being outsourced. In all cases, however, the task of obtaining value for money will be affected by the degree to which the transaction is characterized by asset specificity, switching costs, uncertainty and information asymmetry. Not that all writers on outsourcing agree as to *how* the concepts affect the task of obtaining value for money, as will be seen in the rest of the chapter, which reviews the three aforementioned outsourcing decision-making models.

The strategic partnership model of outsourcing

The first of the three models of outsourcing risk management we are to assess in this chapter is the *strategic partnership model*. This model emerged out of a much wider reassessment of buyer–supplier relationships that took place in the 1980s and 1990s. Traditionally, the management of buyer–supplier relationships was deemed to involve short-term, adversarial, arm's-length exchanges where value for money was achieved through formal negotiation. By the 1980s, however, many writers in the purchasing and supply field recognized that the achievement of value for money required more sophisticated methods. Many had been influenced intellectually by ideas such as the 'hybrid' relationship form put forward by transaction cost economics (Williamson, 1985), and empirically by data from the Japanese automotive experience and the US and UK retail sectors (Hines, 1994; Hughes and Merton, 1996; Palmer, 1996; Womack *et al.*, 1990). In particular, it came to be argued that adversarial and arm's-length approaches to relationship management were counterproductive when purchases were complex, characterized by uncertainty and required asset-specific investments.

Whilst by no means all academics and consultants were advocates, there was, by the mid-1990s a dominant voice within the purchasing and supply field that stated that non-adversarial collaboration represented 'best-practice' purchasing and supply management (Burt and Doyle, 1993; Carlisle and Parker, 1989; Chopra and Meindl, 2001; Hines, 1994; Wilding, 2002). This voice had a big influence on the emerging literature on outsourcing (for example, Andersen Consulting, 1997; Bruck, 1995; Economist Intelligence Unit / Arthur Andersen, 1995; Huber, 1993). So, whilst different objectives were put forward for outsourcing – for example, cost reduction, obtaining access to supplier innovation and improvements in quality – the way in which those objectives would best be achieved was deemed to be through collaborative relationships.

The starting point of the strategic partnership model, as should be the case with all models of purchasing and supply, is the behavioural context to buyer–supplier exchange. There are two main elements to the behavioural context: buyer cognitive capabilities and supplier self-interest orientation. In terms of the former, there is general acceptance outside mainstream economics that economic actors (in our context, buyers) operate under a condition of bounded rationality (Simon, 1947). When constrained by bounded rationality managers intend to act rationally, but are limited in their ability to do so by their capacity for information collection, storage and processing. The existence of bounded rationality is one reason put forward as to why collaboration between buyers and suppliers is necessary – communication between the two parties needs to be extensive.

The latter element of the behavioural context – the self-interest orientation of suppliers – is more contentious. There are three broad types of self-interest orientation that have been identified: altruism, simple self-interest-seeking and opportunism (Williamson, 1985). The first involves actor A considering the welfare of actor B even to the point of reducing its own level of welfare. The second involves actor A pursuing its own self-interest at the expense of actor B, but only in accordance with the initial agreement made by the two parties. The third involves actor A pursuing its self-interest with guile – that is, departing from the initial agreement struck by A and B should the circumstances arise where it is profitable to do so and/or crafting the initial agreement so that such circumstances are more likely to occur. The first two types of self-interest orientation can be seen as situations where the party in question – a supplier, in our context – acts in a trustworthy manner. The latter type is a situation where trust is absent.

The concept of trust has been much discussed over the past 20 years, but we will take our definition from the work of Nooteboom (2002). He defines trust as 'an expectation that… people will not fail us, or the neglect or lack of awareness of the possibility of failure, even if there are perceived opportunities and incentives for it' (Nooteboom, 2002, p. 48). In his work, Nooteboom also separates an actor's behavioural disposition from its behavioural actions. This separation is particularly crucial to the second and third models we are to assess later in the chapter. According to the strategic partnership model, the supplier can be assumed by the buyer to be essentially trustworthy (although not altruistic) in terms of its behavioural disposition (Chopra and Meindl, 2001; Wilding, 2002). This is something that is then reflected in its behavioural actions.

The implications of the decision to base an outsourcing model on an assumption of trust are profound. As Williamson comments:

> [Opportunism] vastly complicate[s] problems of economic organization … if it were not for opportunism, all behaviour could be rule governed. This need not, moreover, require comprehensive preplanning. Unanticipated events could be dealt with by general rules, whereby the parties agree to be bound by actions of a joint profit-maximizing kind.
>
> (Williamson, 1985, pp. 47–48)

Indeed, this is precisely what the strategic partnership model, freed from the assumption of opportunism, proceeds to do. The concepts of asset specificity, switching costs, uncertainty and information asymmetry are merely deemed to be technical problems that are addressed in collaborative relationships based on trust (Chopra and Meindl, 2001).

Collaborative relationships under the strategic partnership model serve two purposes. The first is to facilitate the day-to-day working practices that are required in order to deliver value for money to the buying organization. Effective working practices are secured through the use of, for example, vendor-managed inventory and Internet-based operating linkages that facilitate the efficient exchange of information. The second is to maintain the environment that is conducive to productive working relations. Under this model, this means the maintenance of the trust that exists between the two parties. Therefore, relationships contain also mechanisms such as cost transparency, formal problem-solving forums and the development of norms of behaviour to which both sides are expected to adhere (Hines, 1997; Macbeth and Ferguson, 1994).

In addition to discounting opportunism, the strategic partnership model also plays down the importance of power to buyer–supplier relationships. It is argued that, as both parties will understand the importance to *both parties* of the buying organization being an efficient and effective supplier to its own customers, issues of power will be set to one side (Macbeth and Ferguson, 1994). Therefore, in relationships where there is a need for asset-specific investments and/or high switching costs, neither party exploits any dependence that arises out of asymmetrical lock-in. Likewise, in relationships where there is uncertainty, both parties work together to reduce or live with uncertainty, rather than exploit it in the resultant renegotiations. Finally, in relationships where information asymmetries arise, the two parties share information to reduce those information asymmetries, rather than exploit them by promoting adverse selection, strategic misrepresentation or moral hazard.

The decision to base an outsourcing model on an assumption of trust and a rejection of the use of power advantages does not just affect the manner in which the resultant buyer–supplier relationship is conducted. It also affects the actual decision as to what is outsourced in the first instance. A key assessment made as part of the 'make or buy' decision concerns the level of supply risk that the organization is being exposed to as a result of outsourcing a particular business activity. If one is proceeding from a behavioural assumption of trust, then the scope for outsourcing is much greater as, in the words of Williamson, the absence of opportunism greatly reduces the complications of supply management. Under this assumption, the main emphasis of risk management can be on the strategic issue of retaining 'core' activities and the technical issues of finding capable suppliers and managing the transition, rather than being directed at managing supplier opportunism. It is not surprising then that the idea of the 'virtual organization', floated in the mid-1990s, was usually underpinned by the concepts of partnership and trust (Handy, 1995; Holland, 1998).

The balanced contracting model

The second and third models of outsourcing decision making, the *balanced contracting model* and the *asymmetric power model*, are less sanguine about the behavioural context to purchasing and supply management. However, they draw different conclusions about the managerial implications of this. The *balanced contracting model* of outsourcing is essentially drawn from transaction cost economics (Riordan and Williamson, 1985; Williamson, 1985, 1990, 1995). The main objective of transaction cost economics has been to understand when different governance structures – the main ones being in-house management, hybrid arrangements or arm's-length contracting – are appropriate to different transactional circumstances. Its relevance to outsourcing, therefore, is obvious. Indeed, it seems to be the inspiration for the UK government's ambitious outsourcing and contracting schemes, such as the private finance initiative and public–private partnerships (Office of Government Commerce, 2002).

The starting point of the *balanced contracting model* is very different to that of the strategic partnership model. Whereas the latter is built on the behavioural assumption of trust, the former takes as its assumption the existence of opportunism. As was mentioned earlier, opportunism is defined as 'self-interest seeking with guile' (Williamson, 1985, p. 47). It is said to cover business behaviour, including 'the incomplete or distorted disclosure of information, especially to calculated efforts to mislead, distort, disguise, obfuscate or otherwise confuse' (ibid.). It is said also to cover more extreme forms of behaviour, such as lying, stealing and cheating. Within this behavioural context, outsourcing, and purchasing and supply in general, is a much more challenging task. This is particularly the case with respect to those transactions that are characterized by high levels of asset specificity, switching costs, uncertainty and information asymmetry.

Under the balanced contracting model these concepts do not merely present technical problems. They are features of transactions that, if not managed properly, can leave the buying organization open to commercial exploitation. We have already mentioned the potential risks. Asset specificity and switching costs present the possibility of asymmetric lock-in, which could be exploited by one party 'holding up' the other (Lacity and Willcocks, 1996; Lonsdale and Cox, 1998). In the context of outsourcing, the main concern would be if the outsourcing organization found itself significantly locked in to its supplier, whilst the supplier retained the ability to redeploy its assets relatively easily.

If such asymmetric lock-in is also combined with uncertainty, then the need for renegotiation (the initial contract having been incomplete) will lead to even greater contractual difficulties. This is because all the newly recognized requirements will have to be negotiated under conditions of supplier dominance. Given that many suppliers try to engineer post-contractual lock-in from the start of a relationship (that is, they pursue lock-in or unbundled pricing), it is not surprising that the consequences can often be severe. Finally, if all of this is supplemented by the outsourcing organization suffering an information asymmetry vis-à-vis its supplier, then the ensuing moral hazard can leave it with even worse value for money.

However, despite identifying opportunism as an inherent feature of the business environment, with all of the potential hazards that attend it, the balanced contracting model is quite optimistic that these hazards can be avoided. This is because, under the model, managers are said to be able to develop balanced contracts with suppliers. It is here that the aforementioned distinction between an economic actor's behavioural disposition and its behavioural action is key. Whilst the balanced contracting model assumes that a supplier's *disposition* will always be towards opportunism, it argues that, if a balanced contract is developed between the two parties, its *actions* will remain in accordance with the buying organization's requirements.

The idea behind balanced contracting is the creation of mutual dependence. It is argued that if a buyer and a supplier both make irreversible investments in a relationship, then both will have a disincentive to act opportunistically as both will have an interest in sustaining the relationship. This is because neither party will want to write off the irreversible investments they have made. These irreversible investments can take different forms. First, it could be that the two parties divide equally the responsibility for making the required asset-specific investments. This kind of policy is currently being developed by Rolls Royce plc in its relationships with its suppliers of engine subassemblies (Rolls Royce plc, 2003). However, sometimes an equal division is not feasible, perhaps because the major investments required are in training the buying organization's employees to use a supplier's software system. Under such circumstances, a different way of engineering contractual balance is through one party (the party that is not making the asset-specific investments) posting a 'hostage' – for example, putting down a financial bond that is triggered should the party exit the relationship.

An example of this latter mechanism can be seen in the relationship between the UK government department, National Savings and Investments (NSI), and Siemens Business Services (SBS). The relationship was formed following NSI's decision to outsource the whole of its business operations to SBS. The consequence of this decision was always going to be that

NSI would become significantly locked in to SBS, something that, within an opportunistic environment, raised the potential for a hold-up problem. Recognizing this risk, NSI managed to negotiate, pre-contractually (NSI had significant leverage over the supply market at that stage), a provision in the contract whereby SBS would have paid NSI anything up to £250 million in the event of SBS walking away from the contract. The National Audit Office reported that this liability provision 'places the onus on SBS to improve [should it find itself in a] loss-making position' (NAO, 2003a, p. 27), rather than being able to 'hold up' service provision at the first signs of difficulty. It has also allowed the two parties to manage uncertainty and develop transparency mechanisms to head off any problems of information asymmetry.

So this is how *the balanced contracting model* believes that the risks of outsourcing in transactions of significant asset specificity, switching costs, uncertainty and information asymmetry should be managed. But why can it be assumed that buying organizations possess the wherewithal to develop a balanced contract? Two reasons are offered. First, it is believed that buying organizations usually have access, *ex ante*, to a competitive supply market. As a result, managers can use the pre-contractual competitive tension to negotiate contractual balance – contractual balance is simply made a condition of winning the business.

Second, it is argued that managers possess 'feasible foresight'. This provides them with the ability to undertake 'farsighted contracting' (Williamson, 1990). As a means of explanation, Williamson comments, 'Economic actors have the ability to look ahead, discern problems and prospects, and factor these back into the organisational / contractual design' (Williamson, 1990, p. 226). So, although they will not be able to develop comprehensive contracts because of their bounded rationality, the possession of feasible foresight allows them to develop high-level contractual safeguards. For example, where risk arises out of asset specificity, it is argued that managers will be able to anticipate the risk and ensure that the asset-specific investments are shared or, where that is not practical, ensure that a hostage is posted (Williamson, 1985).

As a result of all this, despite its identification of an opportunistic behavioural context, the balanced contracting model is optimistic about organizations obtaining positive outcomes from their outsourcing. It is argued that, because organizations will usually enjoy competitive pre-contractual supply conditions and because managers within organizations possess feasible foresight, they will be able to engineer contractual balance, even in complex and high-risk contractual situations. This will allow them to secure a commercial outcome that provides good value for money. It means also that the scope for outsourcing is considerable. According to Williamson, most transactions of low and medium asset specificity can be safely managed externally, albeit using different relationship forms (Williamson, 1985).

The asymmetric power model

The final of the three models of outsourcing decision making is the *asymmetric power model*, which has been developed by myself and colleagues (Cox et al., 2002; Lonsdale, 2005; Lonsdale and Cox, 1998). It is in line with, and seeks to build on, the work of Lacity and Hirschheim (1993), Lacity and Willcocks (1996), Ramsay (1996) and MacDonald (2001). The model is the least optimistic about the potential for achieving positive outcomes from outsourcing. Its starting point, as with all of the models, is the behavioural context. Like the balanced contracting model, it sees a condition of bounded rationality being joined by a condition of opportunism on the part of the supplier. Also in line with the previous model, it sees this as potentially problematic in the case of transactions that are characterized by significant asset specificity, switching costs, uncertainty and information asymmetry. The difference between this model and the balanced contracting model is that it casts doubt on the mechanisms that are used by the balanced contracting model to generate positive outcomes – namely, pre-contractual competitive tension and feasible foresight. Instead, a different set of factors are introduced that predict that positive outcomes, whilst still eminently possible, will not be axiomatic, as is the case with the balanced contracting model.

The first of the factors relates to the pre-contractual negotiation. The model questions the assumption that the nature of pre-contractual competition will always, or even usually, provide the outsourcing organization with sufficient leverage with which to negotiate a balanced contract. The use of Richard Emerson's observations about power-dependence relations is well established within the purchasing and supply literature (Campbell and Cunningham, 1983; Cox et al., 2002; Ramsay, 1994). Emerson's work allows us to understand that there are four potential pre-contractual power relations that can characterize a transaction between a buyer and a supplier: buyer dominance, buyer–supplier interdependence, buyer–supplier independence and supplier dominance.

According to the asymmetric power model, in each of these different pre-contractual power situations the outsourcing organization will have different levels of leverage over its supplier. Its ability to engineer contractual balance in situations of supplier dominance will be extremely limited, as the supplier will usually wish to use its dominance to ensure that it is perpetuated post-contractually. In situations of buyer–supplier independence, the outcome is uncertain. For example, in the work of Lacity and Willcocks (1996), it was shown that suppliers in this type of power situation are as likely to 'chance their arm' and try to engineer post-contractual supplier dominance as they are to submit tamely to the disciplines of the competitive market situation they find themselves in (although this is related to their expectations of buyer competence, something discussed below).

A better prognosis for engineering contractual balance exists in situations of either buyer dominance or buyer–supplier interdependence. The former is simply a mirror image of the supplier dominance scenario, only this time the buyer is able to use its pre-contractual leverage to ensure that its dominance is perpetuated post-contractually. In the case of the latter, the pre-contractual mutual dependence that exists between the two parties will provide each with sufficient incentive and leverage to negotiate a contract that sees mutual dependence perpetuated post-contractually. So, contrary to the strictures of the balanced contracting model, the asymmetric power model grants the outsourcing organization the ability to negotiate a balanced contract that is highly contingent on the power relations that exist between itself and its supplier or suppliers pre-contractually. An ability to negotiate contractual balance cannot be assumed in all circumstances.

The second factor that casts doubt on the ability to create contractual balance concerns the relative capabilities and resources of the outsourcing organization and its supplier or suppliers. It is assumed by the balanced contracting model that both parties to the transaction possess similar transactional capabilities and resources – this facilitates the development of contractual balance (Williamson, 1995). However, the asymmetric power model argues that any rudimentary investigation of the business-to-business environment will reveal a reality that is very different. The UK's National Health Service (NHS) is used as an example (Lonsdale, 2005). The structuring and resourcing of the procurement capability in the NHS means that, routinely, commercial managers are managing a portfolio of hundreds of suppliers, many of them multinational corporations that are well resourced on the sales and marketing side of their business. Furthermore, many of the purchases they are undertaking are highly complex and require significant research and analysis in order for a proper negotiation case to be compiled. The idea that commercial managers in the NHS, to any degree of regularity, are able to exercise 'feasible foresight' is risible. There certainly are examples of buying organizations that organize and resource their procurement capability in a manner that allows them to regularly exercise 'feasible foresight' – automotive assemblers and the supermarket retailers come prominently to mind. The point is that it varies between relationship situations and so is a further variable that will be different in different cases. Like pre-contractual power relations, this factor contributes to different outcomes, not the contractual balance taken for granted by the balanced contracting model.

A further doubt that is expressed about the concept of feasible foresight concerns its reliance on rational decision making. The concept assumes that those responsible for decisions related to contracting not only possess feasible foresight but also are motivated towards exercising it in a manner that maximizes the interests of the organization. However, perspectives based on rational decision making have long been questioned by those that stress the existence of power and politics within organizations (for example, Hickson *et al.*, 1971; Pfeffer, 1981). These political perspectives on organizational decision-making inform the asymmetric power model. In the context of outsourcing, this adherence to a political perspective on decision making means that an assumption is inherent in the model that outsourcing decisions, rather than reflecting the imperatives of effective contracting, are subject to the conflicting agendas and relative power resources of the many actors that are often party to them (Lonsdale, 2005). According to the model, it is not realistic to expect that on all, or most, occasions decisions are made by managers who possess both a high level of contractual foresight and an attitude that places contractual concerns ahead of other functional or personal objectives they might hold. This casts a shadow over the concept of feasible foresight and provides a further barrier to the creation of contractual balance.

This view of decision making is supported by a recent investigation into the management of large IT projects, many of which involved outsourcing (Caulkin, 2004). Caulkin collected data from many managers involved in large IT projects, and the following response was typical: 'One senior manager in financial services said he had not seen a successful IT project in 25 years. The reason: internal politics ensured that project teams would be made up of political allies rather than the managerially and technically competent' (Caulkin, 2004, p. 11).

Finally, according to the asymmetric power model, contractual balance can be affected by the fact that the two parties often attach different degrees of importance to a transaction, risking again to the possibility of hold-up. This factor is referred to as the problem of asymmetric transactional salience (Lonsdale, 2005), and, although it can be seen in both sectors of the economy, it is particularly relevant to the public sector where the public body has a statutory duty to provide certain services to the taxpayer and is subjected to political, as well as commercial, pressures. The problem of asymmetric transactional salience favouring the supplier was seen to be a key factor in determining the poor value for money achieved by the outsourcing organization in the recent relationships between the Lord Chancellor's Department, a UK government department, and ICL-Fujitsu and the Inland Revenue and Accenture (NAO, 2003b; NAO, 2001). On both occasions, the government body in question was disadvantaged in its post-contractual negotiations by the fact that it desperately needed the project to be a success – and quickly.

All of these factors lead to the asymmetric power model being less optimistic about the ability of organizations to engineer contractual balance in transactions of significant asset specificity, switching costs, uncertainty and information asymmetry. According to the model, for contractual balance to be achieved there needs to be a very specific set of circumstances in place, which will not always be the case. This, of course, has significant implications for the model's view of the original outsourcing decision. Earlier in the chapter, it was argued that the selection of business activities for outsourcing is affected by either the existence or otherwise of trust, or the ability of managers to successfully deal with its absence. As the strategic partnership model was based on an assumption of trust, the scope for outsourcing was deemed to be significant. The same can be said for the balanced contracting model. Although this latter model discounted trust, it was optimistic about the ability of managers to deal with opportunism. As a result, the scope for outsourcing was also deemed to be significant.

With the asymmetric power model, however, the picture is rather different. Because the model assumes the existence of opportunism and argues that there are limitations on an organization's ability to manage that opportunism, it, not surprisingly, counsels greater caution in the original selection of activities for outsourcing. In particular, it states that where activities are characterized by significant levels of asset specificity, switching costs, uncertainty and information asymmetry, great consideration needs to be given as to whether the activity can be efficiently sourced from the market.

Conclusion

In this chapter, the main features of three alternative models for managing the supply risks attending the practice of outsourcing have been presented. Each model has different views about both the business environment and managerial capabilities and capacities. These different views have an impact on: (a) the extent to which the models believe that organizations can safely outsource their internal activities to suppliers; and (b) the manner in which it is believed that those suppliers should subsequently be managed. As is the case with many issues in the area of purchasing and supply, there is no sign of a convergence of views appearing in the near future. In particular, there is huge disagreement over the concept of opportunism. What this chapter has sought to do, therefore, is merely structure the debate so that practitioners can methodically consider the arguments and assess their options.

References

Andersen Consulting (1997), 'A revolution in outsourcing', paper presented at the SMI Conference, London, June.

Bettis, R., Bradley, S. and Hamel, G. (1992), 'Outsourcing and industrial decline', *Academy of Management Executive*, vol. 6, no. 1, pp. 7–22.

Bruck, F. (1995), 'Make versus buy: the wrong decisions cost', *McKinsey Quarterly*, vol. 1, pp. 29–47.

Burt, D. and Doyle, M. (1993), *The American Kieretsu*, Business One Irwin, Homewood, IL.

Campbell, N. and Cunningham, M. (1983), 'Customer analysis for strategy development in industrial markets', *Strategic Management Journal*, vol. 1, pp. 360–80.

Carlisle, J. and Parker, R. (1989), *Beyond Negotiation*, John Wiley, Chichester.

Caulkin, S. (2004), 'Don't automate – eliminate', *The Observer: Business*, 16 May, p. 11.

Chopra, S. and Meindl, P. (2001), *Supply Chain Management: Strategy, Planning and Operation*, Prentice Hall, Englewood Cliffs, NJ.

Cox, A., Ireland, P., Lonsdale, C., Sanderson, J. and Watson, G. (2002), *Supply Chains, Markets and Power*, Routledge, London.

Economist Intelligence Unit / Arthur Andersen (1995), *New Directions in Finance: Strategic Outsourcing*, Economist Intelligence Unit, New York.

Handy, C. (1995), 'Trust and the virtual organization', *Harvard Business Review*, May–June, pp. 40–47.

Hickson, D., Hinings, C., Lee, C., Schneck, R. and Pennings, J. (1971), 'A strategic contingencies theory of intraorganizational power', *Administrative Science Quarterly*, vol. 6, pp. 216–29.

Hines, P. (1994), *Creating World Class Suppliers*, Pitman, London.

Hines, P. (1997), 'A comparative typology of intercompany networking', in A. Cox and P. Hines (eds), *Advanced Supply Management*, Earlsgate Press, Boston, MA, pp.137–82.

Holland, C. (1998), 'The importance of trust and business relationships in the formation of virtual organisations', in P. Sieber and J. Griese (eds), *Organisational Virtualness: Proceedings of the Vo-Net Workshop, 27–28 April 1998*, Simowa Verlag, Bern, pp. 53–65.

Huber, R. (1993), 'How continental bank outsourced its "crown jewels"', *Harvard Business Review*, January–February, pp. 121–29.

Hughes, D. and Merton, I. (1996), 'Partnership in produce: the J. Sainsbury approach to managing the produce supply chain', *Supply Chain Management: An International Journal*, vol. 1, no. 2, pp. 1–4.

Lacity, M. and Hirschheim, R. (1993), 'The information systems outsourcing bandwagon', *Sloan Management Review*, Fall, pp. 73–86.

Lacity, M. and Willcocks, L. (1996), *Best Practices in Information Technology Sourcing*, Oxford Executive Research Briefings, Oxford.

Lonsdale, C. (2005), 'Risk transfer and the UK private finance initiative: a theoretical analysis', *Policy and Politics*, vol. 33, no. 2, pp. 231–49.

Lonsdale, C. and Cox, A. (1998), *Outsourcing*, Earlsgate Press, Boston, MA.

Macbeth, D. and Ferguson, N. (1994), *Partnership Sourcing*, Pitman, London.

McDonald, F. (2001), 'The role of power relationships in partnership agreements between small suppliers and large buyers', in J. Genefke and F. McDonald (eds), *Effective Collaboration: Managing the Obstacles to Success*, Palgrave Macmillan, Basingstoke, pp.152–68.

NAO (2001), *NIRS 2: Contract Extension*, National Audit Office, London.

NAO (2003a), *National Savings and Investments' Deal with Siemens Business Services: Four Years on*, National Audit Office, London.

NAO (2003b), *New IT Systems for Magistrates' Courts: The Libra Project*, National Audit Office, London.

Nooteboom, B. (2002), *Trust*, Edward Elgar, Cheltenham.

Office of Government Commerce (2002), *Standardisation of PFI Contracts*, HM Treasury, London.

Palmer, C. (1996), 'Building effective alliances in the meat supply chain: lessons from the UK', *Supply Chain Management: An International Journal*, vol. 1, no. 3, pp. 9–11.

Pfeffer, J. (1981), *Power in Organizations*, Pitman, Marshfield.

Porter, M. (1996), 'What is strategy?', *Harvard Business Review*, November–December, pp. 61–78.

Quinn, J. and Hilmer, F. (1994), 'Strategic outsourcing', *Sloan Management Review*, Summer, pp. 43–55.

Ramsay, J. (1994), 'Purchasing power', *European Journal of Purchasing and Supply Management*, vol. 1, no. 3, pp. 125–38.

Ramsay, J. (1996), 'The case against purchasing partnerships', *International Journal of Purchasing and Materials Management*, Fall, pp. 13–21.

Riordan, M. and Williamson, O. (1985), 'Asset specificity and economic organization', *International Journal of Industrial Organization*, vol. 3, pp. 365–78.

Rolls Royce plc (2003), *Annual Report and Accounts 2003*.

Simon, H. (1947), *Administrative Behaviour*, Free Press, New York.

Venkatesan, R. (1992), 'Strategic sourcing: to make or not to make', *Harvard Business Review*, November–December, pp. 98–107.

Wilding, R. (2002), 'The 3Ts of highly effective supply chains', Working Paper, Cranfield School of Management.

Williamson, O.E. (1985), *The Economic Institutions of Capitalism*, Free Press, New York.

Williamson, O.E. (1990), 'Transaction cost economics and organization theory' in O.E. Williamson (ed.), *Organization Theory: From Chester Barnard to the Present and Beyond*, Oxford University Press, Oxford, pp. 207–56.

Williamson, O.E. (1995), 'Hierarchies, markets and power in the economy: an economic perspective', *Industrial and Corporate Change*, vol. 4, no. 1, pp. 21–49.

Womack, J., Jones, D. and Roos, D. (1990), *The Machine that Changed the World*, Rawson Associates, New York.

17 *Use of Service Credits to Mediate Performance in an Outsourcing Agreement*

Dai Davis

Service-level agreements do not exist in isolation but, rather, as part of an outsourcing agreement. Therefore, this chapter begins by considering the types of outsourcing agreements that exist. The chapter then looks at service-level agreements by way of several examples of the different type of agreement. Having examined the variety of service-level agreements, we next examine the drafting, negotiation and enforcement of those agreements with particular reference to the issue of change control. Finally, we look at the relationship between service credits, service debits and limitations of liability.

Types of outsourcing agreement

There are different definitions of outsourcing. At the heart of the broadest is the concept of engaging a third party to take actions necessary for the running of your business that you could otherwise undertake yourself. Bearing this definition in mind, there are two ways of achieving this, and both ways may also involve the transfer of assets to the service provider. Those assets may be tangible, such as computer hardware or personnel, and the service provider may be required to maximize the use of a given set of assets over a given period. Alternatively, the customer may specify only a set of outputs. The former is known as a guaranteed capacity agreement and the second a guaranteed service agreement. Guaranteed service agreements are by far the more common and important type of outsourcing agreement nowadays.

GUARANTEED SERVICE AGREEMENT

As has been said, this is by far the more common form of agreement today. In this model, the parties specify the services to be performed by the service provider. The service provider then determines what assets he needs to use in order to perform those services. Some of those assets may be transferred from the customer, or else the customer may be obliged to provide them. It is in this context that service levels are most relevant. What the customer is buying is defined in terms of a service that is to be performed. Therefore, if the service is not performed, the customer will suffer a loss. In this context, the service levels are used to predefine the nature and extent of the loss the customer suffers in certain circumstances.

GUARANTEED CAPACITY AGREEMENT

In this form of outsourcing agreement, the service provider guarantees that a certain amount of assets will be used exclusively for the customer. These assets may typically comprise a large piece of computer hardware, such as a mainframe, together with a specified number of staff dedicated to using the hardware and associated software. The customer can direct the service provider to use the assets as the customer wants from time to time. The customer can more directly set the priority of the services to be provided. In this type of agreement, therefore, a service-level agreement and associated service credits become less important. The most common comparable obligation might relate to the total number of hours expended by the staff in a given period towards the provision of the service for the customer. Nevertheless, it is possible to find service-level obligations in a guaranteed capacity agreement that are similar to those found in a guaranteed service agreement.

SERVICE-LEVEL AGREEMENTS AND SERVICE CREDITS

A service-level agreement is, and always should be, a key part of an outsourcing agreement. In an outsourcing agreement, the outsource service provider will make a number of promises in respect of the services it is to provide, and these promises will form part of its service provision specification. A service-level agreement provides a means of ensuring that service specifications are actually met.

The service-level agreement will predetermine a variety of ways in which the service may not be properly provided in the manner that the parties originally envisaged. Where the services are not provided as planned, then the service provider will make fixed payments, known as service credits, to the customer. Sometimes, where the service is provided in an exceptional manner then service debits are provided – these are additional monies paid by the customer to the service provider.

SERVICE CREDITS AND DAMAGES

It should be borne in mind that if there is no service-level credit and the service provider fails to perform those services in the manner anticipated by the contract, the customer would have a common law claim for damages. Those common law damages would be open-ended. It is often in both parties' interests to specify the loss that would occur where there is a simple breach of contract. A simple breach of contract would include a relatively minor breach of the service level. In those circumstances, the service-level agreement is a predetermination of the loss that the customer will suffer. It means that the customer will have less difficulty in showing the service provider that he has suffered a loss and the supplier will know that he is not likely to be sued in an open-ended manner. This minimizes the need for either party to have to go to court, arbitrate or invoke some other form of dispute resolution mechanism in the event of a simple breach of contract. The parties can deal with the matter themselves in the preordained fashion that they have decided upon previously.

Service credits are only useable for foreseeable and likely failures in the service. Where there is a gross failure to perform the service or a failure in some unexpected manner, the customer should be free to revert to other legal remedies and to sue the service provider for damages. Indeed, attempts to circumvent or limit the customer's rights in those circumstances will be subject to the law on limitations of liability, which is discussed later in this chapter.

Anatomy of a service-level agreement

The service-level promises that are relevant will depend on the subject matter of the outstanding agreement. However, some straightforward examples, which could be considered, are as follows.

DESKTOP AGREEMENT

Consider an agreement in which the service provider agrees that, for every new member of staff to join the customer, the service provider will supply a new personal computer (PC) with a particular software configuration. The customer will expect the service provider to supply the PC and the associated software within a given timeframe. Typically, the contract might provide that the supplier must do this within, for example, a *maximum* time period of 72 hours.

The contract may go on to provide a service credit, which states that, for each 12 hours or part thereof by which the supplier is late, there will be a fixed monetary amount payable by the service provider and credited to the customer. There could be a *free period* for, say, the first 12 hours for which no service credit is due. There could be a second service credit related to the *average* time period within which the supplier must supply configured PCs on desks. This second service credit could also be relevant where there is a service debit (see below). There could be a cap on the service credit so that there is a fixed amount payable for each (average) hour of delay. This service credit may apply only for delays of up to a maximum of, say, 60 hours. For delays exceeding that, the contract may provide either explicitly or implicitly that damages will apply.

CHEQUE AND PAYMENT CONTROL

Another example may be where a customer outsources the processing of cheques. A customer may receive 1000 cheques per day, which typically total £100 000. The outsource service provider may be required to process these cheques. Clearly, the processing will be time-critical. All the cheques will be entered into the customer's cash ledger and the appropriate discount entries recorded. This may need to be done before 3 p.m. in the afternoon so that the cheques can be paid into the bank before the close of banking business that day.

A service credit may be provided as an incentive to the service provider to process a specific proportion of the monies (perhaps even 100 per cent) before 3 p.m. To the extent that this proportion of cheques is not paid in until after the close of the banking day, there may be a service credit – say, a day's loss of interest suffered by the customer on the proportion of cheques not paid in to the bank on that day. In this instance there is a direct relationship between the service credit and the amount of loss suffered by the customer. Nevertheless, in the extreme position, where a cheque is never paid in – perhaps because it is lost or otherwise misplaced by the service provider – the customer will want to be able to claim damages for the loss of the cheque (to the extent that the customer has not been able to mitigate its loss by other means).

'JUST-IN-TIME' STOCK CONTROL

A further example might involve the outsourcing of a stock control system. The service provider may be required to run overnight routines so that, for example, lorries can be loaded early in the morning with stock for branches of a retailer. The retailer (whether in conjunction with the service provider or otherwise) may be required to input the requirements detailing which stock is required at which branch for delivery a certain time throughout the following day. The service provider will then run a routine that will minimize the time taken by staff to pick the stock from the warehouse so that the lorries can be loaded early in the morning. Such a system is inevitably highly time-critical, with certain tasks having to be undertaken by certain times during the night. There may be, say, about half a dozen different computer programs, which will run to create the stock-picking order.

Unless the stock-picking order is ready by a certain period of time – say 3 a.m., then the trucks will not be loaded by 6 a.m. for their delivery run to the stores. To the extent, therefore, that the service provider is unable to run the routines and have the stock pick list ready by the required time, the customer will suffer loss. In those circumstances, there will again be a service credit, perhaps in this instance in half-hour blocks with fixed credits being payable. Clearly, where the stock pick routine cannot be run at all one night or by a certain time such as 7 a.m., the customer may wish to reserve his right to seek for more substantial damages. Conversely, a service debit may be available to benefit (and to provide an incentive to) the supplier. If the lorries are fully loaded early, the customer may be able to make cost savings in his warehouse – perhaps by paying less overtime.

TELEPHONE CALL CENTRE

It is worth mentioning one very common form of outsourcing these days – that of the telephone call centres and customer care centres operated by many financial institutions and retailers. In such outsourcing models, the service provider provides staff who respond to telephone queries using scripts. The service credits which are appropriate for these circumstances range from technically-driven service credits, such as the availability of free telephone lines, or a requirement that no more than 5 per cent of callers will have to wait more than 30 seconds before a call is answered to value-driven service credits. An example of a value-driven service credit would be to specify the percentage of callers who ring with enquiries and who are subsequently sold a financial package or perhaps sent literature regarding a financial package. Clearly, the latter obligation may be less acceptable to a service provider since whether the service provider will achieve the target will partly depend on the standard of the scripts supplied by the customer to the service provider.

Taking the first obligation, it is relatively easy to see how a service credit may be introduced and measured. For each additional percentage of callers whose calls on average are not responded to within 30 seconds (or whatever the time period set), a service credit would be payable by the service provider. Where there is a catastrophic failure in the service – and, for example, more than 50 per cent of the calls are not answered in 30 seconds, then the customer may reserve the right to sue for more substantial damages rather than rely on a service credit. Conversely, it is easy to build in a service debit to such an arrangement since, where the service provider reduces the average waiting time for callers, this will benefit the customer. Indeed, the average wait time is something that, in these circumstances, is likely to be in the direct control of the service provider.

Drafting the service-level agreement

A service-level agreement is an intrinsic part of a contract. It is therefore important to recognize that, ultimately, it will have a legally binding effect and the parties will wish to rely on it should a dispute arise. Therefore, it is important that the service-level agreement is as clear as possible. One may need to err on the side of length rather than brevity to avoid introducing ambiguities, which may become the source of dispute later. However, like all aspects of a contract, the fact that the service levels are discussed and talked about (and recorded) means that, in practice, the parties are less likely to have an argument about the service level at a later date. The parties are more likely to have an argument about what they fail to discuss and record.

Despite the legally binding nature of a service-level agreement, it is not usually appropriate for a lawyer to draft it because, by its nature, a service-level agreement tends to be relatively technical in nature. Most lawyers are not well suited to writing technical documents. There are, however, many businesses and individuals who specialize in the preparation of service-level agreements, and it is these firms that are usually best placed to write them. Of course, it may also be that, in certain larger organizations, there is sufficient expertise within the organization itself to prepare a service-level agreement. Certainly, if an external consultant is required, the customer should still devote substantial time to assisting the consultant in the preparation of the service-level agreement. Without that assistance, there is a bigger danger that the service-level agreement will not adequately reflect the customer's real requirements.

A service-level agreement should concentrate on those aspects of the service which are most likely to fall down and therefore most likely to give rise to a dispute. In addition, the service-level agreement should concentrate on those areas that are critical to the customer and the customer's business. However, if an aspect of the service is of fundamental importance, it may not be appropriate to deal with it by way of a service credit but rather by recognizing that a failure in that aspect will cause a fundamental breach of contract. In those circumstances, the customer may wish to reserve his or her rights to sue the service provider for damages, should the service provider fail to provide the service in that regard. Indeed, in certain circumstances, the parties may agree that a breach of the agreement in that regard will give rise to the right for the customer to terminate the agreement.

Change control

Invariably, a customer's requirements will change with time. Even in the highly unlikely event that the customer's business does not change in nature, it may change in size. Transactions will decrease or increase. More fundamental changes may occur. The service provider may wish to suggest changes in the way in which the customer runs its business. A mechanism for agreeing the scope of those services may be required as well. There will need to be a change control mechanism to deal with the price at which those new services are supplied. In addition, however, the change control procedure will have to take account of the need to determine the service levels and service credits for those new services.

In English law, it is not possible to have a binding *agreement to agree*. The English courts will not give effect to an obligation requiring the parties to agree a future price increase. Accordingly, if a change control provision depends on the parties agreeing to a change at some future time, and in fact no agreement is subsequently reached, the English courts will refuse to settle the dispute. Instead, they will say that there is no agreement. At worst, and depending upon the precise wording of the contract, this may mean that the entire agreement is lost. At best, it will simply mean that there can be no change. In either circumstance, the outcome is likely to be highly unsatisfactory, perhaps more obviously for the customer than the service provider, but ultimately for both parties. This is in contrast to the approach in certain continental jurisdictions where the courts will enforce an agreement to agree of this type. However, in those circumstances, if there is a disagreement between the parties, the court is more likely to produce a result which neither party wants. The continental court's determination of what is fair and reasonable will not necessarily match what either of the parties view as fair and reasonable.

In essence then, in English law, although it is possible to have a clause that requires both parties to negotiate in good faith, it is not possible to go any further and require that the parties agree a change. If there is a clause requiring both parties to negotiate in good faith and a party refuses to negotiate at all, a claim for damages may ensue. This problem is exacerbated from the customer's perspective, since for many, if not most, changes the customer will be forced to go to the service provider as a sole supplier. So, taking the four examples discussed above:

- if the customer wants a different software configuration, he will be forced to go to the existing service provider;
- if the customer wants to process a greater percentage of cheques by e-payment methods or to take a new type of debit or credit card, he will invariably be forced to go to the original service provider;
- if the customer takes over another business and increases the number of stores to which he delivers to every day, he will be forced to increase the business processed by the service provider;
- if the customer sells a new financial service, he will want to go to the same service provider to agree a new script.

What, then, is the best solution to this 'agreement to agree' issue? There are in fact only three solutions. Ultimately, where there is no agreement between the parties as to the change, one of the three following possibilities should be used as a solution:

- The price and the terms will be those that the service provider, acting reasonably, determines.
- The price and the terms will be those that the customer, acting reasonably, determines.
- The price and the terms will be those that an independent expert determines.

The first two solutions are clearly disadvantageous for one party or the other. Having said that, it is fair to say that many, if not the majority, of outsourcing agreements actually provide for the first alternative.

It is often perceived that it is not sensible to use the third solution and to go to a third party or expert to determine the terms and price of a new service. There is always the danger that the expert determines something that is not related to either of the two parties' wishes. However, an agreement should be constructed in such a way that it is not a foregone conclusion that the parties go to an expert to determine costs, but rather that determination by an expert is a last resort. Essentially, a change control provision, if properly structured, should be drafted so as to force, or at least encourage, the parties to agree, because neither wishes to go to an expert in practice. This is a form of 'shotgun marriage'.

The following elements of a contract can be used to force a shotgun marriage type of arrangement:

1. The expert can have the freedom to award his costs so that his costs are paid by one party to the other as he determines.
2. The expert can be empowered to award the costs incurred by the other side if he believes that one party or the other has acted unreasonably either before or during the process of determination by the expert.
3. The parties can be required to provide sealed bids to the expert. The expert will use these sealed or final bids as a means of determining which party pays the costs. The party whose bid is judged *furthest away* from the decision will have to pay all the expert's costs and possibly also the costs of the other insuring party. In practice, this has the effect of making the parties act in a reasonable manner.
4. Prior to going to an expert, the matter can be escalated within the service provider's organization. For example, the matter may need to be referred to the representatives of the board of each of the parties prior to expert determination. There will be a cost (in the time of board directors) for each of the parties to do this.

All of these and similar provisions can be used in combination to provide a system which, in practice, discourages the invocation of expert determination. Instead, the parties are forced to be reasonable and to determine their dispute without the need to invoke expert determination.

Change control, however, is not just about the price. It is about a number of factors including:

a) a schedule of payments if appropriate;
b) the specification of the change (that is, what new services are to be supplied);
c) what new service levels and service credits are to apply;
d) the timetable for implementation of the change;
e) the acceptance procedures to be used in relation to the change;
f) any amendments required to the terms and conditions of the agreement;
g) agreement as to the personnel to be involved in providing the change.

Limitations of liability

As indicated, service credits are used to deal with foreseeable failures in the provision of a service. The service provider will also wish to consider his liability to the supplier for unforeseen or more catastrophic failures and will do so by including limitations of liabilities. The law in this regard is complex. However, what follows below is a resumé of what the service provider may do and the effectiveness of typical clauses that limit liability in this context.

PREFACE

In many types of outsourcing, a fundamental transfer of risk is taking place. The customer – that is, the user of the service – is relying on a third party (the service provider) to perform part of his business function. If the outsource service provider fails in that provision, adverse consequences can follow. If the consequences are less serious, it is appropriate to look at a more straightforward form of financial recompense, namely service credits to ensure that the user is not out of pocket. One advantage of having a service credit is that, in the case of a minor breach, the parties are less likely to argue about the amount of damages payable. Indeed, the concept of a service credit normally benefits both parties, since neither party would want to have to take the other to court (or invoke some other form of dispute resolution procedure) in order to determine a relatively minor breach of the agreement.

Nevertheless, if the number of minor breaches becomes significant, the user may wish to invoke some greater remedy against the outsource service provider than the payment of a service credit. It is in this context that limitations of liability become important. Similarly, if a more serious default occurs or if the service provider falls well below the service level envisaged, service credits may not be appropriate and the user may seek to sue the service provider for more substantial damages. In this latter situation, the service provider will seek to try to limit his liability.

If the outsource service contract is silent on the matter of limitation of liability, whenever the service provider breached the agreement by failing to perform the agreement the user would be able to sue for damages up to the extent of his loss. There would be no cap on the service provider's liability. Clearly, a service provider is not going to wish to agree to a contract with unlimited liability. However, in order for limitations of liability to apply there must be a liability in the first place. While this may seem to be stating the obvious, it is nevertheless an observation that is frequently overlooked. To put it another way, the best way of limiting one's liability is not to owe the obligation in the first place.

If there is a contractual promise and the promisor breaks the promise, the promisee may sue the promisor for the consequences. It is only then that limitations of liability will come into play – whether they try to exclude or limit the liability that would otherwise arise. The contractual promise may be expressed or implied. While it is possible to have promises implied by custom, these are not usually of importance in outsourcing contracts. The more important implied promises are those that are implied by statute such as, in the case of goods:

- the promise of quiet possession – that is, that the purchaser owns the goods immediately before ownership is transferred under the contract (see Section 2 of the Sale of Goods and Services Act 1982 (SOGA));
- the warranty of satisfactory quality (replacing the old law of merchantable quality (see Section 4(2) of SOGA as amended by the Sale and Supply of Goods Act 1994);
- the warranty as to fitness for purpose (including fitness for any specific purpose that may have been stated by the promisor (see Section 4(5) of SOGA);
- the warranty as to compliance with description (see Section 3 of SOGA);
- the warranty as to compliance with sample (see Section 5 of SOGA).

In the case of services, the most important warranty is that the services will be performed with reasonable skill and care.

Limitations of liability may work in both directions. Although it is usually the service provider who will want to rely on the limitations of liability, there are circumstances in which it is the customer who will wish to do so. For example, the customer may have made a promise regarding the *roll-out* or *scale-up* of the outsourcing to other departments or divisions within the customer. If that promise fails to materialize, the service provider may wish to sue the customer, and the customer may then wish to rely on the limitations of liability.

EXAMPLES OF LIMITATIONS OF LIABILITY

The following are examples of common clauses that are limitations for liability:

- An obligation on the customer to keep his own back-up copy of data, which the service provider is processing. (Provided that the customer is in a position to do this, then this may be regarded as *reasonable*.)
- A complete exclusion of any liability for all types of claims arising from a particular clause such as due to negligence or arising out of misrepresentations. In this regard it should be noted that it is not possible to exclude liability completely for all misrepresentations since it is never reasonable to exclude liability for fraudulent misrepresentations. See the cases of *Thomas Witter Limited* v. *TBP Industries Limited* [1] and *South West Water Services* v. *International Computers Limited*. [2]
- An exclusion of liability for loss of profit, loss of business and similar consequential loss.
- A quantum limitation of liability – that is, a limitation of liability that limits liability up to a fixed amount, such as 'the monies paid by the customer under the contract' or £2 000 000. It should be noted that the first option may not be easily ascertainable, particularly where a variable amount of goods and services are being provided under the contract. Therefore, it is usually preferable to state the limitation as, for example, 'the monies payable by the customer in the first 24 months of the contract'.

The latter quantum limitation of liability is by far and away the most important liability, since it will cover all types of claim that might arise under the contract. The clause is an *all or nothing* limitation. The clause will either work and limit liability as intended or it will be deemed unreasonable, in which case the attempt to limit liability will fail completely. A court will not replace the clause with its own view of what is reasonable in the circumstances. This is the case even if the clause limits liability to '£2 000 000 or in case such amount is held to be an unenforceable limitation of liability, such other sum as the court finds reasonable in the circumstances'.

PRIMARY LEGAL CONTROL

The primary law which controls limitations of liability in the context of outsourcing agreements is the Unfair Contract Terms Act 1977 (UCTA). Although it is not possible to consider in detail all the rules provided by this legislation in this chapter, the following main points may suffice:

- It is not possible to limit liability for death or personal injury caused by negligence.
- Other liability caused by negligence may be limited only in so far as it is *reasonable* to do so.
- Liability when dealing on another party's standard terms and conditions will succeed only in so far as the limitation is *reasonable*. In practice, however, judges are far more generous than this and apply a test of reasonableness even in circumstances where there is a negotiated contract. See, for example, *St Albans City and District Council* v. *International Computers Ltd*, [3] discussed below.

---

1   15 July 1994 (unreported).
2   (1999) BLJ 420.
3   (1996) 4 All ER, 481.

The test for reasonableness depends on all the circumstances but, in particular, includes the following:

- whether each party is able to insure for the relevant loss;
- the relative bargaining powers of the parties;
- whether the customer (technically, whether each party) could have entered into an alternative contract with another service provider but without having to accept that limitation;
- whether the customer was, or ought to have been, aware of the term;
- where the limitation of liability excludes liability if a condition is not met, whether it is reasonable to expect that condition to be met;
- whether any software or other goods have been specially adapted for the customer.

The leading case in limitation of liability is still that of *St Albans City and District Council v. International Computers Ltd*, decided in 1996 by the Court of Appeal. The Court upheld the substantive parts of the judge's decision that ICL had supplied a defective computer system and that the agreement contained an unreasonable, and therefore unenforceable, quantum limitation of liability.

In this case, the claimant, the local authority, entered into a contract with the defendant for the supply of a computer system to be used in the administration and collection of the community charge. The contract was completed in some haste, partly because the poll tax legislation, requiring local authorities to keep population records, was about to come into force.

As a result of an error in the software, the population of the area for which the claimant was responsible was overstated by about 3000 people. The result was that the claimant set its community charge (poll tax) too low, suffering a loss of revenue. The claimant was forced to recoup the lost revenue by setting a higher community charge in the following year.

The claimant, St Albans, sued for breach of contract relying on the:

- express terms of the contract;
- terms implied under the Sale of Goods Act 1979; and
- negligent misstatement by one of the defendant's employees that the claimant could safely take figures for the population from the computer software.

The defendant, ICL, contended that:

- the claimant was wrong to use the computer software in this way and that the claimant should have realized that something was wrong because the computer printout contained many zeros;
- the claimant was not entitled to recover the loss of revenue for the year in which the rate was set too low, because the loss was recovered the following year; and
- its liability, in any event, was limited under the contract to £100 000.

The case was decided in favour of the claimant at first instance. On appeal, the Court of Appeal upheld the first-instance decision on all but one point, namely the extent of the damages recoverable – an issue that was unrelated to the limitation of liability aspects of the case. The Court of Appeal decided the limitations case, based on the following grounds:

- The software provided by the defendant contained an error, which caused the population figures to be overstated. The inclusion of the error was a breach of the contract.
- The defendant misrepresented that the claimant could safely take figures from the computer software. Although the misrepresentation was innocent, it was still negligent and was also a breach of an express term of the contract.
- The claimant was not at fault for failing to appreciate that there was a problem, even though the printout contained many zeros.

The claimant suffered a substantial loss of £685 000. ICL sought to rely on the limitation of liability that was subject to the Unfair Contract Terms Act 1977. The Court of Appeal decided that the claimant had dealt on the defendant's written standard terms even though there had been substantial discussions between the parties. This was because those standard terms remained effectively untouched by the negotiations. This meant that the defendant's limitation of liability (in the sum of £100 000) was valid only if it was reasonable.

On the question of reasonableness, the Court of Appeal found the limitation to be unreasonable for the following reasons:

- ICL had very substantial resources (it was part of the STC plc group of companies worth some £2 billion and with a worldwide annual turnover of £1.1 billion).
- ICL had professional liability insurance in an aggregate sum of £50 million.
- There was an inequality of bargaining power between the parties: in particular, ICL was one of the few companies who could meet the claimant's requirements and was aware that the claimant was constrained by a tight timescale.

This case illustrates one further matter, namely that is always up to the party relying on the limitation of liability (usually the outsource service provider) to prove that the limitation is reasonable. What is reasonable will differ from contract to contract. From the service provider's point of view it is often difficult to choose a limitation of liability to insert in a contract that will work in all contracts – particularly where the service provider uses a *standard* contract.

Until recently, it was commonplace to find contracts in which the service provider included a quantum limitation of liability in which it attempted to limit liability up to the value of the contract. Such a limitation was upheld by the Court of Appeal in the case of *Watford Electronics* v. *Sanderson*.[4] However, that case had two special features: first the customer was suing for £5 500 000, some 52 times the amount of the limitation (the value of the contract) of £104 000; second, the customer was itself also a computer supplier and had a similar limitation of liability in its own standard contract. Therefore it had a high knowledge of the effect of the limitation.

The context of a limitation of liability is all-important. Two contrasting examples of decisions at first instance, involving limitations of liability, are the cases of *Heathmill* v. *BT*[5] and *Motours* v. *Euroball (West Kent)*.[6] In both cases, users of a telecommunication system were suing the suppliers who had failed to supply that system properly. In the first instance, Heathmill was a substantial company with an in-house legal department. It had not reviewed agreement, and in that case a quantum limitation of liability of £20 000 was upheld. In the second case, Motours was a small travel agency making an annual profit of about £125 000. In that case, an exclusion of consequential loss (that is, a loss of profit) was held to be unreasonable.

---

4   (2002) FSR 19, *The Times*, 9 March 2001
5   (2003), unreported.
6   LTL, 26 March 2004.

Nevertheless, there is a growing trend to increase the amount of liability accepted by service providers up to a multiple of the value of the contract, such as 125 per cent or sometimes 150 per cent.

Conclusion

In any outsourcing contract there is an element of risk, which the service provider accepts. If the service is not provided in a manner which the service provider contracts for, the customer will suffer a loss. The service-level agreement attempts to deal with, and quantify, the compensation to be paid should the outsource service not be provided in the manner envisaged. However, the service credits are only intended to deal with predetermined or 'day-to-day' failures by the service provider. In the case of more serious, or even catastrophic, failures on the part of the service provider, general damages limited by agreed limitations of liability are more appropriate. Service credits, service debits and limitations of liability should fairly apportion the risks between the service provider and the customer in any given outsourcing agreement.

18 Critical Requirements for Building and Sustaining a Successful Outsourcing Relationship

Kathleen Goolsby

As outsourcing rises in popularity, the complexities and business criticality of the functions outsourced also increase. Thus, the return on investment (ROI) for successful outsourcing is more dynamic – as are the consequences of failure.[1]

As outsourcing solutions are enveloped in long-term contracts, many arrangements are structured for five, 10 or even 13 years. This can be problematic for a relationship between two separate entities; a rapidly evolving global competitive marketplace and emerging technology ennoblements create as many plot twists as a novel, and no one can predict what business challenges the parties to the agreement will face during a ten-year relationship. To be successful, an outsourcing relationship must be strong enough to handle the load of unanticipated challenges over the years while achieving the original goals and contracted levels of service and ensuring that the relationship produces ROI for both parties.

Analysts and practitioners have written books, journal articles and research papers about the contractual framework and procedural processes essential for success in outsourcing. They focus primarily on the importance of effective change management programmes, effective service-level agreements (SLAs) and accountability, risk mitigation, governance[2] and flexibility almost like separate ingredients in a recipe. Each of these is important but, in tying outsourcing success solely to these legalistic elements, the writers start in the middle and miss the foundation.

The foundational key to successful outsourcing is the creation of a mutually beneficial relationship between a service provider and its client. Indeed, it is the relationship aspect that makes the difference between the outcomes that can be achieved in an outsourcing arrangement as opposed to a contracting[3] arrangement. While actions can be regulated through legalistic frameworks, behavioural attitudes and underlying motivations cannot be regulated. Moreover, obligation is not a healthy basis for a relationship.

---

1   Failure is defined as the point in time when a client or service provider fails to achieve its anticipated outcomes from the outsourcing arrangement. Failure may be evidenced by: (a) the parties behaving in an adversarial manner and having to enter into mediation; (b) the parties terminating the outsourcing contract early; (c) the client being dissatisfied with the outsourcing arrangement but deciding to suffer through the arrangement until the end of the contract term to avoid paying steep early-termination penalties; or (d) the client deciding to go to market at the end of the contract term to select a different provider instead of renewing the contract.

2   Governance is defined as the formal system and principles by which the parties agree to operate and manage their outsourcing relationship.

3   In outsourcing, the buyer turns over to the service provider the control of the outsourcing function(s). In contracting, the buyer retains control and is prescriptive about the way in which the work will be performed.

A mutually beneficial relationship requires a 'partnership mentality'. That mentality is the topic of this chapter, which will explore the nature and practicalities of the mentality and how its impact on an outsourcing relationship is crucial in enabling valuable outcomes.

A partnership mentality can be defined as 'the parties' attitudes and behaviours that motivate them to avoid acting instinctively in an adversarial manner when their interests differ and when they encounter obstacles on the path to their goals'. As will be discussed in more detail later in this chapter, these attitudes include cultural compatibility, commitment, trust and an approach to handling conflicts. The behaviours include effective communication, continual flexibility, collaboration and a continual effort at aligning interests. Together, these attitudes and behaviours (see Figure 18.1) comprise the partnership mentality – essentially, a holistic model for structuring and managing an outsourcing arrangement for success. It must be in place at the outset of the outsourcing arrangement, and it must remain in place as an outsourcing relationship evolves over time.

It is important to note that a partnership mentality is a *mentality*, not a *business model*.[4] Peter Bendor-Samuel, recognized worldwide as a leading authority on outsourcing, states that the parties to an outsourcing agreement are not partners with joint ownership obligations. Rather, they are allies. They have separate business objectives and interests. But they also have a mutually beneficial agenda specified in their outsourcing contract, which allows them to cooperate and take action together for specific purposes tied to that mutually beneficial agenda (Bendor-Samuel, 2000).

The crucial nature of the contribution of a partnership mentality to an outsourcing relationship cannot be overstated. It is a certainty that an outsourcing relationship will encounter numerous problems if the scope, service-level metrics, business objectives and expectations are not clearly described and agreed on; or if the contract is not flexible enough to deal with a changing business environment; or if the roles and responsibilities of the parties are not clearly defined; or if an effective governance structure is not in place. But such problems can be remedied if there is a partnership mentality; indeed, with this approach, the parties will be able to withstand unanticipated challenges and even turn some of them into opportunities.

Conversely, no matter how well an outsourcing arrangement is contractually structured and governed, it will not be truly successful without a partnership mentality. At best, a relationship lacking a partnership mentality will become a contract-centric arrangement, making it easy at contract renewal time for the client to be drawn to a different provider with a lower price for services and/or with newer technology. At worst, the parties in a relationship lacking a partnership mentality will exhibit adversarial behaviours – focusing on each other's weaknesses and who to blame, rather than focusing on getting the work done – thus negatively affecting their ability to achieve anticipated outcomes.

This chapter aims to assist both service providers and buyers of outsourced services in understanding the distinguishing characteristics of a partnership mentality and how it will make their relationships produce more rewarding results. The first section highlights the elements of attitude in a partnership mentality. The second looks at the elements of behaviour in a partnership mentality as well as their impact on the parties' ongoing interaction and ability to achieve their goals in outsourcing; it also provides an overview of governance to ensure these behaviours. The chapter concludes with a summary of the cause-and-effect dynamics

---

4   Partnership – a business model wherein the parties pool their money, resources and skills under a contractual arrangement for sharing profits, loss and other legal liabilities.

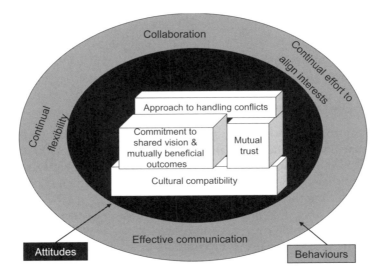

Figure 18.1   Attitudes and behaviours comprising a 'partnership mentality' model

within a relationship built on a partnership mentality and presents recommendations for selecting a service provider or client with a partnership mentality.

All of the information in this chapter is based on two primary data sources: (a) data from 562 private-sector respondents around the world in two separate surveys[5] on business process outsourcing (BPO) considerations and failures; and (b) written information and accompanying in-depth telephone interviews[6] between 1999 and 2004 on approximately 600 successful outsourcing relationships in both public and private sectors worldwide. Almost 400 of these relationships originated as nominations for Outsourcing Center's annual Outsourcing Excellence Awards Program,[7] analysing and recognizing the world's most outstanding outsourcing relationships.

Attitudes in a relationship built on a partnership mentality

An outsourcing relationship built on a foundation of a partnership mentality is distinguished by the fact that it is mutually beneficial. It leverages both organizations' core expertise in the marketplace, which results in revenue for both of them. In such successful relationships,

---

5   'Leading Causes of Outsourcing Failures' (a May 2004 survey conducted by Kathleen Goolsby) and 'Buyer and Supplier Considerations in Outsourcing Services' (a 2003 Outsourcing Center survey, sponsored in part by Richard T. Farmer School of Business Administration, Miami University, Oxford, Ohio); both surveys were analysed by Kathleen Goolsby and F. Keaton Whitlow.

6   Conducted and analysed by Kathleen Goolsby.

7   Outsourcing Excellence Awards is an annual programme developed in 1996 by the Outsourcing Center www. outsourcing-center.com), an online community specializing in thought leadership and education in outsourcing. Companies around the world nominate outstanding outsourcing relationships; the nominees are then studied by the Center and judged by an external panel of industry analysts and experts. Winners are selected for their best practices and innovation in structuring and managing outsourcing relationships for optimal competitive advantage and business-transformational outcomes. The awards programme is sponsored in part by Outsourcing Center's parent company, Everest Group (a global business advisory firm specializing in outsourcing, www.everestgrp.com), and by Forbes magazine. Articles about the awards winners are available at: www.outsourcing-awards.com/ojlist.html.

both organizations grow almost as though they feed off each other. Thus, they nurture their relationship.

The characteristic of being a mutually beneficial relationship begins its formation with four elements based on attitudes shared jointly by a service provider and its client in how they approach their relationship.

ATTITUDE OF COMMITMENT

In approaching outsourcing with a partnership mentality, the parties begin by being committed to a shared vision (their mutually beneficial end objectives), which causes them to approach challenges and opportunities as though they are the same entity, not two different organizations. Their shared vision basically aligns their interests, which is a key factor in their ability to accomplish what they set out to do.

Without working toward a mutually beneficial goal, providers would instinctively focus on efforts to increase their revenue, and their clients would instinctively focus only on manipulating the provider to invest in resources to achieve operational cost reductions and process improvements for the client. These separate endeavours are mutually exclusive. Moreover, when issues arise, both would engage in self-protective (us-versus-them) positioning and smoke-screening behaviours. Conversely, challenges arising in a relationship built on a partnership mentality result in the parties demonstrating their commitment to their shared vision; it motivates them to jointly brainstorm to a workable solution and function as a team in achieving a solution.

Their commitment springs from the recognition that they will lose anticipated ROI if they behave opportunistically towards each other, and they will win (achieve anticipated ROI) only by looking after each other's interests. With a partnership mentality, the parties will not stop to check the small print of the contract, for example, to see how to handle unanticipated issues or opportunities that arise. Over time, their relationship is enhanced by the fact that they have built a history of successfully hammering through obstacles together. This enables them to increasingly value each other's opinions, anticipate each other's proactive recommendations and seek opportunities to collaborate.

ATTITUDE OF TRUST

Trust differs from faith. At the outset of an outsourcing arrangement, the parties have faith in their selection of each other as an alliance partner and faith that each intends to live up to its contractual commitments. Trust is earned. It grows as the parties begin to function together and have to depend on each other to get the work done. (Of course, distrust grows in the same manner in relationships without a partnership mentality.)

In a commodity-outsourcing model (where the buyer simply expects the provider to take over a function and perform the work for a lower cost), trust is not a critical element. It becomes critical in BPO, where a buyer's objectives are more strategic in nature (that is, where innovation is necessary, where integration among systems and processes is necessary, where the buyer's objective is to enter a new market or where the objective is to explore ways of transforming its business). In such strategic BPO initiatives – often lacking a detailed roadmap – deep reserves of trust are necessary so that they can move forward together confidently, not fearing whether the other party will behave opportunistically or overlook the other's needs. They also recognize that when one party pushes back on an issue, it is only because it would not be in their mutual best interest.

Where trust exists, the parties discuss budgets, internal challenges and future strategic plans with each other – matters that they are not comfortable in revealing to other organizations. Thus, an untrusting buyer who is wary of giving a service provider access to in-depth knowledge of its environment builds a roadblock to a partnership mentality. Only when a provider understands its client's business priorities and strategic objectives can the provider contribute ideas and resources aimed at achieving those needs.

CULTURAL COMPATIBILITY

It is difficult to coordinate the actions of groups of people when their values and beliefs differ. Thus, the parties to an outsourcing agreement must ensure their cultural compatibility. Components of cultural compatibility include work ethics, decision-making styles, values and philosophies, risk aversion and adaptability to change. Essentially, these components are motivators for an organization's behaviour and ultimate performance. The degree to which a buyer's and provider's separate corporate cultures have compatible components will determine their ability to jointly adjust to new business pressures, jointly solve problems and jointly achieve goals.

A provider's culture might, for example, have a philosophy of value that focuses on creating innovative approaches to problems; but the impact of such an approach on a relationship will depend on the client's culture. The corporate culture of a client that competes in its marketplace by selling leading-edge products, for example, would be more compatible with such a provider culture and would leverage those innovative capabilities to get products/services to market faster and more cost-effectively. A client with a risk-averse culture, on the other hand, would probably perceive the provider's innovations as just trying to up-sell its scope of services.

Because a buyer turns over control of a business function to its service provider, some cultural components are incompatible when paired in an outsourcing arrangement. As illustrated in Figure 18.2, the pairing of such components is like trying to fit square pegs into round holes.

While cultural components cannot be measured *per se*, they can be evidenced to some extent as the parties interact. However, since some cultural components are masked or under

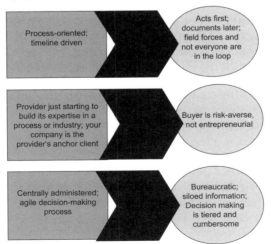

Figure 18.2 Cultural non-compatibilities in outsourcing relationships

the surface at the outset, the parties must ensure early interaction during due diligence and contract negotiation, allowing the people who will be working together some opportunities for decision making and problem solving. Such experiences will bring visibility to deeply ingrained cultural components, revealing how the organizations decide what is worth pursuing and how they go about executing those pursuits.

Blending the cultures of a government entity and a for-profit outsourcing service provider is, perhaps, the ultimate cultural-compatibility challenge. Differing beliefs about enterprise mission, as well as shifts in government policies and funding, can hinder what these outsourcing relationships can achieve even with the best intentions. But changing a government's culture is a steep climb.

There are notable examples of effective public-sector (or non-profit agency) outsourcing relationships that have successfully manoeuvred through these cultural minefields, but they are rare (see Goolsby, 2002a 2002b, 2003a, 2003b, 2004a, 2004b). In each case, the relationship's outcomes must be embedded at the top of the agenda of the government entity's leader; and the required changes in culture and procedures must be strictly enforced from the top down. Dr David Andrew Scott, who develops and advises public- and private-sector strategic alliances, comments:

> In business as in biology, the process of grafting two organisms together can produce undesirable or non-viable mutations. The grafting of a buyer and provider in outsourcing must result in a culturally compatible organism with the desired new traits and possibilities that allow the newly created organism to drive change from which both parties thrive.
>
> It is impossible for a service provider to truly coordinate the actions of people in government 'societies' without a deep understanding of their beliefs. With public-private alliances, it can take years for the government society to learn, change, adapt and feel good about new ways of operating and working with an outside entity.

(Interview with the author, April 2004)

ATTITUDE TOWARDS HANDLING CONFLICTS

Conflicts inevitably arise in outsourcing relationships because of the parties' mutually exclusive interests. When a relationship encounters problems, the natural inclination of a client is to reassert its control and micro-manage the outsourced function(s). This mistake[8] will erode the value outcomes that can be produced by outsourcing. Without a partnership mentality, a buyer has only three options if the relationship encounters trouble:

1. Continue to the end of the contract term, then find another provider.
2. Retain a third-party adviser and enter into mediation.
3. Pay the contractual penalty for terminating the contract early.

Wait, mediate or terminate – each choice is costly, complex and painful.

All relationships encounter problems, so effective risk mitigation includes building an escalating-issues/conflict-resolution plan into an outsourcing agreement. But relationships with a partnership mentality avoid having to resort to such plans; the parties in this type of relationship approach conflicts in a manner that leads to success rather than failure.

---

8   A basic principle of outsourcing is that it does not work unless the provider has 'ownership' control over the way in which the work is performed.

When an issue arises, the parties in a relationship with a partnership mentality first drill down to the root cause of the problem instead of becoming sidetracked on details. They tend jointly to issues as they happen, rather than allowing them to fester. The parties listen to understand each other's point of view, so they can find middle ground. Then they develop a jointly owned solution, ensuring that their interests are still aligned. Such activities produce a history of success in working together, thus strengthening a relationship.

Behaviours in a relationship built on a partnership mentality

In addition to cultural compatibility and attitudes of commitment and trust, a partnership mentality includes four elements of behaviour, which both parties consistently demonstrate throughout their relationship. As will be discussed in this section, these behaviours are the building blocks (or, where lacking, the stumbling blocks) in achieving successful outcomes in outsourcing.

BEHAVIOUR 1: EFFECTIVE COMMUNICATION

Gardens can survive in weedy, rocky soil and a limited water supply; but in such conditions they will not thrive and yield something valuable. Similarly, outsourcing alliances struggle to grow successfully when communication is inadequate. Effective communication is essential in making change happen; it is a tool in building consensus, which helps in turning goals to achievements. When an offshore services component is part of the relationship, learning each other's national/regional styles of speaking, gesturing and conveying messages and intent is even more critical to successful communication.

In outsourcing, building a culture of communication that is clear, honest, proactive, and includes both formal and informal mechanisms is essential. But such communication is dependent on the attitude of trust. The parties must have mechanisms that facilitate feedback and enable discussions of lessons learned and future direction. Thus, people must feel comfortable with talking candidly about what is working well and how to fix what is not working well. Without trust, people will be guarded, fearing that revealing the truth might cause them to come up short in the issues being discussed.

Effective communication includes both formal and informal mechanisms. Sometimes, one is more appropriate than the other in achieving desired outcomes, but both structures for communicating are necessary.

For example, informal communication is better at facilitating brainstorming and collaboration. Bonding at all levels of the two organizations is important, and this usually happens on an informal, personal basis. Informal mechanisms can facilitate faster buy-in on new activities, as they set a sense of urgency and can get beyond bureaucracy in decision making. But formal communication mechanisms, such as joint committees, forums and regulated review meetings (components of a relationship's governance structure) are necessary in setting priorities, monitoring progress and making sure that everyone understands their roles in the new activities. Informal communication is excellent for solving everyday problems at the time they occur; formal communication is necessary for recording any agreements made. Informal mechanisms keep a finger on the pulse, but formal mechanisms help the parties not lose sight of where they are heading.

Because of the level of documentation usually mandated in alliances where the client is a government entity, academic institution or other not-for-profit agency, formal mechanisms are the preferred route for communications. Formal mechanisms and documentation are also preferred for risk-mitigation and change-management communications, as well as resource allocation.

BEHAVIOUR 2: CONTINUAL FLEXIBILITY

Providers and buyers with a partnership mentality build flexibility into their style of interacting with each other. This is not just demonstrated by a provider being willing to customize its one-size-fits-all delivery model or to go the extra mile beyond contractual requirements. Flexibility arising from a partnership mentality means, first, that *both* parties willingly adapt to changing circumstances. Both bend with new requirements and challenges, rather than being rigid about a different priority. As with communication, this behaviour is dependent on the underlying attitude of trust. Second, such behaviour means both parties daily demonstrate operational flexibility by being highly responsive and always accessible to each other (in some circumstances, even beyond work hours); this shortens the lead time required in responding to new opportunities or challenges.

Most importantly, when there is a conflict, both demonstrate flexibility by doing what it takes to make a situation right, without placing blame. They keep the big picture in mind. In an outsourcing alliance, the parties will not always agree on issues or changes or who pays for elements of change. But, ultimately, alliances with a partnership mentality will be flexible enough for each party to move beyond its separate interests and play its part in working towards their mutual goals.

BEHAVIOUR 3: CONTINUAL EFFORT TO ALIGN INTEREST

As discussed earlier, parties with a partnership mentality are both committed to their shared vision of mutually beneficial goals. This essentially means that, throughout their ongoing relationship, both commit to: (a) implement and support change in order to achieve their goals; and (b) continually ensure that their interests remain aligned.

The parties' interests are aligned at the outset of an outsourcing arrangement, as the provider agrees to be paid for performing services which the client wants to purchase. But issues arising from a changed business environment or new objectives will necessitate realigning interests. Risk is always inherent in change, and companies accept risk only in proportion to the level of return (their interest). In such instances, a client needs to reward its provider for taking on a higher degree of risk to accomplish a particular mission.

Monetary incentives for a provider to accomplish a system implementation faster or facilitate speed to market with new products, for example, align both parties' interests. Similarly, in an outsourced procurement function, gain-sharing on savings motivates the provider to achieve the targeted spend reduction sooner.

Reducing a client's operational costs is a primary driver for outsourcing; but, over time, this objective holds inherent risks for both parties, which can cause their interests to move out of alignment. The client risks decreased quality of service if the provider has to cut costs so low that it cannot perform optimally; moreover, if the provider does not make enough profit from the relationship, it will not invest in innovation and resources to provide more capabilities for the client. Gain-sharing on the operational savings achieved is an equitable approach to maintaining aligned interests. Even better, an increased percentage for the provider's portion of the gain-share is an incentive to ensure that service quality does not decrease; thus the incentive aligns their interests.

Often, a provider's best practices and re-engineering of the outsourced process will decrease its revenue, as fewer resources will be needed to perform the work when the process is improved. Rewarding the provider by outsourcing additional functions, thereby increasing the provider's revenue, is an effective means of realigning interests in a scenario where a provider's revenue decreases because of its excellent performance.

Similarly, a client can reward a provider with an expanded scope of services (thus, new revenue). Some companies also find that cross-marketing to each other's clients, or jointly marketing their capabilities to an entirely new market, is an effective means of interest alignment.

BEHAVIOUR 4: COLLABORATION

While enterprises can frequently reap some cost-cutting, productivity and efficiencies with a commodity approach to outsourcing, the 'sweet spots' of value and transformation require collaboration. And the backbone of collaboration is a partnership mentality.

Certainly collaboration means that organizations share ideas and brainstorm on developing innovative services and products. But, in an outsourcing alliance with a partnership mentality, collaboration extends to the way in which the parties look at all issues. Their idea-sharing is rooted in their mutual vision and springs from a perspective of: 'If we do this, what impact it will have on your organization?' or 'What is the best way to make it work for both of us?'.

Collaboration does not happen naturally, and innovation is fraught with risks. It is not simply a matter of both bringing ideas to the table. Collaboration cannot happen at arm's length; both parties need to be shoulder-to-shoulder on the same side of the table. Again, an attitude of trust enables the parties to willingly share the information necessary for a collaborative environment.

RELATIONSHIP GOVERNANCE

Even in situations where the parties to an outsourcing agreement have the right attitudes and best intentions, the challenges that inevitably arise over the long term make it difficult to maintain a successful relationship.[9] Thus, an effective governance (or relationship management) structure must be mutually agreed on and put in place at the outset to govern their way of operating together. This builds stability and ensures that decisions, challenges and opportunities will be handled in an appropriate manner. An effective governance structure suppresses the parties' mutually exclusive instincts that are toxic to ROI in outsourcing and enables partnership-mentality behaviours to thrive. Effective governance takes significant time and effort, but it ensures higher ROI.

Whether the governance agreement is a separate document or part of the overall contractual clauses, its purpose is to encourage both parties to behave in a manner that enables them to do business together for their mutual benefit. Parties with a partnership mentality will ensure that the formal procedures and mechanisms in such an agreement facilitate the desired behaviours and strengthen the desired attitudes. Such procedures include:

---

9   For example, in 1994 the UK Inland Revenue outsourced its total IT infrastructure along with its application development services, to EDS in a ten-year agreement. This outsourcing relationship was nominated for an Outsourcing Excellence Award in 2002. EDS later lost the contract. See BBC News.com (2003); also Cullen (2003).

- a clear description of decision-making authority and financial responsibility for new requests considered out of scope;
- a clear description of the processes surrounding how issues will be addressed quickly and at the right level.

The size of the two organizations, as well as the size and complexity of the outsourcing function(s), will influence the types of forum established to govern various aspects of the relationship. In addition to account/relationship managers, such forums can range from project teams comprising counterparts from both organizations, to steering committees (to ensure organizational priorities and resource support), to executive committees (responsible for the overall strategic direction of the relationship and for ensuring that the parties remain focused on their shared vision and mutual success), to periodic meetings of senior executives and business unit managers to measure and review the performance against business objectives.

In addition to these governance components, many relationships built on a partnership mentality establish a joint forum to generate and manage ideas for creating added value on an ongoing basis.

Conclusion

SELECTING AN APPROPRIATE PARTNER

As in a marriage, outsourcing requires ongoing effort and commitment to make a relationship work, but each party needs to ensure that it selects the right partner with which to begin. It is a mistake to assume that a partnership mentality will just naturally evolve over time. It must be in place at the outset, and both buyers and service providers should seek evidence of the attitudes and behaviours of this mentality in their potential partner during the selection and contract negotiation phases.

Whether a client conducts a competitive bid or a sole-sourced process in its outsourcing initiative, or whether the initiative includes an offshore element, the first clue to the identity of a potentially good alliance partner happens during initial discussions. Buyers should build in several opportunities during the due-diligence phase to get together and talk about what the two parties could do together so that they can observe demonstration of elements of a partnership mentality.

A provider oriented towards a partnership mentality will (a) make the effort upfront to understand the buyer's organization, business and objectives and (b) show how it will align its capabilities and resources with the buyer's goals. A buyer with a partnership mentality will (a) not approach the relationship with a short-term[10] perspective and (b) will establish ongoing forums that include the provider in discussions about the buyer's long-term strategic plans so that the provider can understand when and how it might provide more valuable services. Both parties will clearly reveal not only their needs, but also their expectations regarding each other's attitudes, behaviours and desired outcomes from the relationship.

---

10   To ensure contractual terms that are flexible enough to accommodate changes in the business environment over time, various outsourcing advisory firms and industry analysts recommend that the parties create short-term SLAs for individual objectives and service scope (which can be updated or supplemented easily without impacting on the contract for the entire relationship) but use a long-term, umbrella contract for the overall relationship.

In determining the suitability of a potential alliance partner, the parties should obtain answers to four key questions providing clues as to each other's attitudes and behaviours (buyers should be sure to ask these questions in reference checks with a potential provider's existing and past clients):

1. How do the organization's executives react when unanticipated challenges arise?
2. How do the employees behave under stressful conditions?
3. How open are the organization's communications and is communication proactive or reactive?
4. Does the organization take a collaborative approach to working with its clients?

THE RELATIONSHIP CONTINUUM

In addition to a motivating factor of fulfilling one's needs, the first step in entering into any relationship is to acquire a feeling of security. At this point in an outsourcing relationship, evidence of the attitudes necessary for a partnership mentality will help build that security and will also create chemistry between the parties. With chemistry, they can move forward to achieve goals. As illustrated in Figure 18.3, when the parties demonstrate partnership-mentality behaviours as they work to achieve goals, a ripple effect is created that evolves to a point of synergy, taking the relationship to its peak in creating value.

The partnership mentality is the tie that continues to bind a service provider and client throughout an outsourcing relationship. It is an implacable determination that carries them through challenges, strengthening their synergistic ability to create the desired valuable outcomes.

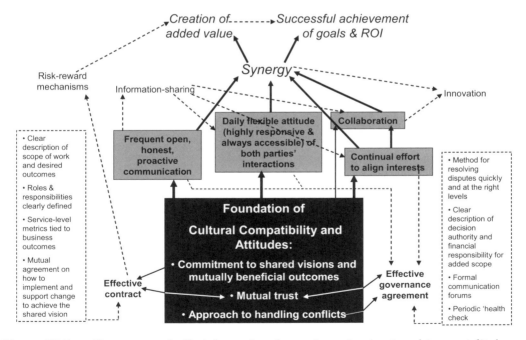

Figure 18.3   The cause-and-effect dynamics of an outsourcing 'partnership mentality'

References

BBC News.com (2003), 'Inland Revenue dumps IT provider', 11 December, available at: http://news.bbc. co.uk/1/hi/business/3310189.stm (accessed September 2004).

Bendor-Samuel, P. (2000), 'Turning Lead Into Gold: The Demystification of Outsourcing', Executive Excellence, Provo, Utah.

Cullen, D. (2003), 'Inland Revenue sacks EDS', The Register.com, 11 December, available at: www. theregister.co.uk/2003/12/11/inland_revenue_sacks_eds (accessed September 2004).

Goolsby, K. (2002a), 'Glasgow City Council and Mitel Networks: Landmark Outsourcing Arrangement Creates World-Class Solution for Scottish Schools', *Outsourcing Journal.com*, June, available at:_www. outsourcing-awards.com/2002-steps2.html (accessed September 2004).

Goolsby, K. (2002b), 'Commonwealth of Pennsylvania and Unisys: Turbo-charged, Friction-free Government – How Outsourcing Turned Pennsylvania into a Technology Champ', *Outsourcing Journal. com*, June, available at: www.outsourcing-awards.com/2002-strategic.html (accessed September 2004).

Goolsby, K. (2003a), 'City of Chicago and Unisys: Mayor Declares Outsourcing is the Way of the Future', *Outsourcing Journal.com*, June, available at: www.outsourcing-awards.com/2003-flexible.html (accessed September2004).

Goolsby, K. (2003b), 'City of Issy-les-Moulineaux and Euriware Group: City Inhabitants Enjoy Partner for Innovation', *Outsourcing Journal.com*, June available at: www.outsourcing-journal.com/jun2003-euriware.html (accessed September 2004).

Goolsby, K. (2004a), 'City of Minneapolis and Unisys: Partnering for Performance', *Outsourcing Journal. com*, June available at: www.outsourcing-awards.com/2004-firststeps.html (accessed September 2004).

Goolsby, K. (2004b), 'University of Florida and Follett Higher Education Group: Academic Outsourcing – Major in Financing, Minor in Risk', *Outsourcing Journal.com*, June, available at: www.outsourcing-awards.com/2004-innovative.html (accessed September 2004).

19 *Outsourcing: Ethical Supply Chain Issues*

Alison Smart

Globalization has given companies the chance to source products and services from many different parts of the world, leading to the opportunity to reduce supply costs by moving to areas of cheaper labour and materials. However, with globalization has come a growing awareness among customers of how the goods and services they buy are produced. Greater disposable income has meant that people are now able not only to factor price and availability into their buying decision, but to consider the social conditions in which the goods and services are produced and delivered. Many people are uncomfortable with the notion that children working in oppressive conditions in a poor country may have produced their expensive shoes.

Business ethics, like all ethics, is concerned with how we behave in particular situations. Ethical questions centre on whether actions are right or wrong, good or bad, bring good or harm, are praiseworthy or worthy of blame. The issue of business ethics is not new, but there has been increased emphasis over the last few years as companies such as Enron, Worldcom and others have been shown to have been involved in what can, at best, be described as unethical behaviour. This chapter considers ethical implications in outsourcing. There is only a very small literature that deals specifically with ethics relating to outsourcing, but many lessons can be drawn from the growing literature on supply chain ethics and corporate social responsibility (CSR). This chapter will not go into detail about the philosophy surrounding ethical behaviour, but will concentrate on how ethical behaviour is considered within a supply chain context, and the factors that organizations may need to consider when making outsourcing decisions. We need also to make the distinction between the ethical decisions that might face an outsourcing manager and what is often referred to as 'fair trade'.

Fair trade

When initially considering ethical behaviour, many managers become confused between ethical transactions and fair trade. The European Fair Trade Association (EFTA) defines fair trade as:

> … *a trading partnership, based on dialogue, transparency and respect, that seeks greater equity in international trade. It contributes to sustainable development by offering better trading conditions to, and securing the rights of, marginalized producers and workers – especially in the South. Fair Trade organisations (backed by consumers) are engaged actively in supporting*

producers, awareness raising and in campaigning for changes in the rules and practice of conventional international trade. [1]

Fair trade in this context is about working with – often marginalized – suppliers in poor regions of the world with the specific goal of assisting in development aims. This often requires specialist skills in partner organizations to bring about economic development and to train producers and workers in practices that will improve their circumstances. This approach to fair trade is not what is being discussed here. Instead, I am focusing on how organizations in a supply chain can ensure that those upstream of them behave in an ethical way towards stakeholders and the environment.

Ethical behaviour

One of the first things that has to be considered when talking about business ethics is what precisely we mean by 'ethics'. Not breaking the law can hardly be regarded as 'ethical': legal behaviour is the *minimum* standard of behaviour that any business might be expected to meet. The *Shorter Oxford Dictionary* defines ethics as 'the science of morals' and as 'the rules of conduct recognized in certain limited departments of human life'. Thus, business ethics might be regarded as the moral practices surrounding business.

Ethical behaviour is often cited in the terms of the organization's social responsibility, and many may find it easier to think in these terms rather than drawing in-depth on the work of the many philosophers who have developed the field of ethics. Here, I draw largely on the literature that has developed in the field of social responsibility within the supply chain, not least because this enables us to think specifically in terms of application, rather than just theory.

A number of difficulties exist in discussing ethical behaviour in a supply chain context. There are some – although they appear to be an increasingly marginalized minority – who argue that ethics have no place in business. They frequently cite the views of Milton Friedman, claiming that he states that the only social responsibility of business is to increase its profits (see, for example, Friedman, 1970). Friedman suggests that executives should be free to use their own money for philanthropic purposes as they see fit but that, as agents of the shareholders of a company, they have no remit to choose for which social purposes money is used, unless it serves the purposes of the corporation – for example, by donations to a community in order to improve the chance of recruiting desirable workers from that community. Friedman states that such reasons for actions are not 'social responsibility', but rather sound business sense, and that to label them as social responsibility represents a misuse of the term. Friedman's stance, however, loses its value to those whose views oppose ethical consideration when we consider that he states that it is the role of management 'to make as much money as possible while conforming to the basic rules of society, both those embodied in the law and those embodied in ethical custom'. It would seem, therefore, that Friedman's views do not oppose what might now be considered as ethical and societal issues, but do require that such behaviour remains consistent with the stockholder's view of the firm (Jones *et al.*, 2002) and does not distract the focus of managers from the imperative to make money for shareholders.

Somewhat in opposition to Friedman's views, Carroll (1991) describes a four-stage pyramid of corporate social responsibility: economic, legal, ethical and philanthropic (see Figure 19.1).

---

1   See www.eftafairtrade.org/definition.asp.

He suggests that the economic responsibility to be profitable is the foundation on which all other responsibilities rest. Organizations also have a requirement to obey the law. Failure to do so is unlikely to be in the long-term interests of the corporation, as the recent Enron affair has demonstrated. Although the problems encountered by Enron have often been cited as demonstrating the need for ethical education in business schools, there is some indication that what happened at Enron was illegal, rather than unethical. This indicates an important distinction. The legal responsibilities of an organization require the agents of the organization to obey the law: ethical responsibilities go beyond what is required in law; they require that we do 'what is right, just and fair' (Carroll, 1991) and to avoid behaviour that harms others.

A further difficulty in discussing ethical behaviour is that there is still no universal agreement about what constitutes ethical behaviour in business. As a consequence, we cannot arrive at a simple prescription of what is ethical and what is unethical. One significant difficulty is that ethical behaviours can be highly contingent on culture. So while some people in Western economies may regard it as highly unethical to employ 13-year-old children, in developing economies these children may provide a significant proportion of a family's income. The question then becomes whether it is more unethical to use a supplier that employs child labour or to develop a policy that prevents families from earning a living wage. However, there are few people who would argue that it is satisfactory for children, in whatever context, to work in unsafe conditions. Husted *et al.*, (1996) studied the difference in beliefs about ethical behaviour between samples of Mexican, Spanish and US MBA students. They found that, while students differed in moral reasoning, there was overlap in a number of practices that all students found morally objectionable, notably unsafe working conditions, unsafe products, pollution and waste, sexual discrimination and favouritism. Husted *et al.* conclude that even when managers from different cultures arrive at the same moral judgements, their underlying reasoning may be different.

In an attempt to address the difficulties raised by cultural differences in the perception of moral behaviours, Dunfee and Donaldson (1994) argued for the need to develop 'hypernorms', which they define as 'principles so fundamental to human existence that they serve as a guide in evaluating lower level moral norms. As such, we would expect them to be reflected in a convergence of religious, philosophical, and cultural beliefs' (1994, p. 265). Hypernorms

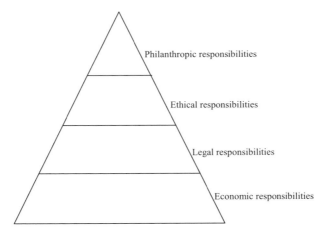

Source: Adapted from Carroll (1991).

Figure 19.1   The pyramid of social responsibility

might therefore be regarded as those principles that are so fundamental they seek to evaluate all lower-order norms, having at their root what is ethical for all humanity (Donaldson and Dunfee, 1999). The difficulty remains as to who decides what constitutes a hypernorm. A number of authors and groups have attempted to develop them (see, for example, Frederick, 1991; the Caux Round Table;[2] the Parliament of World Religions;[3] the United Nations Global Compact, originally comprising nine principles in the areas of human rights, international labour standards and the environment when it was first formulated in 1999, and to which a tenth principle on anti-corruption was added in 2004[4]).

Frederick compared six intergovernmental pacts that he considered the most archetypal of the accords that 'have been intended to put on the public record various sets of principles regulating the activities of governments, groups and individuals' (1991, p. 165). He suggests that, taken together, the codes provide the outline for a 'transcultural corporate ethic'. In other words, the principles enshrined in (i) the United Nations Declaration of Human Rights (1948), (ii) the European Convention on Human Rights (1950), (iii) the Helsinki Final Act (1975), (iv) the International Labour Office Tripartite Declaration of Principles Concerning the Multinational Enterprises and Social Policy (1977), and (v) the incomplete United Nations Code of Conduct on Transnational Corporations together provide a set of guidelines on corporate behaviour and assist in developing appropriate hypernorms. These hypernorms represent a good starting point in identifying what might and might not be regarded as ethical behaviour and are enshrined in both the principles suggested by the Caux Round Table outlined below and the Ethical Trading Initiative code of conduct described later in this chapter.

The Caux Round Table describes itself as 'an international network of principled business leaders working to promote moral capitalism'. It has developed a statement that 'aims to express a world standard against which business behaviour can be measured'. One set of principles deals specifically with stakeholders. In relation to outsourcing, two particular sets of guidelines can be seen as providing guidance: those dealing with employees, and in particular the need to 'be sensitive to the serious unemployment problems frequently associated with business decisions' and those dealing with suppliers (see Figure 19.2). Although the last point in the table talks only about suppliers and subcontractors, outsource providers would certainly be considered as requiring the same conditions.

Thus, although it is not possible for everyone to agree on all aspects of what constitutes ethical behaviour – for example, where does bribery end and the use of small 'greasing' payments to get things to happen become legitimate? – there are some fundamental principles on which most religions and non-governmental organizations agree.

Outsourcing: the outsourcer's perspective

The work that has been carried out on ethics in the supply chain has largely examined the problem from the perspective of ensuring compliance with certain standards by suppliers. However, when any outsourcing decision is made, consideration has to be given to those in an organization who will either find themselves without a job or who will wind up working for a different employer. Breslin (1999) suggests that many public-sector employees fear outsourcing because of the loss of benefits that frequently accompany their transfer to a private-sector

2   See www.cauxroundtable.org.
3   See www.cpwr.org.
4   See www.unglobalcompact.org.

The Caux Round Table principles for dealing with suppliers suggest that:

'The relationship with suppliers and subcontractors must be based on mutual respect. We therefore have a responsibility to:

- seek fairness and truthfulness in all our activities, including pricing, licensing, and rights to sell;

- ensure that our business activities are free from coercion and unnecessary litigation;

- foster long-term stability in the supplier relationship in return for value, quality, competitiveness and reliability;

- share information with suppliers and integrate them into our planning processes;

- pay suppliers on time and in accordance with agreed terms of trade; and

- seek, encourage and prefer suppliers and subcontractors whose employment practices respect human dignity.'

Source: Caux Round Table at: www.cauxroundtable.org/documents/Principles%20for%20Business. PDF.

Figure 19.2   Relevant guidance from the Caux Round Table principles

outsource provider. He cites the statistic that only 34 per cent of private-sector workers in the USA possess a defined benefit pension plan, compared to 84 per cent of public-sector workers. Given that the public sector in many countries is concentrating on outsourcing many 'non-core' activities, this raises the question of whether short-term savings in public-sector expenditure may be at the expense of long-term public spending on pensions and healthcare. Certainly, there is a perception that outsourcing may lead to inferior terms and conditions for workers. Some (who might well include Friedman) would argue that the outsourcing decision is taken in the interests of the shareholders and that the decision should concentrate purely on obtaining the best financial terms, irrespective of the outcome for workers whose roles are outsourced. However, managers considering outsourcing may want to consider whether, in the long term, outsourcing is the best answer. Unions and the press have been heavily critical of the decline in cleanliness in UK hospitals since many health providers outsourced the cleaning service. Although it appears to have resulted in money being saved, some have suggested that hygiene standards have dropped and the level of infections among hospital patients has risen as a consequence. Whether or not the claims are true, the idea has been planted in the minds of the public. Were this a company rather than an essential service, there is no doubt that the adverse publicity would have impacted on the brand and, potentially, the company's profits.

Social responsibility and supply chain relationships

It is clear that sourcing, of both goods and services, is key in considering ethical issues in a supply chain context. It is not enough for the sourcing company to treat its own staff well: the treatment of workers and stakeholders in the companies from which the focus company sources also needs to be considered. As a number of incidents have shown, it is possible for organizations to suffer adverse publicity as the consequence of its suppliers' activities, whether manufacturing subcontractors or outsource providers. Nike suffered a spate of adverse publicity and student boycotts in the USA as a consequence of suppliers which, the media discovered, were using child labour to manufacture Nike products (Maignan *et al.*, 2002; Wootliff and Deri, 2001). In this case, although Nike had not employed child labour directly, they were associated with the practice, even if unwittingly, and consequently suffered adverse publicity. Similarly, Benetton, usually renowned for their use of advertising to promote social causes, was held to be accountable for allegations that one of its Turkish manufacturing subcontractors used child labour. The discovery resulted in an agreement between Benetton and the Turkish supplier about ending the use of child labour. In the process, though, Benetton received some adverse comments in the press.

Thus, as illustrated above, companies selling direct to the final-user (B2C) companies are often seen by consumers to be responsible for activities throughout the supply chain. The increasing activism evident at international meetings, notably those of the World Trade Organization (WTO) coincides with a belief among the general public that companies are no longer required to focus only on business fundamentals: evidence from the Millennium Poll on Corporate Social Responsibility revealed that nearly 60 per cent of consumers form the impression of an organization based on broader issues such as ethics, labour relations, environmental factors and social responsibility. This compares with only just over 30 per cent who mentioned the fundamental business issues such as financial performance, company size and management reputation.[5]

Codes of conduct

Most supply chain managers are not moral philosophers, and deciding what constitutes ethical or unethical behaviour can be a deeply personal decision. Whilst most people recognize the fact that murder is wrong, how can we decide whether or not behaviour is ethical? A number of national and international organizations have developed codes of practice to which members and affiliated bodies commit. These codes of practice have many common factors, based on the International Labour Organization conventions.[6] Figure 19.3 shows the code of conduct to which members of the UK-based Ethical Trading Initiative subscribe.

The code outlined here is very similar to the Apparel Industry Partnership Agreement, set up to try to counter the bad publicity generated by accusations that international sourcing in the textile industry was encouraging sweatshop practices (Emmelhainz and Adams, 1999). The code of practice requires the following in the workplace:

- that child labour should not be used;
- that abuse, harassment and discrimination are eliminated;
- that workers are paid the higher of either the legal minimum wage or the prevailing wage in the industry;
- that workers have the right to associate freely and the right to collective bargaining;
- that workers should have no more than a 60-hour working week and should not be forced to work overtime;
- that workers should have a safe and healthy working environment.

The emphasis in these codes of practice is largely on what would be regarded by many as fundamental workers' rights.

---

5   See www.sustdev.org/journals/edition.02/download/sdi2_1_5.pdf.
6   See www.ilo.org.

1. **Employment is freely chosen.**
   1.1. There is no forced, bonded or involuntary prison labour.
   1.2. Workers are not required to lodge 'deposits' or their identity papers with their employer and are free to leave their employer after reasonable notice.

2. **Freedom of association and the right to collective bargaining are respected.**
   2.1. Workers, without distinction, have the right to join or form trade unions of their own choosing and to bargain collectively.
   2.2. The employer adopts an open attitude towards the activities of trade unions and their organisational activities.
   2.3. Workers representatives are not discriminated against and have access to carry out their representative functions in the workplace.
   2.4. Where the right to freedom of association and collective bargaining is restricted under law, the employer facilitates, and does not hinder, the development of parallel means for independent and free association and bargaining.

3. **Working conditions are safe and hygienic.**
   3.1. A safe and hygienic working environment shall be provided, bearing in mind the prevailing knowledge of the industry and of any specific hazards. Adequate steps shall be taken to prevent accidents and injury to health arising out of, associated with, or occurring in the course of work, by minimising, so far as is reasonably practicable, the causes of hazards inherent in the working environment.
   3.2. Workers shall receive regular and recorded health and safety training, and such training shall be repeated for new or reassigned workers.
   3.3. Access to clean toilet facilities and to potable water, and, if appropriate, sanitary facilities for food storage shall be provided.
   3.4. The company observing the code shall assign responsibility for health and safety to a senior management representative.

4. **Child labour shall not be used.**
   4.1. There shall be no new recruitment of child labour.
   4.2. Companies shall develop or participate in and contribute to policies and programmes which provide for the transition of any child found to be performing child labour to enable her or him to attend and remain in quality education until no longer a child; 'child' and 'child labour' being defined in the appendices.
   4.3. Children and young persons under 18 shall not be employed at night or in hazardous conditions.

5. **Living wages are paid.**
   5.1. Wages and benefits paid for a standard working week meet, at a minimum, national legal standards or industry benchmark standards, whichever is higher. In any event wages should always be enough to meet basic needs and to provide some discretionary income.
   5.2. All workers shall be provided with written and understandable Information about their employment conditions in respect to wages before they enter employment and about the particulars of their wages for the pay period concerned each time that they are paid.
   5.3. Deductions from wages as a disciplinary measure shall not be permitted nor shall any deductions from wages not provided for by national law be permitted without the expressed permission of the worker concerned. All disciplinary measures should be recorded.

6. **Working hours are not excessive.**
   6.1. Working hours comply with national laws and benchmark industry standards, whichever affords greater protection.
   6.2. In any event, workers shall not on a regular basis be required to work in excess of 48 hours per week and shall be provided with at least one day off for every 7 day period on average. Overtime shall be voluntary, shall not exceed 12 hours per week, shall not be demanded on a regular basis and shall always be compensated at a premium rate.

7. **No discrimination is practised.**
   7.1. There is no discrimination in hiring, compensation, access to training, promotion, termination or retirement based on race, caste, national origin, religion, age, disability, gender, marital status, sexual orientation, union membership or political affiliation.

8. **Regular employment is provided.**
   8.1. To every extent possible work performed must be on the basis of recognised employment relationship established through national law and practice.
   8.2. Obligations to employees under labour or social security laws and regulations arising from the regular employment relationship shall not be avoided through the use of labour-only contracting, sub-contracting, or home-working arrangements, or through apprenticeship schemes where there is no real intent to impart skills or provide regular employment, nor shall any such obligations be avoided through the excessive use of fixed-term contracts of employment.

9. **No harsh or inhumane treatment is allowed.**
   9.1. Physical abuse or discipline, the threat of physical abuse, sexual or other harassment and verbal abuse or other forms of intimidation shall be prohibited.

Source: Ethical Trading Initiative at: www.ethicaltrade.org/Z/lib/base/code_en.shtml.

Figure19.3   The Ethical Trading Initiative Base Code

Maignan *et al.* (2002) use the example of Nike to show how the strategies adopted by organizations practising socially responsible buying range along a continuum from reactive through defensive and accommodative to proactive strategies. The reactive strategy seeks to deny that the organization has any responsibility for the activities of its suppliers. Nike was first accused of dealing with suppliers who used child labour in the mid-1990s. The company's initial response was that manufacturing shoes was not its business and that it could not be blamed for the practices of the East Asian manufacturers (reactive strategy). Nike then moved to a defensive strategy, acknowledging that the issue existed but not addressing the concerns. Then, following adverse media comment, the company issued a report suggesting that the workers in the factories concerned enjoyed a satisfactory standard of living, although local activists disputed this view, resulting in more bad press. In the next stage (accommodative strategy), Nike introduced guidelines for its suppliers, covering both workers' rights and environmental standards. Yet, voices within Nike continued to suggest that such initiatives would damage the company's competitiveness. In the final stage – reached by Nike in the late 1990s – an organization will systematically solicit the demands of stakeholders and address the reasonable demands. In Nike's case this resulted in a formal supplier auditing process, to which student representatives and activists were invited in order to observe and make recommendations for better practice. Over the years, Nike moved from denial of any responsibility to accepting that, at least in the eyes of members of the public, they were responsible not only for their own actions, but also for those who supplied them.

The proactive approach requires initiatives to be undertaken by the firm in assessing suppliers. Maignan *et al.* suggest a number of different, but not mutually exclusive, approaches, including:

- *Developing social responsibility goals*. Maignan *et al.* refer to this in a purchasing context, but it is clear that this is equally important for strategically significant decisions such as outsourcing.
- *Identifying people within the organization who are responsible for socially responsible sourcing*. In Nike's case, as a consequence of boycotts, the company created the post of Vice President for Social Responsibility.
- *Educating suppliers (or potential outsource providers)*. Although some suppliers may readily meet required social standards (for example, those laid down by the ETI code of conduct in Figure 19.3), others may require training programmes and changes in practice to enable them to meet the required standards.
- *Monitoring suppliers of products and services*. Alongside with education of suppliers it may be necessary to monitor supplier performance in conforming to standards. There are a number of different approaches to supplier monitoring, including in-house auditors, external consultants who will undertake audits and independent groups established by those purchasing the goods or services.
- *Imposing sanctions*. So that the aspirations for socially responsible activities in the supply chain are taken seriously, sanctions need to be taken against those who fail to meet the criteria set by the sourcing organizations. This does not mean that suppliers who fail to reach the standards set should be dropped immediately. Educating suppliers and giving assistance in meeting the sourcing organization's gaols may be regarded as more socially responsible than simply not giving the contract to a company in a location where the provision of employment can lead to significant social improvements.

- *Communicating achievements to stakeholders*. There is some dispute about whether companies should trumpet their achievements: some are wary of trumpeting achievements for fear of attracting attention and of the possibility that the media will work harder to identify problems. Others wish to draw attention to the fact that their brand can be regarded as 'ethical'.
- *Receiving feedback from stakeholders*. Proactive companies want to find out from stakeholders how they are progressing with particular initiatives. Stakeholders in this process may include the organization's own employees, shareholders and suppliers who have been subjected to the company's policies.

It is important that companies don't just have a written policy but also implement initiatives to ensure that the policy is put into practice.

One of the difficulties that managers face is identifying practices that might be regarded as unethical. It is difficult for managers in sourcing organizations to not take an ethnocentric view of what constitutes ethical behaviour. One study (Carter, 2000, p. 194) identified a range of 'unethical' activities, which included a number of factors that could apply equally to outsourcing contracts and standard purchasing agreements. These practices included:

- writing specifications to favour a particular provider;
- allowing a supplier to bid again after a specified closing date;
- permitting only certain suppliers to bid;
- limiting which suppliers can bid;
- using bribery;
- offering gifts (in excess of a nominal value);
- overcommitting resources;
- deliberately misleading the other party.

The later points indicate that unethical behaviour is not unique to the outsourcing organization. Both sides of an outsourcing relationship may indulge in unethical practices.

Auditing suppliers/outsourcing providers

To protect themselves from allegations of social irresponsibility, organizations need to consider very carefully those companies with which they do business. In order to do this, the outsourcing organization needs to do more than carry out simple financial audits of potential outsource providers. It may sometimes be couched in other terms, but the main purpose of outsourcing is to improve the profitability of businesses, and the prime consideration in selecting outsource providers has traditionally therefore been financial. However, as the stories of Nike, Benetton and others have shown, focusing only on finance in assessing potential partners can ultimately have an adverse impact on the brand and income of outsourcing organization. The implication is that, in considering potential providers of outsourced services, companies also need to consider the potential impact of an association between the outsource provider's brand and their own. Some organizations choose to carry out their own audits, developing processes to ensure that suppliers, if not already complying with the principles outlined by the sourcing company, have the capability to develop appropriate behaviours. Other organizations may employ an external consultant to carry out the evaluations.

For organizations that achieve the required standards in sourcing activity there is the possibility of becoming SA8000 accredited. SA8000 has been described as 'the new social standard' (Leipziger, 2001) and develops performance criteria in very similar areas to those described in the ETI code of conduct in Figure 19.3. SA8000 has been designed to fit within the ISO9000 and ISO14000 accreditation process, making it the most widely adopted social responsibility standard (Miles and Munilla, 2004). This may make it an attractive accreditation for those who already have, or are seeking, the latter two standards. Although the requirement for suppliers to be SA8000 accredited is not yet discernible, it is possible to envisage that it may become a requirement in the award of contracts in much the same way that many companies now require ISO9000 from all those who tender for business.

Ethical/socially responsible behaviour and company performance

A major problem with assessing ethical behaviour and corporate social responsibility in a supply chain setting is that there has been no definitive study on the impact of such initiatives on organizations' financial performance. In addition, there have been no specific studies of corporate social responsibility in outsourcing relationships. It is necessary therefore to draw on studies carried out within a supply chain purchasing setting. One study (Carter and Jennings, 2002b) demonstrated that high levels of social responsibility lead to improved levels of supplier performance. Carter and Jennings' study is one of the first to demonstrate empirical support for the view that cooperation between firms in a supply chain can lead to increased performance within the supply chain. In another paper (Carter and Jennings, 2002a) they indicate that 'several informants specifically mentioned reduced costs as a consequence of Logistics Social Responsibility, while only two informants stated that costs had increased' (2002a, p.167). In both these cases, the increased costs resulted from improved environmental practices that the authors suggest may have resulted in improved relationships with stakeholders, including customers. However other writers, cited by Carter and Jennings (2002b), writing in the 1970s and 1980s, found either no relationship between CSR and performance or that CSR increases. A more recent study by Johnson (2003) suggests that companies that engage in a strategic approach to CSR tend to perform better in financial terms than those whose approach is piecemeal, but the study largely concentrates on CSR activities within the organization and local communities.

Although it currently is hard to identify clear evidence that socially responsible behaviour in the supply chain leads to improved performance, the examples of Nike and Benetton cited earlier provide a reason for engaging in ethical behaviour: failure to do so can result in adverse publicity and damage to brands. There is no doubt that when individuals and organizations boycott brands there is at least an opportunity cost in terms of lost sales.

Conclusion

Although there is currently only limited evidence that consideration of ethics and corporate social responsibility within a supply chain has a positive impact on organization performance, there is a growing awareness that companies who are found to be indulging in what their customers believe to be unacceptable practices can suffer negative publicity and damage to their brand(s). This chapter has shown that there are still a number of issues to be resolved regarding what constitutes ethical or unethical behaviour, but that a range of guidelines exist that can help companies in designing appropriate policies. It is unlikely that requirements for ethical behaviour in outsourcing decisions and practices will decline, but this is an area of literature that is very much in its infancy, and it will be interesting to watch developments.

References

Breslin, D.A. (1999), 'On the ethics of outsourcing: a philosophical look at A-76', *Programme Manager*, pp. 24–26.

Carroll, A.B. (1991), 'The pyramid of corporate social responsibility: toward the moral management of organizational stakeholders', *Business Horizons*, vol. 34, no. 4, pp. 39–48.

Carter, C.R. (2000), 'Ethical issues in international buyer-supplier relationships: a dyadic examination', *Journal of Operations Management*, vol. 18, no. 2, pp. 191–208.

Carter, C.R. and Jennings, M.M. (2002a), 'Logistics social responsibility: an integrative framework,' *Journal of Business Logistics*, vol. 23, no. 1, pp. 145–80.

Carter, C.R. and Jennings, M.M. (2002b), 'Social responsibility and supply chain relationships', *Transportation Research. Part E, Logistics and Transportation Review*, vol. 38, no. 1, pp. 37–52.

Donaldson, T. and Dunfee, T.W. (1999), 'When ethics travel: the promise and peril of global business ethics', *California Management Review*, vol. 41, no. 4, pp. 45–63.

Dunfee, T.W, and Donaldson, T.J. (1994), 'Towards a unified conception of business ethics: integrative social contracts theory', *Academy of Management Review*, vol. 19, no. 2, pp. 252–84.

Emmelhainz, M.A. and Adams, R.J. (1999), 'The apparel industry response to "sweatshop" concerns: a review and analysis of codes of conduct', *Journal of Supply Chain Management*, vol. 35, no. 3, pp. 51–57.

Frederick, W.C. (1991), 'The moral authority of transnational corporate codes', *Journal of Business Ethics*, vol. 10, no. 3, pp. 165–77.

Friedman, M. (1970), 'The social responsibility of business is to increase its profits', *The New York Times Magazine*, pp. 122–26.

Husted, B.W., Dozier, J.B., McMahon, J.T. and Kattan, M.W. (1996), 'The impact of cross-national carriers of business ethics on attitudes about questionable practices and form of moral reasoning', *Journal of International Business Studies*, vol. 27, no. 2, pp. 391–411.

Johnson, H.H. (2003), 'Does it pay to be good? Social responsibility and financial performance', *Business Horizons*, vol. 46, no. 6, pp. 34–40.

Jones, T.M., Wicks, A.C. and Freeman, R.E. (2002), 'Stakeholder theory: state of the art', in N.E. Bowie (ed.), *The Blackwell Guide to Business Ethics*, Blackwell, Oxford, pp. 19–37.

Leipziger, D. (2001), *SA8000: The Definitive Guide to the New Social Standard*, Financial Times/Prentice Hall, London.

Maignan, I., Hillebrand, B. and McAlister, D. (2002), 'Managing socially-responsible buying: how to integrate non-economic criteria into the purchasing process', *European Management Journal*, vol. 20, no. 6, pp. 641–49.

Miles, M.P. and Munilla, L.S. (2004), 'The potential impact of social accountability certification on marketing: a short note', *Journal of Business Ethics*, vol. 50, no. 1, pp. 1–11.

Wootliff, J. and Deri, C. (2001), 'NGOs: The new super brands', *Corporate Reputation Review*, vol. 4, no. 2, pp. 157–64.

5 *The Practical Side of Outsourcing: The Case-Study Approach*

A case-study approach can provide an in-depth assessment of the successes and failures of outsourcing. Part 5 provides a few case studies that will feature the specific processes involved in outsourcing and the different results that arise from such processes. It will provide an opportunity to work through a unique experience retrospectively and generate ways of ensuring that the problem is addressed adequately.

Jane Linder, in the opening chapter, examines the Kinleith mill's outsourcing experience. Kinleith mill was an organization that needed to reduce its overhead costs, improve its productivity and improve its relationship with the workers. The organization decided to outsource one component of its operations to assist with its transformation. This case study outlines the various processes involved in moving the organization forward and achieving its objectives.

In Chapter 21 Anthony Boardman and Ricki Hewitt focus on the practical approach, outlining a practical guide for those public-sector managers who are considering outsourcing a government activity or service. They note that, although the decision on whether or not to outsource has usually been based on transaction cost economics (TCE), this has been developed for use within the private sector. They have therefore adapted the dynamics of the process for the public sector. This has involved them in providing key questions that should be considered before a decision is made.

The final chapter, written by Julian Howison and Amit Mehta, presents an in-depth assessment of an outsourcing relationship between an established information technology (IT) company, the ARRK group, and a small and medium-sized enterprise (SME), the ABC company. The usefulness of an outsourcing relationship with an SME is not usually highlighted in the literature. This case study shows that an SME was able to successfully outsource a vital part of its businesses, while working within financial constraints and being aware of the risks involved in the outsourcing process.

20 *Clean Skin at the Kinleith Mill*

Jane Linder

Kinleith mill had a 50-year history of horrific union contracts characterized by, amongst other things, a culture of entitlement. If I asked you to fill the water cooler, and this was a task that you did not normally do, you felt you were entitled to more pay. When we entered the watershed negotiations of August 2001, our tradespeople were earning twice the New Zealand average for their trades, the mill had not earned its cost of capital for several years running and the world price for pulp and paper was depressed. We were on the edge. It was our last chance to create a sustainable future for the mill.

David King
Kinleith Mill Manager

In July 2004, Juergen Link, ABB Ltd's[1] Kinleith site director, and Ian Whyte, the Kinleith mill's operations manager, met briefly after the monthly governance meeting to chat. The meeting had been more stressful than usual as the Kinleith/ABB joint management team worked to resolve some persistent information technology issues as well as get a grip on the most recent budget challenges. Neither man had any illusions about the magnitude of the task which they had taken on 18 months earlier, and it helped them both to recall how far they had come. Carter Holt Harvey's Kinleith mill was significantly more competitive, and management's radical decision to outsource maintenance to ABB deserved a fair share of the credit.

Background

Kinleith was Carter Holt Harvey Ltd's (CHH) largest paper and pulp mill with an annual capacity of 570 000 tons and sales of NZ$450 million. CHH, headquartered in Auckland and part of the International Paper family,[2] was New Zealand's largest forest products company with 2003 sales of about NZ$4 billion. It owned about 810 000 acres of New Zealand forestlands. In addition to Kinleith, CHH operated four pulp and paper mills; 24 converting and packaging plants; 67 wood products manufacturing and distribution facilities; and six paper and packaging product distribution branches. The Kinleith mill produced a wide range of finished papers to meet the needs of the domestic New Zealand market. It also competed for a share of the price-competitive, chronically overcapacity, global pulp market, shipping most of its output to Australian and Asian destinations.

---

1   ABB Ltd is a global power and automation company headquartered in Zurich, Switzerland. Its 2004 revenues exceeded $20 billion.
2   In 2004, International Paper Company (IPC) owned 53 per cent of CHH.

Originally built in 1953 by New Zealand Forest Products, Kinleith enjoyed tariff protection in its home markets for its first three decades. Cost increases were simply passed along to customers. In 1984, however, a currency crisis convinced the government to embrace radical reforms and adopt free-market principles. Soon import tariffs were lifted, and New Zealand's paper and pulp industry began to consolidate in order to compete. As forest products companies merged and jockeyed for position, the Kinleith mill changed owners three times. CHH took it over in the early 1990s.

From 1987 to 1999, CHH and its prior owners made substantial investments in Kinleith's capacity and productivity to improve its competitive position. Some machines were shut down, and others were modernized. The most recent investment in the late 1990s totalled NZ$300 million and modernized the only remaining paper machine to a position of world-class efficiency. As a result of this and prior investments, Kinleith went from six paper machines and two pulp dryers producing 1200 tons per day in 1987 to one paper machine and one pulp dryer producing 1600 tons per day in 1998. Over the same period, the mill's workforce was reduced from 3000 to 770.

Despite the investments in productivity, Kinleith lagged behind the competition. Large, modern mills in Chile, China, and Russia had an estimated $200 per ton cost advantage. Closer to home, a directly competitive mill, recently commissioned in New South Wales, was reputed to have a cost structure that was 75 per cent that of Kinleith. In 2001 Kinleith carried high overhead costs by international standards,[3] its 2001 EBIT was negative and its five-year cash flow return on investment (CFROI) averaged only 5 per cent against a cost of capital of 12 per cent. Management recognized that the mill's inability even to service long-term debt would ultimately result in its closure.

Kinleith chief executive (CE) Brice Landman promoted David King, a South African, to mill manager to help capture the benefits from the company's recent investment in the mill. King recalled, 'We spent the first two years getting the mill to operate as designed from a technical perspective, and we were successful in that respect. Then I assumed responsibility for managing the mill in 2001, which brought me in direct contact with the union. Unlike most people at Kinleith, I had worked elsewhere so I had an outside benchmark. What I saw was horrific.'

Union–management relations

During the plant's tariff-protected years, the unions had gained considerable power as management learned to acquiesce to their demands in order to avert strikes. Eighty per cent of the mill's 270 maintenance workers and 100 per cent of its 500 production workers were represented by the Engineers, Printing and Manufacturing Union (EPMU). The remainder of the maintenance workers, save a few independent individuals, were represented by the Independent Electrical Workers' Union and five additional minority unions. All of the unions worked through a site committee for collective bargaining with the company.

In management's view, the unions embraced an entitlement culture with a philosophy that said, 'If you want my discretionary capacity, you must pay for it'. To back up their stance, they had become adept at resisting all incremental change initiatives. One manager recalled, 'In a previous restructuring, we reduced headcount. We believed that if we created a vacuum,

---

3   CHH commissioned an international, comparative study of staffing levels in 2000 and communicated excerpts from this analysis to the union in early 2001.

the remaining people would move to fill it. That theory turned out to be wrong. The workers stayed where they were and created holes which we had to fill by recruiting. I found it quite soul-destroying.' Another manager continued, 'The workforce's greed for gold is greater than their fear of death. Wealth generation has become their sole objective in life.'

In 2001, the maintenance workers' contract allowed them all to work on 11 statutory holidays, regardless of work demands. In addition, the contract permitted 25 per cent of the 270 workers to work each weekend, again regardless of the need. For work on these statutory holidays and over weekends, they were paid at an overtime rate. While the average trades person in New Zealand earned about NZ$35 000, Kinleith's maintenance workers received an average of NZ$80 000, in addition to subsidized pensions and free medical care and life insurance.

Union delegates countered that a series of revolving-door managers took short-sighted decisions that did not always serve the mill. They asserted that the workers were unaccustomed to taking the initiative because management had been reluctant to relinquish any authority to them. A union executive explained, 'My advice to new managers is to find out what you have before you try to change it. Managers get offside by not listening to the intellectual property the workers have – 16 000 years of experience in total. It's not uncommon for someone to have 35 years' seniority. And when they trust you, you get their best.'

Since Kinleith's employees made up a substantial fraction of the population of the nearby town of Tokoroa, work issues spilled over into the community. During the 1991 strike, for example, banks and retailers readily extended credit to workers to enable them to sustain their families while they negotiated a new contract. According to an independent study, closing the mill for good would have reduced the local economy by 25 per cent.

2001 contract negotiations

In the summer of 2001, shortly after David King assumed his new role, management and the site committee representatives met to discuss a new contract. Ian Whyte, the engineering and maintenance manager at the time, recalled, 'We went into those negotiations on the back of six consecutive EBIT[4] losses, but we had relatively benign demands.' Management was prepared to offer a 3 per cent wage increase, but they asked for a few things in return. They wanted to stop running buses between the mill and Tokoroa. Each bus carried only two people on average, and eliminating the service would generate savings of NZ$650 000 per year. Management also wanted the plant to operate on Christmas and Boxing Day. Whyte explained, 'Our plant is complex and hard to start up after a shut-down. By not working those two days, we actually lost four days of production. We wanted to get the benefit of those four days, and we were happy to pay for it.'

In addition, management wanted to begin discussing the weekend and holiday maintenance staffing to find a way of whittling down its NZ$3 million price tag. King emphasized, 'This wasn't even a demand. We just wanted to begin to work on this issue during the coming year and within the term of the contract that we wished to renew.'

In responding to management, the site committee threw down the gauntlet. They were looking for a 4.5 per cent wage increase, and they were heard to retort, 'We will not fund our own increase. We have come here to take, not to give. We will simply wait for pulp prices to rise, and then you will give us what we want.'

---

4   Earnings before interest and taxes.

The two sides adjourned negotiations without reaching a new agreement. The contract expired in 2001, and the law required that its terms remain in force until a new contract was signed. Through a series of in-house newsletters, Landman explained the mill's precarious situation to employees, warning that, even at 100 per cent efficiency, the mill was losing money.[5] Subsequently, CHH CEO Christopher Liddell added his weight to the argument saying, 'This is not a fire drill. The mill is not in any great short-term danger, but we need to ensure its medium- to long-term health, in particular as a source for future investment. This is likely to involve some step change from everyone concerned.' At the same time, a CHH spokesperson was quoted on a forest industries website saying that 'all [Kinleith] output is being sold as the mill is one of the lowest cost producers in the world'.[6]

Project Green

In October, King convened an unconventional group of four or five managers to meet with Landman and discuss how to move forward. The hand-picked team included Ian Whyte and Larry Bryers, the manufacturing manager, both of whom were veterans at Kinleith, but new to their roles. Whyte and Bryers took an assignment away from the meeting: assume the plant's physical assets are as is, but history doesn't exist as far as the workforce is concerned. If you were starting with a clean sheet of paper, how would you staff it and what type of collective agreement would you seek? Whyte and Bryers went to work on greenfield exercises for maintenance and manufacturing respectively.

Whyte recalled, 'At that stage, we still had an in-house workforce in mind. But coincidentally, some of ABB's senior people from the US paid us a visit. They presented a viable alternative, so we agreed they should do a survey on the site just to test our own thinking.' In mid-December 2001 the Kinleith management provided ABB's experts with documentation about mill operations, maintenance staffing levels and payroll costs. In order to keep the exercise confidential until any proposals could be released to the workforce, ABB set up a base off-site and visited with Whyte and his colleagues after hours.

Despite being unable to speak directly with the trades people, ABB concluded that it could significantly reduce the cost of maintenance and still make a fair profit by taking over the function from Kinleith on an outsourced basis. Whyte continued, 'There may have been one or two items in the audit I could have taken some exception to, but the rest was exactly what I saw.' Both plans featured cutting the maintenance workforce by about half as well as improving shutdown and system performance. 'We all know what it takes,' Whyte summarized, 'good planning and scheduling, good predictive maintenance, good practices for rebuilding machines. It's not rocket science.'

On 11 and 12 February 2002, King convened an off-site workshop to review both the ABB and in-house proposals and to choose a course of action. An ABB-sponsored facilitator skilled in the Kepner Tregoe method of decision making led the first day's discussion. Over dinner, King fired him, commenting, 'He wasn't allowing me to ask the right questions. The next day, I ran the workshop.'

After reviewing Whyte's in-house proposal and ABB's proposal to provide full service maintenance, Paul Mackay, the employee relations manager, asked his Kinleith colleagues the

---

5   Judgment of Judge G.L. Colgan of the New Zealand Employment Court, Auckland Registry, 30 August 2002. Judgment number 53/02, file number ARC 42/02.
6   Paperloop.com

critical question: 'Which plan has the best chance of success?' Whyte, currently the manager of the function that would potentially be outsourced, answered first. 'ABB! Internally, we had a demonstrated track record of failing to implement our initiatives. The unions would resist until the gains were outweighed by the effort. What we really needed was a change of culture, and ABB presented evidence that they could get it done. It was difficult for me to criticize my own department and my own performance, but it was still the truthful answer.' The team was unanimous.

King turned to ABB and asked them to make a rock-solid commitment to specific deliverables if they got the business: 'I couldn't go forward with a radical strategy based only on high hopes. I needed hard numbers. ABB came back with the cost savings and productivity rates that are now in our contract.'

Shifting gears

In short order, management pulled together two field trips to confirm ABB's capabilities. Their conclusion after visiting several steel, paper and chemical plants – some of which were union strongholds – was that ABB could do what it promised. None of the plants was perfect. In some cases, the operations were no better than those at Kinleith. But Whyte emphasized, 'They were rock-solid on the relationship things.'

With the team confirmed in its intentions, Landman carried a three-point pitch to the CHH board and ultimately to the board of International Paper. Kinleith would, subject to consultation with affected parties:

1. outsource maintenance, reducing staff in that function from 270 to 180;
2. restructure production, making 60 employees redundant;
3. negotiate a new-age collective agreement.

The CHH board, which included representation from major shareholder International Paper, recognized that the decision to outsource would have a major effect on the mill. In gruelling sessions, they pressed for a cold-eyed view of the costs and the risks, as well as information on how the team would handle the potential for a significant mill outage. Based on projected annual savings of NZ$18 million for outsourcing and an additional NZ$12 million for the other changes, they gave Kinleith the approval to proceed.

King also hired a public relations firm to begin crafting communications for the workforce. At this time, only the Project Green team – a handful of individuals – knew about the plans. But on Wednesday 27 March 2002, that changed. All employees at Kinleith Mill received a copy of the 'Day 1 Pack' (see Figures 20.1 and 20.2). Its 87 pages laid out management's radical change agenda as well as a revised employment contract and initiated two distinct processes: collective bargaining with union delegates over the contract and consultation with the entire workforce about the proposed changes in the business structure (Figure 20.3 shows a timeline).

The letter hit Kinleith like a bombshell. One union executive remarked, 'It was devastating. There had been a stand-off for such a long time, and this just pushed the parties farther apart.' In meetings that day, union representatives indicated that all consultation with employees, as well as the contract negotiation, was to be done through the union.

Over the next six weeks, union and management dug in. On the advice of their union leadership, the production and maintenance workers boycotted 30 consultative meetings set

To All Employees
CHANGES AT KINLEITH MILL

A number of significant changes are proposed for Kinleith over the next few months.

The proposed changes include:

- Contracting out the maintenance function to a specialist maintenance company with proven industry expertise.
- A reduction in staffing levels throughout the rest of the business.
- Changes to conditions of employment to reflect the structural changes.

While changes to the business structure will be the subject of consultation, changes to conditions of employment will require agreement from those affected.

Details of the proposed organisational structure and an explanation of how the change process will unfold are part of this information pack. These are proposals only at this stage, albeit serious ones. *No final decisions have been made.* Nor will they be until employees have been consulted and their views considered.

The consultation process will aim to ensure that the best outcomes and processes have been identified in the time available.

Details of the changes the company is seeking to collective conditions of employment will be available to waged employees only from their union representatives in the first instance. The company is legally obliged to deal directly with employees' unions when negotiating for changes to the collective agreement.

The changes we seek to make are large and far-reaching. There is no escaping the fact that many jobs will disappear. It will be tough but, as has been the experience in recent times of many other mills around the world, doing nothing is worse.

There will be fewer jobs, but those who are employed will become relatively higher skilled, and will have greater job portability if they choose to move on in time. Jobs at Kinleith will become more secure than if we had done nothing. The contracting out proposal will provide approximately 150 job opportunities.

The proposed changes will affect the wider community as well. We recognise that Kinleith has and will still have a major economic input into the South Waikato community. We therefore will be building on our already close relationship with the community and local government leaders to ensure that any opportunities for balancing out the impact of the proposed changes are identified.

We will also be providing and staffing an information centre in Tokoroa to give employees and their families the ability to get answers to questions on any aspect of the changes and their impact.

However, before the change process begins I want to tell you why we believe change is necessary, and outline the company's proposals for meeting the challenges ahead. The following pages set out the company's proposals in more detail.

If you have queries about anything in this information pack please contact [the HR representative] or, if appropriate, ask your union delegate to do so on your behalf .

Regards
Brice Landman
Chief Executive
Carter Holt Harvey Kinleith

Figure 20.1 Day 1 Pack cover letter

CONTENTS

Vision for Kinleith
Our Desired Culture
Rationale for Change
Proposed Organisation Structures
• Maintenance & Engineering
• Pulp
• Finished Products
• Steam & Recovery
• Environmental, Health, Safety & Risk
• HR
• Finance
• Marketing
Notes to the proposed structures
Financial Background
Proposed Process
Questions & Answers
Resource Centre Information

Figure 20.2 Day 1 Pack table of contents

up by management to discuss the changes and introduce ABB to the staff. The union site bargaining team delivered written requests to management to share the research information that underpinned the 'Day 1 Pack' assertions that maintenance systems were weak, procedures and work histories were poorly documented, maintenance costs were too high, productivity was poor and that the existing structure was unable to meet the needs of the business. They

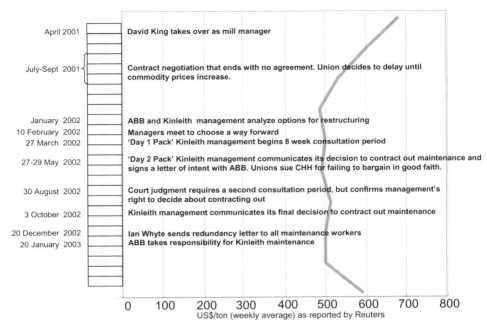

Figure 20.3 Kinleith timeline against a graph of pulp prices

wanted to understand the identities of the mills against which Kinleith had been benchmarked, the standards by which the comparisons were made, more details about the best practices that Kinleith allegedly lacked and specific evidence that showed that outsourcing was the best way to achieve the culture change they sought. In addition, they asked what alternatives management had considered in reaching their conclusion that maintenance should be outsourced. Management responded with documents that described 'ingrained' behaviours including:

- trade demarcation – for example, fitters refusing to do welding
- employees qualified for dual trades but refusal to utilize those skills
- reluctance to engage in a skills assessment survey
- withdrawal from training groups
- reluctance to engage in leave management
- refusal to utilize spares
- refusal to work at Christmas.

It also provided a consulting report that surveyed practices in 31 mills, in addition to a study by International Paper. Management went on to reiterate its intention to conclude consultation on 15 May and then make its decision about restructuring. While the union tried to engage in bargaining on both the contract and the restructuring, the company fielded two separate teams in order to segregate these processes. It continued to reject the union's assertion that it could consult on behalf of the workforce.

Volleys of formal letters did not begin to capture the emotional tone at Kinleith. Workers felt that they were being cast aside as 'rubbish'. One remarked, 'Hot shot university-trained managers drift through here for six or twelve months, rip the guts out and sail off elsewhere. It's the workers who have a deep commitment to the mill. It keeps the town going. It keeps the community going. They tell us the plant is losing money, but it's all creative accounting.' Another pointed out, 'If you really want to know what caused this, look at the millions they spent in the late 1990s when they rebuilt the mill. They didn't do it to the right spec, and now they have to spend more to correct their mistakes.'

Outsourcing affected the salaried supervisors and engineers in the maintenance organization as well as the unionized workers. While these employees did attend ABB's informational meetings, they had some of the same feelings as their hourly-paid colleagues.

During the consultation period, management invited Transfield Services, an Australia-based provider of industrial outsourcing services, to develop a proposal to take over the function. They also considered a proposal submitted by an employee group.

On 16 May, Kinleith management decided to outsource maintenance. They then summarized their position in the 'Day 2 Pack'. Released on 27 May, this document provided details about the decision to restructure the mill. It also laid out a process for management and employees to consult about how the changes were to be implemented. Unionized employees and their representatives declined the invitation to attend the associated briefing.

On 28 May, Kinleith management signed a letter of intent to outsource maintenance to ABB. At that point it agreed not to consider proposals from other parties. King said, 'We did not put them through a competitive tender. We selected them for the company we perceived them to be.'

Shortly after this date the EPMU initiated legal action through the Employment Relations Authority on the basis of two charges: that the process of restructuring should have been subjected to collective bargaining, not consultation; and that management had entered the process with a closed mind. One union leader was heard saying, 'ABB is a marauding disease looking for a victim.' The Employment Authority upheld the rights of Kinleith's management and ruled that they could proceed to restructure the business. This decision was subsequently appealed, to the Employment Court, by the unions.

After hearing arguments from both sides, the Auckland Employment Court judge ruled on the first point in favour of management and on the second for the union. He required management to engage in a 'meaningful' two-week consultation process about the restructuring and an additional two-week process to address how the company would deal with redundancies.

ABB was asked to clear the site to enable consultation to begin in mid-September. King recalled, 'During the second round of consultation discussions, the union delegates acknowledged that workers had been abusing the system. They promised to change their behaviour and work with us hand in hand.' However, the proposals developed by employees during this period could not match ABB's plan for either cost savings or evidence that the culture change could actually be accomplished. Whyte said, 'We looked at the proposals seriously. Then we took them back to the individuals who put them forward and explained where they were short. We did this in a respectful and honest way, but their proposals were short the same way I had been short earlier. They were always going to fail at implementation.'

On 3 October 2002 another information pack reiterating management's decision to outsource maintenance to ABB was issued. ABB's development team returned to Kinleith to continue their due diligence, formal contract negotiations and efforts to recruit both managers and tradespeople from the staff who would be made redundant.

The Kinleith–ABB agreement

With the outsourcing decision made, ABB and Kinleith management began to negotiate the contract that would underpin their relationship. Raymond McNickle, the commercial manager who joined the Kinleith team in 2001, led the effort to create the best financial and contractual structure.

Traditionally, maintenance outsourcing providers positioned themselves as 'ticket clippers', according to McNickle. 'They charge a handling fee for every transaction that flows through them. We knew this would not give us the business efficiency we needed.' McNickle and his ABB counterparts negotiated an arrangement designed to leverage the strengths that each player brought to the deal. 'CHH owns all the stores and all the equipment. We use CHH's size for purchasing capability and capital and ABB's culture and maintenance intelligence. That gives us the most effective model.'

The companies also decided to use CHH business systems, based on SAP, to collect all the inventory and financial records coherently in one database. The exception to this rule was Maximo, ABB's preferred maintenance management system. Kinleith agreed to purchase and implement this software to give ABB site management a tool with which they were already adept.

The two parties first agreed on a philosophy: fairness, communication and no-fault in order to focus both sides on decision making. They also established, according to King, three types of key performance indicators intended to 'balance maintenance thinking and behaviours':

- *Maintenance costs*. The outsourcing contract determined the maintenance budget for each of its five years and ABB was to manage the costs to meet that budget. To make sure that they did not quibble over money, there would be no bonuses or penalties if ABB came in within 2.5 per cent of the target (see Figure 20.4).
- *Overall equipment efficiency (OEE)*. ABB was responsible for making a targeted step-change in this metric each year. (Overall equipment efficiency, a well-established metric in the paper industry, was calculated as availability × speed × quality.) They would receive no

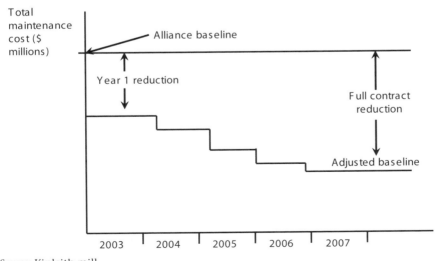

Source: Kinleith mill.

Figure 20.4 Total maintenance cost performance indicator

bonus without year-over-year improvements (see Figure 20.5). (A second component of ABB's bonus was based on the earnings before interest and taxes (EBIT) of IPC at the mill gate, tying ABB's compensation to IPC's market success.)

• *Inventory carrying cost.* ABB received half of the interest saved by reducing inventory, based on a commercially published bank rate.

The negotiators also agreed that neither organization would push the other into a loss position. Managed under an open-book approach, the maximum penalty that ABB would pay was its Kinleith earnings (before interest and taxes); and the mill would not owe bonuses if it were losing money. In addition, to keep both sides focused squarely on making the best operating decisions, Kinleith agreed to pay ABB a baseline profit based on ABB's revenue, which were mainly the salaries and wages of its employees. McNickle explained, 'To create a sustainable model, both parties have to be successful, but not gain in the extreme. ABB set its profit expectations to encourage the engagement and to get the best from the business relationship, so that's what we pay. Our approach also makes some of their decisions better. They have no inherent bias toward using their own people over contract labour. If they were paid based on actual cash costs instead of the budget, they would have an incentive to discriminate toward their own labour.'

In contrast to many outsourcing contracts, the Kinleith/ABB deal featured no automatic adjustments for inflation. McNickle was particularly animated on this point: 'I don't think an automatic inflation up-tick is consistent with fairness. Why should CHH make more funds available for maintenance if the cost of maintenance has not increased? Besides, it's impossible to calculate in the abstract. Which inflation indicator should we use? We import a large portion of our equipment spares from the US. Should we use US inflation? Instead we have adopted a philosophy of requesting variations. Either party can request a variation from the contract amount if they think circumstances warrant it.' McNickle characterized this resolution as the 'fair way, not the easy way'.

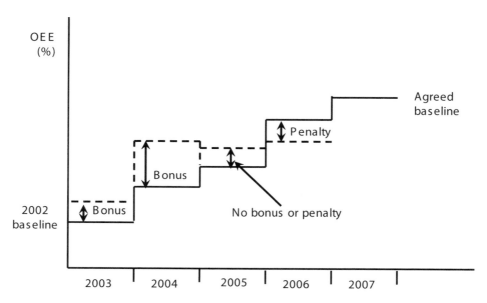

Source: Kinleith Mill.

Figure 20.5   Overall equipment efficiency key performance indicator illustration

The teams also used the contract term and renewal cycle to provide incentives for the right behaviour. They established a five-year rolling contract, renewable annually. In other words, the contract would be reviewed every year. If renewed, an additional year would be added on the end of the term. If it were not renewed, however, it would still have four years to run, during which time it could be brought back on track. This approach helped the provider avoid complacency while underscoring the parties' long-term commitment.

Over the course of four months of McNickle, Whyte and their ABB counterparts worked through the issues both at the negotiating table and outside the room. McNickle summarized, 'You have to innovate on the fly. You have to be prepared to experiment and dream. And to get the contract signed, you may have to push some things outside the deal. As long as I have a vehicle to solve the problem – a way to engage the discussion – I will agree. I trusted the ABB representatives particularly, and we built a strong relationship.' By structuring the model capably, McNickle and his team estimated they saved CHH NZ$8–10 million.

Crossing the line

While the ABB and Kinleith commercial teams worked out the contract, ABB operating management attempted to recruit tradespeople to move over to ABB. Feeling that it had lost the battle, but not the war, the union continued to resist.

All the players recognized that the mill's tradespeople held a wealth of critical tacit knowledge about the operation. In addition, the labour market for skilled trades in the rural central North Island of New Zealand was tight and small. To retain some leverage, the union advised its members to avoid even speaking to ABB about employment opportunities. Some workers reported being intimidated and even threatened with physical harm by the union brotherhood if they agreed to meet with ABB.

Hiring supervisory staff was a challenge for ABB as well. Having been alerted that their jobs were being eliminated, maintenance managers and engineers recognized that they had to do something, but many were unsure how to move forward. 'They were looking for leadership,' Whyte recalled. 'These people represented the brain trust of Kinleith. They had other options, and we were going to give them a bunch of redundancy pay to boot. We worked hard on the three natural leaders of this group to get them to go to ABB.' Whyte and Juergen Link, ABB's new site manager, had personal conversations with each person in the group to 'get them through the period of hurt and make sure they knew we wanted and valued them'. What swung the tide for two of them, according to Whyte, was a re-employment agreement. If the relationship between Kinleith and ABB did not work out, Whyte committed to rehire these individuals at Kinleith.

ABB offered the third key individual, at 58 years old, a two-year fixed contract to carry him to the point at which he would retire. Although, on the face of it, this proposal seemed sensible, to the manager concerned it implied that ABB thought he had limited value. He declined.

Whyte told his ABB counterpart not to accept 'no' as a final answer and to go back and make the manager say 'yes'. Link called on ABB's most senior executive in New Zealand to rescue the situation personally by communicating how important this individual was to their success. 'Once these three people signed up,' Whyte explained, 'all the other salaried people went along too. It was all done in a matter of days.'

With the hourly-paid employees, the story was quite different. A few workers broke ranks with their union colleagues, but by early December ABB had signed up only 10 per cent of the tradespeople it needed.

The dam broke on 19 December 2002. Having signed a formal contract with ABB the night before, Whyte sent a personal letter to each maintenance employee informing him that he would become redundant on 19 January 2003. 'It was the unshackling of the individual,' King pointed out. 'People had to finally admit that the union had failed them. They rushed into the arms of ABB.'

In accordance with the expired collective bargaining agreement, the redundancy pay was generous at about a year's wages, costing Kinleith a total of NZ$27 million. King asserted that paying this price to make all the workers redundant was a critical success factor for the initiative: 'The board asked us why we couldn't just transfer the workers to ABB and save the redundancy costs. Of course that would have meant that all the work conditions and the contract would have been transferred along with them. Instead we created a new beginning for ABB so that they could succeed where we had failed. It was the rebirth of the Kinleith maintenance organization under a new employer – ABB.'

ABB used its newly recruited salaried staff to deal with the onslaught of hiring. When ABB took over maintenance operations on 20 January 2002, it had a full complement of workers and the transition was seamless. Whyte recalled, 'The first weekend, Juergen came to me and said he didn't want any extra people working. They had a small team of six rather than the historical practice of 25 per cent of the workers. Things went just fine. The next weekend we dispensed with the weekend team entirely.' Since maintenance and engineering were now managed by ABB, Whyte accepted a new role as operations manager, with responsibility for the ABB relationship, among other duties.

Taking a strike in production

With maintenance operations finally on the right track, Kinleith management turned its attention to the rest of the transformation agenda: restructuring the production workforce and establishing a new-age contract with them. Their intention was to reduce the production staff by 60 and change the remaining workers from an hourly to a salaried pay system. After six weeks of contentious consultation and contractual negotiation discussions with union representatives, on 7 March 2003, the production workers went on strike, ostensibly because their contract had expired.[7]

The ABB maintenance workers belonged to the same union but, because they worked for a different company, they could not participate in the strike.

Over the next four weeks, the mill was able to ship finished products in stock using salaried employees. This breach of the picket line had never been achieved before in Kinleith's 50-year history. The shipping of paper inventory kept the local packaging industry operational throughout the strike. Management then pulled forward an annual scheduled shutdown[8] – the first ever run without the help of production people. At the time, commodity pulp prices were depressed and electricity costs at a peak. During the strike, plant depreciation was also deferred. As a result, the opportunity cost of the strike was contained. In addition,

---

7   Striking because of health and safety or in pursuit of a contract was lawful in New Zealand. It was unlawful to strike to object to a restructuring decision. The production workers' contract had expired in 2001.

8   By law the plant was required to shut down the boilers every year for a thorough inspection.

the Kinleith site union representative had been granted an interview with a local TV current affairs programme and had revealed that he was already earning NZ$75 000 and was looking for more. In the words of one manager, 'Because of this comment, the union lost the support of the community and the country. Many people in New Zealand would kill to make that kind of money.'

As the strike dragged on, Kinleith management mounted a communications campaign of its own. They spoke with business leaders and politicians, explaining the important role the mill played in the local economy. Towards the end of May 2003, they received a call from the union suggesting that they could work out an agreement. King stepped out of the process and, over the next two weeks, the two sides struck a deal.

The new contract came into effect on 7 June 2003, changing all production workers from an hourly to a salaried pay system. King explained, 'Through 50 years of effort, the union employees had developed 101 ways to abuse the contract. It was a local pastime. If two workers were obligated to swap shifts, they both got an increment in their pay. The new contract pays a salary for doing a job.' In addition, the shift schedule changed from eight-hour days, six on and two off, to 12-hour days, four on and four off. This change, along with a dramatic reduction in overtime hours, gave workers big blocks of free time and improved their lifestyles. King continued, 'People's focus changed from finding ways in which to increase hours and thereby enrich themselves to working smarter and enjoying a greater quality of life.'

The change to salaries also helped improve productivity. Under the old system, one manager noted, it took a gang of ten people 16 hours to change the wire around the perimeter of a drum filter. In the first month of the salaried system, it took five people eight hours. Whyte explained, 'The mindset had changed from "how can I get more hours?" to "how can I get home on time?"'

Results

In the first year of its contract, ABB achieved performance improvements that exceeded its first four years of projections – taking NZ$9 million of maintenance costs out of a budget of NZ$60 million. Overall equipment effectiveness improved by 3 per cent across the business. Despite a difficult start-up following the production strike, the second half of 2003 boasted record production. The first quarter of 2004 was even better and created a new quarterly record. Product quality levels had increased as well.

Satisfying as the production statistics were, the mill's leadership felt that they were overshadowed by early evidence of deeper changes in the culture. King pointed out, 'Management was not respected before. We have regained power and control over the workplace.' 'Normally', Whyte said, 'these projects come down from the top. This was completely the opposite. The whole process was generated by five or six people here. It made us an absolutely formidable force. The passion and commitment were huge. And that feeling has stayed with us. Instead of just trying to hold the line against the union, we now spend our time working on improving things.' King continued, 'The approach we used throughout Project Green was "ready, fire, steer". We knew we had to put our jobs on the line to get the transformation started, but we didn't know full well where it was going. Along the way, we never wavered from the strategy, and we never let go of the primary objectives.' Whyte, Bryers and King agreed that the management team was 'rock-solid'.

McNickle shared a personal example: 'Since negotiating the outsourcing contract, one ABB team-member retired and another member of the start-up team returned to Sweden. Their replacements were not party to the discussions of philosophy so they don't understand the structure of our key performance indicators, and they don't understand the commitment. I'm passionate about this, and I don't want to let it get away. Even though I have shifted out of my role, I consider it my responsibility to educate my successor.'

Contrary to what one might expect, many of the workers were also happier. One union leader called ABB 'a breath of fresh air', and Link was known as 'a most approachable man'. Another remarked, 'We are lucky to have Juergen. He has made himself available to talk.' Several mentioned the positive effects of what they called 'Juergenisms' – helpful analogies that gained a humorous twist from Link's unique use of English (see Figure 20.6). An incident involving the ABB stores manager had also flown through the mill at the speed of gossip. She explained, 'I was walking past the stores counter, and someone from the trades was standing there waiting to get a part he needed. So I got it for him.'

Under Link's guidance, ABB had taken its maintenance workforce for a two-day offsite in the forests of New Zealand. He elaborated, 'When you are taken over by an outsourcing company,

Link, originally from Germany, suggested these were often made more interesting by the fact that English was not his first language.

On managing change
- 'One thing I have learned, if your trousers are down around your ankles you need to pull your trousers up before trying to run, otherwise you just end up flat on your face.'
- 'Your proposal makes me want to bite off my nose and spit it in my face.'
- Commenting on a newly designed process for root-cause failure analysis: 'We build them a Rolls Royce but they still run around naked in the bushes.'
- 'It's a bad idea to ask a beautiful woman to dinner and then tell her the other women in the restaurant are also beautiful.'
- 'There is no point shooting into a grave; he's already dead.'
- 'Systems are like sex, you need to have it before you know what it is really about.'

On dealing with the union
- 'You can lead someone to a table full of food, but they have to feed themselves. Some people, when they are not fed complain there is nothing to eat despite all the food.'
- 'The way you shout into a forest, the forest shouts back at you.'
- 'You know, I cannot extract their brains to see what they think; they must tell us.'
- When a union wanted more money: 'Have you ever found money in the pocket of a naked man?'
- During contract negotiations with the union 'You know, communism is a better idea than capitalism; we just don't have the right people.'

On his own background
- When asked if Germany had any friendly rivalry with other countries like New Zealand and Australia: 'No, we don't have time for being petty. We just invade them all every hundred years or so.'
- 'Consultants are like seagulls; they fly around, poop on your desk, and then leave you to clean up their mess.'
- 'There is an old German saying: Who cares about that stuff I said yesterday.'

On management
- When told that a difficult customer was being pleasant 'This means he made love with his wife last night and is in a good mood. Don't worry; it won't last.'
- On building management teams: 'if you want to hunt a stag you need wolves, not chickens – then you just have to accept that wolves bite each other more often and harder than chickens do.'
- On companies merging: 'You know, if you mate an elephant and a bird – I don't know what you get.'
- On executives who do not value their people: 'They are all as bad as each other, you could put them in a bag, hit it with a stick and you will always hit the right one.'

Figure 20.6 Juergenisms: Analogies and Sayings of Juergen Link

you feel that you have not been good enough to do the job. Those emotional wounds have to be healed. Part of the ABB approach is to spend two days in the woods creating an emotional journey; the workers, together with their new manager, have to find their way to a meeting point in the middle of the woods with only a map and a compass. They struggle through cold rivers and deep valleys, and at the end we bring them together around the fire to talk. We tell them how much we value and rely on them, as they value and rely on each other.'

Link also instituted Kinleith's first Future Leaders group, inviting interested maintenance workers to volunteer. More than 15 individuals had signed up by early 2004. While all workers had experienced income reductions as part of the restructuring process, they had also gained free time. Instead of working every weekend and every statutory holiday, they now had time to spend with their families. Not all, but many, had also adopted the new business-oriented mindset that came with being customer-facing. With these early signs of change to their credit, Link and his ABB management team set about the daily effort to institutionalize a new culture.

21 Key Questions to Ask when Contracting Out Government Services: An Application to Orderly Services

Erica Susan Hewitt and Anthony E. Boardman

This chapter develops a practical guide for public-sector managers who need to decide whether to contract out a government activity or service. The guide consists of a series of five questions. These questions are based on traditional transaction cost economics and reflect the realities of contracting out in the public sector. The contracting-out decision should be based on total (social) costs including production costs, transaction costs and externality costs. Transaction costs are determined by the levels of *ex ante* competition, asset specificity, complexity/uncertainty and public-sector contract management effectiveness (both contracting expertise and subject matter expertise). To illustrate the guide, it was applied to the decision to contract out orderly services at Sir Charles Gairdner Hospital in Western Australia. Values of the key variables were determined through in-depth interviews and an extensive review of documents. The guide indicates that the service should not have been contracted out, but it was contracted out and the result was poor in terms of cost, quality and externalities. Application of the guide to public-sector contracting out could save significant government expenditures and improve service quality.

Introduction

The percentage of a country's GDP spent on healthcare in general, and on hospitals in particular, continues to rise. This trend is likely to continue. Demographic shifts, especially the aging of the baby boomer generation, increases in population and wealth, and rising expectations will increase the demand for hospital services. At the same time, governments in most jurisdictions and in most countries are trying to balance budgets or cut taxes. As the healthcare sector is large and growing, governments naturally target it for ways of cutting costs or improving efficiency.

Following the lead of the Thatcher government in the mid-1980s, many governments turned to privatization. Some privatizations had the dual benefit of raising funds that could be used to reduce both the debt and subsequent liabilities (subsidies). However, most governments are reluctant to privatize healthcare – at least not completely. To try to reduce costs and still retain sufficient control in hospitals, governments have used public–private partnerships (PPPs), which are called private finance initiatives (PFIs) in the UK, or contracting out.

A critical question is: does contracting out public-sector activities or services reduce costs while holding quality constant? The evidence on the benefits of contracting out public-sector services varies considerably. Some early studies identified cost savings in the region of 20 per cent (Domberger et al., 1986; Domberger. 1994; Farago et al., 1994). However, these studies have been criticized on a number of grounds, and more recent studies are much less positive (Boyne, 1998; Hodge, 2000; Walker and Walker 2000). The cost of contracted-out services increased in some studies (Hodge, 1996; Sclar, 1997).

The benefit or success of contracting out depends on the specific circumstances. The most fruitful basis for deciding whether or not to contract out a particular activity is transaction cost economics (TCE). Traditionally, TCE was developed for the private sector. However, as we show in this chapter, it can be 'modified' to make it applicable to public-sector services. This requires two major adaptations. First, the decision maker must recognize that the goals of the public sector are different from those in the private sector – public sector managers should care about allocative efficiency, not technical efficiency (Vining and Globerman, 1999). Second, the analysis should incorporate and place more emphasis on separability, market competitiveness and public sector contract management effectiveness.

The applicability of TCE to public-sector service contracting-out has been identified and discussed in general terms (see, for example, Boardman and Hewitt, 2004; Boston, 1991; Domberger, 1998; Domberger and Jensen, 1997; Domberger and Rimmer, 1994; Globerman and Vining, 1996; Hodge, 2000). However, there is a dearth of theoretically-based models or guides for public-sector managers that have been tested empirically. This chapter modifies traditional TCE to make it more directly applicable to the decision to contract out government services. It argues that public-sector contracting-out decisions can be based on answers to five key questions. The chapter then goes on to discuss the reasons for these five questions and explains how a well-informed manager or decision maker can provide qualitative answers to each question. It also illustrates how to answer each question by reference to the decision to contract out orderly services at Sir Charles Gairdner Hospital (SCGH) in Western Australia. The case study illustrates the usefulness and applicability of the modified TCE approach for public-sector contracting-out decisions in practice.

The second section below presents a brief review of the traditional TCE literature and introduces our suggested 'modifications' to account for key differences between the public and private sectors. This section provides the basis for the five key questions. The third section contains background information about the case study. The fourth section considers each question in turn, provides more information about the rationale for each question and shows how a well-informed decision maker faced with the decision to contract out orderly services at SCGH would have answered each question.[1] The final section contains a brief conclusion and describes what happened after the orderly service was contracted out.

---

1   The third section and the discussion of transaction costs in the fourth section draw on Boardman and Hewitt (2004).

A modified TCE approach for public-sector contracting out

TRADITIONAL TCE

Traditional TCE posits that, for profit-maximizing firms, the decision to produce within a firm or to buy in the market depends on the relative total costs of the two alternatives – that is, the sum of production costs (resource expenditure for inputs) and transaction costs (the costs associated with writing, negotiating, monitoring and enforcing the terms of transactions). Firms will choose the lowest-cost alternative. For many activities it might be advantageous to buy (or outsource) because a supplier might experience greater economies of scale (lower production costs), but this might be dominated by greater transaction costs.

In traditional TCE, transaction costs depend on frequency, asset specificity and uncertainty/complexity (Williamson, 1975).[2] Asset specificity refers to the degree to which a contractor's investments that are essential to serve a contract can be redeployed elsewhere without sacrificing productive value. It is related to the notion of 'sunk cost'. Once a contract has been awarded and the contractor has invested heavily in an asset specific investment, the sunk cost will be high. We discuss uncertainty and complexity in more depth later.

Williamson (1975) also introduced two key behavioural assumptions – opportunism and bounded rationality. Bounded rationality implies that managers cannot write a complete contract (that is, a perfect contract that anticipates and specifies *ex ante* all possible contingencies). Opportunism implies that someone may take advantage of an incomplete contract. Most importantly, one side might be 'held up' after it has made an asset-specific investment.

INCORPORATING THE SPECIFICS OF THE PUBLIC SECTOR

Public-sector managers should pay attention to allocative efficiency, not technical efficiency (Globerman and Vining, 1996). Consequently, holding quality constant, they should minimize social costs, not private (that is, government) costs in public-sector contracting-out decisions. Government production and transaction costs are only part of social costs. Employees, consumers of the service and other citizens may also experience costs (or benefits), which we call externality costs. By including these costs (or benefits), the decision is based on a broad societal perspective rather than being limited to the impact on an individual government agency's budget.

We now consider three factors that affect transactions costs in public-sector contracting out, but which are rarely emphasized in traditional TCE, mainly because they are rarely an issue in the private sector. The first factor is separability. Contracting out begins with consideration of a particular activity or group of activities (a service) that has been chosen for consideration for contracting out. Managers should be able to put a definable boundary around these activities so that they are clear about which activities government will no longer provide, but will be purchasing. In effect, it must be possible to treat the service as a separate business – possibly establishing a separate business unit or even 'corporatizing' it as a precursor to contracting out.

---

2   Williamson (1985) argues that transaction frequency is likely to increase the negotiation and haggling and increases the likelihood of market failure. However, he and other transaction cost economists have not focused on this variable. Furthermore, most studies have found no relationship between transaction frequency and hierarchical governance (for example, Anderson and Schmittlein, 1984; Anderson, 1985). For these and other reasons, we drop this variable from further consideration.

The second factor is market competition. Traditional TCE theory generally assumes that markets are competitive *ex ante*. For example, Williamson (1979, p. 246) assumes that '[p]otential suppliers for any given requirement are numerous – which is to say that *ex ante* monopoly in ownership of specialized resources is assumed away'. In most circumstances, private-sector managers would not consider using the market for the supply of essential goods or services where adequate competition did not exist. However, *ex ante* competitiveness cannot be taken for granted in markets for public-sector activities.

The third factor is contract management effectiveness. This topic is not discussed in the conventional TCE literature. This may be because private-sector managers are experienced at managing outsourcing contracts or can readily hire such expertise. However, contract management represents a relatively new endeavour for many areas of the public sector. In Australia, outsourcing involved a change in the functions of government agencies, away from direct service delivery and regulation to being a purchaser of services (Industry Commission, 1996). Osborne and Gaebler (1993) consider that contracting is one of the most difficult methods of service provision for a public organization because writing and monitoring contracts require so much skill. Contract management effectiveness incorporates two complementary skills – contract management capability and in-house knowledge (and understanding) of the business or activity being contracted out (Yates, 2000).

CONTESTABILITY, HOLD-UP AND TRANSACTION COSTS IN PUBLIC-SECTOR CONTRACTING

One of Williamson's key insights was to recognize that, although a market may be competitive *ex ante* (that is, before the contract has been let), it may not be competitive *ex post* (that is, after the contract has been let *and* a party has made the necessary investments to fulfil the contract). In the public sector, *ex post* competition (and contestability) will depend principally on the *ex ante* market structure and asset specificity.[3] Clearly, *ex post* competition will be low if *ex ante* competition is low. However, even where *ex ante* competition is high, *ex post* competition may be low if asset specificity is high. Williamson argues that, even where there 'high numbers bidding' at the outset, a 'fundamental transformation' can occur in the contracting environment so that a competitive environment can be transformed into one of bilateral monopoly (Williamson, 1985, p. 61). In such circumstances, one of the parties may act opportunistically and attempt to renegotiate the terms of the contract to their own advantage – that is, to engage in 'hold-up' (Klein, 1992; Klein, Crawford and Alchian, 1978; Lyons, 1994; Williamson, 1985). Examples of hold-up include shirking, creaming or refusing to deliver at all. Because of the risk and consequences of hold-up, both parties have an incentive to protect their positions. This can result in large transaction costs.

Transaction costs depend also on the level of complexity/uncertainty and contract management effectiveness. When *ex post* contestability is low, uncertainty/complexity is high, and when contract management effectiveness is low, the risk of hold-up is high and the associated transactions costs will be high. The key variables affecting transaction costs are *ex ante* competitiveness, asset specificity, complexity/uncertainty and public-sector management effectiveness. We refer to these variables as the transaction cost variables.

---

3   Baumol (2002, p. 163) describes contestability as 'a market into which entry is quick and easy and which faces a multitude of potential entrants, each one vigilant for an opportunity to earn profits by opening up for business in the field'. He refers to perfectly contestable markets as those 'where entry and exit can be carried out at zero cost' – that is, no asset specificity and hence no sunk costs.

A MODIFIED TCE APPROACH TO PUBLIC-SECTOR CONTRACTING OUT

The preceding discussion suggests that, when making the decision to contract out a particular activity or service, public-sector managers should ask five questions in the following order:

1. Is the activity separable?
2. Is the market competitive (*ex ante*)?
3. If the activity is contracted out, what will the transaction costs be?
4. Should the service be market tested?
5. Are the expected (post-tender) total costs of contracting out less than the expected (post-tender) total costs of in-house delivery?

If the answer to the first question is yes, the manager can proceed to the second question. If the answer is yes to that question, he/she can proceed to the third question. The expected transaction costs depend on the values of the transaction cost variables. If the transaction cost is not likely to be too high, then the manager can proceed to the fourth question. At this point, market testing should normally go ahead, unless it would be unreasonably costly. Finally, in response to question five, the manager selects the alternative with the lowest total costs.

It is presumed that the manager has a particular contract in mind at the outset. Where answers to a particular question suggest that the manager may have a contracting problem, there are two alternatives. The manager may stop the process and retain the service in-house or may redesign the contract to mitigate potential contracting problems (Globerman and Vining, 1996).

Background information about orderly services at SCGH

Orderly services at Sir Charles Gairdner Hospital (SCGH) in Western Australia were selected as a case study for four main reasons. First, orderly services were a relatively new and untested area of services contracting out and this was the first service contract of its kind in Western Australia. Second, key personnel were available and willing to participate in interviews, including a former manager for the contractor, a union representative and key hospital staff. Third, a substantial body of relevant documentation was available for review. Fourth, this contracting exercise attracted a great deal of public attention.

SCGH is one of Australia's largest public teaching hospitals. Prior to the contracting-out decision, orderlies were employed directly by SCGH. They provided assistance to clinical staff (primarily nurses) with the lifting and positioning of patients within wards and transferring patients throughout the hospital. Orderlies also performed hygiene/rubbish duties including the delivery of clean linen and sterile instruments, and the removal of unsterile instruments and soiled linen. In addition, they provided a hospital-wide courier service for specimens, mail, medical records and pharmacy items.

Under pressure from the government to contract out non-core services and with the help of consultants, SCGH developed a plan to replace the existing orderly service with two new services – an inter-ward courier/delivery type of orderly service that would be contracted out and a multi-skilled, ward-based patient service assistant (PSA) service that would be provided in-house. The courier/delivery orderly service would transfer patients throughout the hospital, and deliver and remove linen and medical instruments. The PSA service would encompass the previous ward-based activities of orderlies, including lifting and positioning of patients, plus a variety of ward-based catering and cleaning duties not previously done by orderlies. On 21 June 1995 SCGH called for Expressions of Interest (EOIs) for the supply of the courier/delivery orderly service.

The orderlies were opposed to the proposed new PSA service, although similar services had been successfully implemented in other public hospitals in Western Australia, using directly employed staff. They were also opposed to contracting out the courier/delivery orderly service. The union held stop-work meetings and placed pickets at the hospital. Negotiations with the union over the introduction of the PSA service broke down, and the matter went to the Australian Industrial Relations Commission (AIRC) for resolution.

While the AIRC was deliberating, SCGH received 12 EOIs for the courier/delivery orderly service. After evaluating these EOIs, the hospital invited three firms to submit tenders. The main elements of the contract specifications in the Request for Tender (RFT) were based on the work of a project team within the hospital with help from a private consultant (FIRM A) that had provided orderly services for many years in New Zealand hospitals (Health Western Australia and Government Health Supply Council, 1995). All firms that were invited to tender did submit bids. Shortly thereafter the AIRC handed down its ruling which was unfavourable towards the PSA model. The hospital decided not to implement the proposed PSA service, but to broaden the scope of the services that were to be contracted out. Essentially, all the traditional ward and departmental orderly tasks (for example, assisting primary care-givers with lifting, transferring and positioning patients within wards and departments, regular lifting and turning of patients in the intensive care unit (ICU), lifting and turning of orthopaedic patients as required and orderly surveillance or patient guarding), and tasks associated with the Emergency Department's internal operation were added. The only orderly services to be excluded were those in operating theatres. The RFT was adapted to reflect these changes, and the three invited tenderers were given the opportunity to submit revised tenders. The selection panel recommended that the three-year contract be awarded to FIRM A – the firm that had assisted SCGH specify the service for the RFT. The Agreement (1995) was signed on 27 October 1995, and the contractor commenced operation on 30 October 1995.

The modified TCE approach to public-sector contracting out

We now consider the five questions to be considered by management presented earlier. We explain the reasons behind each question and determine how a well-informed hospital manager would have answered each question for the orderly service before it was contracted out. These answers are generally of a qualitative nature (for example, high, medium or low). In some cases we compare the hypothetical answers to each question with information obtained after the service was contracted out. This provides some information about the accuracy of the *ex ante* answers.

In the case of SCGH, initial background discussions were held with key hospital managers to help identify the key issues and information sources for this study. A review was then undertaken of many files and documents concerning the contract and delivery of these services, including the RFT, EOIs, tenders, tender evaluation reports, consultants' reports, the Agreement (1995), letters and reports relating to contractor performance, tender preparation working papers, information memos, minutes of internal meetings, quality improvement surveys, media releases, SCGH staff bulletins, SCGH annual reports and newspaper articles. In-depth interviews were conducted with nine, closely involved people: five SCGH managers;

a clinical nurse specialist; a former manager for FIRM A; a representative of the union; and an orderly employed at SCGH until the service was contracted out. Hewitt (2004) provides more information about the study in general and the questionnaires in particular.

QUESTION 1: SEPARABILITY OF THE ACTIVITY

The first question asks: *'Is the activity under consideration separable from the other activities of the organization that will not be contracted out?'* It is important to be able to describe and define the service that is being considered for outsourcing, and to specify what activities are required and what are not required.

Managers' views differed about the ability to separate orderly services at SCGH from other services. Although orderly services appeared to have been successfully treated as a separate marketable service in New Zealand, one survey participant thought that the service in New Zealand could have been a more straightforward, non-ward-based porter/courier orderly service, similar to the one originally identified by SCGH for market testing. Separability was a potential problem because the inclusion of ward-based services, which were integrated with patient care provided by the nursing staff, made the boundaries of responsibility unclear at times. Furthermore, orderlies performed their tasks under the direction and supervision of nurses who were employed by SCGH. This situation created the potential for orderlies to receive conflicting instructions from their own managers and from hospital staff. Also, orderlies often had to wait for nurses to complete their work before they could undertake their tasks. Thus, an informed hospital decision maker would probably have concluded that separability was 'low.'

In fact, defining and providing the orderly service required by SCGH as a separate business proved to be difficult. As one manager said, 'You can't easily break down the work into manageable, bite-size pieces because it's an integrated service that directly impacts on patients and the day-to-day business of the hospital'. There was ongoing tension and argument about contractor responsibilities and performance. As one hospital interviewee commented, 'there were constant discussions about what was and what was not included in the contract'.

If, as in this case, the service under consideration is not clearly separable from activities retained in-house, then managers should consider redesigning the contract. Separability might have been improved by breaking a service into smaller activities or combining it with other activities. For example, instead of contracting out all elements of the orderly service, the contract could focus on patient support services not interconnected with the delivery of clinical services, such as catering, linen supplies and waste removal.

QUESTION 2: *EX ANTE* COMPETITIVENESS

The second question requires the decision maker to ask: *'Is the market for the activity under consideration competitive* ex ante *(that is, before the contract is let)?'* If there is already a well-established market for the activity with low barriers to entry and many competitors, the market will be very competitive. While many private-sector markets are competitive, it cannot be taken for granted in the public sector. If only government has provided the activity in the past, then market competitiveness will be low. Sclar (2000, p. 45) notes: 'if governments have been providing a service for a long time, outsiders rarely have the knowledge or expertise to do the job done by the public agency... Even when private firms provide similar services, they may not have the expertise to operate on the scale or with the scope of service required by government.'

Assessing the level of market competitiveness requires judgement. Managers need to be aware that the number of bids does not necessarily indicate the level of competitiveness. Not all bidders may be potentially acceptable in terms of price nor have the ability to deliver the requisite level of service. In some circumstances, however, only one or two bidders may be sufficient to ensure a reasonably competitive market.

No private-sector contractor was providing the proposed SCGH orderly service in Western Australia. Despite this, the call for EOIs attracted 12 responses. This high response might suggest that *ex ante* competitiveness was reasonably high. However, after evaluating the EOIs, only three businesses were invited to tender for the orderly service.[4] Of these firms, only one (the eventual successful tenderer) had any direct experience operating orderly services and this had not been in Western Australia. Thus, *ex ante* competition was actually 'low'.

If the market for the activity is not very competitive, then managers should consider redefining the activity, redesigning the contract or using other tactics to increase market competitiveness. For example, and depending on the particular circumstances, the activity might be split into a number of smaller contracts or the government agency might combine with other similar agencies to increase the size and value of the contract.

QUESTION 3: THE TRANSACTION COSTS IF THE ACTIVITY WERE CONTRACTED OUT

The third question asks: *'If this service were contracted out, would the expected transaction costs be high?'* Following our earlier discussion, transaction costs depend on *ex ante* competition (which we have already discussed in this case), asset specificity, uncertainty/complexity and contract management effectiveness.

Asset specificity

Asset specificity can pertain to physical assets (for example, specialized machine dies), sites or locations (for example, the close location of a power-generating station to a processing plant), human assets (for example, specialized training and learning by doing) and dedicated assets (for example,, investment in special-purpose plant at the behest of a particular customer). For hospital services and other labour-intensive public-sector activities, human asset specificity is most relevant.[5]

Whilst it was not necessary for orderlies to be highly skilled in a technical or academic sense, they required more initial and ongoing training than catering or general cleaning staff. Their specialized duties included responding to cardiac arrests, performing safe lifts and turns and assembling certain medical equipment. They assisted in life-threatening emergency situations, dealt carefully and sensitively with seriously unwell patients in the presence of blood and vomit, and handled deceased patients. Orderlies worked closely with clinical services (nurses) with whom they needed to share some specialized language.

A site-specific investment, which was identified by all parties interviewed, was the time and resources required to familiarize orderlies and their managers with the SCGH site, given its

---

4   The contractor interviewee noted: 'In reality there were probably only three companies which could have actually provided the service.'

5   Williamson (1991a) emphasized the importance of human asset specificity. It can include tacit skills and knowledge relevant to a particular contract; skills that cannot be easily gained (for example, through manuals and training programmes) but are acquired as a result of holding certain essential personal attributes and/or from performing the work in the specific environment over a period of time – that is, from learning on the job.

vast physical size (33 hectares) and many wards (25) and departments spread across a number of widely dispersed buildings (Health Western Australia and Government Health Supply Council, 1995, p. 29). Also, there were idiosyncratic administrative requirements, specific to the Western Australia public hospital system and to SCGH. In summary, this contract required a fairly substantial investment in recruiting and training which would have been sunk, largely because the job-specific competencies would not be useful in other contracts, such as cleaning or catering, and there was no other hospital in Western Australia contemplating contracting out orderly services. Of course, a private provider would have been able to 'buy' some of these specific skills by taking on existing orderly staff. However, not all SCGH orderlies were willing to transfer to a private contractor and not all would have been considered suitable. Overall, the level of asset specificity was 'medium'.

Complexity/uncertainty

Conceptually, uncertainty and complexity are separate variables. Complexity refers to the extent to which outputs and outcomes can be clearly specified and accurately measured.[6] Uncertainty refers to the extent to which decision makers can predict at the beginning of a contract how the situation will unfold in its entirety – that is, the extent to which they are able to specify a complete decision tree or to put all contingencies in a written contract (Williamson, 1975). While complexity and uncertainty are conceptually different, they are often present at the same time and can be difficult to separate.[7] High levels of complexity can actually create uncertainty and vice versa. Thus they are often combined together.

Complexity
The duties of orderlies may not appear to be particularly complex. Much of the work involves simple tasks such as transferring patients from one area to another, and linen delivery and removal. However, the work of orderlies includes a range of fairly specialized duties as well. Furthermore, the key issue of specifying and measuring service delivery was difficult. There had been no perceived need to specify the service in detail, and it had not been done. There was close interface between orderlies and the hospital-employed nursing staff, as discussed in the section on separability. Also, because of the industrial environment at the time, hospital management was unable to gain the cooperation of orderlies in a job analysis.

Measuring service delivery quality was difficult, too. First, it was difficult to specify and accurately measure the outputs and outcomes. For example, it was difficult to measure the way in which an orderly enhances patients' quality of life. Second, it was hard to know what would be reasonable compliance with performance specifications, such as patient waiting times. According to the interviewed hospital managers, 85 or 90 per cent compliance might have been considered adequate for catering, but not for orderly services where there might be severe financial cost implications attached to delays in collecting patients, not to mention the personal costs to patients. Third, it was difficult to specify acceptable levels of customer satisfaction, given the unpredictable demands at any particular time.

---

6   Williamson (1975, p. 23) originally referred to complexity/uncertainty as if this were only one dimension. He later dropped the reference to complexity and referred only to uncertainty, but more recently he acknowledged that ease of measurement (in other words, complexity) is probably another important transaction dimension (Williamson, 1991b). Other transaction cost economists refer to one, the other or both as variables, often not differentiating between them.
7   A contract that accounts for all possible contingencies can theoretically be written for a highly complex task (albeit extensive in detail and perhaps prohibitively costly), but not where uncertainty exists.

Most interviewees (including the contractor interviewee) rated the level of complexity of the orderly service as 'highly complex' and the others rated it as 'moderately complex'. Overall, it would be fair to rate the level of complexity for this contract as 'medium to high'.

Uncertainty

On average, SCGH had approximately 600 bed moves per day, but there was considerable variation. Unlike nursing homes or community hospitals where most patients are pre-booked for medical procedures, about 75 per cent of patients at SCGH were emergency admissions. Consequently, the numbers and types of patient at any particular time were largely unknown in advance. This uncertainty made orderly rostering difficult. The hospital could not, and did not intend to, specify the actual number of patient movements or specimen deliveries required each day, nor did it intend to specify the number of orderlies or supervisors to be employed. Also, the need for orderly services was based on the nurses' judgements. Thus, the private contractor would have to rely on the ability and professionalism of nurses to rationalize their demand for orderly services.

The scope of the service in terms of the *outcomes* specified in the contract might have been expected to change little over the contract term. However, there would have been considerable uncertainty about the appropriate staffing levels. Other areas of uncertainty were the expected levels of sick leave and workers' compensation claims and, consequently, premiums in subsequent years. Finally, at a broad level, there was also uncertainty associated with advances in technology and clinical methods, changes in government policies, changes in hospital policies and procedures, changes in consumer expectations and outbreaks of disease in the community. Overall, the level of uncertainty was 'medium'.

Public-sector contract management effectiveness

Contract management effectiveness depends on both the agency's contract management capability *per se* and on its understanding and knowledge of the specific business under consideration, both pre- and post-contractually. Agencies contemplating contracting out need both types of skill during contract negotiations and after the contract is let.

Contract management capability

In-house contract management capability depends on both technical skills and on political constraints. Technical skills pertain to writing contracts, undertaking tender processes, and monitoring and enforcing contracts. Because contracting out is a relatively new phenomenon in many areas of the public sector, these skills may be limited. Even if they do exist, public-sector agencies might be constrained from using them in the most effective manner where a government pursues an ideological commitment for or against contracting out.

The orderly contract represented the first major service contract in Western Australia. SCGH had no previous experience in contracting out a comparable service and it had not been formally monitoring the existing orderly service. Given the infancy of contracting for services across government generally and within SCGH specifically, management was not well prepared. Furthermore, politics aggravated the situation. Consistent with government policy, all non-clinical or non-core services provided by the hospital, such as orderly services, catering, cleaning, waste management and linen supplies, had been identified as candidates for contracting out. The orderly service was probably selected as the first one for market testing because it was thought to be less efficient than other non-clinical services and was proving difficult to reform. Given the public interest in this contract there was a perceived imperative for contracting out to 'succeed', thereby potentially limiting the hospital's ability to manage the contract efficiently and increasing transaction costs (and/or production costs). In sum, SCGH did not have the requisite technical contracting skills and was constrained by politics. Thus, the hospital's contract management capability was 'low'.

Knowledge and understanding of the business

Public-sector agencies need to have a sound understanding of, and specialist knowledge and expertise in, the activity they are contracting out. This is necessary in order to specify the requirements and to monitor contractor performance effectively. Retaining adequate knowledge of how to operate the business reduces the potential for information asymmetry in favour of the incumbent contractor once the contract has been let and may ensure also a certain level of *ex post* contestability.[8]

The hospital's understanding of the orderly business and its capacity to directly operate the service was high and was expected to remain high even if the service were contracted out. Although SCGH would no longer directly employ orderly staff, managers retained to manage the contract would have strong clinical and hospital administration backgrounds and a sound understanding of the requirements of the orderly service at SCGH. Also, nursing staff would continue to provide direction and supervision to the private orderlies. Consequently, the hospital's understanding of the requirements and its ability to monitor the implementation would remain 'high'.

Although SCGH's knowledge of the business was 'high', its contract management capability was 'low' and, thus, overall management effectiveness was 'moderately low'.[9]

Overall assessment of expected transaction costs

Ex post contestability (after the contract is let) depends on *ex ante* market competitiveness, which was 'low', and asset specificity, which was 'medium'. Consequently, *ex post* contestability was likely to be 'low' – even lower than *ex ante* competitiveness. The entry barriers for alternative suppliers would have been quite high because of the substantial time and resources that they would need to invest in specific skills and organizational knowledge. Given that *ex post* contestability would be 'low', complexity/uncertainty would be 'medium to high' and public-sector management effectiveness would be 'moderately low', then the risk of hold-up and the expected transaction costs if the service were contracted out would be 'high'.

With limited contestability once the contract had been let, together with the difficulty in clearly specifying and measuring service requirements, there would have been significant potential for an incumbent contractor to behave opportunistically. This problem was exacerbated by a government that required the market testing of all 'non-core' hospital services and was keen to make it 'work'. With one exception, all interviewees (including the contractor interviewee) rated the potential for the contractor to behave opportunistically as 'very high' or 'moderately high'.

The threat of contractor hold-up, even for a brief period, would have presented a serious problem for SCGH. Withholding or otherwise cutting back or shirking on orderly services could seriously compromise clinical services, at least in the short term. For example, as one

---

8   Tactics that can be considered to assure an adequate level of knowledge of the business post- contractually could include retaining some level of operational/technical staff and excluding successful contractors from engaging key agency personnel for a specified period.

9   The combined value of contract management effectiveness variable depends on the multiplicative effect of the two components – each one is critical, and a low value of either one is potentially very damaging.

manager noted, 'surgery would have to be cancelled if clean linen deliveries were stopped or rubbish was not removed'. This would enhance the bargaining power of the incumbent contractor. The difficulty of replacing the contractor at short notice was acknowledged by the former contractor employee who stated that 'because of the size and complexity of the contract, delivering an orderly service was not something that could be done overnight'. Although hospital personnel felt generally that SCGH could have returned the service to in-house delivery, the transition costs and the dislocation and consequences for patients in the interim could have been considerable. In conclusion, the transaction costs of negotiating and writing a tight contract and monitoring, managing and enforcing the contract to minimize the risk of hold-up were 'high'.

QUESTION 4: MARKET-TESTING

The fourth question asks: 'Should the service be market-tested through a formal competitive tendering process?' This question requires the decision maker to sum the anticipated total costs (transaction costs, production costs plus externality costs) for contracting out the activity and for retaining it in-house. If the former are less than the latter, then the activity should be market-tested and the decision-maker should move to the final question.

Estimates of the total cost for each alternative can be obtained after the activity has been put out to tender. Thus one might argue question 4 is unnecessary. However, asking this question before going through the tender process might save the considerable costs that are associated with the competitive tendering and contracting processes in the public sector.

Answering question 4 requires estimates of the production costs and externality costs for the two alternatives. Production costs should include the contractor's expected costs plus transition costs. Externality costs can be estimated by assessing the likely impact of contracting out versus in-house provision on the quality of the service and considering any other third-party impacts (including other branches of government or the contractor). Negative externalities could take the form of cost-shifting to other public-sector agencies, to other levels of government, to other employees or to other members of the community.

At the pre-tender stage, it would have been anticipated that production costs for a contractor (with its potential ability to reduce labour costs, eliminate inefficient workplace practices and increase productivity) would be similar to, or slightly lower than, those for SCGH (with its experience, tacit skills and potential economies of scope). A contractor's expected quality would have been similar to, or slightly lower than, SCGH's given its incentives and lack of localized experience. Perhaps more importantly, the contractor might also create some negative externalities. For example, because of the blurring of some responsibilities between orderlies and nursing staff, and because of the general professionalism of nurses, nurses might take on additional duties in the event of inadequate numbers of orderlies being supplied. There would also be potential negative impacts on former orderlies should they be forced to take redundancies or new jobs with different shift patterns or lower perceived status. Overall, contracting out looked like the higher-cost alternative – it had larger transaction costs, not significantly lower production costs and potentially worse externality costs.

QUESTION 5: EXPECTED (POST-TENDER) TOTAL COSTS OF CONTRACTING OUT VERSUS IN-HOUSE DELIVERY

Question 5 asks: 'Are the expected (post-tender) total costs of contracting out less than the expected (post-tender) total costs of in-house delivery?' Having decided to market-test an activity, managers can use the additional information obtained through the competitive tendering process to make their final estimate of total costs under the two options – contract out or retain in-house.

The Tender Evaluation Committee found that the middle-priced tender was the best value at AU$1 982 840 per year (in 1995 dollars). This bid was significantly lower than the in-house cost, even after taking into consideration the transition costs.[10] The main driver for the lower price was the number of orderlies, not wages, which would be unchanged.[11] The winning bid was based on 56 full-time equivalents (FTEs), 35 per cent fewer than SCGH had identified in the RFT as the number currently performing the duties. Although SCGH recognized that the number of orderlies would be 'tight', the hospital concluded that the contractor should be able to provide the required standard of service, given its previous success in New Zealand. However, not everyone (especially the former orderlies and the union) was convinced that the contractor could perform the service effectively with 56 orderlies. A manager making the contracting-out decision would have reasonably concluded that the transaction costs, quality impacts and other negative externalities would have been worse than previously anticipated. Despite the contractor's lower apparent production costs, based on tender price, the total cost of contracting out was likely to be higher than the total cost of retaining the service in-house. Thus, the modified TCE approach would indicate that the service should not be contracted out.

Conclusion

This chapter suggests that the decision to contract out a public-sector service can be based on the answers to five key questions. Thus, managers can approach a contracting-out decision in a relatively straightforward way. The rationale for the five questions is based on traditional TCE, with modifications to reflect the special characteristics of the public sector. Public-sector managers should retain a service in-house or contract it out, depending on which alternative has the lowest total costs considering production costs, transaction costs and externality costs. The key variables affecting transaction costs are *ex ante* competitiveness, asset specificity, uncertainty/complexity, and contract management effectiveness.

This chapter provides a rationale for each of the five questions and demonstrates how to answer each question by drawing on the decision to contract out orderly services at SCGH. The questions and the answers to each question are summarized in Table 21.1. The answers suggest that the service should not have been contracted out. This was reasonably clear from the answers to the early questions. There were problems with the separability of the service and *ex ante* competitiveness was 'moderately low'. Question 3 requires estimation of transaction costs if the service were contracted out. Given 'low' *ex ante* competitiveness, 'medium' asset specificity, 'medium/high' complexity/uncertainty, and 'moderately low' contract management effectiveness, *ex post* contestability would be 'low', the risk of contractor hold-up would be

---

10   Transition costs are the one-off costs associated with a change to private-sector provision. In this case they included redundancy payments to orderlies displaced by the contract, transition payments to orderlies taking up positions with the private contractor and income maintenance for orderlies who remained as permanent public servants but would be redeployed in lower-level positions with less or no shift/weekend work. Partially offsetting these costs was the revenue from the sale of assets, such as from the sale of equipment to the new service provider.

11   The contractor indicated that it would achieve efficiency gains by having a centralized service and two-way radios, as it did in New Zealand. However, this should have raised questions as the hospital had just successfully switched to a more decentralized orderly service, which had reduced the number of orderlies employed and resulted in significant savings.

'high' and transaction costs would be 'high'. Given the high anticipated transaction costs if the service were contracted out and the similar levels of production costs that would have been predicted at this stage, the service should probably not have been put out to tender. However, it *was* put out to tender, and the price tendered by the preferred contractor was lower than anticipated. Nonetheless, despite the lower contracted production costs, the transaction costs and externalities of contracting out were likely to be high, suggesting that the total cost of contracting out would have been higher than the total cost of retaining the service in-house.

In fact, the service was contracted out. Despite the fixed-price contract, the contractor provided an inferior service at a higher cost than was agreed in the contract. In addition, SCGH incurred large transition costs and substantially higher transaction costs than would have been necessary with in-house delivery. Also there were a number of negative externalities.

Table 21.1   Summary of applying the five key questions to the decision to contract out the SCGH orderly service

Question	Answer (value)
Q. 1: Separability?	Low
Q. 2: *Ex ante* competitiveness?	Low
Comment	Should consider tactical improvements
Q. 3: *Ex post* contestability, risk of hold-up and transaction costs if services are contracted out?	
Ex ante competitiveness	Low (from above)
Asset specificity	Medium
Complexity/uncertainty – complexity – uncertainty	Medium/high – medium/high – medium
Public-sector contract management effectiveness – contract management capability – knowledge of the business	Moderately low – low – high
Ex post contestability	Low
Risk of hold-up	High
Transaction costs	High
Comment	Should consider tactical improvements
Q. 4: Market-test or not?	
Transaction costs	High (from step 3)
Production costs	Similar to in-house
Quality	Adequate but lower than in-house
Externalities	Mostly negative
Comment	Should consider tactical improvements
Q. 5: Expected total cost of contracting out versus the total cost of retaining in-house?	
Transaction costs	High – higher than in-house
Production costs	Lower than in-house
Quality	Lower than in-house
Externalities	Mostly negative
Total (social) costs	Higher
Comment	Should not contract out

The transaction costs for the hospital were very high. It had to spend considerable time monitoring, managing and maintaining the contract. The tender process and negotiations involved many hours of senior hospital staff time and, once the contract commenced, considerable time was devoted to following up incident reports and resolving complaints, as well as discussing performance and dealing with internal users of the service, the contractor and legal advisers. Early in the contract the hospital appointed a full-time contract manager. In addition, numerous directors, the manager of Patient Support Services and finance and administrative support staff spent a great deal of time on the contract. Clinical staff spent also more time than expected in supervising and monitoring the new orderlies and often performed orderlies' tasks themselves. Nurses and patient support staff spent several hours each week at customer liaison meetings identifying problems with the contract and attempting to find solutions.

In addition, the quality of the orderly service was lower than anticipated, and there were many instances when the contractor either engaged in or threatened post-contractual hold-up of services in some way. In order to provide an acceptable level of service, the hospital performed extra work and incurred substantial costs. The hospital agreed to pay the contractor for an additional 4.4 FTEs from 1 January 1997. It also agreed to reduce the work specifications and it performed a number of the contractor's management responsibilities, such as preparing rosters, keeping personnel records, providing personnel advice to orderlies, and monitoring quality through quality surveys and regular liaison meetings. According to one hospital manager, 'the hospital added more money for support and made significant changes to address problems, and get something we could all live with'.

There was a general consensus that the contract should have been terminated early, but legal advice indicated that terminating the contract would be difficult as it was 'not tight enough'. A hospital interviewee stated that 'we used to get a lot of arguments about what was in and what was not, because the contract was not clearly specified'. The contractor interviewee indicated that it was impossible to get an accurate measure of performance, particularly since 'the hospital did not know what they wanted us to measure because they had never measured it themselves'.

This case study indicates that the cost of incorrect contracting out decisions can be considerable. The exercise of contracting out the service did ultimately effect the implementation of a more efficient and effective type of orderly service. However, the total (social) costs were high. This case study suggests that, by answering five key questions, decision-makers can make efficient and effective decisions about contracting out services that have traditionally been provided directly by government. Application of the questions as a practical guide to public-sector managers facing contracting-out decisions could save significant government expenditures and improve service quality.

References

Agreement (1995), *Agreement between [X] Chairman of the Government Health Supply Council (Customer) and [FIRM A] (Contractor)*, 27 October 1995.

Anderson, E. (1985), 'The salesperson as outside agent or employee: a transaction cost analysis', *Marketing Science*, vol. 4, no. 3, pp. 234–54.

Anderson, E. and Schmittlein, D.C. (1984), 'Integration of the sales force: an empirical examination', *Rand Journal of Economics*, vol. 15, no. 3, pp. 385–95.

Baumol, W.J. (2002), *The Free-market Innovation Machine. Analysing the Growth Miracle of Capitalism*, Princeton University Press, Princeton, NJ.

Boardman, A.E. and Hewitt, E.S. (2004), 'Problems with contracting out government services: lessons from orderly services at SCGH', *Industrial and Corporate Change*, vol. 13, no. 6, pp. 917–29.

Boston, J. (1991), 'The theoretical underpinnings of public sector restructuring', J. Boston, J. Martin, J. Pallot and P. Walsh (eds), in *Reshaping the State: New Zealand's Bureaucratic Revolution*, Oxford University Press, Auckland, pp. 1–23.

Boyne, G.A. (1998), 'Competitive tendering in local government: a review of theory and evidence', *Public Administration – An International Quarterly*, vol. 76, Winter, pp. 695–712.

Domberger, S. (1998), *The Contracting Organization: A Strategic Guide to Outsourcing*, Oxford University Press, New York.

Domberger, S. (1994), 'Public sector contracting. Does it work?', *The Australian Economic Review*, 3rd Quarter, pp. 91–96.

Domberger, S. and Jensen, P. (1997), 'Contracting out by the public sector: theory, evidence, prospects', *Oxford Review of Economic Policy*, vol. 13, no. 4, pp. 67–78.

Domberger, S. and Rimmer, S. (1994), 'Competitive tendering and contracting in the public sector: a survey', *International Journal of the Economics of Business*, vol. 1, no. 3, pp. 439–53.

Domberger, S., Meadowcroft, S. and Thompson, D. (1986), 'Competitive tendering and efficiency: the case of refuse collection', *Fiscal Studies*, vol. 7, no. 4, pp. 69–87.

Farago, S., Hall, C. and Domberger, S. (1994), *Contracting of Services in the Western Australian Public Sector*, The University of Sydney, Graduate School of Business, Sydney.

Globerman, S. and Vining, A.R. (1996), 'A framework for evaluating the government contracting-out decision with an application to information technology', *Public Administration Review*, vol. 56, no. 6, pp. 577–86.

Health Western Australia and Government Health Supply Council (1995), *Request for Tender for the Provision of Orderly (Porter) and Courier/Delivery Services to Sir Charles Gairdner Hospital*, Tender Number HSC 560/95.

Hewitt, E.S. (2004), 'A transaction cost approach for evaluating public sector contracting out: evidence from four case studies', DBA thesis, GSM, University of Western Australia.

Hodge, G.A. (1996), *Contracting out Government Services: A Review of International Evidence*, Montech, Melbourne.

Hodge, G.A. (2000), *Privatization: An International Review of Performance*, Westview Press, Boulder, CO.

Industry Commission (1996), *Competitive Tendering and Contracting by Public Sector Agencies*, Report no. 48, 24 January, Australian Government Publishing Service, Canberra.

Klein, B., Crawford, R.G. and Alchian, A.A. (1978), 'Vertical integration, appropriable rents, and the competitive contracting process', *Journal of Law and Economics*, vol. 21, no. 2, pp. 297–326.

Klein, B. (1992), 'Contracts and incentives: the role of contract terms in assuring performance', in L. Wering and H. Wijkander (eds), *Contract Economics*, Blackwell, Oxford, pp. 149–72.

Lyons, B.R. (1994), 'Contracts and specific investment: an empirical test of transaction cost theory', *Journal of Economics and Management Strategy*, vol. 3, no. 2, pp. 257–78.

Osborne, D. and Gaebler, T. (1993), *Reinventing Government: How the Entrepreneurial Spirit is Transforming the Public Sector* (2nd edn), The Penguin Group (Plume), Harmondsworth.

Rimmer, S.J. (1994), 'Competitive tendering and contracting: theory and research', *The Australian Economic Review*, 3rd Quarter, pp. 79–85.

Sclar, E. (1997), *The Privatization of Public Service. Lessons from Case Studies*, Economic Policy Institute, Washington D.C.

Sclar, E.D. (2000), *You Don't Always Get What You Pay For: The Economics of Privatization*, Cornell University Press, Ithaca, NY.

Sir Charles Gairdner Hospital (1998), *Tender Evaluation Report, HSC 234/98 – Provision of Hospital Services Assistants to Sir Charles Gairdner Hospital*.

Vining, A.R. and Globerman, S. (1999), 'Contracting-out health care services: a conceptual framework', *Health Policy*, vol. 46, pp. 77–96.

Walker, B. and Walker, B.C. (2000), *Privatisation: Sell off or Sell out? The Australian Experience*, ABC Books, Sydney.

Williamson, O.E. (1975), *Markets and Hierarchies: Analysis and Antitrust Implications*, The Free Press, New York.

Williamson, O.E. (1979), 'Transaction-cost economics: the governance of contractual relations', *Journal of Law and Economics*, vol. 22 no. 2, pp. 233–61.

Williamson, O.E. (1985), *The Economic Institutions of Capitalism: Firms, Markets, Relational Contracting*, The Free Press, New York.

Williamson, O.E. (1991a), 'Comparative economic organization: the analysis of discrete structural alternatives', *Administrative Science Quarterly*, vol. 36, pp. 269–96.

Williamson, O.E. (1991b), 'Strategizing, economizing and economic organization', *Strategic Management Journal*, vol. 12, Winter, pp. 361–401.

Yates, A. (2000), *Government as an Informed Buyer: Recognising Technical Expertise as a Crucial Factor in the Success of Engineering Contracts*, The Institution of Engineers Australia, Barton.

22 *Offshoring and the SME*
Julian Howison and Amit Mehta

Outsourcing has been recognized as a common business practice for decades. However, over the past decade, global market forces, driven by developments in technology and communications, have changed the nature of competition and, as a consequence, the outsourcing paradigm has taken a more strategic hue. The same forces have also facilitated new opportunities as boundaries and distance have been erased, and the offshore relocation or 'offshoring' of service operations – in particular, information technology (IT) services – has become a compelling way for large Western-based companies to optimize their cost base and improve operational efficiency.

To date, the vast majority of the work done in the IT offshoring field has focused on how the large, multinational corporations (MNCs) have utilized offshore resources to reduce their costs. Research figures estimate that more than 50 per cent of the American Fortune 500 firms and an increasing proportion of Western European and Japanese firms are users of offshoring. Small and medium sized enterprises (SMEs) are relatively new users of offshoring, and little has been done to investigate their drivers and barriers to offshoring. We posited that SMEs face a number of unique challenges in considering offshoring.

This chapter focuses on how a SME managed the process of offshoring software development and, specifically, how it mitigated the risks of offshore outsourcing by breaking down a large project into various distinct phases and then adopting different strategies in each phase. This case study highlights the types of offshoring strategies used, their applicability to specific project scenarios, and their abilities to achieve project and organizational goals.

Introduction

Small and midsize businesses and outsourcers seem to be made for each other. One typically lacks skills and the other specialises in delivering those skills at an affordable price.

(Brown and Browning, 2003, p.1)

Outsourcing, the focus of this chapter, is an arrangement in which one company employs services from another company to achieve a particular function or objective rather than using in-house resources. The outsourcing trend, already well established in areas such as catering, security, payroll and property management, is becoming increasingly common in more complex business functions such as information technology (IT), marketing, human resources (HR) and management accounting. Although outsourcing is an important factor in today's business environment, there is no single and generally accepted definition (De Looff, 1995). Gilley and Rasheed shared similar views and observed that there was confusion in the management literature about the meaning of the term 'outsourcing' and added, 'generally, the definition of outsourcing used in studies of the subject is so broad that it included virtually any good or service that an organization procures from outside firms' (2000, p. 764). Other offbeat definitions include 'giving the ROI without the I,' (Kaiser, 2002, p. 6) and 'spending rather than managing' (Philips, 1992, p. 3).

Globalization in the IT industry has been making headlines in the last couple of years; especially as more and more 'service-sector' jobs are relocated offshore. As the world economy becomes more interdependent and as poorer nations are developing capabilities in line with more advanced Western developed nations, IT offshoring is shaping up to be one of the decade's most important business trends. The rapid growth observed in recent years has been accelerated by the economic downturn in the West and the reduced labour costs that can be obtained by moving service-based business processes to lower-cost countries. As with most complex outsourcing, other factors influencing decisions to outsource IT include not only the availability of skilled resources at lower cost, but also improved flexibility, increased capacity and access to niche expertise and experience.

Van Hoorn (1979) argues that small and medium-sized enterprises (SMEs) lack the managerial experience, financial resources and methodological know-how to manage offshore projects in the way that large firms do. As a result, SMEs may face high levels of risk compared to larger firms when 'going offshore'. Further, for a SME, the failure of an IT project will almost invariably prove to be a major financial setback. This case study focuses on how a SME managed the process of offshoring software development and, specifically, how it mitigated the risks by adopting a number of different models, each suited to the requirements of the different stages of the process.

The chapter is structured as follows. The next two sections briefly describe the two firms – the outsourcing firm and the outsourced firm or the supplier. The factors considered in the outsourcing firm are its intentions and the main drivers for offshoring, as well as its unique capabilities and offshoring methodology. This is followed by a discussion of the risks inherent in offshoring and the specific project details and descriptions of the various phases and strategies that were employed to execute the project. Finally, the chapter ends with the key learning points from the case study, with a short concluding note.

ABC Ltd

ABC is the UK market leader in the provision of construction industry market intelligence. The company is over 70 years old, has over a hundred employees and a turnover of £5-6million. ABC provides information on the profile and status of major construction projects to many of the top construction companies, subcontractors, building suppliers, architects and surveyors throughout the UK. Traditionally, this information was supplied through a combination of paper-based reports (bulletins) and a PC-based software tool. ABC wanted to publish these bulletins online (on the World Wide Web) and to provide extensive 'search' facilities to the end-users. This was a new technology business initiative with a number of constraints, including an initial low budget, and could be successful only if done cost-effectively. Being a small firm with limited resources and a very small IT department, ABC was confronted by an array of bewildering choices in a rapidly changing market. It faced a difficult and challenging task of making the appropriate decisions for its businesses. However, the budgetary constraints and need for additional, niche IT skills drove the company to consider executing this project offshore.

In considering offshoring, a number of barriers and risks were impending, the most significant being the need to identify the right supplier. This was compounded by the fact that ABC had no prior experience in dealing with suppliers located in a different corner of the globe. The advantages that ABC sought from offshore were reduced costs, availability of skilled resources and faster time-to-market for the new service.

ARRK Group

Arrk Group combines the strengths of a local UK-based IT consultancy tightly integrated with a wholly-owned Indian back office, and is thus uniquely positioned to provide a complete solution to the needs of its customers. Arrk's UK consultants and project managers have collectively managed over 600 man-years of offshore development, and its Indian team are tuned in to the needs of UK companies. Arrk offers customers an end-to-end service encompassing strategic planning, change management, transition execution and high-quality, cost-efficient offshore delivery of IT development and support projects.

ARRK'S UNIQUE CAPABILITY

Arrk's unique capability stems from the fact that it is a hybrid UK/Indian company comprising a front-end located in the customer's domain closely coupled with an in-house technical team based in India. The experience that Arrk's UK-based consultants have gained as project managers and delivery technicians, combined with a wealth of knowledge gleaned in creating and managing offshore operations, gives them a unique insight into the day-to-day challenges likely to be faced by ABC's management and staff. Arrk's Indian operation has been carefully tuned and optimized to the needs of the UK market and these two teams, one in the UK and one in India, work hand-in-hand to deliver the customer's needs. These two elements are brought together by a single coherent set of values and processes managed by a single senior leadership team drawn from the UK and Indian companies and collectively responsible for both operations at both sites. This is quite unique in itself and differs significantly from the traditional offshoring model in which the offshore supplier's presence in the customer's domain is little more than a small 'front-end' sales office.

Risk and offshore outsourcing

There are a number of significant risks inherent in the traditional 'direct' offshore engagement model in which a UK customer contracts directly with an offshore-based supplier in a country such as India or Vietnam. These are driven by the supplier's lack of domain knowledge, poor project management skills, differences in language and culture, time and distance issues, infrastructure weaknesses and legal and commercial issues associated with trading overseas. This is often further compounded by the customer's lack of experience in running an end-to-end service delivery operation with an offshore component. These issues are especially acute where the customer is a small firm with limited resources and budgets. In many instances, offshoring is not simply about reducing the maintenance costs of steady-state systems, but also of providing an enhanced capability (quality/capacity/efficiency) that is responsive to business needs. There is a real danger in direct offshoring of the service delivery agents becoming disconnected from the customer, thus making it very difficult for them to serve the needs of the business end-user and thereby making matters worse rather than better. Brown and Browning (2003) argue that, in this sense, the traditional direct offshoring model is ill-suited to smaller organizations.

Lee (2003) mentions five basic approaches to offshoring that are commonly used by multinational corporations (MNCs). Following the right approach to offshoring is extremely crucial for success of the project and can mitigate many of the potential risks. The three primary options are:

1. outsourcing;
2. creating a wholly owned subsidiary also known as captive unit; or
3. partnering with a local company or MNC in a joint venture.

Two lesser-known options are indirect offshoring and purchasing a turnkey operation. Each approach has its own advantage and disadvantage, so choosing the right model is largely a question of risks and priorities (Lee, 2003).

Companies that are prohibited from working offshore – generally due to legislation, public pressure or lack of experience may get round these barriers by use of indirect offshoring. Indirect offshoring involves hiring a local firm that has access to offshore resources. Benefits pass through the hired firm in the form of lower costs, higher quality and reduced development time (Lee, 2003). A rare, but highly desirable, scenario is an integrated end-to-end model that successfully integrates customer and delivery agents within a single organizational framework of common processes, congruent capabilities and synergistic values.

To address the issues outlined above, Arrk has developed a tightly integrated onshore/offshore model that enables its customers to leverage the cost savings associated with offshore outsourcing without compromising on quality or increasing risk. This model is the result of almost six years of working with small to medium-sized businesses and the belief that all types of outsourcing involve defining, identifying and managing risks and issues, implementing solutions to mitigate these risks, and understanding the customer's needs as they evolve.

Project 'Delta'

ABC provides business intelligence services to many of the top construction companies, subcontractors, building suppliers, architects and surveyors throughout the UK. Massive amounts of data are required to drive the production of these services. Until the introduction of Delta, the web-based system launched by ABC, all data were handled by the company's internal system, with paper-based reports (bulletins) being generated manually and distributed by 'snail mail'.

'Generating bulletins was a manual process, which was prone to error. One of the main objectives was to remove the effort and delay caused by the manual process,' commented the director responsible for IT at ABC.

In order for clients and other end-users to access updated information on the various construction projects being executed in the UK, they had to wait until ABC distributed the next report. This caused three main problems:

- The contents of the reports were common to all clients and they often had to wade through massive amounts of useless data to find the information that they were looking for.
- The reports took a long time to generate and thus were often out-of-date by the time they were received by end-users.
- All reporting was done on a 'push' basis – it wasn't possible for suppliers or customers to get data on demand – they simply had to wait until the reports were sent to them.

'We wanted to provide our customers and suppliers the ability to get the information they needed when they needed it,' commented the IT director, 'rather than asking and waiting for it to be compiled.'

ABC decided to build a web-based system that would allow customers to probe the data held in its databases and pull down the information relevant to them on an 'as-needed' basis.

The solution developed by ABC comprised the following distinct parts:

1. the creation of a central data warehouse application to store, search and access all the information;
2. the development and deployment of web-based 'user-defined' templates that would allow users to probe the data and produce reports on an 'as-needed' basis;
3. a document-sharing repository that could be used to sort and distribute project-related documents pertinent to a particular user group, ensuring that all parties working on a project were using the most up-to-date versions of project documents.

Although offshoring was the IT director's initiative, it was welcomed by other senior managers in ABC and well supported by a very strong business case. Having taken the decision to offshore, ABC faced a number of challenges, the first one being with whom and where to offshore. Aside from the possibility of engaging Arrk, ABC also weighed up two other options; insourcing temporary IT staff to expand their in-house team or working directly with an Indian-based offshore vendor. However, insourcing temporary UK-based IT staff would cost more and require a lot of ABC management time. ABC also had no prior experience in offshoring, and instinct suggested that direct offshoring with an Indian company was too risky. This was compounded by the fact that ABC had set a very low budget for the initial pilot project and had a very small in-house IT department with limited experience of large-scale IT development. Hence it was decided to engage Arrk and utilize offshore resources through them.

Over the following four years Arrk developed a large-scale online data warehouse application and an associated complex set of routines that fed data from legacy systems. Users access the data through a number of different web-based tools. The project consisted of three phases. Once the first phase of the Delta product had been developed, Arrk provided maintenance and second-line support for the production system. This included capacity planning, performance tuning, release management, security and disaster recovery procedures. At present, the system has over 2000 users and averages 200 log-ons per day. Arrk now supports and maintains the service from 'ABC's virtual offshore development centre (VODC)' within Arrk's Indian office, which carries out all support and maintenance work and liaises directly with the customer.

PHASE I

The IT department, with the IT director's guidance, prepared detailed requirements for the first phase of this project. They decided to begin by outsourcing a small part as a pilot project. The requirements for the pilot contained all the specifications, including timelines.

ABC and Arrk decided to use the *indirect* offshoring model for this phase, where the project was staffed by a UK-based senior consultant (project manager) and a development team based in India. All development work was carried out offshore with the onshore project manager carrying out account management and other customer-facing activities. The offshore team comprised a project leader, Oracle developers, web developers, DBA/technical architects and testers. This enabled ABC to avoid the most common risks of offshoring. ABC staff and management interacted primarily with Arrk's UK consultants and had limited contact with Arrk's technical team in India. Thus issues related to culture and language differences were avoided. Also, having employed Arrk (a British company), there were no hidden costs in the contract and the issues related to time differences and distance had no direct impact on ABC. However, this was at the cost of increased dependence on the UK-based project manager, which inevitably created an 'added layer' in the communication chain, making some processes more complex and somewhat reducing the potential cost savings.

There were quite a few drivers for this phase, one of the main ones being risk mitigation. The pilot phase was conceived as a low-cost, low-risk way of experimenting with offshoring and with the relationship with the supplier.

Phase I was estimated to be completed in four months and was successfully completed within the deadline, with ABC facing hardly any major issues. This was due mainly to Arrk's tightly integrated onshore/offshore operation managed by a strong, global service delivery management team.

The main benefits to ABC from this phase included greater understanding of the issues surrounding offshoring, which led to increased business confidence. They were geared up to take more challenges in the future. Despite using the indirect model they still achieved substantial cost savings, one of the main objectives. ABC performance risk was mitigated by fixed-price contracting during this phase.

To summarize this phase, Arrk UK, which in turn interacted with Arrk India, provided both the management/control and technical solution. ABC did not interact directly with Arrk India at any time (see Figure 22.1).

PHASE II

After the success of Phase I, ABC took the decision to go ahead with the next phase, which included extending the functionality provided by the pilot project. One of the critical factors of this phase was that the requirements were not as clear as the first phase and the project involved more technical complexities and risks. On the other hand, the budgets were increased slightly as a result of greater confidence and a stronger business case.

The two main drivers for ABC in this phase were increased flexibility and faster time-to-market. ABC wanted to increase rapidly the sophistication of its web-based reporting tools to attract more clients and gain a larger market share. Thus an iterative approach to developing the software was adopted, which allowed the project to be broken down into a number of smaller releases, each happening at two- to three-month intervals. Evolving requirements meant frequent discussions with the development team. Collectively, these measures increased the complexity and risk of the project. This, combined with a strong sense of urgency, resulted

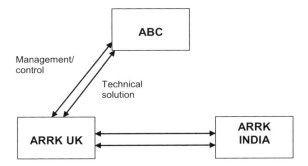

Figure 22.1   The indirect offshoring process used during Phase I of the project

in ABC and Arrk deciding to adopt a different model for this phase, temporarily relocating the entire technical team onshore at Arrk's office in the UK. The UK project manager continued to run the project, mainly because of his strong business analysis capability and knowledge of ABC's business.

As Phase II was broken down into several sub-phases the support element that Arrk was responsible for grew with each sub-phase. In total, Phase II lasted almost 18 months and was successfully accomplished within the budgets. The costing in this phase was based on resources utilized on a time and material (T&M) basis.

One of the main benefits to ABC from this phase were the frequent and direct interactions with Indian programmers, facilitated by Arrk's UK consultants, thus familiarizing them with the Indian work culture. This further increased their confidence in offshoring.

To summarize this phase, Arrk UK provided the project management/control while the technical solution was provided by Arrk India as illustrated in Figure 22.2.

PHASE III

Having successfully completed two phases and the majority of development work, the third phase consisted of supporting and maintaining the system, with limited new development activity. The main tasks included in this phase were minor bug-fixing, error-handling and improving the database efficiency. ABC and Arrk concluded that these activities could be carried out offshore, and thus the entire team was relocated back to India. The main drivers here were a desire for simplified management and technical process and increased cost efficiency.

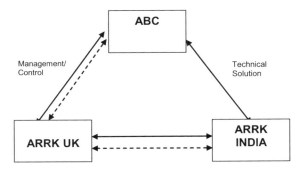

Figure 22.2   The management of the process during Phase II of the project (onshore team with UK-based project management)

The strategy employed by ABC and Arrk was to establish a virtual offshore development centre (VODC) with only minimal UK-based project management. Support was entirely supplied through Arrk's offshore staff, with ABC interacting directly with Arrk offshore team in India. Only the commercial account management and service assurance functions remained in the UK, although the Arrk's UK team continued to provided strategic IT and business advice to ABC's management (see Figure 22.3).

Benefits to ABC

HOW ARRK HELPED ABC

Arrk's initial proposal was to enable ABC to take advantage of offshoring without having to face head-on the risks and issues so often associated with 'first time buyers' in this market. Whereas large companies have the management bandwidth to enable them to learn and, if necessary, make a few mistakes, for smaller companies these risks are often unacceptable. As ABC gained more experience of offshoring, Arrk adapted its proposition to one aimed at recreating Arrk's own integrated service delivery model within ABC. This involved training ABC staff and management over time to adopt the role of Arrk UK. Arrk's framework for this is their Offshore Relocation Roadmap™ methodology that encompasses a number of phases and stages including:

- developing a strategy with ABC which would culminate in ABC having a mature offshore centric capability, enabling them to develop and support high-quality IT systems in a highly cost-effective manner;
- managing the knowledge acquisition process such that appropriate levels of business and IT knowledge were acquired by Arrk's teams in the UK and India in a timely fashion to support the implementation of the strategy;
- supporting and project managing an overall change management programme within ABC, including a focus on organizational and culture synchronization through communication, consultation and team-building;
- end-to-end process synchronization that integrated ABC's business and IT teams with Arrk's onshore/offshore service delivery organization;
- training and mentoring ABC's management and driving offshore process maturity to enable a rapid transition to a highly offshore centric model under controlled risk.

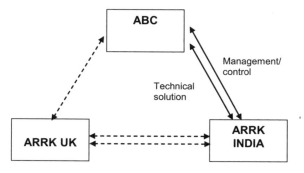

Figure 22.3   The strategy used during Phase III of the project (VODC)

Conclusion

The key learning points from this case study are:

- Do not look at offshoring just as a means of immediate cost savings.
- Have a solid, strong business case – with clearly stated long-term goals – and make sure that all stakeholders not only understand it, but have also 'bought in' to the decision to offshore.
- Managers need to have a holistic view of the entire offshoring process right from conceptualization to execution. If you don't have the in-house capability to develop this find a supplier who can.
- There are various models of offshoring as explained in this chapter. Choose the one that best suits your project requirement and mitigates most of the risks, and do not be afraid to change it as conditions evolve.
- The value realized from any offshoring relationship will be determined by the way in which the three core threads of service quality, cost and risk are executed, but remember offshoring is not just about cost-savings. A good supplier will add much more.

Our conclusion is that offshoring has the potential to add significant value to a very wide range of different companies and organizations, both large and small. However, different companies in different circumstances require different approaches. Small to medium-sized companies need a model that is flexible, affordable and aligned with their business goals and project requirements, irrespective of whether offshoring is *adaptive* or *transformational*.

The *indirect* model is particularly valuable for medium-sized businesses, particularly those entering the offshoring arena for the first time. But a good supplier should be able to help the customer map out a strategy and navigate their way from an early stage (immature) offshore capability to an advanced offshore centric (mature) operation.

Offshoring, if planned and executed efficiently, can be one way for SMEs to grow, to become flexible and to face global competition. As more and more companies have favourable offshoring experiences and they expand their offshoring relationships with providers in different countries, this can lead to more favourable attitudes towards offshoring on the part of SMEs.

References

Brown, R.H. and Browning, J.A. (2003), *SMBs: The Biggest Little Outsourcing Market in the World*, Gartner Research, AV-21-2630, Gartner Inc., Stanford CT, available at: www.gartner.com/resources/118400/118457/118457.pdf.

De Looff, L.A. (1995), 'Information systems outsourcing decision-making: a framework, organizational theories and case studies', *Journal of Information Technology*, vol. 10, no. 4, pp. 281–97.

Lee, P. (2003), *Making the Off-shore Call: The Road Map for Communications Operators*, A Deloitte Research Report, Deloitte Touche Tohmatsu, London.

Gilley, K.M. and Rasheed, A. (2000), 'Making more by doing less: an analysis of outsourcing and its effects on firm performance', *Journal of Management*, vol. 26, no. 4, pp. 763–90.

Kaiser, M.A. (2002), CEO Cendian Corporation quoted in 'Why outsourcing is becoming a strategic tool', *Forbes Magazine* (special section on outsourcing), 11 November, p. 5.

Philips J.T. Jr (1992), 'Outsourcing high tech services', *Records Management Quarterly*, vol. 26, no. 2, pp. 2–34.

Van Hoorn, T.P. (1979), 'Strategic planning in small and medium-sized companies', *Long Range Planning*, vol. 12, no. 2, pp. 84–91.

Index